Public Policy and the
Income Distribution

Public Policy and the Income Distribution

Alan J. Auerbach
David Card
John M. Quigley
Editors

Russell Sage Foundation
New York

The Russell Sage Foundation

Library of Congress Cataloging-in-Publication Data
Public policy and the income distribution. / Alan J. Auerbach, David Card, and John M. Quigley, editors.
   p. cm.
   Includes bibliographical references and index.
   ISBN 0-87154-046-0
   1. Economic assistance, Domestic—United States. 2. Economic security—United States. 3. Poverty—United States. 4. Income distribution—United States. 5. United States—Social policy. I. Auerbach, Alan J. II. Card, David E. (David Edward), 1956- III. Quigley, John M., 1942-

   HC110.P63P69 2006
   339.4'6'0973—dc22

            2005050847

RUSSELL SAGE FOUNDATION
112 East 64th Street, New York, New York 10021
10 9 8 7 6 5 4 3 2 1

This volume is dedicated to Eugene Smolensky
by his many colleagues and students, friends, and admirers.

Contents

Contributors

ALAN J. AUERBACH is Robert D. Burch Professor of Economics and Law at the University of California, Berkeley.

DAVID CARD is Class of 1950 Professor of Economics at the University of California, Berkeley.

JOHN M. QUIGLEY is I. Donald Terner Distinguished Professor and professor of economics at the University of California, Berkeley.

REBECCA M. BLANK is dean of the Gerald R. Ford School of Public Policy and co-director of the National Poverty Center at the University of Michigan.

DORA L. COSTA is professor of economics at the Massachusetts Institute of Technology and research associate at the National Bureau of Economic Research.

JANET CURRIE is professor of economics at Columbia University and research associate at the National Bureau of Economic Research.

GARY V. ENGELHARDT is associate professor of economics in the Maxwell School of Citizenship and Public Affairs at Syracuse University.

JONATHAN GRUBER is professor of economics at the Massachusetts Institute of Technology.

MATTHEW E. KAHN is associate professor at the Fletcher School, Tufts University.

STEVEN RAPHAEL is associate professor of public policy at the Goldman School of Public Policy at the University of California, Berkeley, and research affiliate of the National Poverty Center.

EMMANUEL SAEZ is professor of economics at the University of California, Berkeley, and research associate at the National Bureau of Economic Research.

JONATHAN SKINNER is John French Professor of Economics and professor in the Department of Community and Family Medicine at Dartmouth.

TIMOTHY M. SMEEDING is Maxwell Professor of Public Policy and director of the Center for Policy Research at the Maxwell School, Syracuse University.

WEIPING ZHOU is research associate and statistician at the Center for Evaluative Clinical Sciences, Dartmouth Medical School.

Preface and Acknowledgments

ALAN J. AUERBACH, DAVID CARD, AND JOHN M. QUIGLEY

In December 2003, a conference was organized in Berkeley. We commissioned the eight papers in this volume, seeking out the preeminent expert on each of the related topics treated in this book. Drafts of the papers included here were originally presented at that conference. Each paper was reviewed and discussed by two experts on the topic, and the papers were revised and greatly improved in response to these comments. The discussants for these papers included Sheldon Danziger, Victor Fuchs, Irwin Garfinkel, Robert Haveman, Hilary Hoynes, Ron Lee, Peter Lindert, Robert Plotnick, John Karl Scholz, Joel Slemrod, Michael Stoll, and Barbara Wolfe.[1]

Many institutions and individuals contributed to the completion of this book. Financial support for the research was provided by a number of research institutions at Berkeley: the Robert D. Burch Center for Tax Policy and Public Finance, the Center for Economic Demography and Aging, the Center for Labor Economics, and the Berkeley Program on Housing and Urban Policy. Additional financial assistance was provided by the Russell Sage Foundation. We are grateful to each of these organizations.

We are also grateful for the efforts of Mercedes Arevalo-Romero, Amanda Randolph, Larry Rosenthal, and Henrietta Williams in organizing the conference and providing editorial and logistical support.

Note

1. We regret that space constraints preclude publication here of the pene-
trating insights of discussants and conference participants. The discussants' comments, however, can be easily accessed electronically from the
Robert D. Burch Center for Tax Policy and Public Finance (http://emlab.
berkeley.edu/~burch/).

Chapter 1

Introduction

ALAN J. AUERBACH, DAVID CARD, AND JOHN M. QUIGLEY

The postwar era in the United States has been a time of rising national income and unprecedented gains in the economic well-being of American households. This prolonged period of growth led to a reduction in poverty rates but was also associated with a rise in the inequality of wealth and family income. Concurrent changes in demographics—increased immigration, the baby boom and bust, shifts in marriage and living arrangements, and continued suburbanization—have affected labor markets, the demand for social services, and the overall distribution of well-being. At the same time, changes in transfer and entitlement programs have affected the levels of support offered by the government to the poor, the aged, and the infirm.

The chapters in this book analyze the complex interactions among demographics, poverty, the distribution of income, and public policy from a longer-run perspective, taking stock of our knowledge of trends and causes, and identifying key areas where positive economics can contribute further to our understanding of policy options. In considering these broader linkages, it is important to keep in mind the extent of absolute improvement in the well-being of Americans, their incomes, and their economic circumstances. Figure 1.1 shows the trend in inflation-adjusted income per capita during the period 1960 to 2000. Real national income per person grew by 250 percent over the forty-year period. Figure 1.2 shows how these increases in economic output have translated into trends in

Figure 1.1   Per-Capita Gross National Product of the United States, 1960 to 2000 (2000 Dollars)

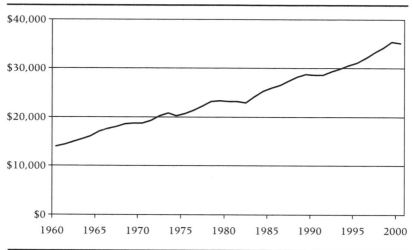

Source: U.S. Department of Commerce (2004, 167, table 1).

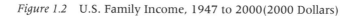

Figure 1.2   U.S. Family Income, 1947 to 2000(2000 Dollars)

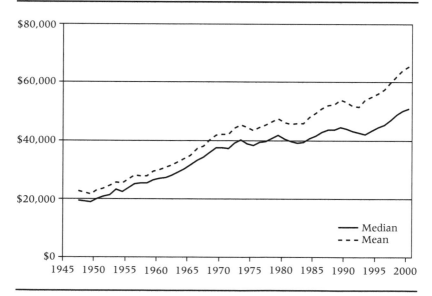

Source: U.S. Census Bureau (2001).

family income. Median family income—the level of income separating the top and bottom halves of the distribution—rose from about $20,400 in 1947 (in 2001 dollars) to about $52,300 at the turn of the century. To be sure, the increases have not been without interruption. Decreases occurred during major recessions—in 1975, for example, and in the early 1980s and early 1990s—but these declines were small, and the reverses were of short duration.

Figure 1.2 also reports the course of mean family income. This measure of family well-being has risen even faster, from about $23,900 to $67,400. The widening gap between mean and median family incomes reflects the increasing inequality in the distribution of family income, which has attracted much attention in recent years. Indeed, the systematic increase in the share of income accruing to upper-income families is shown clearly in Figure 1.3. From the mid-1960s through the end of the century, the share of income accruing to the top quintile of families increased from 43 percent to 50 percent, while the share of income garnered by the richest 5 percent of families increased from 17 percent to 22 percent.

Notwithstanding the widening of the distribution of income, poverty rates among American households have declined systematically.

Figure 1.3   Share of Household Income in Top 20 Percent and Top 5 Percent of Income Distribution, 1967 to 2000

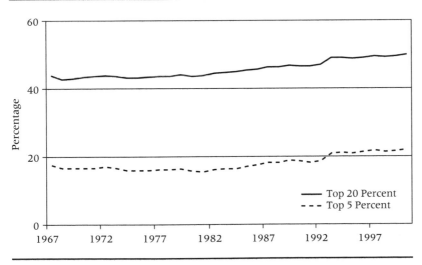

Source: U.S. Census Bureau (2000a).

Figure 1.4 shows the trends during the last four decades. Among whites, the incidence of poverty declined by nearly half, from 18 percent in 1960 to 9.5 percent in 2000. Among nonwhite households, the decline was even larger. In 1960, more than half of nonwhite households in America (56 percent) lived in poverty. By 2000, less than one fifth (19 percent) of nonwhite households had incomes below the poverty line. The declining trends in poverty rates have not been continuous, and there were periods, especially during the early 1980s, when poverty rates increased markedly. Nevertheless, for the period as a whole the reduction in poverty rates was remarkable. Despite this general progress, at the turn of the century differences in poverty rates for blacks and whites remain substantial. As indicated in Figure 1.4, by 2000 the poverty rate among nonwhites was still more than twice that for whites. In fact, at the end of the century the average poverty rate of nonwhites was about equal to the rate of whites forty years earlier.

These changes in the level and distribution of income and the incidence of poverty have arisen from changes in the labor market—the distribution of skills and labor supply and the incidence of unemployment—and from government policies. Secular changes in

Figure 1.4   Poverty Rates for Whites and Nonwhites, 1960 to 2000

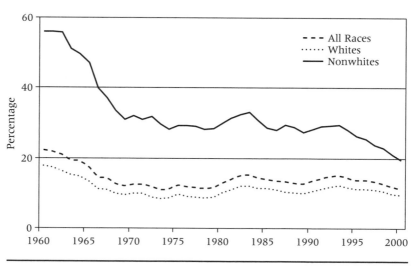

Source: U.S. Census Bureau (2000b).

skills, as proxied by the education levels of adults, have been enormous. As indicated in figure 1.5, in 1962 nearly 40 percent of adults had no more than eight years of formal schooling. By 2004, that percentage had declined to less than 7 percent. Meanwhile, the proportion of adults who have completed high school increased from 46 percent in 1962 to 85 percent in 1988, while the proportion with at least a bachelor's degree rose from 9 percent to 28 percent. Though not shown in the figure, there has also been a rapid rise in the fraction of adults with one to three years of postsecondary education, from 16 percent in 1960 to 51 percent in 2000.

This upgrading of skills has been accompanied by substantial increases in the labor supply of women and a small decrease in laborforce participation among adult men. As indicated in figure 1.6, labor-force participation rates for white and nonwhite males declined from 86 percent to 77 and 75 percent, respectively, from 1960 to 2000. In contrast, labor-force participation rates for nonwhite women increased from 50 percent to 64 percent and participation rates for white women rose from 36 percent to 60 percent. Women with

Figure 1.5 School Completion Rates of Adults Age Twenty-Five and Older, 1962 to 2004

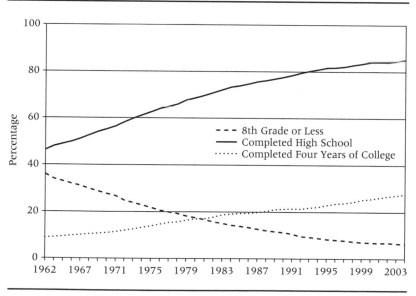

Source: U.S. Bureau of the Census (2003).

Figure 1.6   Labor-Force Participation of Adults Aged Twenty and Older, by Race and Sex, 1960 to 2000

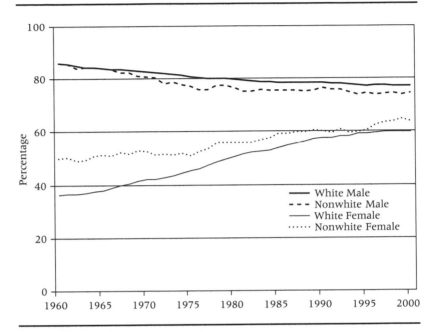

Source: U.S. Bureau of Labor Statistics (2000).

children have accounted for most of the secular rise in female labor supply. Currently, 77 percent of women whose youngest child is between six and seventeen years of age are participating in the labor force, and the participation rate for women with a preschool child is 62 percent. It is interesting that the participation rate of women with no children under eighteen years of age is only 54 percent.

Although the increases in labor-force participation of the adult population have been accompanied by rises in employment rates and per-capita hours of work, unemployment remains a significant concern in the U.S. labor market. As shown in figure 1.7, unemployment rates at the end of the century were at the levels of the mid-1960s. (In the post-2000 recession, rates rose about two percentage points above their 2000 levels.) Unemployment rates for both whites and nonwhites are highly correlated with the business cycle, though over most of the past four decades, unemployment rates for nonwhites have remained about twice the rates for whites.

Figure 1.7 Unemployment Rates by Race, 1960 to 2000

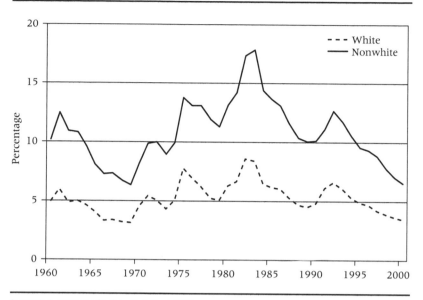

Source: U.S. Bureau of Labor Statistics (2000).

Secular rises in the educational attainment of Americans have been accompanied by equally large changes in the economic returns to these skills. In 1960, the average full-time worker with less than a high school diploma earned $13,300 (in 2000 dollars). The average high school graduate (with twelve to fifteen years of education) earned $19,900, and a college graduate earned $30,600. By the late 1990s, the economic returns to these levels of education were $11,600, $22,700, and $41,100, respectively. The economic disadvantage of less-skilled workers had become much more pronounced. For those without a high school diploma, real incomes actually declined.

The economic changes in the past four decades were accompanied by equally profound changes in the demographic characteristics of the U.S. population. As shown in figure 1.8, life expectancies have risen substantially—by more than 10 percent for both men and women. Estimated life expectancy for men born in 1960 is sixty-seven years and for women, seventy-three years. For people born in 2000 the corresponding estimates are seventy-four years and seventy-nine years. Put another way, a male born in 1960 could expect to live two years beyond the customary retirement age of sixty-five. Males born in 2000 can expect to live nine years beyond the traditional age of retirement.

Associated with increased life expectancies have been pronounced changes in the age distribution of the population. Increased longevity, together with the decline in fertility rates since the end of the baby boom in the mid-1960s, has meant that the fraction of the elderly has risen while the fraction of the population below the age of eighteen has declined. As is evident from figures 1.9 and 1.10, these changes are similar for males and females. The rise in the fraction of the population over sixty-five years of age, from about 8 to 12 percent between 1960 and 2000, has led to increasing attention to the problems of financing private and public pension systems.

An equally important demographic factor has been the greatly increased levels of immigration. Before the elimination of national quotas as a result of the Immigration Act of 1965, foreign migration to the United States averaged about 265,000 per year. As shown in figure 1.11, legal immigration inflows gradually increased over the 1970s and 1980s, reaching a rate of about 600,000 per year in the

Figure 1.8   Life Expectancy at Birth by Sex, 1960 to 2000

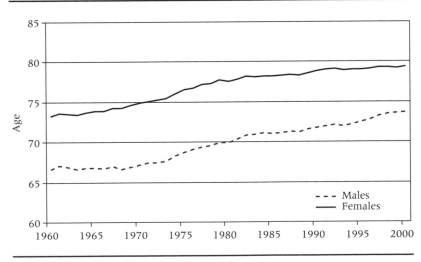

Source: Social Security Administration (2002, 132–36, table 11).

Figure 1.9   Age Distribution of the Female Population, 1960 to 2000

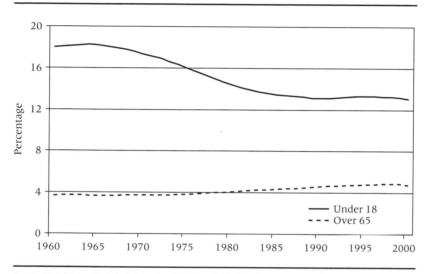

Source: Social Security Administration (2002); calculations by www.mortality.org.

Figure 1.10   Age Distribution of the Male Population, 1960 to 2000

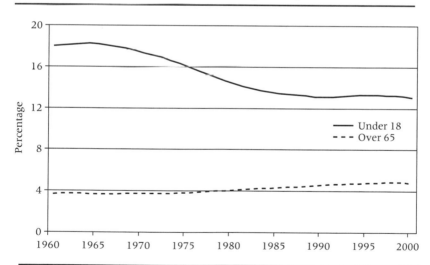

Source: Social Security Administration (2002); calculations by www.mortality.org.

Figure 1.11   Annual Immigration, in Thousands

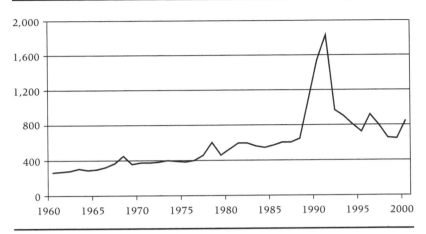

Source: Department of Justice (2001, table 1).

mid-1980s. Illegal immigration flows probably contributed a further 150,000 to 200,000 people per year, many of whom were legalized in the late 1980s (generating the "spike" in the legal-flow data reported in figure 1.11). Over the 1990s, legal inflows have risen to about 800,000 per year—and illegal inflows add as many as 200,000 additional people. Currently, immigration contributes about one-third of the net rate of increase of the U.S. population.

Against this background of fundamental economic and demographic trends, the chapters in this book pose a series of key questions about the role of government policy in altering the level and distribution of economic well-being. To set the stage for the individual chapters, it is helpful to give a brief overview of some of the general trends in overall government spending and taxation that have emerged over the past forty years.

Since the beginning of the Kennedy administration, real spending by the federal government has quadrupled, from $527 billion in 1960 to $2,143 billion in 2004 (in 2000 dollars). Figure 1.12 shows the trends in outlays for national defense and nondefense spending. Beginning in 1969, just after the peak of spending on the Vietnam War, nondefense spending surpassed spending on defense. Defense spending subsequently declined, returning to its 1968 level briefly during the Reagan administration. Figure 1.12 also reports transfers and other payments to individuals, the largest component of non-

Figure 1.12 Federal Outlays by Category, 1960 to 2004 (Billions of 2000 Dollars)

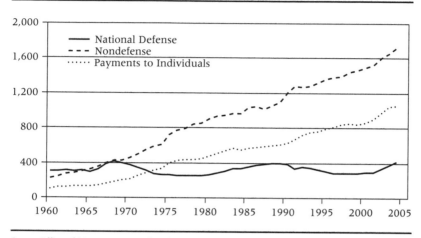

Source: Office of Management and Budget (2005, table 6.1).

defense spending. By the mid 1970s, payments to individuals exceeded military expenditures. Figure 1.13 shows the same series in per-capita terms. By 2004, defense outlays totaled about $1,400 per capita while nondefense outlays amounted to $5,900 per person. Of the latter figure, about $3,600 represented transfers to individuals.

Figure 1.13 Federal Outlays Per Capita by Category, 1960 to 2004 (2000 Dollars)

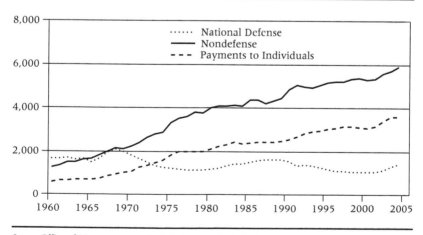

Source: Office of Management and Budget (2005, table 6.1).

More detail on the trends in government spending programs is provided in figure 1.14, which shows spending in five key areas: Social Security payments to individuals (mostly old-age and survivors insurance plus disability insurance); unemployment assistance; payments for public assistance and related programs (mostly welfare payments to individuals, Earned Income Tax Credit payments, and supplemental security payments); medical care (mostly Medicare and Medicaid payments); and housing, food, and nutrition programs. As indicated in the figure, there was a steady increase in federal outlays for all five program areas over the past four decades, though the growth rates vary substantially across areas. Outlays for unemployment assistance increased at the slowest rate, 2.3 percent per year, rising to $38 billion by 2004 (in 2000 dollars). Social Security payments increased by 4.8 percent per year, to $462 billion by 2004, while outlays for public assistance increased by 4.8 percent, from a much lower base, to $101 billion in 2004. Payments for housing, food, and nutrition programs increased by 8.4 percent per year, from an even smaller base, to $67 billion in 2004. The fastest growing program area—outlays for medical care—increased by 10.5 percent per year during this long period, to $477 billion in 2004. Growth in medical-care spending has been particularly rapid in the past five years, rising by $125 billion (in constant 2000 dollars) between 1999 and 2004. Medical payments amounted to almost 23 percent of the $2.1 trillion in federal outlays in 2004. Medical-care and Social Secu-

Figure 1.14   Government Payments to Individuals by Major Category (Billions of 2000 Dollars)

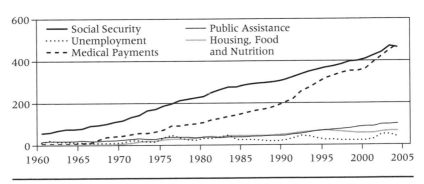

Source: Office of Management and Budget (2004, table 11.3).

rity payments together account for almost 45 percent of federal government outlays.

Finally, figure 1.15 crudely summarizes the course of federal tax policy, indicating the marginal tax rate on the highest-income individuals during the period, as represented by the statutory tax rate on wage income for those with one million dollars of income (in constant 1992 dollars). The recent decline in tax rates stands in sharp contrast to the continued increases in per-capita spending documented in figures 1.12 to 1.14, underscoring the source of concern over the sustainability of current policy directions.

The chapters in this book focus on the linkages and interactions between government programs and policies, on the one hand, and the economic and demographic forces described earlier, on the other hand. Although the scope of the terrain is broad, the chapters are not intended to represent comprehensive surveys of scholarly research. Instead, we asked leading contributors in the fields of public finance

Figure 1.15   Highest Federal Tax Rates on Ordinary Income, 1960 to 2004

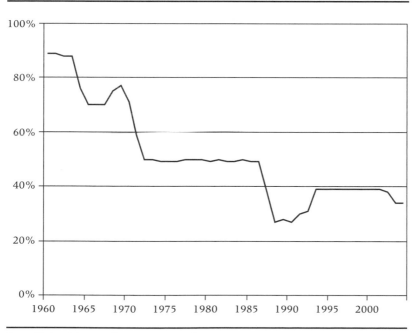

Source: National Bureau of Economic Research (2003).

and public policy to focus on specific issues they found most relevant to assessing these linkages.[1] Several chapters focus on questions related to the distributional impacts of government policies: What determines the take-up rate of benefits offered by different government programs? How are the relative labor-market opportunities of young black and white men linked to incarceration policies? Other chapters present an evaluation of specific policies: the effects of Social Security on poverty among the elderly, and the accomplishments of the welfare reforms of the 1990s. Two of the chapters present historical assessments: What can we learn from the past about public-health expenditures and demographic outcomes? How has the concentration of wealth in industrialized countries been affected by the different tax policies pursued by their governments?

Along with economic, demographic, and policy changes, the past forty years have seen a massive change in social science research, made possible by modern computers and advances in quantitative methods. As a result of this explosion of research, we now know far more than earlier generations about the interactions between demographic and economic trends, public policies, and the distributions of individual and family outcomes. Nevertheless, the authors are careful to emphasize important unanswered questions. The discussion in each chapter makes it clear that there are many open questions and new directions for research that will surely be addressed in the coming years.

In chapter 2, "What Did the 1990s Welfare Reforms Accomplish?," Rebecca Blank considers the far-reaching changes wrought by passage of the Personal Responsibility and Work Opportunity Reconciliation Act (PRWORA) in 1996. She documents the course of welfare reform from the cautious experiments of the 1980s to the more ambitious waiver programs of the 1990s and ultimately to the passage of PRWORA. As Blank indicates, by converting the matching-grant provisions of the old welfare system into a block grant and by introducing time limits, welfare reforms rewarded efforts by the states to encourage the welfare-to-work transition, to increase earnings "disregards" for recipients (amounts not counted against the calculation of their benefits), to impose sanctions, and to impose more stringent time limits on welfare beneficiaries.

Changes in welfare rules weren't the only policy innovations of the 1990s, and any evaluation of the effects of welfare reforms must recognize these other changes in the economic environment. Importantly, the booming economy of the 1990s had an enormous impact on the low-wage segment of the labor market making it easier to implement reforms encouraging labor-force participation.

Blank's chapter documents the dramatic changes brought about by this combination of policy reform and economic good fortune. Her review reveals that welfare caseloads fell by 50 percent in the decade of the 1990s, that labor-force participation rates for single mothers increased sharply through 1999, before declining modestly, and that during the recent downturn, unemployment rates among less-educated women have not risen as fast as rates for other groups. Increases in incomes and declines in poverty rates among single mothers were substantial, but they were less dramatic than changes in caseloads and labor-force participation.

This chapter provides the first systematic research comparing changes in income and poverty rates, caseloads, and labor-force participation among groups of single mothers. Blank presents evidence by race and level of education and by the age of the mother's youngest child. A striking result of these comparisons is the large gains in earnings shares made by women who had little or no earnings in the mid-1990s. There were also large gains in labor-force participation and substantial reductions in poverty among these women. All this suggests that those single mothers who were most disadvantaged in the labor market had no greater difficulty finding work after the rules were changed.

Blank provides a synthesis of the results of the many studies that have sought to interpret these findings—sample surveys of women leaving welfare, analyses of government data such as the Current Population Survey, natural experiments, and a few controlled experiments. Experimental studies suggest, for example, that "work first" programs, which place mothers directly into employment without regard to wages or skill requirements, can be more effective than job-training programs at getting women working. Other studies suggest that work programs can have modest positive effects on the well-being of children.

Finally, Blank considers the important lessons from efforts during the past decade at welfare reform: the importance of interactions and synergies—the strong economy, the Earned Income Tax Credit (EITC), the other changes in policy—in affecting outcomes; the asymmetric responses of labor-force participation during the recent slowdown in the economy; and the interactions among public assistance programs, family composition, and fertility.

Blank's chapter concludes by identifying an important set of unanswered research questions about the effects of these policy changes on outcomes, the effects of macroeconomic conditions on low-wage labor markets, and the longer-run effects of time limits on single-parent households.

In chapter 3, "The Take-Up of Social Benefits," Janet Currie explores the distribution of in-kind benefits to selected recipients—individuals or groups targeted as "deserving" as a result of their demographic attributes or poverty status. Currie's chapter is concerned with an important feature of public-assistance programs long neglected by economists, namely, the imperfect targeting of beneficiaries by the design and execution of programs. These design features matter. If the take-up of benefits by eligible individuals or households is too low, a program will fail to reach its goal of providing assistance to the targeted group. If the take-up of benefits by ineligibles is too high, then a government transfer program is wasteful, or worse, counter productive.

After a review of the received model of social stigma as a deterrent for some eligible households to participate in public programs, Currie finds the model of limited value. She stresses instead the variations in the costs of participation in government programs, including information, transactions, and transport costs, and the problems of principal-agent coordination.

Currie provides a comprehensive survey of the literature on the take-up of means-tested transfer programs in the United States and a more limited survey of analogous programs in the United Kingdom. Her empirical results reveal an astonishing variation in take-up rates across programs, even when entitlement programs offering similar services are compared. Currie deconstructs several of these programs, exploring the extent to which the effects of information and transaction costs can vary.

One important normative question in evaluating these variable take-up rates is: do the barriers to program participation screen out the "undeserving" people? Currie's synthesis of research on disparate programs—Supplemental Social Insurance (SSI), school lunch programs, and Medicaid, for example—indicates the difficulty in devising program rules to target programs only to those who "need" them.

A second and purely positive question is: what can be done to affect take-up rates? Currie suggests that take-up rates for programs will be higher when businesses as well as individuals profit from program participation: commercial tax preparers promote take-up of the EITC; hospitals also benefit if eligible pregnant women are covered by Medicaid before delivery. There may also be some benefit in bundling applications for certain programs—Medicaid and food stamps, for example—so that information costs are reduced.

Currie's survey of the take-up of program benefits in Britain also reveals a large variation in estimates of the fraction of eligible individuals who receive program benefits. Take-up of the British version of the EITC is roughly the same as that across the Atlantic, but take-up of the British version of SSI is a good bit higher than in the United States.

Currie's survey strongly suggests that economists should pay much more attention to rules about program eligibility and to information about how those rules are enforced and disseminated. She also provides anecdotal evidence about natural variation in services and outreach across states or regions which could be exploited to learn more about these important issues.

In chapter 4, "Government Programs and Social Outcomes: Comparison of the United States with Other Rich Nations," Timothy Smeeding produces a comparative analysis of the incidence of poverty in the United States and seven other highly developed countries: Canada, the United Kingdom, Belgium, Germany, the Netherlands, Finland, and Sweden. Smeeding then analyzes the extent to which government programs mitigate the prevalence of poverty in the population as a whole, as well as poverty among key subgroups such as children and the elderly. He concludes with some comments about policies the United States might undertake to reduce the number of households living in poverty.

Measuring poverty is in itself a challenging task that raises questions that have occupied economic researchers for years. First, how does one compare the living standards of families that differ in size and composition? Here, the standard approach is to adjust income using equivalence scales that reflect variations in the per-capita cost of living among family types. Second, should comparisons be made using a relative measure or an absolute one? Smeeding argues that poverty should be viewed as a relative concept, relying primarily on incomes below half the median as an indicator of poverty. Third, how should income and living standards across countries be compared? Smeeding uses not market exchange rates but "purchasing-power parity" (PPP) exchange rates, which measure the relative strengths of currencies in purchasing a constant market basket of goods. Fourth, how broad an income measure should one use in measuring a family's available resources? Smeeding includes not only after-tax disposable income, but also government transfer payments.

The most novel and most challenging aspect of Smeeding's analysis is its cross-country approach. Aside from dealing with the exchange rate issue, Smeeding and his associates have devoted considerable effort over the years to the collection of comparable data for the different countries. This work has been undertaken through the Luxembourg Income Study.

To summarize Smeeding's findings, by the year 2000 the United States was a clear outlier in many respects. It stood out in aggregate economic performance, with per-capita gross domestic product substantially higher than that of the next-highest country, the Netherlands, and an unemployment rate that was substantially lower than that of all but one of the other countries—again, the Netherlands. But the U.S poverty rate also stood out. At 17.0 percent, the rate was substantially higher than the sample average of 9.8 percent, and much higher even than the second-highest poverty rate in the group, the United Kingdom's 12.3 percent. As in most of the other countries, poverty among the U.S. elderly has lessened over the past couple of decades, even as general poverty and poverty among households with children has increased, but the U.S. poverty rates in all subgroups are well above the international average. In certain at-risk groups, the U.S. poverty rate is startlingly high, reaching, for example, 51.3 percent among children living in families with low-education parents.

Why is poverty so prevalent in the United States? Smeeding argues that in the other countries, government intervention, through the tax system, social insurance (universal transfer programs), and social assistance (targeted transfer programs), make the difference. Poverty rates as measured by market incomes—money earned from working—are actually lower in the United States than in most of the other countries. But government interventions are estimated to reduce the poverty rate by 62 percent on average in the other countries, but only by 28 percent in the United States. These measures do not provide precise estimates of the extent to which the programs actually reduce poverty, of course, because one cannot observe what market incomes would have been in the absence of government intervention. But the differences between the United States and all the other countries are nevertheless very suggestive of the lack of government intervention as a key factor in the high U.S. poverty rate.

Smeeding also dismisses the labor market as a source of the discrepancy between poverty rates in the United States and in other developed countries. Indeed, as others have observed, the United States stands out for its high labor-force participation rates and long work weeks. These patterns exist, not only in the aggregate population, but also among lower-income workers. Yet many in the United States who work remain in poverty. For example, among single-parent U.S. families in which the household head works more than 1,000 hours per year, 33 percent remain in poverty; the international average of those who remain poor while working is just 13.5 percent.

Given that the United States has a much higher average living standard than other countries, one might ask whether our high incidence of poverty, relative to our median income, really means that the poor are worse off in an absolute sense. Here, the evidence is mixed. Comparing living standards across countries among the poor, which Smeeding defines as those in the poorest tenth of the population, he finds that the U.S. poor, overall, have about the same income as those in the tenth percentile in other countries. But among children living in one-parent families, the poor in the United States fare worse, even when an absolute standard is used.

Thus, poverty in the United States is widespread, and it is particularly acute in certain subgroups, such as single-parent families. Smeeding blames this outcome—especially when measured against the situation in other countries—on a lack of effective government intervention, and argues that the United States can do considerably more to eliminate poverty.

In chapter 5, "Income and Wealth Concentration in a Historical and International Perspective," Emmanuel Saez provides another international comparison of incomes. Saez's focus differs from Smeeding's in a number of respects—most important, Saez is concerned with activity near the top of the income distribution rather than near the bottom. Economists have a number of reasons for investigating patterns in the concentration and composition of income and wealth among the rich, ranging from a wish to understand the role of entrepreneurship in economic growth to concerns about social cohesion and the distortions imposed by progressive taxation. During the last few decades of the twentieth century, increasing income dispersion in many countries, especially the United States, directed increased attention to the causes and consequences of concentrations of income and wealth. These concerns in some respects echoed those voiced a century earlier.

Saez also departs from Smeeding in the types of data sources used. A key finding of the cross-country research that Saez summarizes (much of which he has produced himself, independently and in collaboration with others) is that there is great heterogeneity among those at the very top. In particular, it is useful to disaggregate even within the top 1.0 percent of the income distribution, as patterns within the top 0.1 percent differ markedly from patterns among those in the "bottom" 0.9 percent of the top percentile. Given how much of a country's income and wealth may accrue to those in the top 0.1 percent of the population, very fine groupings may be productive from a research perspective. But survey data are not very helpful for these purposes because there is scant coverage of the very rich. Thus, following methods first developed in the 1950s by Simon Kuznets, the line of research pursued by Saez uses statistics from income tax returns to measure the incomes of those at the top, and he compares these incomes to aggregate measures based on national accounts. To a lesser extent, with the same methodology, estate tax returns can be used to analyze wealth concentrations.

An advantage of using data from income tax returns is that, although income taxes have grown in their population coverage over time, they applied earliest to those with the highest incomes. Thus, one can observe data going back to early in the twentieth century, when income taxes were first established. A disadvantage is that any researcher is constrained by the components of income covered by the tax system, so that income intentionally or unintentionally excluded from the tax base (through tax evasion, for example) is not directly observable. Nonetheless, the research that Saez organizes and discusses has yielded rich time series for several countries that provide fascinating details on the course of income and wealth concentration during the twentieth century. These time series invite the formulation of hypotheses to explain these patterns.

Saez provides time series on top income percentiles since around World War I for six countries: the United States, Canada, the United Kingdom, France, the Netherlands, and Switzerland. In all countries except Switzerland, the patterns through the end of World War II are similar. First, there was a sharp decline in income concentration over this period. Saez attributes this decline to the successive shocks of the Great Depression and World War II, and also to a reduction in the concentration of capital income. In five of the countries, for those with the highest incomes, capital income has come to represent a much smaller share of income than was true a century ago. Switzerland, by contrast, did not experience a drop in its income concentration, which Saez attributes at least in part to its avoidance of the World War II conflict. This prevented severe economic disruptions and reduced the sharp pressures for increases in progressive income taxation experienced by the other countries.

After World War II, the common trends of all the countries (excluding Switzerland) break down, with income concentration rising sharply in the "Anglo-Saxon" countries, the United States, Canada, and the United Kingdom, but not in the "Continental" countries (France and the Netherlands). The increase in concentration has brought the share of income in the top 0.1 percent of the population back up to levels not seen since World War I, at least in the United States. But the driving force this time is labor income, not capital income, and perhaps because it takes time for accumulations from labor income to translate into wealth, there has yet to be such a sharp rebound in the concentration of U.S. wealth.

How can one explain this divergence between the Anglo-Saxon countries and the Continental countries? One possible explanation is the significant declines in top marginal tax rates in Anglo-Saxon countries, which could have spurred not only increases in actual income but also shifts in the composition of income toward components subject to tax. This explanation is more plausible for the United States and the United Kingdom than for Canada, which did not implement significant reductions in top marginal tax rates. Saez argues that Canada's proximity to the United States may have forced incomes up there as well to keep mobile workers from leaving. But the timing of income increases in the United States does not match perfectly the changes in income tax rates, suggesting that the process may relate more to a long-term tax environment than to specific legislation or particular tax changes. This leaves open alternative, and possibly complementary, explanations, such as changes in the strength of corporate governance that may have permitted surges in executive compensation.

If there is one "success story" in the area of poverty alleviation, it is the reduction in poverty among the elderly that has been accomplished by old-age pension systems. As noted earlier in the discussion of Smeeding's international comparison of poverty, old-age poverty has been trending downward even as the frequency of poverty among children has been rising. Nowhere is this development more noticeable than in the United States, where the establishment and continual growth of the Social Security system has been given credit for a substantial decline in poverty among the elderly. In chapter 6, "Social Security and the Evolution of Elderly Poverty," Gary Engelhardt and Jonathan Gruber ask: how much of this decline is due directly to Social Security, and how much to other factors that have increased economic well-being over the same period?

As Engelhardt and Gruber note, the drop in the U.S. poverty rate among the elderly has been very rapid, from 35 percent in 1960 to 10 percent in 1995, from a rate more than twice that of the non-elderly population to a rate lower than that of the non-elderly population. But there have been many other changes—in the labor market, living arrangements, health status, private and pension saving, and so forth—that could also have exerted important influences on elderly poverty. How is one to determine the separate impact of Social Security? Here, an unintentional variation in policy—a temporary mistake in the structure of Social Security benefits during the 1970s—has provided us with a quite powerful large-scale experiment.

As the United States moved to a regime in which Social Security benefits were indexed for inflation, the indexation scheme initially implemented was inadvertently structured so that recipients' real benefits actually rose with inflation as a result of a "double-indexing" of nominal benefits. This mistake was corrected in 1977, but not before real benefits among those retiring had risen sharply. To deal with the political difficulty of cutting benefits that had resulted from this windfall, the government allowed those born prior to 1917—those who, roughly, had already reached the early-retirement age of sixty-two—to keep the higher level of benefits. Those born after 1921 received benefits based on the corrected formula. For those in the transition birth cohort, born between 1917 and 1921—the so-called "notch" cohort—a transition from higher to lower benefits was implemented. Because the large swing in real benefits affected cohorts born just six years apart and because the changes related only to birth year and not to other circumstances, the variation in benefits can be used to distinguish the effects of changes in benefit rules from other contemporaneous changes.

Using as their measure of poverty an income below 40 percent of the median income among the non-elderly, adjusted for family size, Gruber and Engelhardt estimate the impact of Social Security benefits on the incidence of poverty among different subgroups of the elderly over time. Because actual benefits also may have changed as a result of behavioral changes, such as variations in labor-force participation, the authors construct an instrument for benefits by calculating the benefits that would have been received in each birth cohort by an individual with the work history and real-income profile of a male born in 1916 who earns the median income. Using this instrument for actual Social Security benefits and a number of other controls (such as education) that one would also expect to matter, the authors estimate the impact of changes in Social Security benefits on the poverty rate.

The results, although varying by specification, are very strong, suggesting an elasticity of around 1, that is, a decline of 10 percent in the poverty rate for each 10 percent increase in the level of benefits. This responsiveness is large enough to explain fully the drop in elderly poverty between 1967 and 2000, a period in which the poverty rate fell by more than half. Interestingly, the effect is larger for elderly families, defined as families headed by elderly persons, rather than for elderly households, defined as households in which elderly families live. As Gruber and Engelhardt discuss, this difference can be reconciled by the fact that changes in benefits also influence living arrangements, with higher incomes making it more likely for the elderly to live alone rather than with children or with other non-elderly relatives. To the extent that choices to live alone are voluntary, the apparent increase in household poverty associated with living alone biases downward the observed impact of increased benefits on poverty reduction.

Thus, increases in Social Security benefits have had a powerful effect on the elderly poverty rate and have altered living arrangements as well. The impact of these benefit increases on other aspects of behavior, such as labor-force participation, has been considered in earlier work, but Gruber and Engelhardt identify a further important question to be addressed by future research: How has this poverty alleviation affected consumption and other, broader, measures of well-being?

A key element of well-being is health. This is particularly so among the elderly, for whom significant health problems are common, for whom health expenditures are very large, and among whom health status and life expectancy vary considerably. In chapter 7, "The Measurement and Evolution of Health Inequality: Evidence from the U.S. Medicare Population," Jonathan Skinner and Weiping Zhou analyze trends in health-care inputs—spending—and outcomes in the U.S. elderly population, considering how these measures have varied by income level over time. They present variations in access to health care and the effectiveness of the U.S. health-care system for its users according to their income class. They review changes in these measures over time, especially with the development of the Medicare system.

In the absence of information on individuals' health measures and incomes, Skinner and Zhou used data grouped by postal code, classifying U.S. zip codes by average income, and considered how health measures vary by average neighborhood income.

A more significant problem is that there are no perfect measures of health-care access and effectiveness. One simple measure of access and effectiveness, though an indirect one, is health-care expenditures per capita. Skinner and Zhou do not have direct observations on total per-capita expenditures, but they observe per-capita Medicare expenditures, which account for a large share of health-care spending for the elderly. Of course, health-care spending is not a direct measure of either access or effectiveness. Spending may be higher for one group simply because that group is sicker, or because prices vary geographically. Moreover, as Skinner and Zhou suggest, some increases in health-care spending may be of little benefit to those on whose behalf the expenditures are incurred.

If not all increases in health-care spending translate into improved health-care outcomes, then why not look directly at outcomes instead? Skinner and Zhou do this as well, considering how life expectancy has changed over time among different income groups. But there are problems in relating life expectancy to health-care access and effectiveness, because other factors may lead to variations in mortality, including individual lifestyle choices such as diet and exercise as well as genetic and environmental conditions.

Thus, in addition to analyzing the inputs and outputs of the health-care system, Skinner and Zhou consider a third type of variation in the access and effectiveness of the health-care system, namely, the penetration of significant medical technologies. Given the rapid technological progress in health care, it is often the case that different generations of technology for dealing with serious medical conditions coexist, as the newest and most effective treatments force out older, less effective ones only gradually. In some cases, however, new treatments are deemed so effective, relative to cost, that they quickly become dominant technologies that should be expected to be used on the entire population for which they are applicable. For these treatments, "The target rate approaches one hundred percent regardless of income or demographic group." (An example is mammography screening.) In such a case, lack of usage indicates a failure of the health-care system to provide access to the most effective care, and this provides one dimension by which to gauge how well the health-care system performs.

These three approaches prove useful, because the resulting trends differ. If one considers trends in Medicare spending, then it appears that Medicare growth has effected a remarkable redistribution of resources to the poor elderly over time. Between 1987 and 2001, Medicare spending grew rapidly for all income groups, as did medical spending for the U.S. population as a whole. But spending among the lower-income elderly grew especially fast, so that the dollar change in spending per capita in the bottom income decile exceeded that in the top decile by $1,410. This number is nearly as large as the total increase in median household income over the same period, and it is larger than the average level of per-capita benefits from the EITC, a major income-support program for the working poor.

But this apparently huge transfer of health-care resources to the poor stands in stark contrast to the trend in survival probabilities, which shows a much greater improvement among higher-income groups. Comparing ten-year survival rates in 1992 to those in 1982, Skinner and Zhou find a 0.2-year increase in life expectancy in the bottom decile, a 0.5-year increase in the fifth decile, and a 0.8-year increase in the top decile—a large divergence over so short a period.

It is hard to know how much of the differing trends in inputs (spending) and outputs (life expectancy) are due to trends in other, unmeasured, inputs, such as diet or exercise, and how much is due to the variations in the effectiveness of health-care spending. Skinner and Zhou's results do suggest that a large part of the surge in Medicare spending on home health care was simply wasted. This brings them to their third measure of health-care access and effectiveness, the penetration of cutting-edge treatments. Here the results are mixed. They find that individuals in lower-income deciles are less likely to be exposed to leading technologies, but there is limited evidence that this gap has diminished over time. However, they conclude that these differences alone would account for only a very small fraction of observed differences in mortality.

In chapter 8, "The Socioeconomic Status of Black Males: The Increasing Importance of Incarceration," Steven Raphael provides a sobering assessment of the importance of incarceration in explaining differences in the incomes and labor-force attachment of black males and white males. Raphael documents the alarming trends in incarceration rates among African Americans. Using data from the public use samples of the last four decennial censuses, Raphael estimates that the fraction of employed black males declined from 73 percent in 1970 to 57 percent in 2000; for black high school dropouts, the employment rate declined from 71 percent to 34 percent.

At the same time, the proportion of black males institutionalized increased from 3 to 8 percent. For high school dropouts, the proportion increased from 4 to 19 percent. For black high school dropouts between 26 and 30 years of age, the fraction of those incarcerated increased from 6 percent in 1970 to 34 percent in 2000.

Of course, these static estimates of the prison population substantially underestimate the fraction of prime-age males with a record of conviction and jail time. Raphael makes use of administrative records on all prison terms served in California prisons in the 1990s to estimate the likelihood that individuals of differing sociodemographic characteristics have served a term in prison during the previous decade. Raphael estimates that 17 percent of white high school dropouts between forty-five and fifty-four years of age had served a prison term in the previous ten years. For blacks the estimate is 90 percent.

Raphael observes that "for black high school dropouts, serving time in prison is virtually a certainty." He goes on to estimate the effect of incarceration on the labor-market prospects of workers—estimating the time lost from other labor-market activities and the effects of the stigma of a prison record on the employability of workers.

Finally, Raphael's empirical analysis suggests the extent to which the large differential in black and white employment rates can be attributed to the much higher involvement of blacks with the criminal justice system. His estimates make sobering reading, and his projections suggest that the proportion of black males with criminal records will increase, even if current incarceration rates remain unchanged.

Raphael's analysis suggests that policies about sentencing, in particular differential sentences for apparently similar behavior (such as trafficking in powdered versus crystallized cocaine) and the extent of judicial discretion are relevant. Prisoner reentry programs appear to be crucial to reducing the labor-market consequences of entering the criminal justice system, but these programs are rare.

The final chapter in this volume, "Public Health and Mortality: What Can We Learn from the Past?" by Dora Costa and Matthew Kahn, provides a historical analysis of public assistance in large U.S. cities during the early twentieth century. In this era the United States was spending twice as much on hospitals and health care as it was on public transfers, poor relief, and welfare. Costa and Kahn argue that the role of public infrastructure investments in reducing mortality during the period between about 1910 and 1930 represented "the foremost public policy success of the twentieth century."

Costa and Kahn begin by investigating the determinants of state and local generosity in public programs in the early twentieth century. Analyzing data from large U.S. cities in 1907 and in 1930, the authors conclude that localities with more minorities and immigrants appeared to be more likely to support redistributive expenditures than homogeneous cities. This finding is contrary to the findings of research on more recent periods. The authors attribute these heightened expenditures, not to heightened altruism in the earlier era, but rather to the greater possibilities for contagion and epidemics in the early decades of the last century.

Costa and Kahn investigate a historical version of the "welfare magnet" hypothesis: that immigrants were attracted to cities with more generous redistribution policies. They find little support for this in the historical record. They also investigate whether public spending "crowded out" private philanthropy and find some support for a substitution of public for private provision of redistributive activities.

Costa and Kahn report an extensive series of tests to establish whether these public expenditures "mattered" in improving the health of the populations that were targeted. They present two kinds of evidence: microdata from the 1910 and 1940 censuses and aggregate data for cities. They study mothers' expected experiences with infant deaths and child mortality, and find significant effects of spending upon outcomes for whites and little or no effects for blacks. Public expenditures, sewer connection, and health examinations had important effects on mortality in the first third of the twentieth century, at least for whites.

In summary, the chapters in this book provide a very broad perspective on the role played by government policy in affecting the distribution of income and the prevalence of poverty. Although much of the focus is on the United States today and in the recent past, valuable lessons can be learned from other countries' experiences as well.

A number of conclusions are evident. First, the problems of poverty, particularly among certain groups in the population, have not disappeared with growing affluence and cannot be expected to do so in the future. Second, for a variety of reasons, even extensive policy interventions do not ensure success at poverty reduction. At the same time, though, one can identify clear evidence of successful intervention, from such policy endeavors as improved sanitation, welfare reform, and the expansion of public pensions. The continuing study of intervention successes and failures will help inform future decisions in this most critical area of public policy.

Note

1. Detailed commentary on each of these chapters was provided by two senior researchers in the field. Unfortunately, space limitations preclude

their inclusion in this volume. These comments are available on-line at the Robert D. Burch Center for Tax Policy and Public Finance at the University of California, Berkeley (http://emlab.berkeley.edu/~burch/).

References

Bureau of Labor Statistics. 2000. "Employment Situation Release." A tables, 1960–2000. Washington: U.S. Bureau of Labor Statistics.

Department of Justice. Immigration and Naturalization Service. 2001. *Statistical Yearbook of the Immigration and Naturalization Service, 2000.* Washington: U.S. Government Printing Office. Available at: http://uscis.gov/graphics/shared/aboutus/statistics/Yearbook2000.pdf (accessed September 8, 2005).

National Bureau of Economic Research (NBER). 2003. Internet Taxsim. "U.S. Federal Marginal Income Tax Rates, 1960–2003, by 1992 Real Income." Cambridge, Mass.: NBER.

Office of Management and Budget. 2004. "Budget of the United States Government. Fiscal Year 2004." Washington, D.C.: Office of Management and Budget.

———. 2005. "Historical Tables, Budget of the United States Government. Fiscal Year 2005." Washington, D.C.: Office of Management and Budget.

Social Security Administration. Office of the Chief Actuary. 2002. "Life Tables for the United States, 1900–2000." August. No. 11-11536.

U.S. Census Bureau. 2000a. "Annual Social and Economic Supplements, 1967–2000." Washington: U.S. Census Bureau, U.S. Department of Commerce. Available at: http://www.census.gov/hhes/income/histinc/h02ar.html (accessed September 8, 2005).

———. 2000b. "March Current Population Survey, Annual Social and Economic Supplements, 1960–2000." Washington: U.S. Census Bureau, U.S. Department of Commerce. Available at: http://www.census.gov/hhes/poverty/histpov/hstpov2.html (accessed September 8, 2005).

———. 2001. "March Current Population Survey, 1947–2001." Available at: http://www.census.gov/hhes/income/histinc/f12.html (accessed September 8, 2005).

———. 2003. "March Current Population Survey, Annual Social and Economic Supplements, 1960–2003." Washington: U.S. Census Bureau, U.S. Department of Commerce.

U.S. Department of Commerce. National Income and Product Accounts. 2004. "GDP and Other Major NIPA Series, 1929–2004:11." August. Available at: http://research.stlouisfed.org/fred2/series/GNPC96/downloaddata (accessed September 8, 2005).

Part I

Government Transfer Programs

Chapter 2

What Did the 1990s Welfare Reforms Accomplish?

Rebecca M. Blank

In August 1996, Congress passed and President Clinton signed into law the Personal Responsibility and Work Opportunity Reconciliation Act (PRWORA). Many pieces of legislation are heralded as "pathbreaking reform" when they are passed. PRWORA was an exception in that such a claim has turned out to be correct. The changes that PRWORA initiated, along with several related policy changes that occurred at the same time, have fundamentally altered the ways in which we provide assistance to low-income families in the United States. The implications of these changes are only beginning to be understood. This paper reviews the provisions of PRWORA and its subsequent effects on welfare programs, provides some simple empirical summaries of the changes in behavior and well-being since the mid-1990s, summarizes the existing literature that analyzes the effects of these reforms, and discusses a set of key questions about the effects of these reforms that are still unanswered.

What Did Welfare Reform Do?

Since the Reagan administration, there has been a growing interest in providing welfare recipients with the assistance and the incentives to move rapidly off welfare into employment. Experiments with welfare-to-work programs started in the 1980s. These experiments became more dramatic in the early 1990s under the Clinton administration.

States were encouraged to experiment with major changes to Aid to Families with Dependent Children (AFDC), the cash welfare program that had been created as part of the Social Security Act of 1936. The Department of Health and Human Services received requests from states to run cash welfare programs that violated the federal requirements for AFDC but that tested alternative ways to increase work incentives for women. By 1996, twenty-seven states had major waivers in effect and a number of other states were experimenting with smaller changes. These waivers allowed states to experiment with time limits on cash assistance, with lower earnings disregards (allowing women who went to work to keep benefits for a longer period of time, hence creating incentives for women to take low-wage jobs), or with various other changes designed to encourage work and discourage welfare use.

The 1996 passage of PRWORA enacted federal changes to cash assistance programs.[1] Most notably, it abolished AFDC, and in its place Congress created the Temporary Assistance for Needy Families (TANF) block grant. This had two major effects.

First, it gave states much more discretion over program design. TANF is not a federal welfare program, but a funding stream that the states can use (with restrictions). AFDC was a cash assistance program with a variety of eligibility and pay-out rules determined by the federal government, although program authority was shared and states determined other parameters of the program. A key aspect of AFDC was that it was an entitlement. Any individual who qualified for assistance under the combined federal and state rules had to be given cash assistance. Under TANF, states have a greater ability to design their own cash support programs and to limit benefit availability. No one has an entitlement to cash assistance; for instance, if states are under financial pressure they can simply reduce or eliminate assistance to certain groups.

Second, TANF provides funds to state programs as a block grant, whereas AFDC was funded through a matching grant. When states raised their AFDC spending, they drew down more federal dollars, so state-initiated changes in benefits and eligibility were partially funded by federal dollars. In contrast, the block grant is fixed and does not vary as state spending levels change, meaning that the states bear the financial risk of cycles in the need for assistance. In the years immediately following PRWORA, this worked to the states' benefit as caseloads fell but federal dollars remained unchanged. In times of tight budgets, when demand for assistance rises, the states must finance this without increases in federal dollars. Given the limits of state balanced-budget requirements, most states will not be able to expand their welfare spending in a recession, hence TANF-funded programs are likely to provide less counter-cyclical support than did AFDC.[2]

In addition to the creation of the TANF block grant, the PRWORA legislation had a number of other provisions that limited the availability of cash assistance and increased the incentives for low-income families to move into work. PRWORA increased federal work requirements by mandating that states place an increasing share of their active welfare recipients at work in order to receive their federal funds. By 2002, PRWORA required states to have 50 percent of their caseload at work or in work programs.[3] A provision lowered these requirements on states with falling caseloads, however. Since all states experienced rapid caseload declines after 1996, no state had to meet the original requirement. In 2002, the average state had 38 percent of its caseload at work or in work programs.[4]

PRWORA also enacted time limits, limiting an individual's ability to receive TANF-funded assistance to sixty months (cumulative over a lifetime). States have the ability to exempt a share of the caseload from these time limits and can always extend assistance further using state dollars. The time limits were a particularly important symbol of welfare reform, making a strong statement that cash assistance was no longer an entitlement.

Finally, a variety of PRWORA provisions limited access to income assistance programs for members of certain target groups. Immigrant access to TANF was restricted, as well as to food stamps and Medicaid. (The big cost savings in PRWORA largely came from limiting food stamps.) Certain types of disabilities were removed from eligibility for Supplemental Security Income (SSI), the cash assistance program for the elderly and disabled. Many of these provisions, especially those concerning immigrants, continued to be debated, and a variety of amendments to the 1996 law were enacted in the following years to restore eligibility for certain groups. I will not focus on these issues further in this paper except to note that they reinforced the sense that federal involvement in public assistance programs would be more limited in the future.

How Did States Respond?

The devolution of program authority over cash assistance programs from the federal to the state level provided states with both opportunities and challenges. Many observers (including me) expected that many states would largely continue "business as usual"—would rename their old AFDC programs and make some changes to increase work programs, but would continue to provide cash assistance in much the same way as before. As it turned out, virtually all states made major changes in the structure of their cash assistance programs, promoting work and limiting access. These changes are described in more detail elsewhere;[5] I focus on a few key issues here.

As will be apparent, many states adopted a mix of new programs that reflected the experimental changes that had been tested under waivers, although even those states with waivers typically adopted additional program changes once they had full authority over program design. Hence, for states with major waivers, TANF gave them more discretion to push further in the direction they were already going. For states without major waivers, it gave them authority to enact changes without the same degree of federal oversight that waivers had required.

Welfare-to-Work Efforts

As expected, states greatly expanded their welfare-to-work programs. In many cases, the administrative structure of former AFDC offices was completely changed, so that women received encouragement to look for work from the minute they stepped into the office. States talked about changing the "culture of welfare" and about using TANF funds to create work-support programs rather than the AFDC cash assistance programs.[6]

Earnings Disregards

One way that states supported and encouraged work was to lower the earnings disregards, that is, the rate at which cash benefits were reduced as earnings increased. Under the old AFDC program, for many women earnings gains were offset almost dollar-for-dollar by benefit declines once earnings rose above a (very low) disregard level. Under TANF, the majority of states provided for slower declines in benefits, allowing women to see greater income growth as their earnings grew. Rebecca M. Blank (2002, table 2) shows the enormous variation in earnings disregards among the states by the late 1990s.

Sanctions

Not only did states encourage women to work, they also enacted sanctions, enforcing benefit losses on women who did not participate in state-required programs. Sanctions were imposed most often for noncompliance with work programs, but they could be imposed on recipients for not following others of the state's requirements. States varied widely in the penalty imposed by such sanctions. In some states, repeated infractions could result in permanent disqualification for any future benefits; in other states, sanctions involved benefit reductions of increasing severity. Estimates of the number of families affected by sanctions vary enormously across studies with somewhat different methodologies. Around 20 percent of case closures seem to be due to sanctions (Pavetti, Derr, and Hesketh 2003).

Time Limits

As noted above, the federal government imposed a sixty-month time limit on women's eligibility for TANF-funded programs. A substantial minority of states (seventeen) set shorter time limits. States could choose to continue payments to any family using state funds. Many states did not have administrative systems that easily tracked months on welfare among women with multiple welfare spells. As a result, there appears to be great diversity among states in how they are implementing time limits. As of early 2002, about 230,000 families had reached time limits, of which 40 percent had their cases closed and another 16 percent faced benefit reductions (Bloom et al. 2002).

Cash Benefits

The benefits available to women who qualified for cash welfare support varied as widely across states in the TANF era as in the AFDC era. Under AFDC, states set the benefit levels, resulting in wide variation in the cash payments a woman on welfare could receive. These benefit variations were largely unchanged after PRWORA was passed, with maximum monthly benefits in 2000 ranging from $164 in Alabama to $923 in Alaska for a family of three.

All of these changes have led to enormous divergence in the availability of cash welfare across the states. Prior to 1996, state welfare generosity could typically be measured by state benefit levels. After 1996, simple state rankings of more or less generous states became much more difficult. States with high benefits might have low earn- ings disregards. States with high disregards might have short time limits. Comparative state rankings might be different among women in different life circumstances.

A major effect of these changes has been a major shift in the uses of welfare program dollars. The Department of Health and Human Services (DHHS) estimates that state and federal welfare dollars spent on noncash assistance rose from 23 percent in 1997 to 56 percent in 2002, while the proportion of money spent on direct cash assistance declined from 77 percent to 44 percent.[7]

The Interaction with Other Programs

The transformation of state AFDC programs into TANF-funded pro- grams was not the only policy change occurring in the mid-1990s. A variety of other program changes were implemented at about the same time, many of them closely related to the changes induced by PRWORA. These other changes are important because in most cases they supported and reinforced the effort states were making to move women off welfare and into work.

Major expansions in child-care subsidies were an important part of state changes. As the number of welfare recipients who were work- ing increased, an increasing amount of TANF funds were directed to child-care subsidies. But dollars from the Child Care and Development Fund (created by PRWORA by merging several preexisting programs) also expanded over this time, and in the late 1990s many states also increased their own dollars going to child-care assistance for low- income women. The Urban Institute (2002) estimates that spending on child care increased from 4 percent to 19 percent of all federal and state welfare payments between 1996 and 2000.

AFDC receipt had long been closely tied to food stamp and Med- icaid receipt. In most cases, AFDC recipients were automatically eli- gible for these two other programs. As states eliminated AFDC pro- grams, women moved into work and welfare caseloads fell. It is perhaps not surprising that food stamp receipt and Medicaid receipt fell as well. For instance, between 1996 and 1998 food stamp case- loads fell as rapidly as TANF caseloads, although many women leaving welfare for work still had incomes that should have left them eligible for food stamps. By 1999, states were making major efforts to inform and re-enroll eligible families in Medicaid and food stamps. This required them to reach out to working-poor families with these programs, a group that historically had very low enrollment rates.

In the previous decade, Medicaid eligibility had become increasingly delinked from AFDC eligibility. Legislation enacted in the 1980s provided Medicaid coverage to children in low-income families, sequentially covering older and older children in each year. By 1999, all children in families with incomes below the poverty line were covered by Medicaid.[8] Unfortunately, relatively low usage of Medicaid services by these families suggested that they had little awareness of these eligibility expansions. In 1997, the Children's Health Insurance Program (CHIP) was enacted to provide dollars to states to expand health-care usage among low-income children. Many states used CHIP dollars to help increase the use of health-care services for children whose mothers left welfare for work.

Child-care subsidies, food stamps, and health care all provide in-kind benefits to working low-income families. Two other policy changes in the 1990s directly expanded the cash income received by these families. In 1993, significant expansions in the Earned Income Tax Credit (EITC) were enacted, as a result of the legislative proposals sent by the Clinton administration to Congress to fulfill their campaign promise to "make work pay." The EITC is a refundable tax credit, which means that it can either reduce taxes owed or (if no taxes are owed) pay subsidies to recipients.

The most important aspect of the EITC is that it is paid to low-wage workers in low-income families. By running the EITC through the tax system rather than as a separate program, payment can be made conditional upon total family income. This means that the EITC is extremely well targeted to low-income working-poor families (unlike the minimum wage, which is received by all low-wage workers regardless of their overall family income). The EITC expansions of 1993 turned what had largely been a tax reduction program into a program that provided substantial income subsidies to very-low-income working families. The maximum annual subsidy available rose from $1,730 to $3,888 (in 2000 dollars) for low-wage working families with two or more children between 1993 and 2000. These increased subsidy levels meant that the EITC had to be phased out over a longer income range and affected families much higher in the income distribution. By 2000, families with two children with incomes as high as $31,152 could be eligible for some tax reduction through the EITC.

Furthermore, for single-mother families on welfare, EITC dollars do not count as income when states calculate TANF benefits. Welfare-to-work programs resulted in a growing number of women who combined welfare and work, especially in states with higher benefit levels (where women could work part-time before losing all benefits) or those states that enacted lower benefit disregards (allowing women to retain some benefits as their earnings increased). In these states, the EITC functions like an additional earnings disregard and increases the incentive to work.

Along with the EITC expansions, there were also minimum-wage increases enacted in the mid-1990s as well. Between 1993 and 1998, the minimum wage rose from $4.25 to $5.15. Despite concern that this would reduce employer demand, several studies in the mid-1990s concluded that these increases had small or zero effects on employment of less-skilled adults.[9]

The combined effect of increases in the minimum wage plus increases in the EITC was to substantially increase the number of low-wage workers who returned to work. A mother with two or more children who worked full-time at the minimum wage would have seen her real income increase from $10,568 in 1989 to $14,188 in 2000 (both numbers in 2000 dollars), a 34.3 percent increase. (The equivalent increase for mothers of one child was 19.7 percent, from $10,568 to $12,653.) In 1990 these mothers (whether with one or two children) would have had cash income below the poverty line, while by 2000 they would have been above the poverty line.

The bottom line of all these other program changes is that they largely supported and reinforced the welfare program changes being enacted by states. The minimum-wage and EITC changes increased the returns to work, particularly among low-wage workers. The growth in child-care subsidies provided better in-kind support for single mothers who left welfare for work, as did the expanded Medicaid and health insurance coverage for children in low-income families. The only exception was signaled by the decline in food stamps; if this reflected the (incorrect) belief by single mothers that food stamps were no longer available to them after leaving welfare, this would have made the benefit loss of welfare appear greater and the "cliff" that earnings needed to fill seem even larger, providing less incentive to move rapidly into employment.

The Economy's Role

Policy changes weren't the only news in the last half of the 1990s. Although the economy grew slowly coming out of the recession of 1990 to 1991, starting in 1995 the United States entered a period of sustained high growth, rising productivity, and low unemployment. By the time the expansion ended in 2001, it had become the longest period of continuous economic growth in U.S. history.

The effect of this expansion was particularly noticeable for less-skilled workers. Despite a consensus view in the early 1990s that the expected long-term unemployment rate in the United States was between 5.5 or 6 percent, unemployment remained at or below 5 percent from April 1997 through October 2001. Even among adult high school dropouts—whose unemployment rates were in the double digits in the early 1990s—unemployment fell to less than 7 percent.

Wages also rose throughout the wage distribution. This was particularly good news for less-skilled, especially male, workers, who had experienced substantial wage declines for fifteen years starting around 1979. Although the wage increases after 1995 did not make up all of the ground lost in the previous two decades, they clearly increased the economic returns of work.

The result of this economic boom was a job-rich economy that offered more job availability and better wages to low-skilled workers than at any time in the previous two or three decades. This allowed states to largely ignore job-availability concerns as they redesigned their welfare-to-work programs and encouraged a growing number of welfare recipients to seek work. States could focus on program design and implementation for their new TANF-funded programs.

The Results

A substantial literature documents the dramatic changes in welfare and work behavior over the 1990s. In this section I briefly highlight some of those changes and discuss the research literature that attempts to measure how much of these changes was due to policy efforts and how much to economic expansion.

Caseloads

Most discussed has been the dramatic decline in caseloads in the late 1990s. A sharp increase in caseloads in the early 1990s was a major impetus for states to support welfare reform, but even the strongest supporters of welfare reform did not forecast what actually happened. Figure 2.1 shows caseload changes between 1970 and 2004. After a long period of largely constant levels, AFDC caseloads rose steeply in the early 1990s (one reason behind state support for welfare reform). Caseloads began to fall prior to the 1996 passage of PRWORA, but the decline accelerated in the late 1990s. By the end of 2001, caseloads were at 42 percent of their level in 1994. Every state experienced these dramatic declines.

The economy slowed in 2000 and was officially in a recession through much of 2001; for several years afterward, there was slow growth and continuing higher unemployment rates. Yet although caseload declines appear to have stopped, caseloads have not risen,

Figure 2.1   Total AFDC and TANF Caseloads

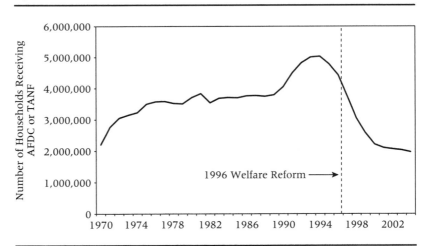

Source: Department of Health and Human Services, Agency for Children and Families (http://www.acf.dhhs.gov).
Note: 2004 data are through June of 2004.

particularly in comparison to the early 1990s, when a mild recession was associated with a large caseload increase. In part, the rise in caseloads in the early 1990s was explained by other factors than the economy, particularly the increase in the availability of AFDC for so-called "child only" cases, where AFDC dollars supported only the child, not the adult, in the family (Blank 2001). Yet, as I shall discuss later, the lack of increase in caseloads in this period of slower economic growth is something of a mystery. In particular, it is unclear if women want cash assistance but are not seeking it because they believe themselves to be ineligible, or if women are remaining employed and are able to avoid returning to the welfare rolls.

One test of whether these caseload changes were significantly correlated with policy changes is shown in figure 2.2. Here I label as the "zero point" on the X-axis the time when either a major waiver was adopted (caseloads among states with major waivers are shown with a solid line) or when a TANF plan was adopted (caseloads among states without a major waiver prior to TANF are shown with a dotted line). Essentially, I align caseload data for each state around the

Figure 2.2   Total Caseloads

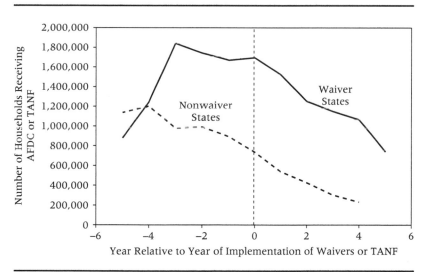

Source: March Current Population Survey. Information on waivers from Council of Economic Advisers (1999, table A1).

point where major policy change was enacted, allowing me to show how caseloads changed in waiver and nonwaiver states immediately before and after new policies were adopted.

It is clear in figure 2.2 that the enactment of waivers or of TANF is not a sufficient explanation for caseload declines. For both groups of states, there were significant caseload declines prior to the change in policy. In both cases, however, caseload decline accelerated after the policy change.

Employment

The goal of welfare-to-work programs was not just to reduce caseloads but also to increase work. Employment rose sharply in the late 1990s, especially among less-skilled single mothers, the group likely to have been most affected by these policies. Figure 2.3 shows the percentage of single mothers who reported any work over the year from 1990 to 2003; the solid line represents mothers with less than a high school degree, the dashed line represents mothers with a high school degree only, and the dotted line represents those with more than a high school degree. As expected, given the very strong economy, employment among all groups of single mothers rises over the late 1990s, but it clearly rose fastest among the less-skilled. (These

Figure 2.3   Percentage of Single Mothers Reporting Work During the Year

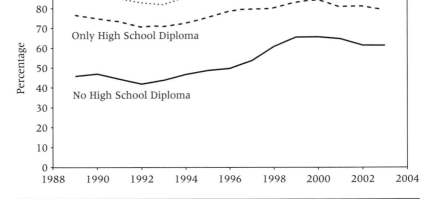

Source: Author's tabulations of the March Current Population Surveys, 1988 to 2004.

data also show faster increases among single mothers than among married mothers.) Employment among single mothers without a high school diploma rose from 42 percent in 1993 to 65 percent in 2000, an enormous increase over a very short period of time. With higher unemployment throughout the economy, employment among less-skilled single mothers falls by four percentage points by 2003, but remains far above its level of a decade earlier.

Figure 2.4 shows this trend in another way, graphing the percentage of single women receiving assistance who report employment in March of each year, among the sample of women who report receiving some form of cash welfare assistance in the previous year. Figure 2.4 shows a dramatic increase in the flow of welfare recipients into employment. (These women may be on or off welfare in March when they make this report; the primary point is that an increasing share of women with recent welfare income were entering work over time.)[10]

The economic slowdown of the early 2000s is clearly visible in these data, combined with the effects of a steady caseload decline. The likelihood of moving into work, conditional on receiving welfare in the previous year, declines in 2001 and 2002 (although it rises

Figure 2.4 Percentage of Single Mothers on Public Assistance in Previous Year Who Report Working in March

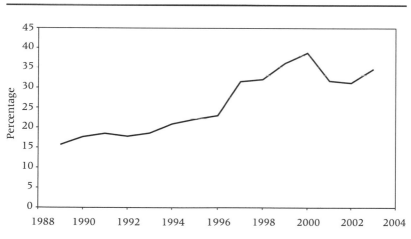

Source: Author's tabulation of the March Current Population Surveys, 1988 to 2004.

again in 2003). In part this reflects higher unemployment rates and a more sluggish economy. In part it reflects the fact that the group of women who report public assistance income in each year is shrinking over time, creating a progressively smaller and more selected base sample.

Studies of women leaving welfare in the 1990s indicate that close to two-thirds of welfare leavers were working at some future point (Cancian et al. 1999; Loprest 2001). Karin Martinson (2000) indicates that only 20 percent of leavers appear to never work in a four-year follow-up of work programs in six sites. Data from 2002 indicate that a substantial number of recent welfare leavers are working, but employment is lower and recidivism is higher than among those who left welfare before 1999 (Loprest 2003).

In all of these studies, however, it is clear that a significant minority of those who leave welfare appear to be jobless. Between 1995 and 2001, welfare caseloads fell by approximately 1.64 million. Employment among single mothers rose by approximately 820,000.[11] This rough calculation suggests that for every 100 families leaving welfare, 50 women entered the labor force.

This calculation almost surely underestimates the overall employment gain for two reasons: First, in 1995 some share of women on welfare were already working and any increase in hours that they experienced would not be captured in this calculation. Second, we know that job turnover is higher among less-skilled workers, implying that some share of this population might be employed over the year but not at work at the time of any specific survey. Even with these caveats, however, these data together with the results from surveys of welfare leavers suggest substantial nonemployment among those leaving welfare. We return to this issue later, because it creates a puzzle about how these women and their children are faring economically.

Income

Increases in employment may not leave women better off economically if their loss of benefits is as great as or greater than their increase in earnings and work expenses. Most evidence suggests that single mothers' income rose over the late 1990s, although overall income rose less than earnings because of the loss of cash benefits. Table 2.1

Table 2.1 Composition of Single Mothers' Income

	Total Income (in 2000 Dollars)	Percentage of Total Income			
		Public Assistance	Own Earnings	Other Earnings	Other Income
1985	$20,417	23.82%	49.03%	5.49%	21.66%
1986	19,842	24.96	49.58	5.44	20.02
1987	18,445	23.55	51.94	3.86	20.65
1988	18,301	23.24	52.95	3.98	19.83
1989	19,090	20.72	54.78	3.92	20.58
1990	18,412	22.63	53.32	4.15	19.90
1991	18,442	23.81	53.22	3.37	19.60
1992	17,878	22.79	52.82	3.14	21.25
1993	18,155	22.70	52.07	2.97	22.26
1994	19,222	19.47	54.82	3.52	22.20
1995	20,026	16.46	56.52	3.63	23.39
1996	19,832	14.85	58.09	3.75	23.31
1997	20,593	12.13	61.32	3.68	22.87
1998	21,765	8.63	65.31	4.18	21.89
1999	22,953	7.10	66.21	4.50	22.19
2000	23,654	5.27	68.77	4.19	21.77
2001	23,741	4.71	67.56	4.29	23.45
2002	23,805	4.45	67.18	3.98	24.40

Source: Author's tabulations of the March Current Population Survey.
Note: Total income is the mean dollar value (in 2000 dollars) before taxes. Public assistance is composed primarily of AFDC and TANF benefits. These calculations are pretax and do not include the imputed value of any in-kind benefits.

provides a snapshot of income and its components among single mothers from 1985 through 2002.[12]

As the first column of table 2.1 indicates, inflation-adjusted income rises very little among this group during the economic expansion of the late 1980s. During the expansion of the 1990s, however, income increases almost one-third between 1992 and 2000. These higher income levels are maintained in the economic slowdown, with average income of $23,805 in 2002 among single mothers. There is an amazingly large change in the components of total income over the 1990s as well. Public assistance falls from almost 25 percent of total income to less than 5 percent. Own earnings by the mother increases from just over half to two-thirds of income.

There is a slight rise in earnings by other members of the household as well. "Other income," which includes other transfer dollars (such as SSI or unemployment insurance), child support, as well as any reported gifts or transfers from other households, also increases.

Between 1990 and 2002, mothers' earnings in single-mother households rise by 63 percent, driving the increase in overall income levels. But declines in public assistance offset these earnings gains so that total income rises by only 29 percent. From table 2.1 one can calculate the average changes in welfare benefits, earnings, and overall income among single mothers. Between 1995 and 2002, single mothers who lost $100 in welfare benefits experienced a $209 rise in average and a $59 increase in other sources of income. The net result was a significant increase in income, with a $168 increase in income for every $100 decline in welfare benefits over these years.[13]

Of course, averages can obscure distributional changes. Since only a share of single mothers received welfare income, the benefit losses were concentrated among welfare leavers, while women with more skills or better labor-market connections were probably able to make greater earnings gains. Yet the evidence suggests that most single mothers, even the least-skilled, experienced some income increases in the years after welfare reform was enacted.[14] Poverty rates among single-mother households declined to 25.4 percent by 2000 and remained near this through 2002 (rising to 28.4 percent by 2004). This is the lowest rate ever recorded and is well below the 38 percent average poverty rate of single-mother households over the 1980s and early 1990s. At worst, it appears that a small share of less-skilled women might have experienced income losses. For instance, the limited evidence available on women who left welfare because of sanctions or time limits seems to indicate that they experienced income losses (Kalil, Seefeldt, and Wang 2002).

One of the difficulties in interpreting these income changes, however, is that our data are incomplete. First, particularly for working single mothers, work expenses might be quite significant, primarily because of child-care costs. Increases in earnings among these families might be entirely used up by increased child-care payments, leaving them no better off. We have no fully adequate data set that allows us to calculate income changes net of work expenses. The substantial expansion in child-care subsidies described earlier suggests that some of these work expenses are being offset. Linda

Giannarelli, Sarah Adelman, and Stefanie Schmidt (2003) indicate that 34 percent of employed low-income families with recent welfare histories received some government assistance for child care in 1999, but more than half of these also incurred out-of-pocket child-care expenses. Fully 18 percent of income went to child-care expenses in 1999 among all employed families with children whose incomes were below the poverty line.

Second, tax and transfer benefits might also be very important to this population. The expansion of the EITC benefits might add as much as $3,000 to the income of some of these families, which the income data in most surveys do not account for. Offsetting this, the decline in food stamp participation would take more resources away from these households over the late 1990s than cash income suggests.

Third, cross-household transfers might be significant for this population, including child-support payments received by these mothers, particularly as many states continue to try to increase child-support collection. But it also includes support from relatives and boyfriends. The strong economy of the 1990s would have provided more income to all low-wage workers and might have increased the inclination and ability of others to share income with single-mother families to which they felt an attachment. This may be how welfare leavers who were not employed were surviving economically.

In order to assess the overall well-being effects of the changes of the 1990s, better data for all of these issues are needed. One alternative is to look at consumption rather than income data, since consumption should reflect all of the concerns mentioned. Bruce D. Meyer and James X. Sullivan (2004) find that total consumption of single mothers increased in the mid-1990s, both in absolute terms and relative to women without children or to married mothers.

Overall, the changes of the late 1990s were very dramatic for single-mother families. There were dramatic declines in caseloads, dramatic increases in work, and (measured with less certainty) moderate increases in overall economic well-being. It is striking that these gains do not appear to have been entirely eroded (according to data available in early 2004) despite a mild recession and an extended period of low growth and higher unemployment. Indeed, unemployment rates among less-skilled women have remained low, relative to their past historical levels. In 1994, at the end of the 1990s recession, unemployment among women without a high school diploma was 16 percent. This fell to 11 percent by 2000 and was at 12.5 percent in 2002.[15]

Did Some Groups Gain More Than Others?

An important question is whether the average numbers for single mothers hide a great deal of variation in the experiences of specific groups. In this section, I disaggregate some of these results by race and ethnicity and by education level of the mother, and by children's ages in the household. Table 2.2 provides comparisons among different groups of single mothers between 1995 and 2002.

Part 1 of table 2.2 compares changes in earnings as a share of family income with changes in public assistance as a share of family income, categorizing groups by education, race, and age of youngest child. The results indicate whether some groups are better able than others to offset changes in public assistance with increases in work. Column 1 of part 1 shows that different groups were substantially more reliant on earnings in 1995. Single mothers with infants received only 45 percent of their income from earnings, whereas single mothers with no preschoolers received over 60 percent of their income from earnings. Reliance on public assistance as a share of family income in 1995 (column 3) is the reverse of earnings reliance; groups with high earnings shares have low public assistance shares and vice versa. Not surprisingly, it is those with high public assistance shares who experience the greatest declines in public assistance between 1995 and 2002 (column 4), and these are also the groups who gain the most in terms of earnings shares (column 2).

The final column (column 5) shows the ratio of changes in earnings shares to changes in public assistance shares. Because earnings increase while public assistance declines, all of these ratios are negative. (If public assistance income were entirely replaced by wage income and nothing else changed, these ratios would all be −1.0.) The ratios in column 5 range between −0.711 and −1.062. Women with younger children and less education have slightly lower earnings gains relative to their loss of public assistance. It is surprising, however, how similar the ratios in column 5 appear. Despite very different starting levels of earnings reliance and public assistance usage, the ratio of welfare declines to work increases among groups is quite similar. (Realize that the fact that these ratios are largely just below 1.0 does *not* imply that public assistance losses were greater than

Table 2.2 Changes in Single Mothers' Income, 1995 to 2002

	Earnings as a Share of Family Income (1995)	Change from 1995 to 2002	Public Assistance as a Share of Family Income (1995)	Change from 1995 to 2002	Ratio of Column(2) to Column (4)
	(1)	(2)	(3)	(4)	(5)
Part 1					
All by education					
No high school diploma	.366	.169	.342	−.213	−0.793
Only high school diploma	.582	.098	.173	−.131	−0.748
More than high school diploma	.648	.069	.084	−.065	−1.062
	.531	.091	.018	−.128	−0.711
All by race					
White (non-Hispanic)	.613	.064	.105	−.076	−0.842
Black (non-Hispanic)	.529	.151	.232	−.179	−0.844
Hispanic	.479	.176	.284	−.197	−0.893
All by age of the youngest child					
No preschooler	.605	.075	.100	−.074	−1.014
Preschooler(s) (less than six)	.510	.150	.265	−.187	−.802
Infant(s) (less than two)	.451	.162	.331	−.225	−.720

(Table continues on p. 52.)

Table 2.2   Changes in Single Mothers' Income, 1995 to 2002 (Continued)

	Share Working (1995)	Change from 1995 to 2002	Share on Welfare (1995)	Change from 1995 to 2002	Ratio of Column (2) to Column (4)
	(1)	(2)	(3)	(4)	(5)
Part 2					
All by education					
No high school diploma	.735	.065	.274	-.182	-.357
Only high school diploma	.487	.127	.465	-.274	-.464
More than high school diploma	.752	.058	.272	-.183	-.317
	.854	.032	.173	-.118	-.271
All by race					
White (non-Hispanic)	.818	.024	.197	-.129	-.186
Black (non-Hispanic)	.671	.125	.356	-.249	-.502
Hispanic	.599	.147	.369	-.240	-.613
All by age of the youngest child					
No preschooler	.808	.037	.188	-.126	-.294
Preschooler(s) (less than six)	.646	.110	.381	-.245	-.449
Infant(s) (less than two)	.560	.114	.425	-.245	-.465

	Share Below Poverty Line (1995)	Change from 1995 to 2002	Share Working (1995)	Change from 1995 to 2002	Ratio of Column (2) to Column (4)
	(1)	(2)	(3)	(4)	(5)
Part 3					
All by education					
No high school diploma	.402	−.075	.735	.065	−1.154
Only high school diploma	.682	−.109	.487	.127	−0.858
More than high school diploma	.413	−.057	.752	.058	−0.983
	.241	−.051	.854	.032	−1.594
All by race					
White (non-Hispanic)	.291	−.039	.818	.024	−1.625
Black (non-Hispanic)	.510	−.117	.671	.125	−0.936
Hispanic	.566	−.168	.599	.147	−1.143
All by age of the youngest child					
No preschooler	.305	−.052	.808	.037	−1.405
Preschooler(s) (less than six)	.522	−.104	.646	.110	−0.945
Infant(s) (less than two)	.584	−.093	.560	.114	−0.816

Source: Author's tabulation of the March Current Population Survey.

earnings gains. This is because income levels were rising at the same time. If you look at table 2.1, you can see how rising incomes mean that greater share declines in public assistance are more than offset by smaller share increases in earnings.)

Part 1 of table 2.2 shows the strikingly large gains in earnings shares among women who have relatively low earnings shares in 1995. Single mothers without high school diplomas increase their earnings share by seventeen percentage points, those with infants by sixteen percentage points, and black and Hispanic single mothers by fifteen to eighteen percentage points. The result is a convergence over the late 1990s in income sources (as well as in work and welfare behavior, seen in part 2) among all these groups of single mothers.

Part 2 of table 2.2 compares changes in the share of single mothers working to changes in the share on welfare, essentially looking at participation effects rather than income share effects. Again, there are substantial differences in the share working, ranging from 0.489 of those without a high school diploma to 0.854 of those with more than a high school diploma. Those groups with a high share working have a low share on welfare. As before, the groups that are more welfare-using in 1995 are likely to experience greater welfare declines and bigger employment increases. Again, column 5 shows the ratio of changes in the share working to changes in the share on welfare. This column indicates whether some groups were less able to find jobs relative to their rate of welfare leaving. More-disadvantaged women—the less-skilled (no high school diploma), black and Hispanic mothers, and mothers with small children— clearly make greater employment gains (relative to their movement out of welfare) than do other groups. Some of this is because more-advantaged groups of single mothers are already working at high levels (above 80 percent) in 1995. Even though these more-advantaged women significantly decrease their welfare usage (almost all of those on welfare go off, according to these data), they may simply be constrained by how much more they can move into work. Many of these more advantaged women who were on welfare may already have been working in 1995.

The question part 3 of the table tries to answer is whether increases in work are mirrored by comparable declines in the poverty rate for all of these groups. It compares changes in poverty rates to changes in the share of single mothers who are working. Among all single mothers there is almost a one-for-one relationship between increases in work and declines in the poverty rate. This varies significantly across groups, however, with more-disadvantaged groups being less able to translate work increases into poverty declines. For instance, among those with no high school diploma, the share working rises by .127 points, but their poverty rate declines by only .109 points. In contrast, among those with exactly a high school degree, the increase in work is almost exactly matched by the decline in poverty. Similar patterns exist by age of the youngest child, with single mothers with preschoolers less able to escape poverty as their work increases than single mothers with older children. Among different ethnic groups, there are fewer differences in the changes in work versus changes in poverty.

Table 2.2 suggests that there is little evidence that single mothers who were more disadvantaged in the labor market—who were less skilled, were members of an ethnic or racial minority, or had younger children—had greater difficulty finding work than those without these disadvantages. It is striking how much public assistance usage and income shares converged across these different groups. In fact, these more-disadvantaged groups seemed better able to increase their work share relative to their declines in welfare participation than other groups. These women did, however, have greater difficulty translating their employment increases into poverty declines, perhaps because they were further below the poverty line to start with and hence needed greater gains before they could escape poverty.

Interpreting These Results

A small industry has sprung up around estimating the impact of welfare reform in the late 1990s. This work is well summarized in several other places.[16] Here I simply highlight some of the main points of this literature.

Studies of Welfare Leavers

One body of research has concentrated on following individuals over time after they leave welfare to see how they are faring. This research is interesting, because it often has involved collecting new data by locating women who were identified as being on welfare at some point in the past. Many studies like this were done within the states in the late 1990s, often with quite small samples and limited follow-up.

Several of these surveys have been much more extensive and useful, however. Because these researchers actually fielded a new survey, it allowed these studies to collect some information not typically available in our larger national data sets. For instance, the National Survey of America's Families (NSAF) has collected three waves (1997, 1999, and 2002) of national survey data on about forty thousand households, with a focus on changes affecting the low-income population. These data have provided us with detailed information on the experience and well-being of low-income and welfare-leaver families.[17] A very different snapshot is provided by the Women's Employment Survey (WES), which has followed about seven hundred single mothers in an urban Michigan county who were all on welfare in February 1997. The survey, now in its fifth wave, has very detailed information on these women's lives, with particularly good information on mental health issues.[18]

These leavers studies are quite useful in providing information about the women most directly affected by welfare reform, namely, those on welfare in the mid-1990s. They provide clear evidence about work behavior, welfare recidivism, and income changes within this population. For instance, the WES data suggest that close to 80 percent of their sample are working in August 2001 (the last available survey point), although slightly less than 50 percent continue to receive some welfare-related assistance. The NSAF indicates that point-in-time employment among welfare leavers in the late 1990s was around 50 percent, whereas welfare leavers in the early 2000s only had a 42 percent employment rate in 2002.

These leaver studies are less useful in providing any sort of overall evaluation of welfare reform, since they provide no information on other populations that welfare reform should have affected. If more limited availability of cash assistance and stronger enforcement of work rules discouraged welfare entrants, or changed the behavior of non-welfare-recipients, then leavers studies provide only a very partial answer to the question "What were the overall effects of welfare reform?"

Furthermore, the leavers studies do not make any effort to separate the effect of policy changes from other changes occurring at about the same time. Some welfare leavers would have left even in the absence of reform, particularly with the strong economy of the late 1990s. These papers provide no good way to separately estimate the behavioral changes resulting from policy and those resulting from economic or other factors. In the end, the information they provide is largely descriptive—which does not mean it is not useful or interesting!

Regression Estimates on Existing National Data Samples

An alternative approach has been to use large national databases (such as the Current Population Survey) to try to analyze the effects of welfare reform. The primary question in this research has been to identify the role that policy played in reducing caseloads and raising employment. Most papers explore this by looking at caseload and employment levels using state panel data over the 1980s and 1990s, and controlling for both state and year effects, as well as state unemployment rates and various demographic measures.[19] "Policy" is specified by a series of dummy variables, indicating when states enacted waivers or when TANF plans were implemented. Identification of the policy effect depends upon variation in the timing of state enactment of reforms. Blank (2002) and Jeffrey Grogger, Lynn Karoly, and Jacob Klerman (2002) provide a much more detailed discussion of these studies and their contribution. Essentially, these studies use regression techniques to do (in a more sophisticated way) exactly what figure 2.2 does, that is, measure caseload change following a major policy change.

This estimation strategy creates some problems. The impact of waivers on caseloads is relatively well determined, since different states implemented waivers between 1992 and 1996, providing quite a bit of variation in timing. But TANF plans are all implemented between September 1996 and the end 1997. Hence, the identification of TANF policy effects depends upon small variations in the timing of enactment. Not surprisingly, TANF effects have been harder to identify.

The studies that rely upon these sort of estimations have somewhat inconsistent results. Most of them tend to indicate a significant role for both the policy changes as well as economic trends over the 1990s. But several papers show little effect on policy (Figlio and Ziliak 1999; Ziliak et al. 2000). These papers tend to use somewhat shorter data periods as a basis for estimation, and more complex specifications with multiple lagged variables.

Two alternative approaches are perhaps slightly more persuasive. Robert F. Schoeni and Blank (2000) not only look at the variation over time but also compare the differential effects among more and less educated women.[20] Their results show larger caseload and employment effects among the least-skilled, consistent with the expected effect of welfare reform. Like other studies, however, these studies have more difficulty identifying the effects of TANF than of waivers.

An even better approach is to move from estimating levels to estimating changes in the flows into and off welfare. Klerman and Steven Haider (2004) indicate that the papers with data on caseload levels are incorrectly specified, if one believes that the flows in and out of welfare are the appropriate thing to model. Unfortunately, good data on entries and exits from welfare are hard to come by. While states were required to report the number of persons entering and leaving welfare in each month for AFDC, it is clear that states defined these flows in different ways and the data across states is noncomparable. Klerman and Haider have data for the state of California and estimate their model for that state. Jeffrey Grogger (2003b) uses multiple waves of the Survey of Income and Program Participation to look at entry and exit data. Both of these papers find that both policy and economy matter in explaining caseload changes.

It is very difficult to evaluate the effects of TANF policy implementation because TANF was implemented in most states at about the same time. Nevertheless, one might note that "TANF" means different things in different states, and this should lead to ways to evaluate the effects of welfare reform components on the basis of the variation across states in the types of reforms that different states enacted. Although this is a theoretically promising approach, it has proved hard to implement in a regression framework.

Several papers have included a series of variables that describe the type of policy components enacted as part of welfare reform (earnings disregards, time limit information, types of sanctions, and so forth) in lieu of a dummy variable indicating the overall implementation of welfare reform.[21] For such a strategy to be convincing, the researcher needs to be able to fully parameterize the set of welfare reform components, and this has proved difficult. For instance, although we have relatively good information on the earnings disregard rules across states, we have very limited information on the ways in which states are running their mandatory welfare-to-work programs and how many people are being assigned into such programs. Because there appear to be correlations in the types of welfare reforms that states are enacting, if we only include information on the earnings disregards without including information on the stringency of welfare-to-work mandates, the earnings-disregard coefficient may be biased if states with high earnings disregards also happen to be states with more stringent work enforcement.[22] In short, it's hard to draw policy conclusions about the included policy components in the absence of a full set of components. In addition, only a limited number of states have implemented specific policies, and many policies have been implemented simultaneously, so that there are serious problems identifying the effects of different policy components. Perhaps for this reason, many of the papers that try to estimate the effects of policy components often find perverse results on at least some of the coefficients.

One way around this problem is to search for some sort of natural experiment that allows one to investigate the effect of a single policy component. Grogger (2003a) has been successful in doing this to analyze the effects of time limits. Grogger notes that families with younger children are more likely to hit future time limits than are families with older children (whose welfare eligibility is likely to end even without an impending time limit as the children age out of the household). He compares the effects of time limits in families with younger and older children and finds much stronger effects on the behavior of families with younger children, as expected.

Despite their limitations, these regression results may be as close as we can come to estimating the overall impact of the 1996 legislation. In general, they suggest that both the economy and policy have played an important role in the caseload reductions and the employment increases of recent years. Even with relatively complete specifications, however, controlling for a large number of economic, demographic, and policy-related changes as well as for a host of fixed effects, these models still do not explain the full magnitude of the behavioral changes among single mothers in the 1990s. For example, the Council of Economic Advisers (1999) estimates a range of models and computes the share of caseload change explained by these models. The models with the greatest explanatory power indicate that 36 percent of the caseload changes between 1993 and 1996 appear to be explained by economic factors, and 15 percent by policy changes; between 1996 and 1998, 10 percent are explained by economic factors and 36 percent by the implementation of TANF. This is roughly similar to other estimates. A recent contribution to this field (Grogger 2003b) finds that changes in TANF, the Earned Income Tax Credit, and a host of other economic variables explain only 31 percent of caseload changes between 1993 and 1999.

In the next section, I discuss possible hypotheses about why we have been so unsuccessful in fully explaining the caseload changes of the late 1990s in these econometric efforts. At a minimum, it is hard to evaluate the effects of policy and economic changes when they all occur essentially simultaneously. Between 1995 and 2000, we implemented TANF, raised the minimum wage, and implemented major EITC expansions, and at the same time the economy went into one of its strongest periods of growth. We lack the tools to fully untangle the consequences of events that occurred everywhere almost simultaneously.

Experimental Data

No discussion of welfare reform evaluations is complete without a discussion of the experimental evaluations. These evaluations grew out of the federal requirement that states seeking to experiment with revised welfare plans in the early 1990s had to provide a serious evaluation of the impact of their program changes. The staff within DHHS, which oversaw these waivers, enforced this requirement in a rigorous way. Rather than allowing states to simply tabulate administrative data, in most cases they required randomized experiments. Their goal was to truly learn from these waivers and obtain highly credible evidence of which state experiments were working more effectively than others. The result was a host of experiments across the states between 1992 and 1996 in which one group of AFDC recipients were allowed to continue as before while another group was placed into a revised program with various provisions such as stronger work efforts, greater earnings disregards, and strict enforcement of sanctions.

All of these experiments were conducted on policy changes implemented through state waivers. When the 1996 PRWORA legislation was passed, states were mandated to implement a new TANF-funded plan. States were not required to evaluate the implementation of their TANF plans (nor did they have much interest in doing so in most cases). Hence, our experimental evidence is from the waiver period, although states with waivers in place when PRWORA was passed were allowed to choose to continue the waiver for some time before they had to implement an explicit TANF plan. States with more extensive waivers typically chose this route, although many of them made other changes to their welfare programs as well.

The results of these experiments have been summarized elsewhere.[23] The waiver experiments (and a host of predecessor experimental evaluations of welfare-to-work programs in the 1980s) were quite important to the passage of PRWORA itself, since they showed that welfare-to-work efforts could increase employment, decrease AFDC participation, and could also save states money.

Because a wide variety of states ran experimental evaluations, we have evidence on quite different programs. MDRC, a research evaluation firm that implemented many of these evaluations, has worked to provide comparative information from across multiple evaluations. Some of the key findings from this comparative work are interesting.

The research suggests that "work-first programs"—programs that place women directly into employment without regard for the wage or skill level the job required—can be more effective than programs that provide job training. In part, of course, this is because women placed immediately into jobs increase their employment faster and use less public resources than women who spend a period of time in a training program before entering employment. Even three-to-five-year follow-ups, however, suggest that the women in job-training programs do not do better than the women in work-first programs (and the job-training programs were much more expensive to operate).[24] Most interesting, these results suggest that "combined" programs—those that provide job training to a selected group of welfare recipients and place the others in work-first—are more effective than only work-first or only job-training efforts. This result indicates the importance of labor-market experience in helping less-skilled women build employment and wage records. The human capital acquired through experience seems to be worth at least as much as the human capital acquired through more formal training.

In a few cases, experimental evaluations focused on quite radically different programs than AFDC. For instance, Minnesota's Family Investment Program (MFIP) combined a strong work-mandate program (enforced with sanctions) with a significantly lower earnings disregard. The results from MFIP suggested that this combination was particularly effective in both increasing employment and reducing poverty.[25] The employment increase was primarily due to the work mandates (which had little effect on income, since public assistance declined as earnings increased), while the lower earnings disregard helped reduce poverty (by providing an ongoing subsidy to very-low-wage work). A variety of researchers have written about the MFIP program and other so-called "financial-incentive" programs that provide positive incentives to work as well as negative incentives through sanctions and time limits (Blank, Card, and Robins 2000; Michalopoulos and Berlin 2001).

One of the most important results of these financial-incentive programs is the fact that there are policies that can both increase work and increase income. This is in stark contrast to the evaluations of the older Negative Income Tax programs, which assumed a trade-off between labor-force involvement and income subsidization. With a combination of earnings subsidies and work mandates, these programs raise employment and reduce poverty at the same time (albeit often with somewhat higher costs).[26]

Another contribution the experiments have made is data they generated on the link between work programs and child well-being. A variety of the experimental studies included special surveys designed to capture any changes in children's school performance or behavioral outcomes as their mothers increased their work effort as a result of welfare reform programs.[27] Since we had virtually no prior information on the effects of work programs on the children in single-mother families, this research received a great deal of attention. The general results suggest relatively few effects on smaller children. Some positive effects on behavior and achievement are visible for children who are placed in higher-quality childcare settings as a result of their mothers' employment. Among adolescents, the picture is more mixed, with some negative behavioral and achievement effects visible. This attention to the effects of welfare policies on children is a long-overdue addition to the research literature.

Overall, the experimental evaluations of welfare reform have added a great deal to our detailed knowledge of these programs' overall effects and more detailed insights into how they have worked in various states. The experimental design gave credibility to their conclusions, and were important in convincing many skeptics that welfare-to-work programs could be implemented by states and could produce employment gains without major increases in economic need among mothers in the program.

The limitations of these experiments are also clear. They are expensive to run and are best at evaluating a relatively simple program change. When used to evaluate more complex programs, there is no easy way to distinguish the effects of different program components. Hence, although the experiments evaluated programs in a number of states that implemented time limits, we cannot use the experimental data to separate out the effects of time limits on employment from the effects of other policy changes in these states.

Experiments tend to be less than ideal for evaluating major national reforms. Even if there had been funding to evaluate the implementation of full TANF plans in the mid-1990s, it is not clear that experiment evaluations would have been useful. Experiments need credible counterfactuals. Those in the control group (for example, remaining on AFDC) have to believe that this program is stable and unchanging, while those in the experimental group (the reform group) have to understand the new program and believe that it will continue for the near future. In a time of major debate about national welfare reform, the control group is likely to realize that the world is changing around them and may adapt their behaviors even if they are not personally facing program changes.

Nonetheless, the welfare reform experiments of the past have been highly useful for our understanding of which changes work in which ways. It would be useful for federal and foundation funders to continue to invest in future experimental evaluations, particularly through demonstration projects.

What Have We Learned from Welfare Reform?

Despite limitations to all of our evaluation techniques, a number of important lessons have emerged from the last decade's efforts at welfare reform, some of which I've highlighted above. As with many research projects, however, the answers to the first round of questions lead to a second round of questions. In this section, I summarize both what we've learned in some key areas and three of the major research issues that are now in front of us.

Interpreting the Caseload Decline and Employment Increase

Everyone was surprised by the magnitude of change in caseloads and employment in the mid-to-late 1990s. Caseloads declined further and employment increased more than anyone would have predicted . . . and I venture that this would have been true even if we had known in 1996 just how good the U.S. labor market would be in the late 1990s. One major lesson from the 1990s was the extent to which low-skilled single mothers could enter employment. Even research that focused on measuring the barriers to employment found that 62 percent of welfare recipients with two to three barriers to employment entered the labor force after welfare reform (Danziger et al. 2000).

The evaluation literature suggests that policy alone was not the primary reason for this. The experimental studies from the early 1990s did not suggest that serious welfare-to-work efforts would produce caseload or employment changes as large as those that actually occurred in the late 1990s. And as noted, the regression analyses suggest that policy explains only a part of the caseload decline. But the strong economy does not fully explain these changes either. For example, with a rich specification of state-level economic and policy variables, Grogger (2003b) concludes that these variables explained only 31 percent of the caseload change between 1993 and 1999.

This leaves us uncertain as to what actually did cause these dramatic behavioral changes. At least two hypotheses have been advanced. The first is that the 1990s produced a moment of incredible synergy between economy and policy. All effects were driving in the same direction. The long and sustained economic boom increased jobs and wages. This interacted with the growing incentives for employment produced by expansions in the EITC and in minimum wages, and with the increased program efforts to reduce welfare use among low-skilled women (sanctions, time limits, earnings disregards, verbal encouragement by caseworkers, and so forth). The strong economy made it easier to implement work-oriented welfare reforms and created a sense of optimism about employment opportunities. This led women to respond to the positive incentives more quickly and to the negative incentives with less resistance. The policies in turn created greater incentives for this population to learn about labor-market opportunities and to take advantage of the rise in job availability. Our evaluation techniques are not well designed to measure these interactive effects and are designed to estimate separate economy and policy effects, which may result in understating their full causal impact.

A second hypothesis focuses on the extent to which low-skilled women (particularly those on welfare) made a behavioral shift, as they internalized the strong antiwelfare message of the 1990s. This message—communicated implicitly and explicitly inside welfare offices and through the public media—told women that cash welfare was becoming increasingly limited and welfare usage was publicly disapproved. As figure 2.2 shows, caseloads fell even before reforms were enacted, consistent with some sort of "pre-announcement" response to the local publicity about welfare reform proposals designed to get women off welfare and into work.

Some of this response may be due to misinformation rather than a proactive early response to expected changes. Hearing about time limits, many women may have assumed they were subject to them. Dan Bloom and Charles Michalopoulos (2001) note that in all the experiments, some control-group members thought they were facing time limits, even though they were not.

Many state and federal officials discussed the need to "change the culture of welfare." The evidence on caseload and employment changes is at least consistent with the interpretation that they were successful. Furthermore, the fact that participation has remained low even in the more sluggish economy of the 2000s is also consistent with this behavioral-shift story.

Dramatic behavioral shifts such as we observed in the mid-1990s are relatively unique. Policy alone rarely produces such a response. The 1990s give us an opportunity to study exactly how and why such behavior changed. This is particularly crucial in understanding the potential persistence of these changes into the future, the subject to which I turn next.

Understanding the Effects of an Economic Slowdown Under the New Policy Regime

Those who were most critical of the welfare reforms predicted that these changes would have strong negative effects on the well-being of families as soon as jobs became less available. Welfare reform both pushed women into work (often with only limited assistance for child care or other work-related needs) and limited women's ability to return to cash assistance (due to time limits, diversion, sanctions, and greater state discretion). When jobs were readily available, it is not surprising that women's earnings rose. Low-wage work has always been strongly cyclical, however, and moderate increases in overall unemployment typically translate into much larger unemployment increases among the less-skilled. Thus, it is puzzling that by 2002 there was not a greater return to welfare nor a greater increase in economic need among women who became unemployed.

The effects of the economic slowdown continue to appear relatively limited among this population. Although caseloads are no longer declining, they have risen little and remain far below where they were a decade ago. Although employment among less-skilled single women has fallen, it still remains four to five percentage points below where it was a decade ago. Although poverty rates are up, among single mothers or persons of color they are still very close to their historical lows and are far below where they were a decade ago. At this point, the interpretation of these data are unclear. Three quite divergent hypotheses are possible.

First, some claim that this is exactly what welfare reform promised. Women have found jobs and built job experience and now have a strong incentive to stay employed; hence, they are retaining their jobs. Survey evidence from employers suggests that they found ex-welfare recipients to be as good or better employees than other workers in similar low-skilled jobs (Holzer, Stoll, and Wissoker 2004). Perhaps less-skilled women have responded in exactly the right way to the changed public assistance system, which supports work more than it provides support to nonworkers.

Second, some claim that the economic slowdown has been relatively mild—a short recession followed by low levels of growth. Unemployment among women has remained relatively low; the sectors with the greatest economic problems have been manufacturing and traded goods, not the retail and service sectors where women are disproportionately employed. Hence, perhaps it is not surprising that less-skilled women are retaining jobs. The current economy has not yet tested how well the new welfare programs work in a truly job-short economy.

Third, there are those who claim that the data on caseloads and employment hide economic pain that we are not measuring. The well-being of less-skilled women, forced to move in with boyfriends or family members in order to survive on low wages and unstable employment, may be poorly measured in our surveys. More crowded households may create personal stress, or parenting tension between multiple adults. It may mean increased domestic violence and abuse. Unwilling to see their children suffer from hunger, women may be taking multiple jobs (or working in the illegal economy), and meanwhile subjecting their children to the stress of a too-often-absent parent and unreliable child care. We have few adequate or timely measures of many of these potential problems, which may mean that these effects are relatively invisible to the research community.

Closely related to the effects of the economic cycle on the behavior and well-being of low-income families are the effects of state budget crises on the structure of state welfare programs. As of late 2003 there was limited evidence of major restructuring of state welfare programs. Since most states had claimed their revised welfare programs were major policy successes only a few years before, there may be a reluctance to quickly revise them. As a larger share of state dollars to low-income families are spent on work support rather than cash assistance to nonworkers, it may cause recipients to be seen as more deserving and thus deserving also of protection from cuts. Furthermore, the state dollars in welfare remain relatively small compared to the dollars spent on Medicaid and other big budget categories. Nonetheless, many states are facing deficits that will require major cuts in virtually all budget categories, and public assistance has long been a target of state cuts in times of tight budgets. It will be very interesting to see how this plays out in the years ahead.

The economic slowdown of the early 1990s seems to have had relatively mild effects as reflected in the data on employment, caseloads, and poverty that are available so far. Unfortunately, however, the detailed studies and data necessary to fully assess the effects of a slower economy on less-skilled women are still unavailable. Whatever the final assessment, this particular period of slower growth has lessened but not undone the increases in work, declines in welfare participation, and declines in poverty that occurred over the late 1990s.

Public Assistance Programs and Family Composition and Fertility

Some of the supporters of welfare reform were more concerned with reducing nonmarital fertility and increasing marriage than they were with work incentives. By making cash welfare less available to non-working single mothers and by promoting work, welfare reform should have reduced the incentives to bear children as a single mother, since children increase the difficulty and the expenses associated with finding and holding a job.

There has long been a debate in the research literature about the extent to which AFDC encouraged out-of-wedlock births. Charles Murray (1994) argues that the aggregate trend in out-of-wedlock births matches the aggregate trend in AFDC benefits, but with a lag. More methodologically nuanced microdata analysis shows smaller and more mixed results. Hilary Williamson Hoynes (1997) claims that AFDC benefit levels have no effect on fertility once state and individual effects are controlled for. Mark R. Rosenzweig (1999) uses an alternative method to control for heterogeneity among welfare recipients and finds small positive effects. In summarizing the research literature on AFDC, Robert A. Moffitt (1998, 5) states, "If there were a sizable effect of welfare on demographic behavior it would probably be more evident with the available statistical methods than appears to be the case in the research literature."

Figure 2.5 shows the trend in birth rates among unmarried women aged fifteen to forty-four. The solid line indicates the overall trend. After many decades of slowly increasing, nonmarital birth rates peaked around 1994 and appeared to level off. The steady nature of this trend made it hard to identify the effects of changing variables over this time period. Nonmarital births among black women have long been much higher, as figure 2.5 shows. Birth rates among unmarried black women peaked in 1989 and have fallen substantially since then, so that white and black nonmarital birth rates are closer today than they have been for several decades.

Trying to discern the relationship between these recent changes in fertility and the recent welfare reforms is probably even more difficult than trying to discern the relationship between employment

Figure 2.5   Live Births to Unmarried Women per 1,000 Unmarried
Women, Aged 15 to 44

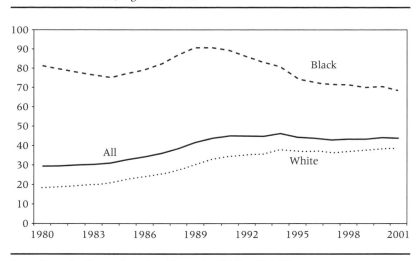

Source: Center for Disease Control and Prevention (2002, table I-18).

changes and recent welfare reforms.[28] The timing of changes in non-marital birth rates among black women does not coincide with welfare reform efforts, although the decline in nonmarital births among white women starts just as waivers and welfare reform became major topics of public discussion. Ann Horvath-Rose and H. Elizabeth Peters (2001) indicate that waivers had negative effects on nonmartial births. In one of the few papers to use post-1996 data, however, Theodore Joyce, Robert Kaestner, and Sanders Korenman (2004) find that neither waivers nor TANF appear to have consistent effects on nonmarital births.[29]

Fertility is also closely linked to household composition, cohabitation, and marriage. Evidence on the effects of welfare reform on household composition is mixed and still quite limited. For instance, John M. Fitzgerald and David C. Ribar (2004) find waivers had few effects on female headship, while Schoeni and Blank (2000) find a negative effect. This issue is particularly important because of the Bush administration's emphasis on marriage-promotion policies. As of late 2005, there is pending legislation, which most observers expect to pass, that will provide substantial funds to operate and evaluate demonstration projects designed to promote marriage and marital stability.

Our ability to link policy changes with family structure and fertility changes remains limited, in part because family-structure choices are often affected by deeply ingrained community and family norms. Thus, sexual or marriage behavior may respond much more slowly to policy changes than does employment behavior. The data often lack the nuanced control variables (such as the availability or willingness of potential marriage partners) that allow us to control for an individual's expectations and environment and to specify full models of fertility and marriage behavior. Furthermore, the data often include only small samples of women making fertility or family choices in any given year, making it hard to nail down affects within subpopulations of interest by age, race, or education level.

Interest is likely to remain high, both regarding the effects of policy changes as well as the potential effects of future policies designed to explicitly encourage marriage or discourage nonmarital fertility. Finding ways to credibly evaluate future pro-marriage policies is important, given the difficulty we've had in the past evaluating the impact of welfare policies on marriage or fertility. Experimental evaluations of demonstration projects are likely to be highly important.

Conclusions

Welfare reform provides an interesting case study not only because it provides a way to understand the specific changes in behavior and well-being that it induced among low-income populations but also because it is an example of major policy reform. Following the enactment of PRWORA, state public assistance programs changed fundamentally in a wide variety of ways. Combined with other policy changes enacted at about the same time, this nation transformed its assistance programs to poor families with children from cash assistance–oriented programs aimed at providing income support to work assistance programs aimed at encouraging and supporting work.

This transformation is hardly complete. Critics can argue that the changes have left us with an inadequate safety net, in which an increasing number of families will be unable to return for assistance because of time limits, past sanctions, and limited state funds. Meanwhile, work requirements force women into unstable, difficult work situations with low wages and inadequate support for child care, health care, or other family needs.

Supporters can argue that the system has now worked for seven years. Owing to a mix of economic good fortune and well-designed policies, a substantial number of women who would previously have been receiving welfare are now in employment, building a record of experience and demonstrating to their children the importance of work preparation. Dire predictions about deep poverty and greatly increased homelessness have not come to pass. Even if the work-support system is far from perfect, it may be preferable to the poorly functioning AFDC welfare system of the past.

It is striking that these arguments are as unsettled now as in 1996. In part this is because the five years after PRWORA was enacted were economically so unusual that it is difficult to know if the behavioral changes during that time period were unique and subject to erosion or whether they signal a permanent change in the landscape of behavior and expectations among less-skilled families.

One message that everyone should draw from the last decade of welfare reform efforts is the importance of the economy to any discussion about low-skilled workers. The availability of jobs is a necessary precondition for less-skilled women or men to find work. Sustained high unemployment, such as we experienced in the late 1970s and early 1980s, would unavoidably erode the gains from the 1990s. Policy choices have clearly been very important over the past decade, and the major policy changes that were enacted appear to have been an important causal factor behind the behavioral change. But a very important tool of antipoverty policy remains economic-growth policies. The healthier the overall U.S. economy, the lower the unemployment rate; the greater the demand for less-skilled workers, the stronger the incentives for the less-skilled to find jobs and the easier it will be for our direct antipoverty programs to support low-skilled families through work subsidies.

As highlighted earlier, there remain a number of unanswered questions regarding the impact of the policy changes in welfare in the mid-1990s—in particular there are four areas for future research. First, it remains unclear whether we can separate the effects of welfare reform from other economic and policy changes in the mid-1990s. Over time, however, it may be increasingly possible to analyze the impact of specific policy components, such as time limits, benefit-reduction rate changes, or particular work requirements. Indeed, some of the more interesting recent work has done a better and more detailed job of collecting specifics on policy components and estimating their particular effects.[30] Creative research efforts that push further along these lines can be important in allowing us to compare the impact of different state welfare program choices.

Second, having shown that it is possible to substantially increase women's labor-market involvement and decrease their welfare use, we now need to better understand the long-term implications of this greater reliance on labor-market earnings. This includes studies of the stability of employment and earnings among these single mothers as well as information on their opportunities for wage progression over time. A primary question is whether, having increased the share of working poor families, we might expect, over time, to see more of these families leave poverty. We should be particularly concerned with following those groups of relatively more-disadvantaged women (as seen in table 2.2) whose earnings shares have increased substantially while their welfare usage has plummeted.

Third, all evidence continues to show that a substantial minority of single mothers are not on welfare and not reporting employment. We need to know more about how these women are managing to survive economically, and monitor broader measures of their and their children's well-being. This will almost surely require new research on income sharing and household composition choices.

Last, there remains a series of questions about the impact of these program changes, directed primarily at welfare and labor market behavior, on other aspects of women's lives and the lives of their children. Will these women work harder to retain jobs and remain off welfare? Will this affect their future fertility and marriage choices? Will their children be more likely to pursue labor market skills and future employment? Any long-term evaluation of the effectiveness of the welfare changes in the mid-1990s will require answers to these questions.

This paper was written for the Berkeley Symposium on Poverty and Demographics, the Distribution of Income, and Public Policy, a conference honoring Eugene Smolensky. Thanks are due to Heidi Shierholz and Cody Rockey for excellent research assistance.

Notes

1. R. Kent Weaver (2000) provides a detailed description of the history that led to the passage of PRWORA.
2. For a more extended discussion of these issues, see Howard Chernick (1998).
3. Work programs are typically designed to help welfare recipients prepare for or search for jobs.
4. See www.acf.hhs.gov/programs/ofa/particip/2002/table01a.htm.
5. For instance, see Blank and Ron Haskins (2001) for a description of state changes and their consequences, or (for more technical information) see U.S. House of Representatives (2000).
6. These administrative changes are discussed in more detail in Thomas L. Gais et al. (2001).
7. These numbers are from a tabulation done by DHHS for the *New York Times* and reported in an article by Robert Pear on October 13, 2003 (p. A1). They are consistent with estimates from the Urban Institute (2002) that indicate 76 percent of federal and state welfare went to direct cash assistance in 1996; by 2000 this had fallen to 41 percent.
8. Children under five were covered if they lived in families with incomes below 133 percent of the poverty line. States had the option to set higher eligibility lines and many states covered children in families with incomes up to 185 percent of the poverty line. For more information on Medicaid, see Jonathan Gruber (2003).
9. Jared Bernstein and John Schmitt (1998) find no evidence of employment-related effects following the minimum-wage increases of the mid-1990s. David Neumark (2001) finds effects only among young workers, not among adult men or women.
10. If you break the data for figure 2.4 into those who received welfare in almost every month of the past year and those who received it only a few months, both groups show large increases in work over time.
11. These calculations are based on the Current Population Survey, March 1996 and 2002, respectively.
12. Top-coding of earnings changes over this period. For consistency, I top-code earnings for every year at its lowest level (in real dollars). This never affects more than forty observations in any year, but does reduce the impact of a few high earners on these overall averages. Since my focus is on lower-income women, I view this as a plus rather than a minus. (I use averages rather than medians since I want to show how income component shares are changing within total income.)
13. As discussed later, calculations that focus only on gross income may obscure important changes in disposable income. I could impute estimated EITC income, but to be accurate in estimating after-tax income, I would need to impute other state and federal taxes as well (in some

states, state taxes on low-income families are significant). Similarly, I could impute Food Stamps, although there is substantial non-take-up of this program. To be accurate about in-kind income, I would also need to take account of child-care subsidies, health insurance, and housing subsidies as well. In short, coming up with an accurate disposable-income calculation is quite difficult, which is the point made in the next few pages.

14. See Haskins (2001) for tabulations of cash income; Meyer and Sullivan (2004) for tabulations of consumption.

15. Author's tabulations of the Current Population Survey; this includes all less-skilled women ages sixteen to sixty-four. The equivalent unemployment rates for single mothers with less than a high school diploma are 29 percent in 1994, 16 percent in 2000, and 18 percent in 2002.

16. See Blank (2002) and Grogger, Karoly, and Klerman (2002).

17. For more information about the NSAF, see www.urban.org/Content/Research/NewFederalism/NSAF/Overview/NSAFOverview.htm.

18. For more information about the WES, see www.fordschool.umich.edu/poverty/wes/index.htm.

19. For example, see Council of Economic Advisers (1999), Geoffrey Wallace and Blank (1999), David N. Figlio and James P. Ziliak (1999), Robert A. Moffitt (1999), or Robert F. Schoeni and Blank (2000).

20. Kaushal and Kaestner (2001) use a similar method, but focus on the effects of individual policy changes rather than on overall TANF implementation.

21. See, for example, Council of Economic Advisers (1999), Moffitt (1999), or Ziliak et al. (2000).

22. For example, Neeraj Kaushal and Robert Kaestner (2001) control only for the implementation of time limits and family caps (a policy that limits cash payments to mothers who have additional nonmarital births). Since other changes were implemented at the same time, this almost surely attributes some of the effects of these other changes to the two included policies.

23. See Blank (2002) and Grogger, Karoly, and Klerman (2002). See also Bloom and Michalopoulos (2001), Gayle Hamilton (2002), and Hamilton et al. (2001).

24. V. Joseph Hotz, Guido W. Imbens, and Jacob A. Klerman (2000) indicate that the two groups tend to converge in a nine-year follow-up. But for much of this period the controlled experiment was no longer operating and the previous control group was encouraged to enter the new program; this may bias the results.

25. For a full report on MFIP, see Cynthia Miller et al. (2000).

26. Blank (2002) discusses the evidence behind this conclusion in much greater detail.

27. This literature is described and summarized in more detail in Pamela Morris et al. (2001) and Hamilton, Stephen Freedman, and Sharon McGroder (2000).
28. Thomas J. Nechyba (2001) shows how complex the relationship between welfare benefit levels and fertility changes might be.
29. Both Blank (2002) and Grogger, Karoly and Klerman (2002) review this literature in more detail. Kristin S. Seefeldt and Pamela J. Smock (2004) provide a broad summary of the recent research literature on family behavior and composition post welfare reform.
30. For instance, see Jeffrey Grogger (2003a), Caroline Danielson and Jacob Alex Klerman (2004), or Hanming Fang and Michael Keane (2004).

References

Bernstein, Jared, and John Schmitt. 1998. "Making Work Pay: The Impact of the 1996–97 Minimum Wage Increase." Washington, D.C.: Economic Policy Institute.

Blank, Rebecca M. 2001. "What Causes Public Assistance Caseloads to Grow? *Journal of Human Resources* 36(1): 85–118.

———. 2002. "Evaluating Welfare Reform in the United States." *Journal of Economic Literature* 40(4): 1105–66.

Blank, Rebecca M., David Card and Philip K. Robins. 2000. "Financial Incentives for Increasing Work and Income Among Low-Income Families." In *Finding Jobs: Work and Welfare Reform,* edited by Rebecca M. Blank and David Card. New York: Russell Sage Foundation.

Blank, Rebecca M., and Ron Haskins. 2001. *The New World of Welfare.* Washington, D.C.: Brookings Institution.

Bloom, Dan, Mary Farrell, Barbara Fink, and Diana Adams-Ciardullo. 2002. *Welfare Time Limits: State Policies, Implementation and Effects on Families.* Report submitted to the Department of Health and Human Services. New York City: MDRC.

Bloom, Dan, and Charles Michalopoulos. 2001. *How Welfare and Work Policies Affect Employment and Income: A Synthesis of Research.* New York: Manpower Demonstration Research Corporation.

Cancian, Maria, Robert Haveman, Thomas Kaplan, Daniel R. Meyer, and Barbara Wolfe. 1999. "Work, Earnings, and Well-Being After Welfare." In *Economic Conditions and Welfare Reform,* edited by Sheldon H. Danziger. Kalamazoo, Mich.: W. E. Upjohn Institute for Employment Research.

Center for Disease Control and Prevention. 2002. *Vital Statistics of the United States, 2000, Volume I, Natality.* Hyattsville, Md.: U.S. Department of Health and Human Services. Available at: http://www.cdc.gov/nchs/datawh/statab/unpubd/natality/natab2000.htm (accessed September 8, 2005).

Chernick, Howard. 1998. "Fiscal Effects of Block Grants for the Needy: An Interpretation of the Evidence." *International Tax and Public Finance* 5(2): 205–33.

Council of Economic Advisers. 1999. "Economic Expansion, Welfare Reform, and the Decline in Welfare Caseloads: An Update." Technical report. Washington: Executive Office of the President.

Danielson, Caroline, and Jacob Alex Klerman. 2004. "Why Did the Welfare Caseload Decline?" RAND working paper WR-167. Santa Monica, Calif.: RAND.

Danziger, Sandra, Mary Corcoran, Sheldon Danziger, Coleen Heflin, Ariel Kalil, Judith Levin, Daniel Rosen, Kristin Seefeldt, Kristine Siefert, and Richard Tolman. 2000. "Barriers to the Employment of Welfare Recipients." In *Prosperity for All? The Economic Boom and African Americans,"* edited by Robert Cherry and William M. Rodgers. New York: Russell Sage Foundation.

Fang, Hanming, and Michael Keane. 2004. "Assessing the Impact of Welfare Reform on Single Mothers." *Brookings Papers on Economic Activity,* vol. 1, edited by William C. Brainard and George L. Perry. Washington, D.C.: Brookings Institution.

Figlio, David N., and James P. Ziliak. 1999. "Welfare Reform, the Business Cycle, and the Decline in AFDC Caseloads," in *Economic Conditions and Welfare Reform,* edited by Sheldon H. Danziger. Kalamazoo, Mich.: W. E. Upjohn Institute for Employment Research.

Fitzgerald, John M., and David C. Ribar. 2004. "Welfare Reform and Female Headship." *Demography* 41(2): 189–212.

Gais, Thomas L., Richard P. Nathan, Irene Lurie, and Thomas Kaplan. 2001. "Implementation of the Personal Responsibility Act of 1996." In *The New World of Welfare,* edited by Rebecca M. Blank and Ron Haskins. Washington, D.C.: Brookings Institution.

Giannarelli, Linda, Sarah Adelman, and Stefanie Schmidt. 2003. *Getting Help with Child Care Expenses.* Assessing the New Federalism Project, occasional paper no. 62. Washington, D.C.: Urban Institute.

Grogger, Jeffrey. 2003a. "The Effect of Time Limits, the EITC, and Other Policy Changes on Welfare Usage, Work, and Income Among Female-Headed Families." *Review of Economics and Statistics* 85(2): 394–408.

———. 2003b. "Welfare Transitions in the 1990s: The Economy, Welfare Policy, and the EITC." National Bureau of Economic Research working paper no. 9472. Cambridge, Mass.: National Bureau of Economic Research.

Grogger, Jeffrey, Lynn Karoly, and Jacob Klerman. 2002. *Consequences of Welfare Reform: A Research Synthesis.* Document DRU-2676-DHHS, prepared by RAND for the Agency for Children and Families, Department of Health and Human Services. Santa Monica, Calif.: RAND.

Gruber, Jonathan. 2003. "Medicaid." In *Means-Tested Transfer Programs in the United States,* edited by Robert A. Moffitt. Chicago: University of Chicago Press and National Bureau of Economic Research.

Hamilton, Gayle. 2002. *Moving People from Welfare to Work: Lessons from the National Evaluation of Welfare-to-Work Strategies.* Report prepared for the U.S. Department of Health and Human Services. New York: MDRC.

Hamilton, Gayle, Stephen Freedman, Lisa Gennetian, Charles Michalopoulos, Johanna Walter, Diana Adams-Ciardullo, and Anna Gassman-Pines. 2001. *National Evaluation of Welfare-to-Work Strategies: How Effective Are Different Welfare-to-Work Approaches? Five-Year Adult and Child Impacts of Eleven Programs.* Report prepared for the U.S. Department of Health and Human Services. New York: MDRC.

Hamilton, Gayle, with Stephen Freedman and Sharon McGroder. 2000. *Do Mandatory Welfare-to-Work Programs Affect the Well-Being of Children? A Synthesis of Child Research Conducted as Part of the National Evaluation of Welfare-to-Work Strategies.* Report prepared for the U.S. Department of Health and Human Services. New York: MDRC.

Haskins, Ron. 2001. "Effects of Welfare Reform on Family Income and Poverty." In *The New World of Welfare,* edited by Rebecca M. Blank and Ron Haskins. Washington, D.C.: Brookings Institution.

Holzer, Harry J., Michael A. Stoll, and Douglas Wissoker. 2004. "Job Performance and Retention Among Welfare Recipients." *Social Service Review* 78(3): 343–69.

Horvath-Rose, Ann, and H. Elizabeth Peters. 2001. "Welfare Waivers and Non-Marital Childbearing." In *For Better and For Worse: Welfare Reform and the Well-Being of Children and Families,* edited by Greg J. Duncan and P. Lindsay Chase-Lansdale. New York: Russell Sage Foundation.

Hotz, V. Joseph, Guido W. Imbens, and Jacob A. Klerman. 2000. "The Long-Term Gains from GAIN: A Re-Analysis of the Impacts of the California GAIN Program." National Bureau of Economic Research working paper no. 8007. Cambridge, Mass.: National Bureau of Economic Research.

Hoynes, Hilary Williamson. 1997. "Does Welfare Play Any Role in Female Headship Decisions?" *Journal of Public Economics* 65(2): 89–117.

Joyce, Theodore, Robert Kaestner, and Sanders Korenman. 2004. "Welfare Reform and Non-Marital Fertility in the 1990s: Evidence from Birth Records." *Advances in Economic Analysis and Policy* 3(1): n.p. Available at http://www.bepress.com/bejeap/advances/vol3/iss1/art6 (accessed September 8, 2005).

Kalil, Ariel, Kristin S. Seefeldt, and Hui-Chen Wang. 2002. "Sanctions and Material Hardship Under TANF." *Social Service Review* 76: 642–62.

Kaushal, Neeraj, and Robert Kaestner. 2001. "From Welfare to Work: Has Welfare Reform Worked?" *Journal of Policy Analysis and Management* 20(4): 699–719.

Klerman, Jacob, and Steven Haider. 2004. "A Stock-Flow Analysis of the Welfare Caseload: Insights from California Economic Conditions." *Journal of Human Resources* 39(4): 865–86.

Loprest, Pamela. 2001. *How Are Families That Left Welfare Doing? A Comparison of Early and Recent Welfare Leavers.* Assessing the New Federalism Project, series B, no. B-36. Washington, D.C.: Urban Institute.

————. 2003. *Fewer Welfare Leavers Employed in Weak Economy.* Snapshots of America's Families, no. 5. Washington, D.C.: Urban Institute.

Martinson, Karin. 2000. *The National Evaluation of Welfare-to-Work Strategies: The Experience of Welfare Recipients Who Find Jobs.* Report. Washington: Department of Health and Human Services.

Meyer, Bruce D., and James X. Sullivan. 2004. "The Effects of Welfare and Tax Reform: The Material Well-Being of Single Mothers in the 1980s and 1990s." *Journal of Public Economics* 88(7–8): 1387–1420.

Michalopoulos, Charles, and Gordon Berlin. 2001. "Financial Work Incentives for Low-Wage Workers." In *The New World of Welfare,* edited by Rebecca M. Blank and Ron Haskins. Washington, D.C.: Brookings Institution.

Miller, Cynthia, Virginia Knox, Lisa A. Gennetian, Martey Dodoo, Jo Anna Hunter, and Cindy Redcross. 2000. *Reforming Welfare and Rewarding Work: Final Report on the Minnesota Family Investment Program.* Volume 1, *Effects on Adults.* New York: MDRC.

Moffitt, Robert A. 1998. Introduction to *Welfare, the Family, and Reproductive Behavior.* Washington, D.C.: National Research Council.

————. 1999. "The Effects of Pre-PRWORA Waivers on Welfare Caseloads and Female Earnings, Income, and Labor Force Behavior." In *Economic Conditions and Welfare Reform,* edited by Sheldon H. Danziger. Kalamazoo, Mich.: W. E. Upjohn Institute for Employment Research.

Morris, Pamela, Aletha Huston, Greg Duncan, Danielle Crosby, and Hans Bos. 2001. *How Welfare and Work Policies Affect Children: A Synthesis of Research.* New York: MDRC.

Murray, Charles. 1994. "Does Welfare Bring More Babies?" *The Public Interest* 115: 17–30.

Nechyba, Thomas J. 2001. "Social Approval, Values, and AFDC: A Reexamination of the Illegitimacy Debate." *Journal of Political Economy* 109(3): 637–72.

Neumark, David. 2001. "The Employment Effects of Minimum Wages: Evidence from a Pre-Specified Research Design." *Industrial Relations* 40(1): 121–44.

Pavetti, LaDonna, Michelle K. Derr, and Heather Hesketh. 2003. *Review of Sanction Policies and Research Studies: Final Literature Review.* Report prepared for the Department of Health and Human Services. Washington, D.C.: Mathematica.

Rosenzweig, Mark R. 1999. "Welfare, Marital Prospects, and Nonmarital Childbearing." *Journal of Political Economy* 107(6, part 2): S3–S32.

Schoeni, Robert F., and Rebecca M. Blank. 2000. "What Has Welfare Reform Accomplished? Impacts on Welfare Participation, Employment, Income, Poverty, and Family Structure." National Bureau of Economic Research working paper no. 7627. Cambridge, Mass.: National Bureau of Economic Research.

Seefeldt, Kristin S., and Pamela J. Smock. 2004. "Marriage in the Public Policy Agenda: What Do Policy Makers Need to Know for Research?" National Poverty Center working paper no. 04-02. Ann Arbor: University of Michigan, National Poverty Center.

Urban Institute. 2002. *Fast Facts on Welfare Policy: How Are TANF Dollars Spent?* Washington, D.C. Available at http://www.urban.org/content/Research/ NewFederalism/Newsroom/FastFacts/Fiscal/FF_Fiscal.htm

U.S. House of Representatives, Committee on Ways and Means. 2000. *2000 Green Book.* Washington: Government Printing Office.

Wallace, Geoffrey, and Rebecca M. Blank. 1999. "What Goes Up Must Come Down? Explaining Recent Changes in Public Assistance Caseloads," In *Economic Conditions and Welfare Reform,* edited by Sheldon H. Danziger. Kalamazoo, Mich.: W. E. Upjohn Institute for Employment Research.

Weaver, R. Kent. 2000. *Ending Welfare As We Know It.* Washington, D.C.: Brookings Institution.

Ziliak, James P., David N. Figlio, Elizabeth E. Davis, and Laura S. Connolly. 2000. "Accounting for the Decline in AFDC Caseloads: Welfare Reform or the Economy?" *Journal of Human Resources* 35(3): 570–86.

Chapter 3

The Take-Up of Social Benefits

JANET CURRIE

This chapter offers a review of recent literature regarding the take-up of social programs in the United States and the United Kingdom. A few general conclusions are drawn: First, take-up is enhanced by automatic or default enrollment and lowered by administrative barriers, although removing individual barriers does not necessarily have much effect, suggesting that one must address the whole bundle. Second, although it may be impossible to devise a definitive test of the hypothesis that eligible people fail to take up benefits because of stigma, other, more concrete types of transactions costs are probably a good deal more important. Third, although people generally have means-tested programs in the United States in mind when they discuss take-up, low take-up is also a problem in many non-means-tested social insurance programs and in other countries.

Historically, economists have paid little attention to rules about eligibility, and virtually no attention to how these rules are enforced or made known to eligibles. Hence, the marginal return to new data about these features of programs is likely to be high in terms of understanding take-up. In an era of social experiments, it might also prove useful to consider experimental manipulations of factors thought to influence take-up.

Virtually all developed countries and many developing countries have a system of income maintenance. In countries with universal programs, the aim of these systems is to maintain a minimum level of income for all individuals, at a reasonable cost to government. In the United States, the goal is to maintain such a standard for selected groups of vulnerable or "deserving" individuals, such as children, the elderly, and the disabled. One of the main problems with designing such programs is that the government typically has imperfect information about the income-generating capacity of any given individual. Hence, a central problem is to design a system that aids the vulnerable while minimizing work disincentives, given these information asymmetries. For example, Timothy Besley and Stephen Coate (1995) present a model in which a negative income tax policy supplemented by workfare for the lowest-earning individuals is optimal.

Besley and Coate (1991) argue that redistribution from rich to poor can also be achieved through the provision of in-kind goods at a quality level such that the rich "opt out" and purchase the good privately, while Charles Blackorby and David Donaldson (1988) show that in-kind provision provides a way to get people with special needs to self-select into the group receiving aid, and can thus be a second-best optimum in a world in which the government cannot judge needs perfectly. Neil Bruce and Michael Waldman (1991) offer a third, dynamic scenario, in which persons offered a cash transfer in the first period have incentives to spend it in a way that maximizes their eligibility for additional transfers in future periods. Offering a "tied" (in-kind) transfer to the target group in the first period avoids this problem. These papers build on insights from early work by Donald Nichols, Smolensky, and T. Nicolaus Tideman (1971) that discusses the way waiting times can be used to ration public goods; by George Akerlof (1978), who argues that appropriate "tagging" of benefits to individuals might result in larger transfers to low-income individuals, and Albert Nichols and Richard Zeckhauser (1982), who show that in-kind transfers can be used to make sure that a higher percentage of welfare transfers goes to the intended population.

Notwithstanding this literature on optimal targeting, most developed countries other than the United States continue to provide many social programs universally rather than targeting them to particular groups. Smolensky, Siobhan Reilly, and Eirik Evenhouse (1995) offer an in-depth discussion of targeting and outline several costs that may offset the potential budgetary benefits. First, targeting may in fact be administratively expensive, though costs can be reduced by means of applying categorical screens and providing benefits in a way that causes the target group to select into the program while others select out. Second, targeting may be socially divisive to the extent that it divides society into those who give and those who receive. Conversely, programs that offer universal benefits may enjoy greater political support.

The third problem with targeting is the subject of this essay, and that is the fact that targeting will always be imperfect. Some of those who take up benefits will not "deserve" them, and some of those who are eligible for benefits will not take them up. If take-up by eligible individuals is low, then the targeted program may fail to reach its main goal of providing a minimum bundle of goods for the target group. If take-up by ineligibles is too high, then government revenues will be diverted from other productive uses.[1]

This chapter reviews what we know about the take-up of social programs, most of which offer in-kind benefits in a targeted fashion. The first section provides some comments about an economic model of take-up. Next I review the literature on the take-up of means-tested programs in the United States with an eye toward what we can learn about the way program characteristics affect participation. In the third and fourth sections I also consider what can be learned from the take-up of several important non-means-tested, or universal, programs in the United States and provide a brief survey of the evidence regarding take-up of programs in the United Kingdom, the country outside the United States that has inspired the most work on these questions. Finally, I offer some conclusions and directions for future research.

An Economic Model of Take-Up

Robert A. Moffitt (1983) was one of the first to model nonparticipation in social programs as a utility-maximizing decision. His model emphasizes "stigma" as the main cost of participation in a means-tested program, but the model can easily be extended to include other types of costs, such as transaction costs. In Moffitt's model, utility is given by:

$$(3.1) \qquad U = U(Y + aPB) - bP$$

Here, Y is income in the absence of the program, and B is the benefit derived from the program. P is an indicator equal to 1 if a person participates, and 0 otherwise. Moffitt distinguishes between "flat" stigma, which is a fixed cost associated with participation in the program, and "variable" stigma, which is a function of the size of the benefit received. Flat and variable stigma correspond to b and a, respectively.

The two types of stigma (costs) have different implications for participation, since with only flat stigma, participation will always be increasing in the size of the benefit, whereas with variable stigma, this may not be the case. If $B = G - tWH - rN$, where G is the guarantee level, t is the marginal tax rate, W is the wage, H is hours of work, r is the marginal tax rate on non-wage income, and N is non-wage income, then flat stigma implies that the probability of participation is increasing in G, and decreasing in t, W, H, r, and N, holding Y constant. If there is variable stigma, then the individual will only participate if $a > 0$.

Moffitt goes on to add the individual's leisure to the utility function, and to consider the fact that eligibility for targeted welfare programs is contingent on being below an income threshold. (As Gary Burtless and Jerry Hausman [1978] show, the latter gives rise to a nonlinear budget, which creates work disincentives.) In this model, stigma increases the cost of participating in the program, so that some households who would participate in the absence of stigma choose not to participate.

The review of the literature suggests that other costs associated with the take-up of social programs are more important than stigma. Individuals eligible for means-tested programs face costs of learning about and applying for the programs. These costs may be sufficient to deter some individuals from using them. Moreover, the costs may be highest for precisely those individuals in greatest need, and in cases where the beneficiary is a young child or an infirm adult, the costs may be borne by an individual other than the beneficiary. To the extent that the principal's agent bears the costs of utilizing the program while the principal receives the benefit, agents may be less willing to bear the costs than the principals would be if they were in a position to choose for themselves. Agency problems provide an additional rationale for providing benefits in kind rather than in cash.

This basic cost-benefit framework has remained the basis for empirical investigations of nonparticipation in social programs. Recently, however, there have been two interesting additions to the basic model. First, there is growing interest in the role of social networks in potentially reducing the costs of participation. For example, Marianne Bertrand, Erzo Luttmer, and Sendhil Mullainathan (2000) show that a woman's propensity to use welfare increases with the number of coethnics in the area, if those coethnics have a high propensity to use welfare nationally. This work builds on earlier research by George Borjas and Lynette Hilton (1996), which showed that the types of benefits received by earlier immigrants influenced the types of benefits received by newly arrived immigrants from the same origin country. Hence, they speculated that there might be ethnic networks that transmitted information about the availability of particular benefits to new immigrants, or reduced stigma.

However, as Charles Manski (1993, 2000), William Brock and Steven Durlauf (2001), Moffitt (forthcoming) and others have highlighted, these correlations could reflect an endogenous effect where the propensity of an individual to behave in a particular way is causally influenced by the behavior of other members of the group; an exogenous effect where the individual's behavior is influenced by an exogenous characteristic that defines group membership; or a correlated effect where individuals from the same group tend to behave the same way because they have similar individual characteristics, or face similar constraints.

Anna Aizer and Janet Currie (2004) attempt to distinguish between these effects by exploiting a rich panel of Vital Statistics data from California, and by examining the propensities of women in different groups to use publicly funded prenatal-care services. They find that the use of public programs is highly correlated within groups defined using race or ethnicity and zip codes. These correlations persist even when the researchers control for many unobserved characteristics by including zip code-year fixed effects, and when they focus on the interaction between own-group behavior and measures of the potential for contacts with other members of the group (Bertrand, Luttmer, and Mullainathan's [2000] concept of "contact availability").

However, the richness of our data allows us to go further and to test the hypothesis that networks affect take-up through information sharing. In particular, we find that the estimated effects among women who have previously used the program are as large as or larger than those among first-time users. Thus, these effects cannot represent information sharing, since women who have already used the program already know about it.

It is also worth noting Esther Duflo and Emmanuel Saez's (2001) experimental study of the effects of information on the take-up of a retirement-plan option by employees. Employees were randomly selected to receive payments if they attended a workshop providing information about the benefit. Duflo and Saez then looked at whether giving information to one person in a group affected the behavior of other members of that employee's work group. They found effects that are statistically significant, but small.

A second theoretical insight comes from the growing field of "behavioral economics." Ted O'Donoghue and Matthew Rabin (1999) argue that conventional economic models incorrectly assume exponential discounting—that is, that "a person's relative preference for well-being at an earlier date over a later date is the same no matter when she is asked" (103). They further argue that a more accurate model would allow time inconsistency in the sense that people tend to put more weight on the present than on the future in making decisions. The model allows for this feature by adopting hyperbolic rather than exponential discounting.

The model has an obvious application here, in that many of the costs (though perhaps not the stigma) of enrolling in social programs are borne immediately, whereas the benefits are in the future. Hence, a person with time-inconsistent preferences might put off enrolling in the program, even though she would find it utility-maximizing to be a participant at some later date. This might be particularly true of programs such as public health insurance, where the benefit might not even be needed until a future health shock occurs.

So far, there has been little research investigating the applicability of this model to participation in public programs. Some of the most convincing evidence in favor of the model comes from studies of the participation in private benefit programs, such as 401(k) plans. For example, Brigitte Madrian and Dennis Shea (2001) analyze a change in one company's policies toward 401(k) plans that replaced a system in which employees had been required to elect participation in the plan to one in which they were automatically enrolled in a default plan. They find that participation was significantly higher after the change, and that a substantial fraction of the enrollees stuck to the default plan, even though most enrollees prior to the change had not selected the default. These results suggest substantial stickiness in behavior, even though enrollees could have changed their plan at any time with a simple phone call.

These results are striking, but they do not necessarily imply hyperbolic discounting rather than high costs of changing the default rule. Although it is true that a phone call is not costly, most people would have to spend substantial time and mental effort to inform themselves about the various options available and make a decision. This, too, can be regarded as a cost. Moreover, in the context of nonparticipation in social programs, it is not clear that the two hypotheses (that nonparticipants in social programs are "irrational" in the sense that they have time-inconsistent preferences, or that nonparticipants just face high costs of enrollment) have different policy implications. Both suggest that reducing the immediate costs associated with enrollment, or adopting default enrollment, would increase participation. Of course, if participants in social programs are on average more "present-oriented" than other people, this may still have implications for the appropriateness of paternalistic government policy (see O'Donoghue and Rabin 2003).

Take-Up of Means-Tested Programs in the United States

Table 3.1 provides a selective overview of the literature about the take-up of means-tested transfer programs in the United States, focusing on more recent studies. Most of these programs are surveyed in more detail in Moffitt (2003c). Table 3.1 provides a thumbnail sketch of each program: when it started, what it does, whom it serves, and at what cost. The programs are grouped by type and expense.

Perusal of the table suggests several broad conclusions. First, take-up varies a great deal across programs. In the case of programs that are not entitlements, take-up often appears to be constrained by the amount of funding available (for example, public housing programs and child-care subsidies). However, even among entitlement programs offering similar services, there is a good deal of variation both across programs and across different groups eligible for the programs.[2]

For example, take-up of the new State Children's Health Insurance Program (SCHIP) has been very low (8 to 14 percent), with the result that the number of uninsured children has changed relatively little since the introduction of the program. Estimates of the take-up of Medicaid coverage among children also suggest that it is low. For example, Currie and Jonathan Gruber (1996b) estimated that although the fraction of children eligible for Medicaid increased by 15.1 percentage points between 1984 and 1992, the fraction actually covered increased only 7.4 percentage points; David Card and Lara D. Shore-Sheppard (2004) find that expansions of eligibility to all poor children born after September 30, 1983, led to about a 10 percent rise in Medicaid coverage for children born just after the cutoff date. In contrast, they estimate that the further extension of Medicaid to children under six in families with incomes below 133 percent of the poverty line had relatively small effects.[3]

On the other hand, 35 to 40 percent of all U.S. births are now paid for by the Medicaid program, suggesting extremely high take-up of that program by eligible women who are delivering. Interestingly, take-up of Medicaid-covered prenatal care lags behind take-up of Medicaid-covered delivery services (Ellwood and Kenney 1995).

Explanations for Variations in Take-Up

Three explanations for low take-up are generally offered in the literature: stigma, transaction costs, and lack of information. Of course, these are not entirely separate explanations. In particular, a person's incentive to obtain information about a program may be influenced by the size of the benefit relative to the transaction costs or stigma associated with applying. For example, Beth Daponte, Seth Sanders, and Lowell Taylor (1999) find that people are more likely to know about the Food Stamp Program when they are entitled to larger benefits. It has also proved difficult to define stigma and transaction costs as completely separate constructs. For example, a person who is required to fill in a thirty-page application form that asks about a great deal of personal and seemingly irrelevant information may well feel stigmatized. So what is known about the relative importance of these factors?

There is considerable evidence that transactions costs are important determinants of take-up rates. For example, Currie's (2000) finding that enrollments in Medicaid among immigrant children increase with family size strongly suggests that what matters is benefits relative to transaction costs (or stigma). Those with more children benefit more while facing a similar cost of enrollment. Moreover, her

Table 3.1 Take-Up of Means-Tested Programs in the United States

Means-Tested Program	Take-Up Estimates	Reasons for Low or High Take-Up	Selected Literature
Medicaid Established in 1965. Provides health insurance for low-income women and children, the disabled, and the elderly in nursing homes. Eligibility for the program greatly expanded throughout the 1980s and 1990s to women and children who were not on welfare. Income cutoffs depend on child age and state. Projected to serve 34 million people at a federal cost of $159 billion dollars in 2003; state matching cost will be > $100 billion (Centers for Medicare and Medicaid Services 2002).	• As of the early 1980s, children on welfare were automatically eligible and take-up in this group was close to 100 percent. • By 1996, 31 percent of children were eligible, but only 22.6 percent were enrolled, for an average take-up rate of 73 percent (Gruber 2003). • Cutler and Gruber (1996) and Currie and Gruber (1996a; 1996b) estimate that of newly eligible children and women of childbearing age, only 23 percent and 34 percent, respectively, took up coverage, but many of these eligibles were already covered by other insurance.	• Applicants who are not on welfare may be required to show birth certificates or citizenship papers, rent receipts, and utility bills to prove residency, and pay stubs as proof of income. Many states have a time limit on the number of days the applicant can take to provide documentation, and applicants are often required to return for several interviews. Up to a quarter of Medicaid applications are denied because applicants do not fulfill these administrative requirements. They cannot produce the necessary documentation within the required time or they fail	• Currie and Gruber (1996a) find that the take-up was higher among newly eligible women who were likely to have had contact with other welfare programs than among newly eligible women of higher income levels. May reflect slow diffusion of information about coverage among new eligibles. • Currie (2000) found that immigrant children are more likely to be eligible for Medicaid but less likely to participate, if eligible. Probability of participation is higher in larger families, and there is a strong seasonal effect in participation, with peo-

- Over 35 percent of births in the United States are now covered by Medicaid (National Governors' Association 2002).
- No take-up estimates are available for the elderly and disabled, although these groups account for over two-thirds of Medicaid spending.

to attend all of the required interviews (U.S. General Accounting Office 1994).
- Eligibility may need to be reestablished as often as every six months.
- Many physicians do not treat publicly insured patients because of low reimbursement rates.
- Conversely, those who are sick may be able to retroactively obtain Medicaid coverage.
- The newly eligible may not be aware of the benefits they have a right to, particularly if they have not previously used public programs.

ple most likely to take up benefits prior to the start of school each year (when immunizations and checkups for school are mandated).
- Currie and Grogger (2002) find that loss of welfare leads to loss of Medicaid coverage among pregnant women, although most women leaving welfare remain eligible. They find little impact of state efforts to reduce non-price barriers to Medicaid coverage, such as shortening enrollment forms.
- Aizer (2003a, 2003b) compares the effects of application assistance and advertising on enrollments in California's Medicaid program. She finds that a positive impact of application

(Table continues on p. 90.)

Table 3.1 Take-Up of Means-Tested Programs in the United States *(Continued)*

Means-Tested Program	Take-Up Estimates	Reasons for Low or High Take-Up	Selected Literature
			assistance is found for children of all ages, but the effect of advertising is limited primarily to infants.
			• Aizer and Grogger (2003) find that making parents eligible for Medicaid increases child coverage. Effects were largest among black and Hispanic children.
			• Card and Shore-Sheppard (2004) find that the expansion of eligibility to all children born after September 30, 1983, in poor families led to about a 10 percentage point rise in Medicaid coverage for children born just after the cutoff date, and a similar rise in overall health insurance coverage.

Program		
State Children's Health Insurance Program (SCHIP) A block grant to states begun in 1998, SCHIP provides funds to cover health insurance for children in families with incomes below the state's Medicaid-eligibility threshold but more than 200 percent of poverty. States may either expand Medicaid or develop stand-alone programs. It is not an entitlement program.	• LoSasso and Buchmueller (2002) estimate take-up rates that range from 8.1 to 14 percent of the newly eligible. • The newly eligible may not be aware of their right to benefits, particularly if they have not previously used public programs.	• Expansions to children under six in families with incomes below 133 percent of the poverty line had relatively small effects. • LoSasso and Buchmueller (2002), using CPS data from 1996 to 2000, found that SCHIP had a small but statistically significant positive effect on insurance coverage. • Aizer (2001) finds that gains in enrollment were larger in states that contracted out outreach for SCHIP.
Supplemental Security Income Program (SSI) Enacted in 1972, SSI began paying cash benefits in 1974. It provides federal assistance for aged, blind,	• Burkhauser and Daly (2003) calculate that participation among the poor elderly declined from 78.5 percent in 1974 to 53.6 percent in 1982. • Low enrollment among the elderly could be due to lack of knowledge about the program and eligibility criteria, stigma, or transaction costs.	• Coe (1985) reported that of the persons classified as SSI-eligible who were nonparticipants (48 percent of all eligible individuals), a significant

(Table continues on p. 92.)

Table 3.1   Take-Up of Means-Tested Programs in the United States (*Continued*)

Means-Tested Program	Take-Up Estimates	Reasons for Low or High Take-Up	Selected Literature
and disabled individuals with low incomes. It has grown to become the largest federal means-tested cash assistance program, serving 6.5 million people in January 2003. Total costs for 2002 were $31.6 billion (Social Security Administration 2003).	Since then, participation rates have fluctuated from year to year, but have remained well below the highs recorded in the early years. • Recipiency rates among poor working-age adults rose from 14.8 percent in 1974 to 20.7 percent in 1998. • Recipiency rates for poor children also increased rapidly during the 1990s, rising from 2.1 percent in 1989 to 6.6 percent in 1998, owing to a change in the definition of disability for children resulting from Sullivan v. Zebley in 1990. • Estimated participation rates among the poor	• Participation among low-income working-age adults and among children is also likely to be affected by the benefits and costs of participation in SSI relative to other programs.	fraction were not aware of the program or did not think they were eligible. Coe also found that benefit levels were positively and significantly related to participation. • Warlick (1982) concluded that lack of program information and difficulty applying were the primary reasons for low participation rates among the eligible elderly. • McGarry (1996) used detailed asset and income information from the U.S. Census Bureau's 1984 Survey of Income and Program Participation (SIPP) to more accurately identify eligibility. She concluded that participa-

elderly range between 45 and 60 percent (Menefee, Edwards, and Schieber 1981; Warlick 1982; Coe 1985; Shiels et al. 1990; and McGarry 1996).

tion is determined primarily by the financial situation of eligible individuals and by their health status and finds little evidence that welfare stigma or informational program costs affect participation.

- Burkhauser and Daly (2003) concluded that the elderly poor are not generally constrained by transaction costs.

- Bound, Kossoudji, and Ricart-Moes (1998) found that two-thirds of new applicants for SSI in Michigan between 1990 and 1991 were people who had been terminated from General Assistance. The fact that these people had not applied for more generous disability payments to begin with suggests that it is onerous to apply.

(Table continues on p. 94.)

Table 3.1 Take-Up of Means-Tested Programs in the United States *(Continued)*

Means-Tested Program	Take-Up Estimates	Reasons for Low or High Take-Up	Selected Literature
			• Daly and Burkhauser (1998): Two-thirds of children found eligible for SSI in the early 1990s were in families already receiving some type of welfare assistance. • Kubik (1999): A 10 percent increase in SSI benefit increases the probability of SSI participation among families with less-educated heads by 0.39 percentage points. • Benítez-Silva, Buchinsky, and Rust (2004) estimate that 28 percent of SSI or DI applicants who get benefits are not disabled, and that 61 percent of applicants who are denied are disabled.

Garrett and Glied (2000) found that the larger SSI benefits are relative to AFDC, the more likely it is that children switched programs after Sullivan v. Zebley made it easier for them to qualify. There was no effect on adults, who were not affected by Sullivan v. Zebley.

Earned Income Tax Credit (EITC)

Established in 1975, EITC is now the largest cash antipoverty program. There were three large expansions of the credit in 1986, 1990 and 1993. The EITC grew from $3.9 million in 1975 ($99) to $31.5 billion in 2000. It is estimated that 5 million people were raised out of poverty by the credit in 1999 (National Governors' Association 2002).

- Scholz (1994) calculates that 80 to 86 percent of taxpayers eligible for the EITC received it in 1990.
- The IRS (U.S. Department of the Treasury 2002a) estimated that between 82.2 and 87.2 percent of eligible households filed tax returns and hence claimed the EITC.
- Scholz (1997) reports that roughly 95 percent of EITC claimants are either legally required to file tax

- The marginal cost of obtaining the EITC for someone who is filing is simply the cost of filling out Schedule EITC.
- Claiming the credit becomes more likely in cases where the potential credit is larger and where the filer's familiarity with the program and the U.S. tax system is greater.
- Commercial tax preparation firms can reap substantial profits by targeting

- IRS (U.S. Department of the Treasury 2002b) calculations suggest that the EITC changes between 1990 and 1996 had relatively little net effect on EITC participation.
- Holtzblatt (1991), McCubbin (2000), and others found that a significant fraction of taxpayers receive the EITC when they are not technically eligible. Misreporting a child—a violation of the

(Table continues on p. 96.)

Means-Tested Program	Take-Up Estimates	Reasons for Low or High Take-Up	Selected Literature
	returns or would file to recover the over-withheld taxes.	those eligible for EITC and offering "rapid refunds." • The IRS notifies all tax-payers who do not claim the credit but, on the basis of their filing information, appear to be eligible for it.	qualifying child-eligibility criteria—is a major reason. • Hotz, Mullin, and Scholz (2000, 2002) find that the EITC has large positive effects on the employment of adults from welfare families in California. The implied elasticity of labor-force participation with respect to net income ranges from .97 to 1.69. • Similarly, Meyer and Rosenbaum (2001) find that the EITC is responsible for much of the recent rise in labor-force participation among low-income single mothers. • Liebman (2002) matches tax records to CPS data and finds that most over-payments went to families

The Temporary Assistance for Needy Families Program (TANF)

Created in 1996 to replace the Aid to Families with Dependent Children (AFDC) program. To be eligible, one's income must be less than a state-determined needs standard. In contrast to AFDC, the TANF program, which has a block grant financing structure, has strong work requirements, time limits on receipt, options for provision of noncash assistance. Through 2002 the annual federal block grant was

- The number of recipients fell from 11.5 to 7.2 million between 1990 and 1999. In 1990, 12.1 percent of all children were on AFDC, compared to 7.2 percent of all children on TANF in 1999 (House Ways and Means Committee 2000).

- Blank (2001) estimates AFDC take-up rates among families with female heads over time. They range from 80 to 90 percent when she uses administrative data, and from 60 to 70 percent when she uses CPS data

- The cost of being on welfare is raised by many rules that TANF recipients must obey.

- With a few exceptions, the studies show that pre-TANF waivers allowing states to impose work requirements and other requirements on AFDC recipients had a negative effect on participation.

with children and that ineligible families are likely similar to eligible ones.

- Hotz and Scholz (2003) provide an overview of the recent literature.

- Blank and Ruggles (1996) estimated that single mothers used AFDC in 62 to 70 percent of the months in which they are eligible. Women who are eligible but do not participate tend to be older, white, and nondisabled, with fewer children and more education. Higher benefits also encouraged participation. These results suggest that the AFDC was used by those with the greatest long-term need whose alternative earning opportunities were limited.

(Table continues on p. 98.)

Table 3.1 Take-Up of Means-Tested Programs in the United States (*Continued*)

Means-Tested Program	Take-Up Estimates	Reasons for Low or High Take-Up	Selected Literature
$16.8 billion. States must contribute an additional $10.4 billion to $11.1 billion (see Moffitt 2003a).	• for twelve states (two-thirds of the caseload). Blank (2002) summarizes literature investigating whether the decline in the caseload should be attributed to welfare reform or to economic expansion. Welfare reform accounts for between one-third and two-thirds of the decline. • Moffitt (2003b) shows TANF participation rates over time for single mothers and for poor single mothers. Both decrease over time, and are about 40 percent for single mothers and 50 to 55 percent for poor single mothers. Moffitt (2003c) shows that nonfinancial factors		• Hoynes (1996) and Moffitt (1998) estimate participation equations which confirm that participation is positively affected by a guaranteed level of benefits and negatively affected by the marginal tax rate on benefits. Participation is also negatively affected by the hourly wage rate available and by nonprogram, nonlabor income. • Grogger and Michalopoulos (2003), using data from a randomized experiment, the Florida Family Transition Program, found that time limits affect welfare use before they become binding (people save their five years of eligibility for a "rainy day").

In the absence of other reforms that increased welfare use, FTP's time limit would have reduced welfare receipt by 16 percent. Grogger (2003) finds that time limits had a much greater effect on women with younger children, since women with older children had no incentive to conserve eligibility for benefits.

- Wallace et al. (1981) compare the fraction of eligible households and participants in the Section 8 Existing Housing and New Construction programs. For Section 8 Existing Housing they find that in 1979 the percentage of participants who were elderly was about the same as the percentage of eligibles in this category,

(Table continues on p. 100.)

had a large effect on entry and exit from TANF.

- For the entire system of housing subsidies, the participation rate among eligible households is far below 50 percent for each combination of income and family size (Olsen 2003).
- Reeder (1985) examines the percentage of households in each income and family-size class who participated in any Housing

Housing programs

Began in 1937. Programs typically reduce rent to a third of the families' income. Most assistance is reserved for households with incomes less than 50 percent of the local median income. Early programs built public housing. Since 1982, most new assistance has been in the form of voucher programs.

- Assistance is available to only a fraction of eligible households, and many housing authorities have lengthy waiting lists, or closed waiting lists.
- Participants whose income rises above the thresholds for admission are rarely terminated, and local housing authorities are allowed to admit people with incomes higher than

Table 3.1 Take-Up of Means-Tested Programs in the United States *(Continued)*

Means-Tested Program	Take-Up Estimates	Reasons for Low or High Take-Up	Selected Literature
In 2000, 5.1 million households were assisted at a cost of $20.3 billion (House Ways and Means Committee 2000).	and Urban Development (HUD) program in 1977. The highest participation rate in any of the 77 classes was less than 25 percent. For unknown reasons, the poorest households of each size have very low participation rates. Within each income class, participation rates are highest for one-person households, reflecting the strong preference received by the elderly in housing programs.	the 50 percent of median income cutoff. So persons of higher income may crowd out persons with lower income.	that minorities were a slightly larger fraction of participants than eligibles, and very-low-income households were a noticeably larger fraction of participants than eligibles. For the Section 8 New Construction Program, elderly, white females and small families were greatly overrepresented in the sense that they were a higher fraction of participants than eligibles. • Olsen and Barton (1983) find that in public housing in New York City in 1965, blacks had a much higher participation rate (about 20 percentage points) than whites with the same characteristics.

Food Stamp Program (FSP)
Established in 1961 as a
pilot program, it became

- Only 69 percent of households eligible for food
stamps participated in

- Possible reasons for nonparticipation include: lack
of knowledge about eligi-

- Crew (1995) used data
from eleven metropolitan
areas in 1987 and found
that the poorest house-
holds—nonwhites, food
stamp and welfare participants, the unemployed,
and the elderly—had
higher participation rates.

- Currie and Yelowitz (2000)
conclude that the participation in housing pro-
grams increases with the
size and is influenced by
the sex composition of the
family (owing to program
rules). It declines with the
age of the head of the
family, is much lower for
married heads, and is
highest among blacks and
those with less than high
school education.

- Three-quarters of nonpar-
ticipating households said
that they were not aware
(*Table continues on p. 102.*)

Table 3.1 Take-Up of Means-Tested Programs in the United States (*Continued*)

Means-Tested Program	Take-Up Estimates	Reasons for Low or High Take-Up	Selected Literature
nationwide in 1975. It serves households with gross incomes less than 130 percent of poverty, without other categorical requirements. FSP provides coupons that can be redeemed for food with few restrictions on the type of foods. The federal cost is $19 billion ($1998); in 1998 the program served 20.8 million persons per month (Currie 2003).	1994. A 40 percent increase in enrollments between 1988 and 1993 was due mainly to a higher participation rate among eligibles rather than to an increase in the number of eligibles (Currie 2003). • Take-up of the Food Stamp Program is high among some subgroups of eligibles, but low among others. In 1994, 86 percent of eligible children participated, but only one-third of eligible elderly persons. Virtually all eligible single-parent households were enrolled compared to only 78 percent of eligible households with children and two or	bility; transaction costs associated with enrolling in the program; and stigma associated with participation. • Transaction costs: The average Food Stamp Program application took nearly five hours of time to complete, including at least two trips to an FSP office. Out-of-pocket application costs averaged about $10.31, or 6 percent of the average monthly benefit (Currie 2003).	that they were eligible. Only 7 percent of nonparticipating eligible households gave stigma as their main reason for nonparticipation, but half answered affirmatively to at least one of the survey questions about stigma (Currie 2003). • Haider, Schoeni, and Jacknowitz (2002) found that many elderly people who are eligible for food stamps say that they do not need benefits, which may indicate that there is stigma associated with using the program unless one is very needy. • Currie and Grogger (2002) show that recertification intervals have a

more adults. Participation rates were higher in some states than in others. Participation rates also tended to fall as income rose (House Ways and Means Committee 1998).

- Blank and Ruggles (1996) found that participation in the Food Stamp Program increased with the size of the benefits. They also estimate take-up rates that range from 54 to 66 percent of all eligibles.

negative effect on participation. The introduction of electronic debit cards instead of coupons, which might have reduced stigma, had little effect.

- Daponte, Sanders, and Taylor (1999) found that informing people about their eligibility increases participation. The larger the benefit that people are eligible for, the greater the effect.

- Yelowitz (2000) estimates that for every ten newly eligible families who took up Medicaid benefits, four also took up food stamps. This fact suggests either that those who applied for Medicaid learned about the program, or that it was more worthwhile to apply for both programs than to apply

(Table continues on p. 104.)

Table 3.1 Take-Up of Means-Tested Programs in the United States (Continued)

Means-Tested Program	Take-Up Estimates	Reasons for Low or High Take-Up	Selected Literature
			for only one (that benefits relative to the cost of applying matter).
National School Lunch Program (NSLP) Established in 1946. It cost 5.8 billion and served 27 million lunches in 1998 (Currie 2003). Lunches are free to those with incomes less than 130 percent of poverty.	• 99 percent of public schools and 83 percent of all (public and private) schools participate. Nationally, 92 percent of students have the program available at their school (Burghardt, Gordon, and Devaney 1995). • In 1996, 57 percent of the children enrolled in participating institutions participated in the NSLP. Eighty-six percent of these participants received free lunches. • 87.2 percent of children aged five to seventeen with incomes less than	• In addition to the usual reasons for nonparticipation, families may not enroll in the program if their children are unlikely to eat the meals.	• Participation in the program is higher among children from the poorest families. • Gleason (1995) found that the characteristics of the meals are important determinants of participation. Glantz et al. (1994) found that if children indicate that they will not eat the meals, then parents do not apply. • Burghardt, Gordon, and Chapman (1993) found that over half of eligible nonparticipants believed they were ineligible, 10 percent thought the

The Special Supplemental Nutrition Program for Women, Infants and Children (WIC)

WIC began in 1972 as a pilot program and became permanent in 1974. Offers nutrition education, supplemental food, and referrals to health and social services to children under five, pregnant women, and nursing mothers with incomes less than 185 percent of poverty. The federal cost is $4 billion (1998 dollars); it served 7.4 million people per month in 1998 (Currie 2003).

130 percent of poverty participated in 1998 (Currie 2003).

- The USDA estimates that 75 percent of eligible persons participated in the program in 1995. Among infants take-up has been estimated to exceed 100 percent (Rossi 1998).

- Bitler, Currie, and Scholz (2003) include those who were adjunctively eligible through participation in other programs and calculate that 58 percent of all infants in any given month in 1998 were eligible for WIC. The take-up rate among eligible infants was 73.2 percent. Among children 1 to 4, 57 percent were eligible for WIC and 38 percent of eligible children received benefits. Estimates for pregnant

- Possible reasons for non-participation include lack of knowledge about eligibility, transaction costs associated with enrolling in the program, and stigma associated with participation.

- In addition, WIC is not an entitlement program, so that funds may not be sufficient to serve all eligibles who present. However, in practice, there have been no waiting lists in recent years (National Research Council 2003). Estimates of take-up are complicated by the fact that one must be at nutritional risk to qualify. However, it appears that virtually everyone who

certification process was onerous, and 20 percent cited stigma.

- Brien and Swann (1999) show that administrative barriers such as requiring income documentation discourage people from applying for WIC.

- Chatterji et al. (2002) show that in addition, restrictions on the type of food that can be purchased discourage participation.

- Bitler, Currie, and Scholz (2003) find that requiring more frequent visits to WIC offices also has negative effects on participation.

(Table continues on p. 106.)

Means-Tested Program	Take-Up Estimates	Reasons for Low or High Take-Up	Selected Literature
	and post-partum women are less accurate because of lack of information about infant feeding practices: It is estimated that 54 percent of all pregnant and post-partum women are eligible for WIC and that 66.5 percent of these women received benefits.	meets income criteria is likely to meet nutritional risk criterion (National Research Council 2003). • Participants in other programs, including Medicaid, are automatically eligible for WIC. The Department of Agriculture has ignored this linkage, resulting in underestimates of the number of eligibles and overestimates of participation rates.	
Child-care subsidy programs First established in 1954, in 1996, PRWORA consolidated four major programs into the Child Care Development Fund. Provides subsidies to working and training families with	• It is estimated that the Child-Care Subsidy Program serves only 15 percent of eligible children (Administration for Children and Families 1999). There is no systematic information available on	• The enrollment process may be particularly difficult for working parents. • Some child-care providers do not accept state subsidies. • It may be difficult to maintain continuous eligi-	• Meyers and Heintze (1999) examined a sample of current and former welfare recipients in four counties of California in 1995. Sixteen percent of employed mothers received a child-care sub-

income less than 85 percent of the state median income (or lower cutoff). The average per-month number of families served in 1998 was 907,351, at a cost of $5.1 billion (House Ways and Means Committee 2003).

- how program funds are allocated among eligible children, though information is available on type of care subsidized.
- No figures are available on the percentage of eligible children served by other subsidy programs.
- Witte (2002), using administrative data and survey data for states that guarantee subsidies for all eligible families, estimates the family-level take-up rate for child-care subsidies to be around 40 percent in early 2000. There are large variations across states.

- bility for the subsidy if income is variable.
- It is difficult to get information about the various programs available.
- There is insufficient funding to meet the demand. In addition to the block grants, states reallocated a billion dollars of their TANF block grants to child care in 1998.

sidy, 30 percent of mothers enrolled in education or training programs received a subsidy, and 34 percent of mothers in neither activity received a subsidy. The acceptance rate of mothers who applied for a subsidy was 72 percent.

- Fuller et al. (1999), using data collected in San Francisco, San Jose and Tampa in 1998, estimated a model of the child-care subsidy take-up decisions of mothers enrolled in TANF. Of the women in their sample who used any nonmaternal child care, 37 to 44 percent received a subsidy, depending on the site.

Head Start
Established in 1964. Head Start is a preschool pro-

- In 2000, about two thirds of poor three- to four-year-old children were

- Most programs are part-day, which means that they do not satisfy all

- Currie and Thomas (1995, 2000; Garces, Thomas, and Currie 2002) investi-

(Table continues on p. 108.)

Table 3.1 Take-Up of Means-Tested Programs in the United States (*Continued*)

Means-Tested Program	Take-Up Estimates	Reasons for Low or High Take-Up	Selected Literature
gram for mostly poor three- and four-year-old children. In 2000, Head Start served 860,000 children at a cost of $5.3 billion (see Currie and Neidell 2003).	served. It is not known how many of the remaining children were constrained by lack of supply. • Black and Hispanic children participate at higher rates than other children. • Programs are required to identify and take the most disadvantaged applicants.	child-care needs of working families. • The program has never been fully funded and many programs have waiting lists.	gated Head Start participation. Participation falls with income and maternal AFQT test scores, but is higher at all income levels for blacks than for whites. • Currie and Neidell (2003) find little evidence that children in high-spending programs are selected differently than children in low-spending programs.

Source: Author's compilation.

finding that enrollments follow a seasonal pattern, with enrollments spiking before school entry in the fall, also suggests that transactions costs or stigma rather than information plays the dominant role, since people are apparently timing their window of enrollment to coincide with a period when they know that they will need services.

Rebecca Blank and Patricia Ruggles's (1996) study of participation in AFDC (Aid to Families with Dependent Children) and the Food Stamp Program showed that participation increased with the size of the benefits people were eligible for, suggesting an important role for transactions costs or stigma. Daponte, Sanders, and Taylor (1999) conducted an experiment, and found that informing people about their eligibility for the Food Stamp Program increased the probability of participation. However, people eligible for larger benefits were more likely to take them up, once again suggesting a nontrivial role for transactions costs and stigma.

On a cautionary note, both sets of authors also find that it is likely to be difficult to assess eligibility for most social programs accurately using survey data. An important problem is that most surveys have little information about assets. For example, Wei-Yin Hu (1998) found that adding asset information increased estimated take-up of Supplementary Social Insurance (SSI) by 60 percent (since people who were ineligible because of their assets were excluded from the denominator). This problem may be particularly acute in the low-income population, where even employment and wages are often inaccurately reported (Haveman and Wallace 2003).

Currie and Jeffrey Grogger (2002) focus directly on transaction costs and show that reducing recertification intervals had a negative effect on participation in the Food Stamp Program, particularly among single heads of families and people in rural areas, both groups that could be expected to have relatively high transaction costs. It is possible that single mothers and people in rural areas feel more stigmatized by participation in the Food Stamp Program than others; but, the available evidence for rural areas suggests the reverse (McConnell and Ohls 2000). Moreover, the introduction of electronic debit cards in place of paper food "stamps," which might have been expected to reduce the stigma associated with food stamps by allowing people to use the program more discreetly, had no detectable effect on food stamp take-up rates, suggesting that stigma is not a major cause of low take-up of the Food Stamp Program.

There has been a great deal of debate over the extent to which the dramatic decline in the roles of AFDC and Temporary Assistance for Needy Families (TANF) over the 1990s can be attributed to welfare reforms that increased the stigma and transition costs of being on welfare rather than to favorable economic conditions (see Blank 2002 for a summary), but most studies suggest that at least a third and possibly as much as two-thirds of the decline is due to "reforms" that increased the cost of using the program. Moffitt (2003b) examines specific policies that accompanied welfare reform and documents that nonfinancial factors—including work requirements, sanctions, and "diversion" (the practice of trying to prevent people from applying for welfare by meeting an immediate need on a short-term basis)—were important determinants of entry into and exit from the TANF program in Boston, Chicago, and San Antonio.

Jeffrey Grogger (2002) and Grogger and Charles Michalopoulos (2003) examine the effect of the Personal Responsibility and Work Opportunity Reconciliation Act (PRWORA) provisions that limit the receipt of benefits to five years, and provide evidence that this change had a profound effect on the way that women used their benefits. In models that interact child age with time limits, they found that women with young children were less likely to use their benefits, other things being equal, presumably because they wanted to conserve benefits "for a rainy day." On the other hand, for women with older children the benefits have a "use it or lose it" quality, so there was no reduction in the probability of benefits receipt in this group. These results suggest that women make fairly sophisticated cost-benefit calculations when deciding to participate in this program, and that such decisions are not driven primarily by stigma (which presumably would be larger for mothers of older children than for mothers of young children).

Medicaid, AFDC and TANF, and the Food Stamp Program are large, well-established programs, and it is likely that most low-income people know of them. Therefore, to the extent that information is lacking, it is likely to be very specific information about exactly how one qualifies or applies for the program.

Lack of information could be a greater problem for take-up of some of the smaller programs. For example, in their study of current and former welfare recipients, Marcia Meyers and Theresa Heintze (1999) asked mothers eligible for employment-related child-care subsidies why they were not receiving them. The majority replied that they were not aware of the programs. Still, given that transaction costs associated with the program have not been systematically examined, it is impossible to draw any clear conclusion about their importance relative to lack of information.

The finding (Bound, Kossoudji, and Ricart-Moes 1998) that in Michigan, two-thirds of the people applying for SSI 1990 to 1991 had just been kicked off of general assistance is particularly striking since the benefits available under SSI were always much higher than those available under general assistance. Apparently, people doing the cost-benefit calculation did not find it worthwhile to pursue SSI when general assistance was an option. It is also possible that the state helped direct people who had been kicked off of general assistance onto the federally funded SSI program, thereby changing the relative transaction costs associated with the two programs. One would expect the stigma associated with general assistance—welfare for the truly indigent—to be much greater than the stigma associated with SSI, so stigma cannot explain the John Bound, Sherri Kossoudji, and Gema Ricart-Moes results.

Finally, there is considerable evidence that transaction costs associated with the Special Supplemental Nutrition Program for Women, Infants, and Children—better known as the WIC Program—matter. Michael J. Brien and Christopher A. Swann (1999) show in cross-sectional data that requiring income documentation of WIC applicants reduced participation rates. Marianne Bitler, Janet Currie, and John Karl Scholz (2003) find that requiring more frequent visits to the WIC office also reduces participation, while Pinka Chatterji et al. (2002) find that restricting the types of foods that can be purchased—which reduces the value of the benefit—discourages take-up. Hence, even in smaller programs, transactions costs relative to benefits appear to be very important determinants of take-up rates.

These observations about the importance of transactions costs and other nonfinancial barriers to participation raise two questions: (1) Are the nonfinancial barriers screening out the "right" people? That is, are the various administrative requirements attached to these transfer programs succeeding in getting benefits to their targets, the neediest eligibles? (2) To the extent that needy individuals are not being served, what can be done to increase their take-up rates?

Do Nonfinancial Barriers Screen Out the Right People?

In many cases attempts to answer this question are hampered by the fact that we do not have a very precise idea of who is eligible. For example, in the case of SSI, we need to know not only that someone has low income but also that the person is "disabled," a concept that is socially determined and liable to change over time. Hugo Benitez-Silva, Moshe Buchinsky, and John Rust (2004) look at "classification errors" in the SSI and Social Security disability insurance (DI) programs (for information on DI, see table 3.2) under the assumptions (1) that the individual's report to the Health and Retirement Survey about their disability status is the truth and (2) that both the Social Security Administration's assessment of the individual's disability status and the self-report are noisy but unbiased measures of true disability. Under either assumption, they find that 28 percent of the SSI or disability insurance applicants who are ultimately awarded benefits are not disabled (by their own reports to the Health and Retirement Survey). Conversely, 61 percent of the applicants whose applications are denied are genuinely disabled.

The authors construct a computerized model of disability based on a subset of relatively objective health indicators and argue that it may be possible to do better than the current regime in terms of reducing both instances where needy people are turned away, and instances where non-disabled people receive benefits. In any case, taken at face value, their results suggest that the SSI system does not do a very good job of identifying and assisting the neediest individuals, perhaps because the neediest people are least likely to be able to endure a lengthy and complicated application process. Similarly, William J. Reeder (1985) finds that the poorest households are less likely than slightly better-off households to live in public housing, again perhaps because these vulnerable households are unable to get through the application process.

Evidence about racial and ethnic differences in participation also suggests that programs are not always reaching the neediest people. Mark G. Duggan and Melissa Schettini Kearney (2005) have found that conditional on being poor, black children are more likely to be enrolled in the SSI program. Similarly, Currie (2000) finds that among immigrant children, many of whom are Hispanic, the eligible children are less likely to be enrolled in Medicaid. This finding mirrors a large literature on the determinants of welfare participation among immigrants, which generally finds that while immigrants are more likely to be eligible for welfare, they are less likely to take it up, other things being equal. With assimilation, however, immigrants become more likely to take up benefits (see Blau 1984); Borjas and Stephen Trejo (1991, 1993); and Borjas and Lynette Hilton (1996); Michael Baker and Dwayne Benjamin (1995) and Regina Riphahn (1998) find similar results for Canada and Germany, respectively.

An interesting exception is that, as Hu (1998) documents, elderly immigrants have similar welfare take-up rates to elderly native-born persons, and have higher overall usage of these programs. The difference is particularly pronounced among immigrants who arrived after age fifty-five. It is possible that barriers to participation are less formidable for elderly immigrants than for prime-age immigrants with children, or that elderly immigrants are selected differently than prime-age ones. For example, the elderly immigrants might come intending to take up benefits, while prime-age immigrants come primarily to work.

On the other hand some programs do seem to serve the neediest applicants. For example, participation in the federally assisted National School Lunch Program is higher among children in poor families, and Head Start, which is required to serve the neediest children first, seems to fulfill this mandate. This may be because Head Start programs are required to set out specific criteria for identifying needy children. Similarly, the WIC program guidelines lay out a very clear hierarchy for which groups should be served if funds are insufficient to serve all eligibles, and WIC participants appear to be much more disadvantaged than other eligibles, on average. Hilary Hoynes (1996) and Moffitt (1998) provide evidence that take-up of AFDC decreased with expected wages, suggesting that at least on average, it is the poorest who take up the benefits. Hence, the evidence regarding whether the neediest are being served is somewhat mixed, and program specific.

Households may also be receiving aid when they do not appear to be eligible, but it is important not to assume that all these households are in violation of program rules. Recertification intervals provide a potential reason for households with incomes above the thresholds to be on public assistance. We know, for example, that households tend to seek out public assistance when their income is unusually low (see Ashenfelter 1983). In this case, we might expect household income to rise after program enrollment, whether or not the family was involved in a public program. Since families tend to be certified for a fixed period, such a pattern might lead us to observe many families in a cross section who participated in a public program even though their incomes were above the threshold. In some programs, families are required to report any improvement in their incomes, but enforcement of this provision is often weak. In other programs, such as WIC, families are certified for fixed periods, regardless of what happens to their income during this period.

The question of whether benefits have been reaching those they target has recently been perhaps most exhaustively studied in the case of the Medicaid program. Many authors have attempted to judge the extent to which expansions of the Medicaid program led to increases in the take-up of public insurance by the target group: people who would otherwise have been uninsured. These authors have also attempted to gauge the extent to which the expansions led people who would otherwise have had private insurance to take up Medicaid. The latter phenomenon has been dubbed "crowd-out."

Despite the dramatic increases in eligibility for public insurance coverage documented in Currie and Gruber (1996a, 1996b) the fraction of children without insurance coverage has stayed remarkably constant in recent years because private health insurance coverage has decreased by about the same amount that public insurance coverage has increased (U.S. General Accounting Office 1994). However, private health insurance coverage has also been falling among groups that one would not expect to be affected by the Medicaid expansions, such as single men (Shore-Sheppard 1996). Thus, it is not obvious to what extent the relationship between increases in public insurance and decreases in private insurance is causal.

Estimates of the extent of crowd-out are sensitive to the methods used to control for possibly preexisting trends in the provision of private health insurance coverage. At the high end of the spectrum of estimates, David Cutler and Gruber (1996, 1997) estimate that for every two people covered by the Medicaid expansions, one person lost private health insurance. However, some of these people

(such as household heads who decided they would no longer purchase health insurance once their children became eligible) were
not themselves eligible for Medicaid—so not all of the people crowded
out ended up getting insurance at public expense. They calculate
that in fact about 40 percent of those crowded out ended up on
Medicaid.

Other observers have posed the question somewhat differently,
and come up with correspondingly different estimates. For example,
Lisa Dubay and Genevieve Kenney (1997) find that about 22 percent
of the increase in Medicaid coverage came from people who used to
be privately insured. Since not everyone who became eligible for
Medicaid did so as a result of the expansions, this number is necessarily smaller than Cutler and Gruber's estimate. Finally, one might
ask what share of the overall decline in private insurance coverage is
a result of the Medicaid expansions. The answer to this question is
about 15 percent, which suggests that a great deal of research
remains to be done on the causes of this decline.

One issue obscured by the focus on crowd-out is the fact that Medicaid insurance coverage may be better than what is privately available to many families. For example, many private policies do not
cover routine pediatric preventive care such as immunizations, and
most have co-payments and limits on what they will pay. Hence, the
substitution of Medicaid for private insurance coverage may improve
children's health care, and this improvement should be valued when
the costs and benefits of the expansions are weighed. Also, from a
societal point of view, it does not matter whether private or public
insurers pay for health care, except in so far as taxation creates a
dead-weight loss, and public insurance transfers resources to families
with children. Still, policymakers reluctant to raise (or eager to cut)
taxes remain deeply concerned about crowd-out. The crowd-out literature suggests that it is extremely difficult to target programs only
to those who need them, such as children who would not otherwise
have health insurance.

What Can Be Done to Increase Take-Up?

Turning to the second question, what can be done to increase take-
up among the "deserving" eligibles, the research summarized in table
3.1 suggests some hypotheses but yields few definitive answers. For
example, it may be the case that the high take-up of the Earned

Income Tax Credit (EITC) program and of Medicaid among pregnant women reflects the fact that businesses as well as individuals have a stake in promoting take-up of these programs. In the case of the EITC, anecdotal evidence suggests that commercial tax preparers have moved into low-income areas in response to the EITC. Many preparers advertise instant cash back, which is essentially the person's EITC credit less the preparer's fee. Wojciech Kopczuk and Cristian Pop-Eleches (2004) show that the introduction of state electronic filing programs significantly increased participation in the EITC, and they interpret this as evidence for the role of commercial tax preparers. Subsidies for H&R Block may not be the most desirable use of government funds, but the example does illustrate the potential role of institutions in enhancing take-up.

In the case of Medicaid, hospitals have a stake in getting pregnant women who are eligible signed up, because if the hospitals accept any payments from Medicare, they are required to serve women in active labor whether or not the women can pay. There is evidence that pregnant women were responsible for much of the uncompensated care provided by hospitals prior to the Medicaid expansions (Saywell et al. 1989). Many hospitals have subsequently established Medicaid enrollment offices on site. These offices assist people in completing applications and tell them how to obtain necessary documentation. Hospitals in at least thirty-two states and the District of Columbia began to employ private firms to help them enroll eligible patients in the Medicaid program (U.S. General Accounting Office 1994).

Conversely, Medicaid enrollment rates may have remained low for other groups despite increases in income cutoffs because of lack of support for the program among vendors of medical services. Baker and Anne Royalty (1996) use data from a longitudinal survey of California physicians observed in 1987 and 1991 and found that expansions of Medicaid eligibility to previously uninsured women and children increased the utilization of care provided by public clinics and hospitals but had little effect on visits to office-based physicians. This is consistent with much previous evidence that many providers either do not accept Medicaid payments, limit the number of Medicaid patients in their practice, or otherwise limit the amount of time that they spend with Medicaid patients (Sloan, Mitchell, and Cromwell 1978; Decker 1992).

This failure of private providers to "take up" the Medicaid program is likely to be related to the costs of doing business with the states relative to the benefits represented by reimbursement levels. Ralph Andreano, Eugene Smolensky, and Thomas Helminiak (1986) document the problems that some vendors in Wisconsin had getting reimbursed from the Medicaid program. Gruber (2003) summarizes the literature relating Medicaid reimbursement levels to physician participation (starting with Currie, Gruber, and Fischer 1995) and concludes that there is a strong relationship.

These examples suggest that giving businesses (or other entities) a stake in getting people enrolled could boost participation rates. This approach has been tried recently in California. Aizer (2003a) studies a program of application assistance in which community organizations were paid $50 per successfully completed Medicaid application. Aizer finds that this program had a large impact on Medicaid enrollments, particularly in the Hispanic and Asian communities, and that the increase in Medicaid coverage resulted in fewer hospitalizations for preventable illnesses among eligible children. In contrast, statewide advertising of Medicaid and the Healthy Families program seemed to have effects only on the enrollment of infants. It appears that people with older children already knew about these services.

Direct attempts to reduce the barriers to participation by government have not always been as successful. Currie and Grogger (2002) show that prior to welfare reform, receipt of Medicaid by pregnant women was closely tied to receipt of cash welfare, even though earlier expansions of eligibility meant that most low-income women were eligible for coverage of their pregnancies even if they were not on welfare. The key seems to be that women who are on welfare are automatically eligible for Medicaid, and do not have to undergo the Medicaid application process. One might think, then, that measures states took to make it easier for pregnant women to apply for Medicaid would have had some impact. These measures included presuming that pregnant women were eligible for Medicaid while their applications were being processed or expediting the processing of applications for pregnant women; "outstationing" Medicaid eligibility workers in hospitals that serve low-income women; dramatically shortening and simplifying application forms; and eliminating the requirement for face-to-face interviews by allowing mail-in applications from pregnant women. However, Currie and Grogger (2002) were unable to find any consistent effects of these measures, suggesting either that they were insufficient or that they were ineffective.

Aaron Yelowitz (2000) provides evidence that altering enrollment requirements for one program can have spillover effects onto the enrollments in other programs. He estimates that for every ten newly eligible families who took up Medicaid benefits, four also took up the Food Stamp Program. It is possible that families learned about their eligibility for the Food Stamp Program when they went to the welfare office to apply for Medicaid. Alternatively, it may be more worthwhile to bear the application costs in the case of Medicaid and the FSP together than in the case of FSP alone. Thus, making it easier to apply for multiple programs might increase take-up among eligibles.

Conversely, reductions in the welfare caseload have impacted enrollments in other programs. For example, Sheila Zedlewski and Sarah Brauner (1999) and Currie and Grogger (2002) found that these reductions reduced enrollment in the Food Stamp Program. And changes in other programs can also affect AFDC (TANF) caseloads—Bowen Garrett and Sherry Glied (2000) find that many families switched from AFDC to SSI after the 1990 case of *Sullivan v. Zebley* expanded eligibility for the SSI program among children. Moreover, families were more likely to switch from AFDC to SSI where the difference between SSI and AFDC benefit levels was greatest.

In summary, it can be inferred that take-up will be higher (1) the more people want the service; (2) the fewer the barriers that are placed in their way; and (3) the more institutions (including private ones) have incentives to assist individuals in taking up their benefits.

Take-Up of Non-Means-Tested Programs

Take-up is generally considered to be a problem associated with means testing. Therefore, it is worth considering whether anything further can be learned about take-up from studying a few large non-means-tested programs in the United States. For example, one might expect the stigma involved in participating in a non-means-tested program to be less than the stigma associated with participation in a means-tested one. Hence, if participation rates were universally higher in the former than the latter, then this might be taken as indirect evidence of the importance of stigma costs.

Table 3.2 provides an overview of four large social security programs in the United States that are not means-tested. The most striking thing about this table is that there is almost as much variation in the take-up of these non-means-tested programs as there is in that of the means-tested programs that were reviewed in table 3.1, which would seem to provide some indirect evidence against the stigma hypothesis.

For example, Medicare forms an interesting contrast to Medicaid, because there is almost 100 percent take-up of the optional part B coverage of outpatient services. This is perhaps surprising because it is not free—people have to pay premiums for part B insurance, even though those premiums are highly subsidized. A key difference between the two programs is that when people turn sixty-five, they have to fill out a form in order to decline part B coverage—that is, if they do not fill out the form they will get part B automatically—whereas people have to go through a complicated process in order to apply for Medicaid coverage. Thus, part B works very much like the 401(k) intervention studied by Madrian and Shea (2001).

The three other programs outlined in table 3.2 all suggest that take-up may be a problem even for non-means-tested programs. It is difficult to estimate the size of the eligible pool for Social Security Disability Insurance (DI) and Workmen's Compensation (WC), given that we do not know which people are truly disabled or injured. However, table 3.2 summarizes a good deal of evidence that participation in these programs varies with the size of the benefits, suggesting that take-up is more likely when benefits are higher relative to costs of enrollment. Similarly, take-up of unemployment insurance is generally much less than full (generally similar to take-up of programs such as AFDC and food stamps), and varies with the size of the expected benefit, as well as with the tax treatment of benefits (Anderson and Meyer 2003).

These less-than-full take-up rates suggest that eligibles perceive substantial costs associated with participation even in non-means-tested programs (otherwise, one could assume that take-up would be 100 percent for any positive benefit). If those costs were driven primarily by stigma, the evidence would suggest that the stigma associated with non-means-tested social insurance programs is of the same order of magnitude as stigma associated with using "welfare" pro-

Table 3.2 Take-Up of Non-Means-Tested Programs in the United States

Means-Tested Program	Take-Up Estimates	Reasons for Low or High Take-Up	Selected Literature
Medicare Signed into law in 1965, Medicare provides health coverage for the elderly and disabled. It consists of two parts. Part A, for mandatory hospital coverage, and part B, which provides optional outpatient insurance. Since 1997 part C has provided optional insurance for services not included in the traditional package. In 2001, 40.1 million persons were covered, of whom 34.4 million were elderly and 5.7 million disabled. Expenditures in 2001 totaled $241 billion, or $6,199 per enrollee.	• In 2002, 33,410,000 people were enrolled in part A and 32,000,000 in part B. So the implied take-up of part B is 96 percent. See http://www.ssa.gov/OACT/STATS.	• One reason for high take-up of part B is that everyone is automatically enrolled in part A when they turn 65. Even though part B is not mandatory, take-up is high, because those who have become eligible for part A have to fill out a form to decline part B.	• McGarry (2002) provides an overview of Medicare: part A is financed by a payroll tax instituted for this purpose and accounts for about 60 percent of Medicare spending. Part B is financed from general revenues and a monthly premium paid by beneficiaries. In 2002, the premium was $54 per month, and represented about 25 percent of the cost of the insurance. In addition, enrollees pay deductible and co-payments on most services covered by part B.

Social Security disability insurance (DI)

The largest U.S. income replacement program directed toward nonelderly adults. Established in 1956, it is an insurance program that provides monthly cash benefits to workers who are unable to work because of long-term severe disabilities. In 2001, it provided benefits to 6.7 million individuals at a cost of $55 billion.

- After the 1984 liberalization of the Federal Disability Insurance Program, the number of nonelderly adults receiving DI rose by 60 percent (Autor and Duggan 2003).
- The number of beneficiaries increased from 2.8 million in 1988 to 5.5 million in 2002. The number of applications increased from 1 million to 1.7 million and the number of awards from 409,000 to 750,000 (see http://www.ssa.gov/OACT/STATS/disStat.html). These figures suggest that take-up increased, since it is unlikely that the number of disabled was rising so rapidly.

- Applicants provide detailed medical, income, and asset information to the Social Security Administration office. Individuals currently in the labor force are not normally eligible. It is difficult to estimate the size of the eligible group. Some work suggests that minorities and low-socioeconomic status people are more likely to be disabled (Bound, Schoenbaum, and Waidman 1995, 1996), though self-reports of disability status may be biased (Bound 1991).
- Benítez-Silva, Buchinsky and Rust (2004) provide an overview of the long and complicated application process.
- Yelowitz (1996) concludes that rising health insur-

- Bound and Waidman (1992) find that half of the decline in labor-force participation among men 45 to 54 between 1949 and 1987 could be due to the expansion of programs such as DI.
- Mitchell and Phillips (2002) find that older people initially in poor health and of low economic status are more likely to apply for DI.
- Autor and Duggan (2003) find that DI benefits impact labor supply. State-level reductions in benefits induced large increases in labor-force participation of male and female high school dropouts from 1979 to 1984, followed by large declines during the DI expansion from 1984 to 1998.

(Table continues on p. 122.)

Table 3.2 Take-Up of Non-Means-Tested Programs in the United States (*Continued*)

Means-Tested Program	Take-Up Estimates	Reasons for Low or High Take-Up	Selected Literature
		ance costs between 1987 and 1993 were an important reason for participation in DI, since DI recipients are automatically eligible for Medicaid.	• Benítez-Silva, Buchinsky, and Rust (2004), assuming that self-reports of disability status are correct, look at the magnitude of classification errors in the award process and find that 28 percent of the SSI or DI applicants who are ultimately awarded benefits are not disabled, while 61 percent of applicants who were denied benefits are disabled. This is consistent with Bound's (1989) earlier finding that less than 50 percent of rejected DI applicants work.
Unemployment insurance (UI) An unemployed worker must (1) not be holding a job in the covered sector	• Blank and Card (1991) estimate a take-up rate of 70.7 percent in 1977, falling to 65.8 in 1987.	• Blank and Card (1991) find that at least half of the decline in take-up rates over the past decade	• Although Blank and Card (1991) find that about one quarter of the decline in take-up is still unex-

and be searching for work, (2) observe a minimum waiting period, and 3) have previously accrued a minimum level of earnings, weeks of work, or hours. Approximately, 97 percent of all wage and salary workers are in jobs that are covered by unemployment insurance. These benefits are typically paid on a weekly basis, and typically replace 50 to 60 percent of lost earnings. Federal law levies a 6.2 percent tax on the first $7,000 in wages per year and the law provides a credit of 5.4 percent to employers that pay state taxes under an approved UI system. In 2002, the UI system paid out $41.6 billion in benefits, and took in $21.4 billion in revenues

is due to a shift in unemployment from high- to low-take-up states. Benefit levels and state unionization rates have a strongly positive effect on take-up, while the disqualification rate reduces take-up. The average number of weeks worked in the last year in the unemployed pool also has a negative impact. In individual-level data, there is little evidence that declining take-up is due to increasing administrative strictness by state programs or changes in eligibility. Instead, demographic variables and household characteristics are significant determinants. Krueger and Meyer (2002) note that individu-

They also find that rates vary widely across states. From 1980 to 1982, they find a take-up rate of 83 percent (if microdata are used) and 72 percent (using state data).

• Less than 40 percent of the unemployed received UI in recent years, because many do not meet eligibility requirements (Krueger and Meyer 2002).

plained, Anderson and Meyer (2003), using administrative data from the late 1970s and early 1980s from the UI system in six states, find that a change in the tax treatment of UI benefits could be totally responsible for the unexplained portion of the decline over the early 1980s. (In 1979 UI became subject to income taxes.)

• Card and Levine (2000) study the effects of changes in the duration of unemployment insurance on the behavior of UI claimants. They find that the New Jersey Extended Benefit Program, under which claimants got thirteen additional weeks for the large majority who

(Table continues on p. 124.)

Means-Tested Program	Take-Up Estimates	Reasons for Low or High Take-Up	Selected Literature
(see http://workforce-security.doleta.gov/unem-ploycontents/data_stats).		als who are new entrants or reentrants to the labor force, who have irregular work histories, or who quit or are fired are typi-cally ineligible. Meyer (1995) surveys a series of experiments that paid bonuses to people who left unemployment and concludes that such eco-nomic incentives affect the speed with which people leave unemploy-ment insurance. • Lemieux and MacLeod (2000) find that response to a 1971 increase in the generosity of the Cana-dian UI system increased with an individual's expe-rience of the system, lead-	were initially eligible for twenty-six weeks of bene-fits, raised the fraction of UI claimants who exhausted their regular benefits by one to three percentage points. More-over, for individuals who were receiving UI when the extension was passed, the rate of leaving UI fell by about 15 percent. • Anderson and Meyer (2003) estimate that a 10 percent increase in the weekly benefit amount would increase the take-up rate by 2.0 to 2.5 per-centage points, while a similar increase in the potential duration of the benefits would increase

Workers' compensation (WC) Each state runs its own program. Employers are required to purchase insurance or self-insure to provide a specific amount of cash benefits, medical care, and in some cases rehabilitation services to workers who are disabled. In 1985, this program covered 87 percent of the workforce and paid out a total of 22.5 billion in benefits (Krueger 1990).

- Krueger and Meyer (2002) state that about 97 percent of the nonfederal labor force is covered, plus all federal employees. However, many workers ineligible for UI are eligible for WC, since workers are eligible when they begin work. It is difficult to estimate take-up, given the difficulty in accurately identifying the eligible.

ing to long-term increases in unemployment as individuals who became unemployed discovered their new entitlements.

- Benefits are about twice those of UI and are not taxable; hence the actual replacement rate may be near 1 (Krueger and Meyer 2002).

take-up by .5 to 1.0 percentage points. A tax increase that decreased the value of after-tax benefits by 10 percent would lower take-up by 1.0 to 1.5 percentage points. Assuming take-up rates of 40 to 60 percent, they estimate benefit elasticities between .33 to .60.

- Krueger (1990) finds that higher workers' compensation benefits are associated with greater participation in the case of men, and that the waiting period has a substantial negative effect on participation. In particular, a 10 percent increase in temporary total benefits would lead to a 4.6 to 6.7 percent increase in workers' compensation recipiency overall.

(Table continues on p. 126.)

Table 3.2 Take-Up of Non-Means-Tested Programs in the United States *(Continued)*

Means-Tested Program	Take-Up Estimates	Reasons for Low or High Take-Up	Selected Literature
			• Card and McCall (1996) ask whether workers' compensation is covering uninsured medical costs. They find that workers without medical coverage are no more likely to report a Monday injury than other workers, and that employers are no more likely to challenge a Monday injury claim, even for workers who lack medical insurance.
			• Krueger and Meyer (2002) summarize the empirical evidence on WC and say that more generous WC is associated with higher reported injury rates, but that the effect is small.

Source: Author's compilation.

grams. If we believe, on the other hand, that the stigma associated with using non-means-tested social insurance programs is less than that associated with means-tested programs, then we would have to conclude that transactions costs are major determinants of participation in all types of programs.

Take-Up in the U.K.

Low take-up of social programs is also often perceived as a peculiarly American problem, possibly because of the United States' heavy reliance on means-tested programs in its social security system. Hence, it is also of interest to examine take-up of social benefits in another country, such as the United Kingdom.[4] Table 3.3 provides a brief overview of the main social benefits available in the United Kingdom. It is less complete than tables 3.1 and 3.2, given this author's relative unfamiliarity with these programs, and less emphasis on the take-up issue in the British literature (although see Peter Craig [1991] for an early survey).

The main point is that many U.K. programs also exhibit less than full take-up. Estimates of take-up of the Working Families' Tax Credit (which is similar to the American EITC) by single mothers range from 67 to 81 percent, which is comparable to Scholz's estimate of 80 to 87 percent for the EITC in table 3.1. Take-up of Income Support among nonpensioners, which (at least for lone mothers) corresponds roughly to AFDC, seems to be higher in the United Kingdom than in the United States, though at 80 percent, is still much less than full. Take-up of Income Support for Pensioners, which corresponds to SSI for the elderly, is somewhat higher than in the United States, at between 64 and 78 percent, but again, is much less than full.

These rough comparisons suggest that perhaps American researchers should pay more attention to factors determining take-up of social benefits outside the United States. It is interesting to note that the one U.K. program with near universal take-up is the Child Benefit. Mothers receive the application materials for this program in hospital, which presumably greatly reduces application transaction costs.

The introduction in the United Kingdom of several new programs, such as the "New Deal" for the unemployed in 1998, would

Table 3.3 Take-Up Rates of Programs in the United Kingdom

Means-Tested Program	Take-Up Estimates	Reasons for Low or High Take-Up	Selected Literature
Working Families' Tax Credit A refundable tax credit for low-income families with children and an adult who works sixteen hours a week or more. It began in 1999 as a replacement for the Family Credit (introduced in the late 1980s). It is more generous than Family Credit in terms of maximum benefits, the income level where the phase-out begins, and the phase-out rate. Once granted, entitlement continued for six months, regardless of whether the family's financial circumstances changed. It includes a new nonrefundable Childcare Tax Credit. In	• Clark and McCrae (2001) find that official estimates of take-up of the Family Credit (72 percent) are much higher than what they simulate using the TAXBEN simulation model, 48 percent. Take-up rates vary widely depending on marital status—67 percent of single parents compared to 40 percent of couples. Take-up also increases with the size of the benefit. • Brewer, Clark, and Wakefield (2002) estimate take-up rates over time: 77 percent in 1993 to 1994 and 81 percent in 1998 to 1999 for single parents and 66 percent	• Because the credit operates through the tax system, stigma effects should be minimized (Blundell 2002). • Dorsett and Heady (1991) note the close relationship between the Family Credit and Housing Benefit (see "Housing Benefit," this table). They find that the "Housing Benefit" entitlement is an important determinant of take-up of both Family Credit and Housing Benefit.	• Clark and McCrae (2001) find that 26 percent of people who received the Family Credit benefit were not eligible. This may reflect the fact that the entitlement period is six months regardless of changes in family circumstances.

Program	Findings
addition, a nonrefundable Children's Tax Credit provides income support to low-income families with children.	and 58 percent for couples for the two time periods, respectively. • Brewer and Gregg (2001): There has been little change in the Child Benefit over time.
Child benefit Begun in 1945, it is a universal transfer program for families with children whereby families receive fifteen pounds a week for the first and ten pounds a week for each subsequent child. Normally paid to the mother. When a child is born, the mother receives the claim package at the hospital.	• Brewer (2000): Take-up of the child benefit was almost 100 percent in 2000 to 2001.
Income support Formerly called Supplemental Benefit, it's a means-tested benefit paid to the household head in workless families, to make	• According to Brewer (2000), Income Support take-up is estimated to be around 80 percent. • Duclos (1995) says that take-up among eligibles in • Duclos (1995) finds that take-up is higher when the value of the benefit is greater. Less than full take-up reflects transaction costs. • Brewer and Gregg (2001): Income Support benefit rates have greatly increased since 1998.

(Table continues on p. 130.)

Table 3.3 Take-Up Rates of Programs in the United Kingdom

Means-Tested Program	Take-Up Estimates	Reasons for Low or High Take-Up	Selected Literature
up the difference between income and a minimum guaranteed income level.	1985 was 64 percent, but about 82.8 percent of the value of the benefit was received. About 6 percent of recipients are ineligible.		
Job seeker's allowance Begun in 1995, it replaced income support among the unemployed. Benefits are tied to previous wages. Recipients must be eighteen or older and have savings of less than 8,000 pounds and be working less than seventeen hours per week.		• Recipients must abide by a "job seekers agreement" or risk losing benefits.	
"New Deal" Programs Introduced in 1998, these are means-tested programs for the unemployed. For those eighteen to fifty years of age, it includes personal advisers, a "gate-	• At the end of June 2003, 91,380 youths eighteen to twenty-four were partici- pating (Blundell 2002).	• Participation is compul- sory after six months of unemployment for eigh- teen-to-twenty-four-year- olds and after eighteen months for those twenty- five to fifty. Eligible indi-	

way" period of four months, then either training or education, subsidized work, volunteer work, or public-sector employment. Help with child-care and travel costs. Less intensive services are offered to those over fifty, single parents, and the disabled (Brewer, Clark, and Wakefield 2002).

viduals who refuse to participate lose their entitlement to benefits.

Pension credit
Earlier called Income Support for Pensioners, and then Minimum Income Guarantee, Pension Credit, introduced in 2003, provides the difference between one's weekly income and a minimum benefit level. It is expected that roughly half of the elderly will be eligible for Pension Credit (Hancock et al. 2003).

- Among those pensioners eligible for income support in 2000 to 2001, between 64 percent and 78 percent received the benefit (Department of Social Security, 2001; Department of Work and Pensions 2003).

- Forms are complex, so those eligible for only small amounts may not apply. Also, stigma may be greater for Income Support than other forms of support such as the Council Tax Benefit (Hancock et al. 2003).

- Income Support for pensioners rose considerably from 1997 to 2002—by 31 percent for a single pensioner under seventy-five, and by 25 percent for a pensioner couple where one is aged seventy-five or over (Brewer, Clark, and Wakefield 2002).

(Table continues on p. 132.)

Table 3.3 Take-Up Rates of Programs in the United Kingdom

Means-Tested Program	Take-Up Estimates	Reasons for Low or High Take-Up	Selected Literature
Programs for the disabled *Incapacity benefit:* A social insurance program that pays fixed benefits to people unable to work. Requires medical evidence. *Severe disablement Allowance and Disability living allowance:* Noncontributory, non-means-tested programs that also make small fixed payments. Those unable to work may also be eligible for Income Support. *Disability working allowance:* eligibles must be in paid work for more than sixteen hours per week, with an illness or disability that creates a disadvantage in securing employment, have			

- savings of 16,000 pounds or less, and be in receipt of a qualifying benefit such as Disability Living Allowance.

Housing programs
Housing benefit: A means-tested payment designed to subsidize the rent of those with low incomes. It is paid by local councils.
Council tax benefit: A means-tested program that pays the local taxes (council "rates") of eligible families. It is the most commonly used means-tested program in Britain.

- Brewer, Clark, and Wakefield (2002) estimate take-up rates for housing benefits in 1999 to 2000 of 89 percent for pensioners, 99 percent for nonpensioners with children, and 92 percent for nonpensioners without children.
- The Department for Work and Pensions (2003) estimates that 7 percent of the elderly who are eligible for Housing Benefit do not receive it, compared to 31 percent of elderly eligible for the Council Tax Benefit.

- Clark, Giles, and Hall (1999) note that the Council Tax Benefit is very complex, which discourages take-up. However, those entitled to Income Support are automatically entitled to Housing Benefit and Council Tax Benefit and forms are issued together, which is likely to increase take-up for Income Support (Hancock et al. 2003).

- Blundell, Fry, and Walker (1988) use the 1984 Family Household Survey and find that there is positive relationship between take-up and the level of entitlement. This supports the view that there may be significant costs (ignorance or stigma) associated with claiming. Household characteristics affect take-up rates. The effect of extra household income is to reduce take-up significantly. Those in rented accommodation owned by local housing authorities are more likely to take up their entitlement than

(Table continues on p. 134.)

Table 3.3 Take-Up Rates of Programs in the United Kingdom

Means-Tested Program	Take-Up Estimates	Reasons for Low or High Take-Up	Selected Literature
			those in private rented and rent-free accommodation. Among those either in or seeking employment, part-time workers and unemployed with no record of occupation are more likely to take-up. Those under retirement age are substantially less likely to take-up than those over that age. Both age and education have a negative effect on take-up for the employed and unemployed. The presence of both additional adults and older children in the family increases the probability of take-up, although younger children appear to have no significant impact.

Source: Author's compilation.

seem to offer an interesting opportunity for research. The New Deal made participation in jobs programs compulsory for many groups of unemployed. It would be interesting to know what effect this had on the probability of participating, and which categories of recipients dropped out. More generally, cross-country collaboration between researchers might uncover variations in transaction costs and other factors that affect take-up, and could help to isolate their effects.

The discussion of social benefits in the United Kingdom might also lead us to think beyond the question "Who takes up programs?" to "Do recipients make optimal use of programs that they have taken up and if not, why not?" Research on the National Health Insurance Program suggests that although there is universal take-up, the rich receive more services than the poor, conditional on their health status. Possible reasons range from higher transaction costs for the poor, such as lack of transportation, or inability to take time off from work; superior connections and communication skills or better rapport with medical providers; and differences in attitudes toward illness and medical care (Dixon et al. 2003). This example suggests that the same factors that inhibit take-up may also affect utilization of universal social programs.

Summary and Conclusions

It is generally agreed that people do not take up benefits if the costs outweigh the benefits, but after many years of research, we still have relatively little insight into precisely what types of costs matter most, and what types of measures are most likely to reduce them. A few general conclusions can be drawn, however. First, take-up is enhanced by automatic or default enrollment and lowered by administrative barriers, although removing individual barriers such as reducing the length of forms or increasing the number of offices that process forms does not necessarily have much effect, suggesting that one must address the whole bundle.

Second, although it may be impossible to devise a definitive test of the "stigma hypothesis," it seems clear that stigma cannot be the only cost facing participants. Other, more concrete types of transaction costs are probably a good deal more important to most people than stigma or lack of information.[5] Third, although people generally have means-tested programs in the United States in mind when they discuss take-up, low take-up is also a problem in many non-means-tested social insurance programs and in other countries.

Historically, economists have paid much attention to rules about eligibility and virtually no attention to how these rules are enforced or made known to participants. This review suggests that the marginal return to new data about these features of programs is likely to be high in terms of understanding take-up. Anecdotal evidence suggests that there is a great deal of variation in the ways that similar types of programs are implemented both within and across countries, and this variation could be exploited to identify the most important barriers to participation.

For example, some states implemented SCHIP as an extension of their Medicaid programs, while others created separate stand-alone programs in order to reduce the stigma associated with receiving public insurance. To my knowledge, the difference has not been exploited to investigate the "stigma hypothesis." About half of the 109 Food Stamp Program offices surveyed in a recent U.S. Department of Agriculture study of program access provided services such as extended hours, whereas a small number of programs required applicants to attend a series of meetings before they were even permitted to sign their application forms (Gabor et al. 2003). Procedures such as requiring third-party verification of income are not standardized across locations either, and could easily explain variation in take-up across areas. More systematic collection and analysis of this type of data would add a great deal to the study of take-up.

In an era of social experiments, it might also prove useful to consider experimental manipulations of factors thought to influence take-up. For example, it might be possible to design an outreach program that would directly test the hypothesis that take-up is influenced by information exchange among members of social networks. Similarly, parameters such as application procedures, recertification intervals, payments for community enrollment assistance, and incentives to service providers to give application assistance could be varied across areas in order to study their effects.

This paper was prepared for a conference in honor of Eugene Smolensky held at Berkeley, December 12 and 13, 2003. The author thanks Alan Auerbach, Jeffrey Biddle, David Card, Sheldon Danziger, Irving Garfinkel, Robert Haveman, John Quigley, and conference participants for helpful comments. Princeton's Center for Health and Well-Being provided financial support. Graciana Rucci provided excellent research assistance.

Notes

1. In his comments, Irving Garfinkel (personal communication) identifies another cost of targeted transfers, which is that they create disincentives for the poor to work and to marry. There is a large literature on the labor supply and demographic effects of such programs, which is beyond the scope of this survey.
2. An entitlement program is one in which all qualified applicants are served, whereas nonentitlement programs have fixed budgets and cannot serve more people than the funding allows.
3. The Card and Shore-Sheppard (2004) estimates of take-up are lower, because they include child age-specific trends in their model, whereas Currie and Gruber (1996a; 1996b), and Cutler and Gruber (1996), discussed later, did not. Nevertheless, all three sets of authors emphasize the low take up of the Medicaid expansions, relative to take up of many other social programs.
4. Take-up estimates for various other countries and programs are also available. See, for example, Ruud Koning and Geert Ridder (1997), who study a rental assistance program in the Netherlands and find a 64 percent take-up rate, and Paul Storer and Marc Van Audenrode (1995) for a summary of take-up of unemployment insurance in Canada. David Coady and Susan Parker (2004) look at take-up of the Oportunidades program in Mexico and find that a third of those eligible who do not take up lack information about the program. This may be due in part to the novelty of this program.
5. Dahlia Remler and Sherry Glied (2003) arrive at the same two conclusions in their overview of the take-up literature aimed at identifying factors that might increase the take-up of public health insurance programs.

References

Administration for Children and Families. 1999. "Access to Child Care for Low-Income Working Families." Available at http://www.actf.dhhs.gov/programs/ccb/research/ccreport/ccreport.htm.

Aizer, Anna. 2001. "Covering Kids: Improving the Health Insurance Coverage of Poor Children." Unpublished paper (photocopy). Los Angeles: University of California, Los Angeles, Department of Economics.

———. 2003a. "Got Health? Advertising, Medicaid, and Child Health?" Unpublished paper (photocopy). Los Angeles: University of California, Los Angeles.

———. 2003b. "Low Take-Up in Medicaid: Does Outreach Matter, and for Whom?" *American Economic Review Papers and Proceedings* 93(2): 238–41.

Aizer, Anna, and Janet Currie. 2004. "Networks or Neighborhoods?" *Journal of Public Economics* 88(12): 2573–85.

Aizer, Anna, and Jeffrey Grogger. 2003. "Parental Medicaid Expansions and Health Insurance Coverage." NBER working paper no. 9907. Washington, D.C.: National Bureau of Economic Research.

Akerlof, George. 1978. "The Economics of Tagging as Applied to the Optimal Income Tax and Other Things." *American Economic Review* 68(1, March): 8–20.

Anderson, Patricia M., and Bruce D. Meyer. 2003. "Unemployment Insurance Takeup Rates and the After-Tax Value of Benefits," *Quarterly Journal of Economics* 112(3): 913–37.

Andreano, Ralph, Eugene Smolensky, and Thomas Helminiak. 1986. "The Economics of Information Exchange: Medicaid in Wisconsin." *Health Care Financing Review* 8(1): 64–79.

Ashenfelter, Orley. 1983. "Determining Participation in Income-Tested Social Programmes." *Journal of the American Statistical Association* 78: 517–25.

Autor, David H., and Mark G. Duggan. 2003. "The Rise in the Disability Rolls and the Decline in Unemployment." *Quarterly Journal of Economics* 118(1): 157–207.

Baker, Laurence, and Anne Royalty. 1996. "Medicaid Policy, Physician Behavior, and Health Care for the Low-Income Population." Unpublished paper (photocopy). Palo Alto, Calif.: Stanford University, Department of Economics. December 1996.

Baker, Michael, and Dwayne Benjamin. 1995. "The Receipt of Transfer Payments by Immigrants to Canada," *Journal of Human Resources* 30(4): 650–76.

Benítez-Silva, Hugo, Moshe Buchinsky, and John Rust. 2004. "How Large Are the Classification Errors in the Social Security Disability Award Process?" NBER working paper no. 10219. Washington, D.C.: National Bureau of Economic Research.

Bertrand, Marianne, Erzo Luttmer, and Sendhil Mullainathan. 2000. "Network Effects and Welfare Cultures." *Quarterly Journal of Economics* 5(140): 1019–56.

Besley, Timothy, and Stephen Coate. 1991. "Public Provision of Private Goods and the Redistribution of Income" *The American Economic Review* 81:979–84.

————. 1995. "The Design of Income Maintenance Programs." *Review of Economic Studies* 62(2): 187–221.

Bitler, Marianne, Janet Currie and John Karl Scholz. 2003. "WIC Participation and Eligibility." *Journal of Human Resources* 38: 1139–79.

Blackorby, Charles, and David Donaldson. 1988. "Cash Versus Kind: Self-Selection and Efficient Transfers." *American Economic Review* 78: 691–700.

Blank, Rebecca. 2001. "What Causes Public Assistance Caseloads to Grow?" *Journal of Human Resources* 36(1): 85–118.

————. 2002. "Evaluating Welfare Reform in the United States." *Journal of Economic Literature* 40(4): December 2002.

Blank, Rebecca, and David Card. 1991. "Recent Trends in Insured and Uninsured Unemployment: Is There an Explanation?" *Quarterly Journal of Economics* 106: 1157–90.

Blank, Rebecca, and Patricia Ruggles. 1996. "When Do Women Use AFDC and Food Stamps? The Dynamics of Eligibility vs. Participation." *Journal of Human Resources* 31(1): 57–89.

Blau, David, and Janet Currie. 2005. "Who's Minding the Kids? Preschool, Day Care, and After School Care." In *Handbook of Education Economics,* edited by Finis Welch and Eric Hanushek. New York: North Holland.

Blau, Francine. 1984. "The Use of Transfer Payments by Immigrants." *Industrial and Labor Relations Review* 37(2): 222–39.

Blundell, Richard. 2002. "Welfare-to-Work: Which Policies Work and Why." Keynes Lecture in Economics. London: Institute for Fiscal Studies.

Blundell, Richard, V. Fry, and Ian Walker. 1988. "Modeling the Take-Up of Means-Tested Benefits: The Case of Housing Benefits in the United Kingdom." *Economic Journal* 98: 58–74.

Borjas, George, and Lynette Hilton. 1996. "Immigration and the Welfare State: Immigrant Participation in Means-Tested Entitlement Programs." *Quarterly Journal of Economics* 111(2): 575–604.

Borjas, George, and Stephen Trejo. 1991. "Immigrant Participation in the Welfare System." *Industrial and Labor Relations Review* 44(2): 195–211.

————. 1993. "National Origin and Immigrant Welfare Recipiency." *Journal of Public Economics* 50(3): 325–44.

Bound, John. 1989. "The Health and Earnings of Rejected Disability Applicants." *American Economic Review* 79(3): 482–503.

————. 1991. "Self-Reported vs. Objective Measures of Health in Retirement Models." *Journal of Human Resources* 26: 106–38.

Bound, John, Sherri Kossoudji, and Gema Ricart-Moes. 1998. "The Ending of General Assistance and SSI Disability Growth in Michigan: A Case Study." In *Growth in Disability Benefits: Explanations and Policy Implications,* edited by Kalman Rupp and David C. Stapleton. Kalamazoo, Mich.: W. E. Upjohn Institute for Employment Research.

Bound, John, and Timothy Waidman. 1992. "Disability Transfers, Self-Reported Health, and the Labor Force Attachment of Older Men: Evidence from the Historical Record." *Quarterly Journal of Economics* 107(4): 1393–1419.

Brewer, Michael. 2000. "Comparing In-work Benefits and Financial Work Incentives for Low-Income Families in the U.S. and the U.K." Working paper 00/16. London: Institute for Fiscal Studies.

Brewer, Michael, Tom Clark, and Matthew Wakefield. 2002. "Five Years of Social Security Reform in the U.K." Working paper 02/12. London: Institute for Fiscal Studies.

Brewer, Michael, and Paul Gregg. 2001. "Eradicating Child Poverty in Britain: Welfare Reform and Children since 1997." Working paper W01/08. London: Institute for Fiscal Studies.

Brien, Michael J., and Christopher A. Swann. 1999. "Prenatal WIC Participation and Infant Health: Selection and Maternal Fixed Effects." Unpublished paper (photocopy). Richmond: University of Virginia, Department of Economics.

Brock, William, and Steven Durlauf. 2001. "Interactions Based Models." In *Handbook of Econometrics,* edited by James Heckman and Edward Leamer. Vol. 5. Amsterdam: North Holland.

Bruce, Neil, and Michael Waldman. 1991. "Transfers in Kind: Why They Can be Efficient and Nonpaternalistic." *The American Economic Review* 81(5): 1345–51.

Burghardt, J., A. Gordon, and N. Chapman. 1993. *The School Nutrition Dietary Assessment Study: Social Food Service, Meals Offered and Dietary Intake.* Alexandria, Va.: U.S. Department of Agriculture, Food and Nutrition Service.

Burghardt, J., A. Gordon, and Barbara Devaney. 1995. "Background of the School Nutritional Dietary Assessment Study." *American Journal of Clinical Nutrition* 61(1 supp.): 178S–181S.

Burkhauser, Richard, and Mary Daly. 2003. "The Supplemental Security Income Program." In *Means Tested Transfer Programs in the United States,* edited by Robert A. Moffitt. Chicago: University of Chicago Press and National Bureau of Economic Research.

Burtless, Gary, and Jerry A. Hausman. 1978. "The Effect of Taxation on Labor Supply: Evaluating the Gary Negative Income Tax Experiment." *The Journal of Political Economy* 86(6): 1103–30.

Card, David, and Philip Levine. 2000. "Extended Benefits and the Duration of UI Spells: Evidence from the New Jersey Extended Benefit Program." *Journal of Public Economics* 78(1–2): 107–38.

Card, David, and Brian P. McCall. 1996. "Is Workers' Compensation Covering Uninsured Medical Costs? Evidence from the 'Monday Effect.' " *Industrial and Labor Relations Review* 49(4): 690–706.

Card, David, and Lara D. Shore-Sheppard. 2004. "Using Discontinuous Eligibility Rules to Identify the Effects of the Federal Medicaid Expansions on Low Income Children." *Review of Economics and Statistics* 86(3): 752–66.

Centers for Medicare and Medicaid Services. 2002. "Program Information on Medicare, Medicaid, SCHIP, and Other Programs of the Centers for Medicare and Medicaid Services." Washington D.C.: Centers for Medicare and Medicaid Services, Office of Research Development and Information.

Chatterji, Pinka, Karen Bonuck, Simi Dhawan, and Nadnini Deb. 2002. "WIC Participation and the Initiation and Duration of Breast-feeding." Working paper no. 1246-02. Madison, Wis.: University of Wisconsin, Institute for Research on Poverty.

Clark, Tom, Christopher Giles, and John Hall. 1999. "Does Council Tax Benefit Work?" London: Institute for Fiscal Studies.

Clark, Tom, and Julian McCrae. 2001. "Issues Arising in Tax and Benefit Modelling: The Case of Family Credit." London: Institute for Fiscal Studies.

Coady, David, and Susan Parker. 2004. "Combining Means-Testing and Self-Selection Targeting: An Analysis of Household and Program Agent Behavior." Working paper. Hills of Santa Fe, Mexico: CIDE Mexico, Department of Economics.

Coe, R. 1985. "Nonparticipation in the SSI Program by Eligible Elderly." *Southern Economic Journal* 51(3): 891–97.

Craig, Peter. 1991. "Costs and Benefits: A Review of Research on Take Up of Income-Related Benefits." *Journal of Social Policy* 20(4): 537–65.

Crew, Amy D. 1995. "Self Selection, Administrative Selection, and Aggregation Bias in the Estimation of the Effect of In-Kind Transfers." Ph.D. dissertation. Richmond: University of Virginia.

Currie, Janet. 2000. "Do Children of Immigrants Make Differential Use of Public Health Insurance?" In *Issues in the Economics of Immigration,* edited by George Borjas. Chicago: University of Chicago Press and National Bureau of Economic Research.

———. 2003. "U.S. Food and Nutrition Programs." In *Means-Tested Transfer Programs in the United States,* edited by Robert A. Moffitt. Chicago: University of Chicago Press and National Bureau for Economic Research.

Currie, Janet, and Jeffrey Grogger. 2001. "Explaining Recent Declines in Food Stamp Program Participation." In *Brookings-Wharton Papers on Urban Affairs,* edited by William Gale and Janet Rothenberg-Pack. Washington, D.C.: Brookings Institution.

———. 2002. "Medicaid Expansions and Welfare Contractions: Offsetting Effects on Maternal Behavior and Infant Health." *Journal of Health Economics* 21: 313–35,

Currie, Janet, and Jonathan Gruber. 1996a. "Health Insurance Eligibility Utilization of Medical Care and Child Health." *Quarterly Journal of Economics* 111(2): 431–66.

———. 1996b. "Saving Babies: The Efficacy and Cost of Recent Changes in the Medicaid Eligibility of Pregnant Women." *Journal of Political Economy* 104(6): 1263–96.

Currie, Janet, Jonathan Gruber, and Michael Fischer. 1995. "Physician Payments and Infant Health: Effects of Increases in Medicaid Reimbursements." *American Economic Review* 85(2): 106–11.

Currie, Janet, and Matthew Neidell. 2003. "Getting Inside the 'Black-Box' of Head Start Program Quality: What Matters and What Doesn't." NBER working paper no. 10091. Washington, D.C.: National Bureau of Economic Research.

Currie, Janet, and Duncan Thomas. 1995. "Does Head Start Make a Difference?" *American Economic Review* 85(3): 341–64.

———. 2000. "School Quality and the Longer-Term Effects of Head Start." *Journal of Human Resources* 35(4): 755–74.

Currie, Janet, and Aaron Yelowitz. 2000. "Are Public Housing Projects Good for Kids?" *Journal of Public Economics* 75(1): 99–124.

Cutler, David, and Jonathan Gruber. 1996. "Does Public Insurance Crowd Out Private Insurance?" *Quarterly Journal of Economics* 111: 391–430.

———. 1997. "Medicaid and Private Insurance: Evidence and Implications." *Health Affairs* 16(1): 194–200.

Daly, Mary C., and Richard V. Burkhauser. 1998. "How Family Economic Well-Being Changes Following the Onset of a Disability: A Dynamic Analysis." Unpublished manuscript. Syracuse, N.Y.: Syracuse University.

Daponte, Beth, Seth Sanders, and Lowell Taylor. 1999. "Why Do Low-Income Households Not Use Food Stamps? Evidence from an Experiment." *Journal of Human Resources* 34(3): 612–28.

Decker, Sandra. 1992. "The Effect of Physician Reimbursement Levels on the Primary Care of Medicaid Patients." Unpublished paper (photocopy). New York: New York University School of Public Service.

Department for Work and Pensions. 2003. "Income-Related Benefits: Estimates of Take-Up in 2000–2001." London: Department for Work and Pensions, Information and Analysis Directorate.

Dixon, Anna, Julian Le Grand, John Henderson, Richard Murray, and Emmi Poteliakhoff. 2003. "Is the NHS Equitable? A Review of the Evidence." Health and Social Care discussion paper no. 11. London: London School of Economics.

Dorsett, Richard, and Christopher Heady. 1991. "The Take-Up of Means Tested Benefits by Working Families with Children." *Fiscal Studies* 12(4): 22–32.

Dubay, Lisa, and Genevieve Kenney. 1997. "Did Medicaid Expansions for Pregnant Women Crowd out Private Coverage?" *Health Affairs,* January–February, pp. 185–93.

Duclos, Jean-Yves. 1995. "Modelling the Take-Up of State Support." *Journal of Public Economics* 54: 391–415.

Duflo, Esther, and Emmanuel Saez. 2001. "The Role of Information and Social Interaction in Retirement Plan Decisions: Evidence from a Randomized Experiment." Unpublished paper (photocopy). Cambridge, Mass.: Harvard University, Department of Economics.

Duggan, Mark G., and Melissa Schettini Kearney. 2005. "The Impact of Child SSI enrollment on Household Outcomes: Evidence from the Survey of Income and Program Participation." NBER Working Paper No. 11568 (August).

Ellwood, Marilyn, and Genevieve Kenney. 1995. "Medicaid and Pregnant Women: Who Is Being Enrolled and When?" *Health Care Financing Review* 17(2): 7–28.

Fuller, Bruce, Sharon L. Kagan, J. McCarthy, G. Caspary, D. Lubotsky, and L. Gascue. 1999. "Who Selects Formal Child Care? The Role of Subsidies as Low-Income Mothers Negotiate Welfare Reforms." Paper presented at the meeting of the Society for Research in Child Development. Albuquerque (April).

Gabor, Vivian, Brooke Hardison, Christopher Botsko, and Susan Bartlett. 2003. "Food Stamp Program Access Study: Local Office Policies and Practices." Document no. E-Fan-03-013. Washington D.C.: United States Department of Agriculture Economic Research Service.

Garces, Eliana, Duncan Thomas, and Janet Currie. 2002. "Longer Term Effects of Head Start." *American Economic Review* 92(4): 999–1012.

Garrett, Bowen, and Sherry Glied. 2000. "Does State AFDC Generosity Affect Child SSI Participation?" *Journal of Policy Analysis and Management* 19(2): 272–95.

Glantz, Fredrick B., Regina Berg, Diane Porcari et al. 1994. *School Lunch Eligible Nonparticipants.* Cambridge, Mass.: ABT Associates.

Gleason, P. M. 1995. "Participation in the National School Lunch Program and the School Breakfast Program." *American Journal of Clinical Nutrition* 61(1 Supp): 213S–220S.

Grogger, Jeffrey. 2002. "The Behavioral Effects of Welfare Time Limits." *American Economic Review* 92(2, May): 385–89.

———. 2003. "The Effects of Time Limits, the EITC, and Other Policy Changes on Welfare Use, Work, and Income Among Female-Headed Families." *Review of Economics and Statistics* 85(2): 394–408.

Grogger, Jeffrey, and Charles Michalopoulos. 2003. "Welfare Dynamics Under Time Limits." *Journal of Political Economy* 111(3): 530–54.

Gruber, Jonathan. 2003. "Medicaid." In *Means Tested Transfer Programs in the United States,* edited by Robert Moffitt. (Chicago: University of Chicago Press for National Bureau of Economic Research).

Haider, Steven, Robert Schoeni, and Alison Jacknowitz. 2002. "Food Stamps and the Elderly: Why Is Participation so Low?" Santa Monica: RAND/Xerox.

Hancock, Ruth, Stephen Pudney, Geraldine Barker, Monica Hernandez, Holly Sutherland. 2003. "The Take-Up of Multiple Means-Tested Benefits by British Pensioners: Evidence From the Family Resources Surveys." Working paper. Leicester, England: University of Leicester, Department of Economics.

Haveman, Robert, and Geoffrey Wallace. 2003. "Work and Earnings of Low-Skill Women: A Sobering Comparison of Survey Responses and Administrative Records." Unpublished paper (photocopy). Madison: University of Wisconsin, Institute for Research on Poverty.

Holtzblatt, J. 1991. "Administering Refundable Tax Credits: Lessons from the EITC Experience." *Proceedings of the Eighty-Fourth Annual Conference on Taxation* 1991: 180–86.

Hotz, V. Joseph, Charles H. Mullin, and John Karl Scholz. 2000. "The Earned Income Tax Credit and Labor Market Participation of Families on Welfare." Unpublished paper (mimeographed). Los Angeles: University of California, Los Angeles, Department of Economics.

———. 2002. "Welfare, Employment, and Income: Evidence on the Effects of Benefit Reductions from California." *American Economic Review* 92(2, May): 380–84.

Hotz, V. Joseph, and John Karl Scholz. 2003. "The Earned Income Tax Credit." In *Means-Tested Transfer Programs in the U.S.*, edited by Robert Moffitt. Chicago: University of Chicago Press and National Bureau of Economic Research.

House Ways and Means Committee. 1998. *Green Book 1998.* Washington: U.S. Government Printing Office.

———. 2000. *Green Book.* Washington: U.S. Government Printing Office.

Hoynes, Hilary. 1996. "Welfare Transfers in Two-Parent Families: Labor Supply and Welfare Participation under AFDC-UP." *Econometrica* 64: 295–332.

Hu, Wei-Yin. 1998. "Elderly Immigrants on Welfare." *Journal of Human Resources* 33(3): 711–41.

Koning, Ruud, and Geert Ridder. 1997. "Rent Assistance and Housing Demand." *Journal of Public Economics* 66: 1–31.

Kopczuk, Wojciech, and Cristian Pop-Eleches. 2004. "Electronic Filing, Tax Preparers, and Participation in the Earned Income Tax Credit." Working paper. New York: Columbia University, Department of Economics.

Krueger, Alan. 1990. "Incentive Effects of Workers' Compensation Insurance." *Journal of Public Economics* 41(1): 73–99.

Krueger, Alan, and Bruce D. Meyer. 2002. "Labor Supply Effects of Social Insurance." In *Handbook of Public Economics*, volume 4, edited by Alan J. Auerbach and Martin S. Feldstein. Amsterdam: North Holland.

Kubik, J. 1999. "Incentives for the Identification and Treatment of Children with Disabilities: The Supplemental Security Income Program." *Journal of Public Economics* 73: 187–215.

Lemieux, Thomas, and W. Bentley MacLeod. 2000. "Supply Side Hysteresis: The Case of the Canadian Unemployment System." *Journal of Public Economics* 78(1–2): 139–170.

Liebman, Jeffrey. 2002. "Who Are the Ineligible EITC Recipients?" *National Tax Journal* 53(4): 1164.

LoSasso, Anthony, and Thomas C. Buchmueller. 2002. "The Effect of the State Children's Health Insurance Program on Health Insurance Coverage." Working paper no. 9404. Washington, D.C.: National Bureau of Economic Research.

Madrian, Brigitte, and Dennis Shea. 2001. "The Power of Suggestion: Inertia in 401(k) Participation and Savings Behavior." *Quarterly Journal of Economics* 116(4): 1149–1525.

Manski, Charles. 1993. "Identification of Endogenous Social Effects: The Reflection Problem." *Review of Economic Studies* 60(3): 531–42.

———. 2000. "Economic Analysis of Social Interactions." *Journal of Economic Perspectives* 14(3): 115–36.

McConnell, Sheena, and James Ohls. 2000. "Food Stamps in Rural America: Special Issues and Common Themes." Washington, D.C.: Mathematica Policy Research.

McCubbin, J. 2000. "EITC Noncompliance: The Determinants of the Misreporting of Children." *National Tax Journal* LIII(2): 1135–64.

McGarry, Kathleen. 1996. "Factors Determining Participation of the Elderly in SSI." *Journal of Human Resources* 31(12): 331–58.

———. 2002. "Public Policy and the U.S. Health Insurance Market: Direct and Indirect Provision of Insurance." *National Tax Journal* 55(4): 789–827.

Menefee, John, Bea Edwards, Sylvester Schieber. 1981. "Analysis of Nonparticipation in the SSI Program." *Social Security Bulletin* 44(6): 3–21.

Meyer, Bruce. 1995. "Lessons from the U.S. Unemployment Insurance Experiments." *Journal of Economic Literature* 33(1): 91–131.

Meyer, Bruce, and Dan Rosenbaum. 2001. "Welfare, the Earned Income Tax Credit, and the Labor Supply of Single Mothers." *The Quarterly Journal of Economics* 116(3): 1063–1114.

Meyers, Marcia K., and T. Heintze. 1999. "The Performance of the Child Care Subsidy System: Target Efficiency, Coverage Adequacy and Equity." *Social Service Review* 73(1): 34–64.

Mitchell, Olivia S., and J. W. R. Phillips. 2002. "Applications, Denials, and Appeals for Social Security Disability Insurance." Working paper 2002-032. Ann Arbor: University of Michigan, Michigan Retirement Research Center.

Moffitt, Robert A. 1983. "An Economic Model of Welfare Stigma." *American Economic Review* 73(5): 1023–35.

———. 1998. "The Effect of Welfare on Marriage and Fertility." In *Welfare, the Family, and Reproductive Behavior,* edited by Robert A. Moffitt, Washington, D.C.: National Academy Press.

———. 2003a. "The Temporary Assistance for Needy Families Program." In *Means Tested Transfer Programs in the United States,* edited by Robert Moffitt. Chicago: University of Chicago Press and National Bureau of Economic Research.

————. 2003b. "The Role of Non-Financial Factors in Exit and Entry in the TANF Program." Unpublished paper (photocopy). Baltimore: Xerox, Johns Hopkins University, Department of Economics.

————. ed. 2003c. *Means Tested Transfer Programs in the United States.* Chicago: University of Chicago Press and National Bureau of Economic Research.

————. Forthcoming. "Policy Interventions, Low-Level Equilibria and Social Interactions." In *Social Dynamics,* edited by Steven Durlauf and Peyton Young. Cambridge, Mass.: MIT Press.

National Governors' Association. 2002. "Earned Income Tax Fact Sheet." Washington, D.C.: National Governors' Association.

————. 2003. "MCH Update 2002: State Health Coverage for Low-Income Pregnant Women, Children, and Parents." Washington, D.C.: National Governors' Association.

National Research Council. 2003. *Estimating Eligibility and Participation for the WIC Program.* Washington, D.C.: National Academy Press.

Nichols, Albert, and Richard Zeckhauser. 1982. "Targeting Transfers Through Redistribution on Recipients." *American Economic Review* 74(2): 373–77.

Nichols, Donald, Eugene Smolensky, and T. Nicolaus Tideman. 1971. "Discrimination in Waiting Time in Merit Goods." *American Economic Review* 61(3): 312–23.

O'Donoghue, Ted, and Matthew Rabin. 1999. "Doing It Now or Later." *American Economic Review* 89(1): 103–24.

————. 2003. "Studying Optimal Paternalism, Illustrated by a Model of Sin Taxes." *American Economic Review* 93(2): 186.

Olsen, Edgar. 2003. "Housing Programs for Low-Income Households." In *Means Tested Transfer Programs in the United States,* edited by Robert Moffitt. Chicago: University of Chicago Press and National Bureau of Economic Research.

Olsen, Edgar, and D. M. Barton. 1983. "The Benefits and Cost of Public Housing in New York City." *Journal of Public Economics* 20: 299–332.

Reeder, William J. 1985. "The Benefits and Costs of the Section 8 Existing Housing Program." *Journal of Public Economics* 26: 349–77.

Remler, Dahlia, and Sherry Glied. 2003. "What Other Programs Can Teach Us: Increasing Participation in Health Insurance Programs." *American Journal of Public Health* 93(1): 67–74.

Riphahn, Regina. 1998. "Immigrant Participation in Social Assistance Programs: Evidence from German Guestworkers." IZA working paper no. 15. Bonn, Germany: Institute for the Future of Labor.

Rossi, Peter. 1998. *Feeding the Poor: Assessing Federal Food Aid.* Washington, D.C.: American Enterprise Institute Press.

Saywell, Robert M., Terrell W. Zollinger, David K. Chu, Charlotte A. Macbeth, and Mark E. Sechrist. 1989. "Hospital and Patient Characteristics of Uncompensated Hospital Care: Policy Implications." *Journal of Health Politics, Policy, and Law* 14: 287–307.

Scholz, John Karl. 1994. "The Earned Income Tax Credit: Participation, Compliance, and Anti-poverty Effectiveness." *National Tax Journal*, March, pp. 59–81.

Shiels, J. F., Burt Barnow, Kathy Chaurette, and Jay Constantine. 1990. "Elderly Persons Eligible for and Participating in the Supplemental Security Income Program." Final report prepared for the U.S. Department of Health and Human Services, 1990.

Shore-Sheppard, Lara. 1996. "The Effect of Expanding Medicaid Eligibility on the Distribution of Children's Health Insurance Coverage." Working paper no. 369. Princeton, N.J.: Princeton Industrial Relations section.

Sloan, Frank, Janet Mitchell, and Jerry Cromwell. 1978. "Physician Participation in State Medicaid Programs." *Journal of Human Resources* 13: 211–45.

Smolensky, Eugene, Siobhan Reilly, and Eirik Evenhouse. 1995. "Should Public Assistance be Targeted?" *Journal of Post Keynesian Economics* 18: 3–29.

Social Security Administration. 2003. *Annual Report of the Supplemental Security Income Program.* Washington D.C.: Social Security Administration.

Storer, Paul, and Marc Van Audenrode. 1995. "Unemployment Insurance Take Up Rates in Canada: Facts, Determinants and Implications." *Canadian Journal of Economics* 29(4a): 822–35.

U.S. Department of the Treasury. Internal Revenue Service. 2002a. *Participation in the Earned Income Tax Credit Program for Tax Year 1996.* Washington, D.C.: Department of the Treasury.

———. 2002b. *Compliance Estimates for Earned Income Tax Credit Claimed on 1999 Returns.* Washington, D.C.: Department of the Treasury.

U.S. General Accounting Office. 1994. *Food Stamp Program: Various Factors Have Led to Declining Participation.* Publication no. GAO/RECD-99-185. Washington: U.S. Government Printing Office.

———. 2001. "SSI Disability: Other Programs May Provide Lessons for Improving Return-to-Work Efforts." Report to Congressional requester. No. GA0-01-153.

Wallace, James E., Susan P. Bloom, W. L. Williamson, Shirley Mansfield, and Daniel H. Weinberg. 1981. *Participation and Benefits in the Urban Section 8 Program: New Construction and Existing Housing.* Volumes 1 and 2. Cambridge, Mass.: ABT Associates.

Warlick, Jennifer L. 1982. "Participation of the Aged in SSI." *Journal of Human Resources* 17(2): 236–60.

Witte, Ann Dryden. 2002. "Take-Up Rates and Trade-Offs After the Age of Entitlement: Some Thoughts and Empirical Evidence for Child Subsidies." Working paper no. 8886. Washington, D.C.: National Bureau of Economic Research.

Yelowitz, Aaron. 1996. "Why Did the SSI-Disabled Program Grow So Much? Disentangling the Effect of Medicaid." Discussion paper no. 1090-96. Madison: University of Wisconsin, Institute for Research on Poverty.

———. 2000. "Did Recent Medicaid Reforms Cause the Caseload Explosion in the Food Stamps Program?" Unpublished paper. Los Angeles: University of California, Los Angeles, Department of Economics.

Zedlewski, Sheila, and Sarah Brauner. 1999. "Declines in Food Stamp and Welfare Participation: Is There a Connection?" Washington, D.C.: Urban Institute.

Chapter 4

Government Programs and Social Outcomes: Comparison of the United States with Other Rich Nations

TIMOTHY M. SMEEDING

The United States has a long tradition of measuring income poverty and income inequality and weighing the effectiveness, successes, and failures of government policies aimed at poverty reduction. In our own way we have created a unique set of social policies that support widely held values and provide stories of both success and failure in reaching goals of poverty reduction and improved social outcomes for all Americans. But still our idiosyncrasies leave many questions to be answered.

One can ask whether, in fact, Americans have "left no child behind." And the answers depend very much on who one asks and where one looks for evidence. One can find claims that the 1996 Welfare Reform Act is a major "accounting" success story, with the AFDC and TANF (Aid to Families with Dependent Children and Temporary Assistance for Needy Families) caseloads falling from over 5 million units in 1994 and 4.5 million in 1996 to 2 million cases (and less than 5 million persons) by June 2003, less than one-third of the 6.9 million units that benefit from the Supplemental Security Income (SSI) program, which is up from 5.9 million recipients over this same period (U.S. Department of Health and Human Services 2003; Social Security Administration, Office of Policy 2003; Smeeding 2001). The question of whether and to what extent this dramatic change in caseloads has provided better outcomes for those who have entered or left each program is also widely debated. And even in areas where the case for policy success seems overwhelming, such as the dramatic decline in poverty among the aged over the last half century, there is still room for serious policy debate over the remaining poor elders and their future prospects for better conditions under impending Social Security reform.

For the most part, these examinations of domestic policy are inherently parochial, for they are based on the experiences of only one nation in isolation from the others. The estimation of cross-nationally equivalent measures of poverty and the comparison of programs that support these groups of the poor provide a unique opportunity to compare the design and effectiveness of American social policy and antipoverty policy with other nations' policies and experience. The Luxembourg Income Study (LIS) database, which undergirds this paper, contains the information needed to construct comparable poverty measures for more than thirty nations. It allows comparisons of the level and trend of poverty and inequality across several nations, along with considerable details on the programs and policies that in large part produce these outcomes. In this paper we use cross-national comparisons made possible by the LIS to examine the United States' experiences in fighting poverty in the face of substantial and growing inequality, in a cross-national context. In so doing, we compare the effectiveness of United States antipoverty policies to those of similar nations elsewhere in the industrialized world.

If lessons can be learned from cross-national comparisons, there is much that American voters and policymakers can learn about antipoverty policy. Every nation has its own idiosyncratic institutions and policies, reflecting its values, culture, institutions, and history, and wide differences in success and failure are evident from the comparisons that follow. Previous research has shown that the United States has one of the highest poverty rates of all the thirty rich countries participating in the LIS, whether poverty is measured using comparable absolute or relative standards for determining who is poor, and despite the fact that (with the exception of tiny Luxembourg itself), the United States is the richest of all nations on earth (Smeeding and Rainwater 2004; Smeeding, Rainwater, and Burtless 2001).[1]

All nations value low poverty, high levels of economic self-reliance, and equality of opportunity for younger persons, but they differ dramatically in the extent to which they reach these goals.

Most nations are remarkably similar in their sources of social concern: births outside of wedlock and single-parent families, older women living alone, high unemployment, immigration pressures, low wages, and the sustainability of social expenditures in the face of rapid population aging. They also exhibit differences in the extent to which working-age adults mix economic self-reliance (earned incomes), family support, and government support to avoid poverty.

This chapter is designed to examine these differences in greater detail. We begin by reviewing international concepts and measures of poverty, as they relate to the main measures of income and poverty used in domestic United States discourse. In so doing, we examine basic differences in aggregate measures of well-being and social expenditure, while also identifying a number of criteria that we can use to examine the success and failure of antipoverty policy in a cross-national context. Next, we present cross-national estimates of both absolute and relative well-being for several subgroups of the population, including the elderly and different types of families with children. Measures of both poverty and inequality are presented and the comparative results are noted. After examining the level and trend in poverty rates, we explore some of the factors that are correlated with national poverty rates and examine the effectiveness of government programs aimed at reducing poverty and equalizing opportunity. Specifically, we examine the effects of work, education, family structure, and social policy in achieving these outcomes. In examining these findings, we use the criteria of adequacy, self-sustainability, and cost effectiveness to identify promising international lessons for the United States. We conclude with a discussion of the relationship between policy differences and outcome differences among the several countries, and consider the implications of our analysis for research and for antipoverty policy in the United States.

Measuring Cross-National Comparisons of Poverty and Inequality

Differing national experiences in social-transfer and antipoverty programs provide a rich source of information for evaluating the effectiveness of alternative social policies. As hinted above, policymakers in the industrialized countries share common concerns about social problems such as poverty and social exclusion. Poverty measurement is an exercise that is particularly popular in the English-speaking countries, and more recently in Europe; in addition, most rich nations share a concern over distributional outcomes and the well-being of the low-income population. Few Northern European and Scandinavian nations calculate low-income or poverty rates, since most recognize that their social programs already ensure a low poverty rate under any reasonable set of measurement standards (Björklund and Freeman 1997).[2] Instead, they concentrate their efforts on studying social exclusion, mobility, and inequality (see Atkinson et al. 2002; Erikson and Goldthorpe 2002).

Although there is no international consensus on guidelines for measuring poverty, international bodies such as the United Nations Children's Fund (UNICEF), the United Nations Human Development Report (UNHDR), the Organization for Economic Cooperation and Development (OECD), the European Statistical Office (Eurostat), the International Labor Office (ILO) and the Luxembourg Income Study (LIS) have published several cross-national studies of the incidence of poverty in recent years. The large majority of these studies are based on LIS data.[3]

There is considerable agreement on the appropriate measurement of poverty in a cross-national context. Most of the available studies and papers share many similarities that help guide our research strategy when confronting measurement issues:

- For purposes of international comparisons, poverty is almost always a relative concept. A majority of cross-national studies define the poverty threshold as one-half of national median income. In this study, we use 50 percent of median income to establish our national poverty lines. We could have selected 40 percent of national median income as our relative poverty threshold because it is closest to the ratio of the official United States poverty line to median United States household (pretax) cash income (42 percent in 1998 and 2002),[4] but we have decided to stay with the conventional level. Alternatively, the United Kingdom and the European Union have selected a poverty rate of 60 percent of the median income (Atkinson et al. 2002; Bradshaw 2003). The results we show at the 50 percent poverty standard can be generalized to the lower poverty standard of 40 percent (see Burtless, Rainwater, and Smeeding 2002). The differences between the United States and other nations are much larger at the 60 percent of median line, which is about 45 percent above the United States poverty line.

- The United States likes to think of itself using an "absolute" poverty measure, but in fact there is no one absolute poverty measure. All poverty measures are, in some sense, relative and are chosen to be appropriate for the context in which they are used. The World Bank defines poverty in Africa and Latin America using an income threshold of one or two dollars per person per day, and in Central and Eastern Europe a threshold of two or three dollars per day (Ravallion 1994, 1996). In contrast, the absolute United States poverty line is six to twelve times higher than these standards and the European poverty line is almost 50 percent higher than the United States line. To satisfy the desire for "real income" comparisons, we instead turn to measures of the real living standards of persons in each nation.

- To estimate real living standards in different countries, researchers must convert national currencies into units of equal purchasing power or "purchasing power parity" (PPP) exchange rates for the currencies (Summers and Heston 1991; Organization for Economic Cooperation and Development 2003). PPP exchange rates were developed to permit accurate comparison of gross domestic product across countries rather than incomes or consumption of lower-income households. This means that even though PPPs are appropriate for comparing national output or output per capita, they are less appropriate for establishing consistent income differences across nations (see also in Relative and Real Economic Well-Being).[5] Moreover, construction of PPP adjusted levels of living standards across countries is problematic, because the results are sensitive to the quality of the micro-data and to the specific PPP that is chosen. Our estimates of real-income distributions are based on a single set of PPP rates, the most recent set benchmarked by the OECD for the year 1999, extended back or forward to cover the period from 1997 to 2000. We use the OECD estimates of PPP exchange rates to translate household incomes in each country into 2000 United States dollars adjusted for family size (using an equivalence scale that is equal to the square root of household size) and then compare income distributions for different household types relative to the United States median disposable income per equivalent person. For 2000, this figure is $24,416 per equivalent United States person.

- Poverty and income measurement is based on the broadest income definition that still preserves comparability across nations. The best such definition of income is currently "disposable cash and noncash income (DPI)," which includes all types of money income, minus direct income taxes and payroll taxes, and including all cash transfers and near-cash transfers (such as food stamps and cash housing allowances) and refundable tax credits (such as the Earned Income Tax Credit, or EITC).[6] This is also called "post-tax-and-transfer income." To determine the antipoverty effects of social transfers and tax policy, we begin with a measure of Market Income (MI), which includes earnings, income from investments, private transfers, and occupational pensions only. This is also called "pre-tax-and-transfer income." By tracing the effects of income-transfer policy from MI poverty to DPI poverty, we determine the effects of two bundles of government programs: social insurance and taxes (universal and social insurance benefits, minus income taxes and payroll taxes) and social assistance (income-tested benefits targeted at poor people, including refundable tax credits such as the EITC). Again, in making these comparisons for all persons and for groups, we use one set poverty line, half of median disposable income (DPI), for all persons throughout.[7]

- For international comparisons of poverty, the household is the single best unit for income aggregation. It is the only comparable income-sharing unit available for most nations to measure. Whereas the household is the unit used for aggregating income, the person is the unit of analysis. Household income is assumed to be equally shared among individuals within a household. Poverty rates are calculated as the percentage of all persons of each type who are members of households of each type with incomes below the poverty line. In some cases we also calculate the poverty rate for elders and children regardless of their living arrangements. Further, we use the available LIS data to separate annual hours worked, marital status (married or living together as married, known as "cohabiting"), and education level of the household head (reference person).

- A variety of equivalence scales have been used in cross-national comparisons in order to make comparisons of well-being between households with differing compositions. Equivalence scales are used to adjust household income for differences in needs related to household size and other factors, such as the ages of household members. In the United States poverty literature, a set of equivalence scales is implicit in the official poverty lines, but these are neither consistent nor robust (Citro and Michael 1995). For the cross-national analysis of *relative* poverty rates, however, we use a consistent scale, which is much more commonly used in international analyses. After adjusting household incomes to reflect differences in household size, we compare the resulting adjusted incomes to the 50 percent of median poverty line. The equivalence scale used for this purpose, as in most cross-national studies that include both children and elders, is a single parameter scale with a square-root-of-household-size scale factor.[8]

Our measure of the diversity of both relative and real living standards is based only on disposable incomes, but allows us the luxury of examining incomes for persons at various levels of living in society. Comparing points in the distribution allows us to examine differences across children within nations as well as across nations, all expressed in 2000 United States PPP dollars and all relative to the median disposable income in the United States in 2000. We use these data to compute the real income of low-income persons and high-income persons in each nation. The low-income person is measured at the 10th percentile (median of the bottom quintile) while the high-income person is measured at the 90th percentile (median of the top quintile). We refer to the difference between persons with high and low incomes as "economic distance" in making comparisons here. This distance can be measured in ratio format (for example, the income of a child in the 90th percentile relative to one in the 10th percentile), in bar graph format, or with the real-income distance between these points measured in PPP-adjusted dollars per equivalent person.

When thinking about this measure of economic distance for families with children, we can interpret it as a measure of equality of opportunity within each nation. Nations with smaller economic distances (or smaller decile ratios) have higher levels of "equal opportunity" across the population of children. We might also think of the distance between the middle-income child and the low-income child as a measure of "fair chance." Researchers have shown that both income and family structure affect children's life chances; thus, the real-income level of children and their parents is of serious social concern (Sigle-Rushton and McLanahan 2004; Duncan et al. 1998). And so, whereas measures of equality of opportunity capture the relative economic distance between the high- and low-income children, we are also vitally interested in the absolute level of resources available to the low-income child relative to similar children in other nations. Children in nations with relatively higher real-income levels for "low-income children" have given their poor children more of a "fair chance" in that nation, when compared to similar children in other nations.

Finally, we need to examine the question of mobility and that of economic opportunity. All of the comparisons in this paper are based on cross-sectional data, not longitudinal data. Opportunities for children are measured by their parents' incomes. Hence, one might ask if there is a strong or weak correlation between parental well-being (as measured by income) and child well-being (as measured by the child's income). In fact, several recent studies that use both national and cross-national data suggest that intergenerational mobility is lower in the United States than in almost every other rich country except for the United Kingdom (Solon 2002). Thomas Hertz (2004) finds that a child born into the bottom decile of income has a 31 percent change of ending up there as a result and an over 50 percent chance to end up in the bottom quintile of adult income. The same comparisons for a top decile child indicate a 30 percent chance of remaining in this decile and a 43 percent chance of being in the top quintile of incomes as an adult. Hence, while there is some intergenerational income mobility across the income distribution, it is lower in the United States than elsewhere (as measured by correlation of father and child earnings), while a child's chances of emulating parental income success (or lack thereof) are also strongly correlated. Hence, our measures of children's opportunities for economic success by their parental incomes are also good measures of their future economic status. As Alan Krueger (2002) has remarked, the available data "challenge the notion that the United States is an exceptionally mobile society. If the United States stands out in comparison with other countries, it is in having a more static distribution of incomes across generations with fewer opportunities for advancement."

Data, Countries, and Macroeconomic Comparisons

The data we use for this analysis are from the Luxembourg Income Study (LIS) database, which now contains almost 130 household-income data files for thirty nations covering the period 1967 to 2000 (see www.lisproject.org). We can analyze both the level and trend in poverty and low incomes for a considerable period across a wide range of nations. Because we are computing the level and trend in relative poverty and real living standards for several major policy-relevant groups, we have selected just eight nations to focus on in this paper, each with a recent 1997-to-2000 LIS database: the United States, two Anglo-Saxon nations (Canada and the United Kingdom), three Central European nations (Belgium, Germany, and the Netherlands), and two Scandinavian nations (Finland and Sweden). These were chosen to typify the broad range of rich nations available within LIS and to simplify our analysis.[9] We include all of Germany, including the eastern states of the former German Democratic Republic, in most of our analyses.[10]

We begin by comparing three features of the economic and social institutions of each nation: standard of living, as measured by gross domestic product (GDP) per capita in 2000 PPP-adjusted dollars; unemployment, as measured by OECD and standardized unemployment rates; and cash and near-cash social expenditures for the non-elderly (OECD 2002). Table 4.1 shows that the United States is far and away the richest nation that we observe among our set, with 2000 GDP per capita of $34,100. Comparisons of microdata-based real incomes per equivalent adult and GDP per capita (shown in appendix table 4A.1) reveal a similar ranking and relationship of average microdata-based income levels across nations. All other nations lie within a tight nine-percentage-point range, from 69 to 78 percent of the United States level GDP per capita. The United States also enjoyed the lowest unemployment rate of all nations except the Netherlands during the 1997-to-2000 period. Canada, Finland, and Belgium all had unemployment rates more than twice

Table 4.1   Macroeconomic Comparison

| Nation (Year) | Average Standard of Living | | OECD Standardized Unem-ployment Rate | OECD Social Expenditures on Non-Elderly[b] |
	GDP per Capita (in 2000 US$)[a]	Index		
United States (2000)	34,106	100	4.0	2.8
Netherlands (1999)	26,517	78	3.2	10.5
Sweden (2000)	25,363	74	5.6	12.6
Germany (2000)	25,329	74	7.8	8.9
Canada (1997)	25,044	73	9.1	6.0
Finland (2000)	24,530	72	9.8	12.1
United Kingdom (1999)	23,723	70	5.9	6.4
Belgium (1997)	23,541	69	9.2	8.9

Source: U.S. Bureau of Labor Statistics (http://www.bls.gov); OECD (http://www.oecd.org); and Organization for Economic Cooperation and Development (2002).
[a]Using 2000 PPPs, price adjusted in each nation to correct year.
[b]Countries with data year 2000 are given the most recent (1999) values available from OECD. Non-elderly social expenditures includes all cash plus near-cash spending (such as food stamps) and public housing but excludes health care and education spending.

the U.S. rate, with the variance in unemployment far exceeding the differences in incomes across these select nations.[11]

The United States is unique not only in both its high standard of living and its low unemployment rate but also in the tiny amount of its resources devoted to cash and near-cash social-transfer programs. In 1999, the latest year for which data are available, the United States spent less than 3 percent of GDP on cash and near-cash assistance for the non-elderly, families with children and the disabled. This is less than half the amount, measured as a percent of GDP, spent by Canada or the United Kingdom; less than a third of spending by Germany, the Netherlands, or Belgium; and less than a quarter of the amount spent in Finland or Sweden. Despite the known rough correlation between social spending and unemployment, the differences we see here are not cyclical, but rather are structural.

In order to examine structural differences, we show the generosity of income-transfer programs by tracing the trend in non-elderly cash and near-cash (food, housing) benefits for OECD countries back over the past twenty years, using data from the OECD (2002). We present these estimates in comparable format in figure 4.1. Here the seventeen OECD nations—all of the major nations except for the Central and Eastern Europeans—have been grouped into six clusters: Scandinavia and the Nordic nations, Northern Europe, Central and Southern Europe, Anglo-Saxony, the United States, and Mexico. (Our eight nations are shown in boldface type at the bottom of the figure.)

We show only non-elderly patterns because elder benefits, especially retirement benefits, depend heavily on the design of systems of income support in each nation (see note 8). Figure 4.1 illustrates the wide differences that one can find for both levels and trends in social spending, using figures that abstract from financing of health care, early-childhood education, and retirement for the elderly. They also correspond very closely to the measures of money and near-money income transfers used in the analytic literature in this area, including that presented here.

The Scandinavian and Northern Europeans shown in figure 4.1 follow similar patterns—high levels of spending that varied with the recession of the early 1990s in Sweden and Finland (when transfers rose and GDP fell), and a tapering of outlays after these events. The Central and Southern Europeans and the Anglo-Saxon nations show remarkably similar spending patterns, again rising in the early 1990s but overall at a level distinctly below that the other two groups. The United States is significantly below all these others and by the late 1990s is spending at a level closer to Mexico than to the other richer OECD nations, in terms of per-capita fraction of GDP. Even before the "Bush revolution," we are a distinct lower-boundary outlier in cash and near-cash social spending on the non-elderly.

Results: Levels and Trends in Poverty

In addition to overall poverty rates, we examined many subgroups. We separately estimated poverty among two vulnerable populations, children (in both one- and two-parent units) and the aged.[12] We examined the antipoverty effect of government policy for each of these groups. We also delved deeply into the situation of poor children, examining the amount of work by parents, family status,

Figure 4.1   Total Non-elderly Social Expenditures in Six Groupings of
Seventeen Nations, as Percentage of GDP[a]

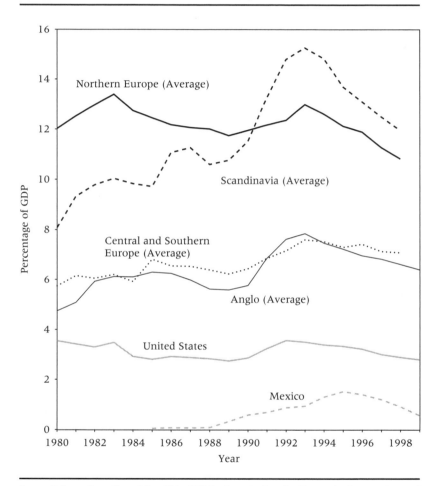

Source: Osberg, Smeeding, Schwabish (2004); Organization for Economic Cooperation and
Development (2002).
[a] Includes all cash plus near-cash spending (such as food stamps) and public housing but excludes
health care and education spending. Anglos: Australia, U.K., Canada; Scandinavia: Finland,
Norway, Sweden; Northern Europe: Belgium, Denmark, Netherlands; Central and Southern
Europe: Austria, France, Germany, Italy, Luxembourg, Spain.

and education level of parents for low-income children in each nation. We conclude with a brief summary of what we have learned about how government support affects poverty for the vulnerable in comparative perspective.

Overall Levels and Trends in Relative Poverty

Relative poverty rates in the eight nations are given in table 4.2. In addition to the overall percentage of the population who are poor, we show poverty rates for five subgroups: children and adults in one-parent households; children and adults in two-parent households; childless non-elderly adults; persons living in a household headed by an aged person; and all other, or "mixed," households. The latter group includes multigenerational households with elders and adult children, unrelated adults living together, and three-generation households where grandparents of any age live with their children and grandchildren. The basic distribution of persons by household types for each group is given in appendix table 4A.2. There one can see that persons living in households with two parents and children, and childless adults are the most predominant household types in each nation. Persons living with elders and single parents—two key vulnerable groups—are smaller fractions in each country, with 9 to 17 percent of persons in household units headed by the elderly and 4 to 11 percent of persons in units headed by a single parent across these eight nations. Mixed households hold 8 percent or less of all persons in each nation. The United States has the largest percentage of persons living with single parents (10.6 percent) and in mixed households (8.4 percent), the lowest percentage of persons living with elders (8.7 percent) and childless non-elderly adults (29.8 percent), and is in the middle of the pack in terms of persons living with two parents (42.5 percent).

The overall poverty rate for all persons using the 50 percent poverty threshold varies from 5.4 percent in Finland to 17 percent in the United States, with an average rate of 9.8 percent across the eight countries. Higher overall poverty rates are found in Anglo-Saxon nations with a high level of overall inequality (United States, Canada, and the United Kingdom) and in geographically large and diverse countries (United States, Canada). Still, Canadian and British poverty rates are both about 12 percent of the population and are, therefore, far below the United States levels. The lowest poverty rates

Table 4.2 Poverty Rates in Eight Rich Countries, by Age Group, at the End of the Twentieth Century

| | Poverty Rate[a] | | | | | | Rank of Country | | | | | |
| | Overall[b] | Children and Their Parents[c] | | Elders[d] | Childless[e] | Mixed[f] | Overall | Children and Their Parents | | Elders | Childless | Mixed |
Nation (Year)		One-Parent	Two-Parent					One-Parent	Two-Parent			
United States (2000)	17.0	41.4	13.1	28.4	11.1	14.9	1	1	1	1	2	1
United Kingdom (1999)	12.3	31.3	8.9	24.6	7.7	7.0	2	4	3	2	6	4
Canada (1997)	11.9	38.9	9.5	5.2	12.1	5.9	3	2	2	7	1	6
Netherlands (1999)	8.9	26.8	7.9	3.2	9.5	14.2	4	5	4	8	4	2
Germany (2000)	8.2	31.6	2.8	12.2	9.0	7.5	5	3	6	4	5	3
Belgium (1997)	7.9	12.5	6.6	13.1	7.3	6.3	6	6	5	3	8	5
Sweden (2000)	6.4	11.3	2.1	8.2	9.7	2.4	7	7	8	6	3	7
Finland (2000)	5.4	7.3	2.2	10.1	7.6	2.1	8	8	7	5	7	8
Overall average	9.8	25.1	6.6	13.1	9.3	7.5						

Source: Author's calculations based on Luxembourg Income Survey files.

[a] Poverty is measured at 50 percent median adjusted disposable income (ADPI) for individuals. Incomes are adjusted by E = .5 where ADPI = unadjusted DPI divided by household size (s) to the power E: ADPI = DPI/s^E.

[b] All types of persons regardless of living situation.

[c] Children are under age eighteen. They and the non-elderly adults living with them in the same household are separated into one- and two-parent columns.

[d] Adults aged sixty-five and over living in units with a head aged sixty-five and over.

[e] Childless are couples or singles where the reference person is under age sixty-five.

[f] Mixed households include persons living in multiple generation families.

are more common in smaller, well-developed, and high-spending welfare states (Sweden, Finland), where they are about 5 or 6 percent. Middle-level rates are found in major European countries where unemployment compensation is more generous, where social policies provide more generous support to single mothers and working women (through paid family leave, for example), and where social-assistance minimums are high. For instance, the Netherlands, Belgium, and Germany have poverty rates in the 8 to 9 percent range. On average, single parents and their children and elders have the highest poverty rates, while those in two-parent units and mixed units and the childless experience the least poverty. Mixed-household poverty rates are lower on average and reflect the economies of scale gained by sharing living arrangements in multigenerational households. Privacy is sacrificed for lower-cost housing.[13] In general, elder poverty rates are somewhere between those of single parents, who are less well off, and two-parent units, which are better off, but this is not universally the case.

The United States has the highest poverty rate in each category except for childless adults, where our 11.1 percent is below the 12.1 percent in Canada (where unemployment was 9.1 percent in the survey year). In all types of household cases, the United States poverty rate is above average; in most cases Canada or the United Kingdom has the second highest poverty rate (for elders, single-parent households, two-parent households).

The trends in poverty are shown in table 4.3. These data use the same definitions as those in table 4.1, and are taken directly from the LIS website. They reflect between ten and twenty years of history in each nation. The trend findings are similar to those in other recent LIS papers with different percentage of median poverty rates and wider ranges of countries (see, for example, Burtless, Rainwater, and Smeeding 2002). In general, poverty is higher in most nations at the end of the relatively prosperous 1990s than it was in the 1980s. (This trend does not conflict with the observation that many nations' poverty rates, including those in the United States, rose in the early 1990s and fell in the later 1990s.) In general, child poverty is increasing, whereas elder poverty has been falling over the ranges of years shown here. Upward changes are least in the "low-poverty" nations, and in Canada. The United States trends do not stand out as being especially different from those in other nations, except that ris-

Table 4.3 Trends in Poverty in Eight Rich Countries, by Age Group: Percentage-Point Change from Initial Year

Nation	Years	Overall	Children	Aged
United States	1979 to 2000	+1.2	+1.5	−2.6
United Kingdom	1979 to 1999	+3.3	+2.9	−0.5
Canada	1981 to 1997	−0.5	+0.9	−16.7
Netherlands	1991 to 1999	+2.3	+1.5	0.0
Germany[a]	1984 to 2000	+1.0	+0.8	−1.1
Belgium	1985 to 1997	+2.5	+3.3	+0.5
Sweden	1981 to 2000	+1.1	−0.7	+0.5
Finland	1987 to 2000	0.0	+0.1	−3.4

Source: Author's calculations using LIS files based on 50 percent of median poverty thresholds. Numbers show actual change in poverty rates at 50 percent of median (in each year) calculated as the change from the initial year. See also http://www.lisproject.org/keyfigures/povertytable.htm.
[a]Only West Germany is included here.

ing United States child-poverty rates come from an already high base. This may be troubling if it suggests that national institutions, morals, and beliefs are such that poverty levels across countries bear some policy-invariant relationship to one another.

We hasten to mention that the trends noted in poverty are different from the changes found in income inequality (measured on a scale from zero to one using the Gini coefficient) over this same period in these same nations. In many of the more equal nations, most of the rise in inequality noted over this period has taken the form of higher incomes at the top of the distribution rather than by falling lower incomes at the bottom (Förster and Vleminckx 2004; Smeeding and Grodner 2000).

The Antipoverty Effect of Taxes and Transfers

In every nation, benefits from governments, net of taxes, reduce income poverty. Figure 4.2 and table 4.4 contain the basic overall patterns. Poverty rates computed using before-tax-and-transfer household income do not differ among countries as much as do those calculated after taxes and transfers (figure 4.2). Here we find that the United States before-tax-and-transfer poverty rate is actually below average, but not as low as in high spending nations such as Finland and the Netherlands. This finding implies that different levels and

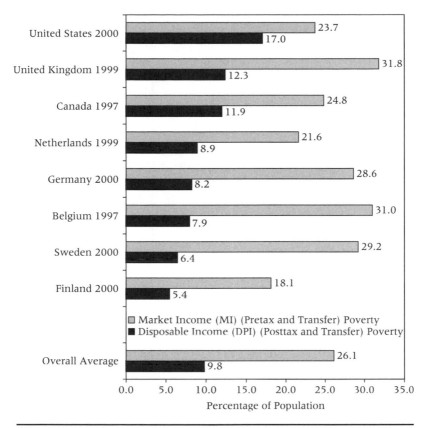

Figure 4.2 Relative Poverty Rates and Antipoverty Effects in Eight Nations at the End of the Twentieth Century (Percentage of Persons with Market Income and Disposable Income Less than Half of Adjusted National Disposable Median Income)

Source: Author's calculations based on Luxembourg Income Study.

mixes of government spending on the poor have sizable effects on national poverty rates (Burtless, Rainwater, and Smeeding 2002). In fact, detailed analysis shows that higher levels of government spending (as in Scandinavia and Northern Europe) and more careful targeting of government transfers on the poor (as in Canada, Sweden, and Finland) produce lower poverty rates (Kenworthy 1998; Kim

Table 4.4 The Antipoverty Effect of Government Spending: Percent of All Poor Persons,[a] by Income Source

Nation (Year)	Market Income[b]	Social Insurance (and Taxes)[c]	Social Assistance[d]	Percentage Reduction of Poverty	
				Social Insurance[e]	Overall[f]
United States (2000)	23.7	19.3	17.0	18.6	28.3
Netherlands (1999)	21.6	10.9	8.9	49.5	58.8
Sweden (2000)	29.2	11.6	6.4	60.3	78.1
Germany (2000)	28.6	9.9	8.2	65.4	71.3
Canada (1997)	24.8	13.8	11.9	44.4	52.0
Finland (2000)	18.1	11.4	5.4	37.0	70.2
United Kingdom (1999)	31.8	22.8	12.3	28.3	61.3
Belgium (1997)	31.0	8.7	7.9	71.9	74.5
Average	26.1	13.6	9.8	46.9	61.8

Source: Author's calculations based on the Luxembourg Income Study.

[a]Poverty rates are for persons living in households with adjusted incomes below 50 percent of median adjusted disposable income.

[b]Market income includes earnings, income from investments, occupations (private- and public-sector) pensions, child support, and other private transfers.

[c]Includes effect of taxes.

[d]Refunds from the Earned Income Tax Credit (U.S.) and the Family Tax Credit (U.K.) are treated as social assistance, as are near-cash food and housing benefits such as food stamps and housing allowances.

[e]Market-income rate minus social insurance rate as a percentage of market-income rate.

[f]Market-income rate minus social assistance rate as a percentage of market-income rate.

2000), a finding that we verify. Unemployment is not well correlated with either market income–based poverty or disposable income–based poverty (table 4.1). Rather, earnings and wage disparities are important in determining both market-income and disposable-income poverty rates, especially among families with children (Jäntti and Danziger 2000; Bradbury and Jäntti 1999). Countries with an egalitarian wage structure tend to have lower child-poverty rates, in part because the relative poverty rate among working-age adults is lower when wage disparities are small.

Greater details as to the effects of different types of spending are shown in table 4.2. Here we split the antipoverty effect into two components: social insurance and taxes, and social assistance. The former is not income- or means-tested and includes universal benefits such as child allowances and child tax credits; the latter is targeted to the otherwise poor using income tests. One can see that most nations make effective use of both types of instruments. As one might expect, the United States shows the least antipoverty effort of any nation. We reduce poverty by 28 percent compared to the average reduction of 62 percent. The nation closest to the United States in terms of overall effect is Canada. But even there, government programs reduce market income–based poverty by 52 percent. Our social insurance and direct (payroll and income) tax system is weak and our safety net and social-assistance system, including the effect of the EITC in the social-assistance category, reduces only another ten percentage points of poverty. Social insurance also has a relatively low antipoverty effect in the United Kingdom and Finland. All other nations get at least a 40 percent poverty reduction from social insurance, and in heavily insured countries such as Sweden, Belgium, and Germany, social insurance reduces poverty by 60 to 70 percent. In the case of social assistance, large effects of targeted programs are evident in Finland and the United Kingdom (33 percent reductions), and lower effects (under 10 percent) in the more socially insured nations where the heavy lifting has already been done (Germany, Belgium, the Netherlands, and Canada). It should be apparent that different nations use different instruments and different "income packages" to achieve their antipoverty effects. There is no one program or one type of policy instrument that is universally generous and common across these eight nations. Hence, we turn to the detail found by examining critical subgroups: elders and households with children.

Antipoverty Effects for Elders and Children

Relative poverty rates can vary across age groups within a nation as much as they do across nations. Comparing poverty among children and the elderly (see table 4.2), we find large imbalances in several nations. Elderly poverty exceeds child poverty in most two-parent units and is generally below poverty in one-parent units by large amounts. Only in the United States and the United Kingdom is poverty relatively high among both the young and the old. In both the Netherlands and Canada the elderly show less poverty than children; the elderly do the worst in Finland and Belgium. Each group is examined separately below.

Elder Poverty   Great strides have been made in reducing poverty among the elderly in most rich countries over the past forty years, but pensioner poverty has not been eradicated, especially in the two major Anglo-speaking nations, the United States and the United Kingdom. As expected, the effects of social insurance on elder poverty are very large in all nations, including the United States. In addition, social assistance is also a powerful antipoverty tool in Sweden, Finland, and the United Kingdom. In other nations, especially in the United States, social assistance—especially Supplemental Security Income (SSI) and food stamps—have almost no effect on elder poverty.[14] Poverty among younger pensioners is no longer a major policy problem. Poverty in old age is almost exclusively an older women's problem. Poverty rates among older women (not shown) rise with both age and changes in living arrangements. Three quarters of the poor elders aged seventy-five or older in each rich nation are women; almost 60 percent of all poor aged seventy-five and over in each nation are older women living alone (Smeeding 1999, 2003). Countries that do best in the fight against elder poverty are those with high minimum "first tier" traditional—that is, defined-benefit type—social retirement plans for all elderly, such as Germany, Belgium, Sweden, and Finland. But population aging in coming decades will put pressure on these governments to reduce exactly these benefits and to turn their systems more toward defined-contribution pension plans, as are now found in the United Kingdom. Unfortunately, the changeover to this system in the United Kingdom has left that nation with a relatively high elder poverty rate.[15] In either case, targeted income-tested benefit strategies, as in Canada, can be extremely successful in reducing elderly female poverty at a much lower overall cost. Such schemes as these should be considered for supplementing both traditional social-retirement schemes and national pension systems of a defined-contribution variety (Osberg 2002; Smeeding and Weaver 2001).

The Canadians combine their social retirement, the Canadian Pension Plan, with an income-tested benefit, the General Income Supplement, at source. The elderly, therefore, receive a "topped up" minimum benefit. This benefit has an almost universally high take-up rate, because the benefits are determined and checks are combined into one payment by the Canadian Social Security office on the basis of the previous year's income-tax filing. There is no test for liquid assets, that is cash or assets that can easily be converted into cash. As can be seen in table 4.3, this highly effective and well-targeted benefit has produced a 16.7 percent decrease in elder poverty since 1981. The Canadians now have the second lowest poverty rate of the eight nations shown in table 4.5.

Despite gains, pensioner poverty, instead of being a "past problem," may rise again in the coming decades. In systems without an adequate safety net, poverty rates among older women are highest among the divorced, widowed, and never married. These are groups whose prevalence within the elder population will rise significantly over the coming decades, as the members of the baby boom retire and grow old, because of changing patterns of divorce and nonmarriage among this cohort. For instance, in the United States, divorced and never-married women were 10 percent of all older United States women in the 1990s; this group will be over 25 percent of all aged in the 2020s (Smeeding 1999). And these groups have poverty rates more than double the overall elder population poverty rates in America, despite the high labor-force participation rates and increasingly higher pension benefits of other women in similar cohorts. The challenge will be to design systems of retirement benefits that guarantee minimum standards of living for very elderly women—especially those who are survivors, divorcees, or who have never been married—and are sustainable in the face of the severe budgetary pressure coming to bear on traditional social-retirement systems due to population aging. The Canadians have shown us how this can be done.

Table 4.5 The Antipoverty Effect of Government Spending: Percentage of Poor Elders,[a] by Income Source

A. Elders Living Alone[b]

Nation (Year)	Market Income[c]	Social Insurance (and Taxes)[d]	Social Assistance[e]	Percentage Reduction of Poverty	
				Social Insurance[f]	Overall[g]
United States (2000)	67.1	28.9	28.4	56.9	57.7
Netherlands (1999)	63.1	4.1	3.2	93.5	94.9
Sweden (2000)	86.2	21.6	8.2	74.9	90.5
Germany (2000)	82.9	12.3	12.2	85.2	85.3
Canada (1997)	68.5	6.7	5.2	90.2	92.4
Finland (2000)	35.4	13.9	10.1	60.7	71.5
United Kingdom (1999)	76.8	38.2	24.6	50.3	68.0
Belgium (1997)	91.5	14.3	13.1	84.4	85.7
Average	71.4	17.5	13.1	74.5	80.7

B. All Elders[b]

Disposable-Income Poverty at Specified
Percentage of Adjusted Disposable Income

Nation (Year)	40%	50%	60%
United States (2000)	15.0	24.7	33.3
Netherlands (1999)	0.4	1.6	21.4
Sweden (2000)	2.1	7.7	21.2
Germany (2000)	5.2	11.6	21.2
Canada (1997)	1.4	5.1	17.3
Finland (2000)	1.1	8.5	24.7
United Kingdom (1999)	10.2	20.9	34.9
Belgium (1997)	1.7	8.7	22.7
Average	4.6	11.1	24.6

Source: Luxembourg Income Study, key figures http://www.lisproject.org/keyfigures/povertytable.htm.

[a] Poverty rates are for persons aged 65 and over, living in households with a reference person 65 or over, and with adjusted incomes below 50 percent of median adjusted disposable income.

[b] Poverty rates are percentage of persons 65 and older regardless of household arrangement with adjusted incomes below the specified percentage of median income.

[c] Market income includes earnings, income from investments, occupations (private- and public-sector) pensions, child support, and other private transfers.

[d] Includes effect of taxes.

[e] Refunds from the Earned Income Tax Credit (U.S.) and the Family Tax Credit (U.K.) are treated as social assistance, as are near-cash food and housing benefits such as food stamps and housing allowances. The poverty rates in this column are the same as those in table 4.2.

[f] Market-income rate minus social insurance rate as a percent of market-income rate.

[g] Market-income rate minus social assistance rate as a percent of market-income rate.

We should also note that the poverty rate of the elderly is particularly sensitive to the income cutoff used to determine poverty because the elder-income distribution is very densely clustered at or near the poverty-line cutoffs. In Europe, the European Statistical Office (Eurostat) has recommended a 60-percent-of-median-income standard for measuring poverty and social exclusion (Eurostat 2000). The United Kingdom has adopted this same standard for its antipoverty efforts with regard to children, but not the elderly (Bradshaw 2003). The United States elder poverty line is just about 40 percent of the median. Although aged poverty rates are on average below overall national poverty rates when poverty is measured using the 40-percent-of-median-income standard, they average five percentage points higher when the 50-percent-of-median-income standard is used, and fifteen points higher when the 60-percent standard is calculated.[16] Raising the poverty threshold from 40 percent to 50 percent of national median income increases the poverty rate of the elderly from 4.6 percent to 11.1 percent on average in the eight countries examined here (table 4.5, section B). This increase is the largest of any age group and suggests that social-protection systems for the elderly often provide income guarantees that are no more than between 40 percent and 50 percent of median national income. In fact, at a 60-percent-of-median-income cutoff, we find 24.6 percent of the aged are poor, on average. Once again, the United States and the United Kingdom have the highest rates at any poverty standard, while the Canadians very cost-effectively fight poverty up to the 60 percent line.

Child Poverty Recently, Ron Haskins and Isabel Sawhill (2003) have suggested that work and marriage are the solution to both poverty and welfare. If all American parents married and if the head of the family worked full-time the full year at the wages paid for high school graduates, and each family had only two children each, our official poverty rate would be 3.7 percent. No account was taken of the cost of child care (since presumably the nonworking parent could be in charge of child care), and no account was taken of the mental and physical health of children or parents. Unfortunately, none of us in the United States or any of the other countries studied here live in such a world. And since none of us will soon be in this simulated world, it is important to ask how policy deals with the world in which we do live: with single parents, undereducated parents, and parents who work. In fact, in the United States, where only 2.0 million families with children are still on welfare, we still have 12 million to 15 million families who work but nevertheless are poor (Shapiro and Parrott 2003).

The effect of antipoverty programs on children is best examined here by splitting the analysis between children with two adults, almost always married parents, in the unit and children in a single-parent family. The experience of these two groups differs markedly both within and between nations (table 4.6). On average, single-parent poverty rates are about four times larger than two-parent rates, measured by either market or disposable income. Also on average, both social insurance and social assistance reduce poverty by another 25 percent for both groups. But once we leave averages behind, the variance across nations and groups is very large.

Among single parents, all nations begin with market-income poverty rates of 41 percent or more. Market income alone does not guarantee any acceptable level of poverty for single parents in any nation. Income transfers better the situation; still, only three nations manage to end with disposable-income poverty rates of 12.5 percent or lower. In five of the nations observed here, at least 25 percent of children in single-parent families are poor after taxes and transfers. When considering the poverty-reduction effects of social programs, the United States is an extreme outlier. We begin with a below-average 49 percent market-income (MI) poverty rate for single parents, but we end with the highest after-benefits (DPI) poverty rate of 41.4 percent. Our social insurance and payroll taxes largely cancel out, so poverty falls by less than 1 percentage point. Even including the EITC, we end up with less than a 15 percent poverty reduction for low-income single parents. Canada does a bit better, with a 27 percent overall transfer effect; Germany ends up with a 38 percent reduction. It should, however, come as no surprise that German and Canadian single-parent poverty rates after benefits are not much better than are American rates. All other nations do much better, with a 51 percent or higher reduction.

In the case of child poverty in two-parent households, the situation is both different and similar. It is different because most two-parent families earn enough to be non-poor to begin with, but then

Table 4.6 The Antipoverty Effect of Government Spending: Percentage of One- and Two-Parent Households with Poor Children,[a] by Income Source

A. One-Parent Households

Nation (Year)	Market Income[b]	Social Insurance (and Taxes)[c]	Social Assistance[d]	Percentage Reduction of Poverty	
				Social Insurance[e]	Overall[f]
United States (2000)	48.6	48.2	41.4	0.8	14.8
Netherlands (1999)	55.2	44.0	26.8	20.3	51.4
Sweden (2000)	48.3	22.9	11.3	52.6	76.6
Germany (2000)	51.0	40.3	31.6	21.0	38.0
Canada (1997)	53.3	44.8	38.9	15.9	27.0
Finland (2000)	41.2	27.4	7.3	33.5	82.3
United Kingdom (1999)	75.6	71.1	31.3	6.0	58.6
Belgium (1997)	45.1	18.3	12.5	59.4	72.3
Average	52.3	39.6	25.1	26.2	52.6

B. Two-Parent Households

Nation (Year)	Market Income[b]	Social Insurance (and Taxes)[c]	Social Assistance[d]	Percentage Reduction of Poverty	
				Social Insurance[e]	Overall[f]
United States (2000)	13.9	15.2	13.1	(9.4)	5.8
Netherlands (1999)	9.9	8.4	7.9	15.2	20.2
Sweden (2000)	9.6	5.2	2.1	45.8	78.1
Germany (2000)	7.4	4.5	2.8	39.2	62.2
Canada (1997)	15.6	11.1	9.5	28.8	39.1
Finland (2000)	10.7	7.0	2.2	34.6	79.4
United Kingdom (1999)	17.8	16.5	8.9	7.3	50.0
Belgium (1997)	12.6	6.9	6.6	45.2	47.6
Average	12.2	9.4	6.6	25.8	47.8

Source: Author's calculations based on the Luxembourg Income Study.

[a]Poverty rates are for all persons living in households with one or two non-aged parents, with adjusted incomes below 50 percent of median adjusted disposable income.

[b]Market income includes earnings, income from investments, occupations (private- and public-sector) pensions, child support, and other private transfers.

[c]Includes effect of taxes.

[d]Refunds from the Earned Income Tax Credit (U.S.) and the Family Tax Credit (U.K.) are treated as social assistance, as are near-cash food and housing benefits such as food stamps and housing allowances.

[e]Market-income rate minus social insurance rate as a percent of market-income rate.

[f]Market-income rate minus social assistance rate as a percent of market-income rate.

it is similar in that the United States benefit system reduces this market-income poverty rate by only a meager .8 percent (19.9 versus 19.1). In fact, since most low-income two-parent households pay more in payroll tax than they receive in unemployment or workers' compensation, the initial effect of the tax-transfer system is to *raise* child poverty by 9.4 percent! The EITC and food stamps more than make up for this effect, however. In all, other nations' benefits systems, especially social insurance in all but the United Kingdom, and social assistance, bring about much larger reductions in child poverty. It seems that, especially for two-parent units, we simply do not provide the programs to help the working poor escape poverty.

Education and Work Effort Among Parents

There are striking differences across countries in the level and configuration of social safety nets and in the outcomes we find when comparing disposable-income poverty for families with children. It is natural to ask how differences in child poverty are tied to systematic differences not only in social spending but also in labor-market performance, as typified by education and work effort. We begin with differences in child poverty according to the education of the parent (table 4.7). In order to isolate an education effect, in panel A of the table we have combined one- and two-parent units and present poverty rates for all children.[17] In panel B we have been able to separate only those children whose parents have the least education. In the United States, this comes down to parents where at least one has not finished high school. (Owing to education coding differences, we had to exclude the Netherlands.) In panel C, these children are compared to all other children whose parents have had more education.[18]

The results of this exercise are striking. In all nations, market-income and even disposable-income poverty rates are more than twice as high for the poorly educated than for the highly educated. About 16 percent of all United States parents did not finish high school, and their children's poverty rate is over 50 percent, even after taking account of taxes and benefits—which, as stated, produce little effect on their incomes.[19] American children with more highly educated parents have much lower market- and disposable-income poverty rates, but the rates are still the highest among the nations

Table 4.7 Pre- and Posttax and Transfer Rates by Education Level: Percentage of Poor[a] Children, by Head or Reference Person, Across Education Levels

A. All Children

Nation (Year)	Market Income[b]	Social Insurance (and Taxes)[c]	Social Assistance[d]	Percentage Reduction of Poverty	
				Social Insurance[e]	Overall[f]
United States (2000)	24.7	25.2	21.9	(2.0)	11.3
Sweden (2000)	18.7	9.4	4.1	49.7	78.1
Germany (2000)	14.2	9.5	6.8	33.1	52.1
Canada (1997)	23.6	17.9	15.6	24.2	33.9
Finland (2000)	16.7	10.6	2.8	36.5	83.2
United Kingdom (1999)	34.1	32.0	15.4	6.2	54.8
Belgium (1997)	17.4	8.5	7.6	51.1	56.3
Average	21.3	16.2	10.6	28.4	52.8

(*Table continues on p. 178.*)

Table 4.7 Pre- and Posttax and Transfer Rates by Education Level: Percentage of Poor[a] Children, by Head or Reference Person, Across Education Levels (*Continued*)

B. Children with Lowest Education Level Parents[g]

Nation (Year)	Market Income[b]	Social Insurance (and Taxes)[c]	Social Assistance[d]	Percentage Reduction of Poverty		
				Social Insurance[e]	Overall[f]	Percentage Parents in Lowest Level
United States (2000)	55.5	56.8	51.3	(2.3)	7.6	15.7
Sweden (2000)	30.7	17.7	5.9	42.3	80.8	17.4
Germany (2000)	17.2	10.7	6.6	37.8	61.6	28.4
Canada (1997)	43.5	34.1	29.8	21.6	31.5	14.4
Finland (2000)	30.6	19.6	6.1	35.9	80.1	20.2
United Kingdom (1999)	46.9	41.9	18.7	10.7	60.1	21.9
Belgium (1997)	47.4	28.9	24.7	39.0	47.9	9.9
Average	38.8	30.0	20.4	26.4	52.8	18.3

C. Children with Other Education Level Parents

Nation (Year)	Market Income[b]	Social Insurance (and Taxes)[c]	Social Assistance[d]	Percentage Reduction of Poverty	
				Social Insurance[e]	Overall[f]
United States (2000)	19.1	19.4	16.5	(1.6)	13.6
Sweden (2000)	16.1	7.6	3.8	52.8	76.4
Germany (2000)	12.9	9.1	6.9	29.5	46.5
Canada (1997)	20.2	15.2	13.2	24.8	34.7
Finland (2000)	13.1	8.3	2.0	36.6	84.7
United Kingdom (1999)	31.3	29.8	14.6	4.8	53.4
Belgium (1997)	14.2	6.3	5.8	55.6	59.2
Average	18.1	13.7	9.0	28.9	52.6

Source: Author's calculations based on the Luxembourg Income Study.

[a] Poverty rates are for persons living in households with adjusted incomes below 50 percent of median adjusted disposable income.

[b] Market income includes earnings, income from investments, occupations (private- and public-sector) pensions, child support, and other private transfers.

[c] Includes effect of taxes.

[d] Refunds from the Earned Income Tax Credit (U.S.) and the Family Tax Credit (U.K.) are treated as social assistance, as are near-cash food and housing benefits such as food stamps and housing allowances.

[e] Market-income rate minus social insurance rate as a percent of market-income rate.

[f] Market-income rate minus social assistance rate as a percent of market-income rate.

[g] Lowest level is less than a high school degree in the United States.

shown. One reason for our high poverty rates is low transfers; the second reason must, therefore, be low earnings—due to either low work hours or low wages or both. Indeed, American children born to single parents with little education have the highest market-income poverty rate by almost 10 percentage points. Belgium and Canada have similar but smaller poverty penalties for the poorly educated parent. In the other five nations, the poverty rates for poorly educated parents are not much different from those found among highly educated parents; consequently, the poverty situation of children is not so dependent on the education level of their parents. In both the United States and Canada, a high percentage of workers earn low wages, whereas Belgium is a high-wage country (Burtless, Rainwater, and Smeeding 2002).

Among more highly educated parents, the United States is about average in its level of market-income poverty. Once taxes and benefits are accounted for, we have the highest child poverty rates, followed more closely by the United Kingdom and Canadian children. Again, our transfer programs do least to help these families with children.

We can begin to understand whether it is wages or hours that lie at the heart of the problem by looking at the data in table 4.8. To make the analysis manageable, we have shown annual work hours for only three groups: all heads and spouses, single parents only, and the head of the unit in two-parent units, broken down by quintile of disposable income. Households in which both parents work more than 1,000 hours and households where only spouses work more than 1,000 hours are not shown. In order to make comparisons easier, in panel B we norm each panel's hours to the average hours worked in the middle quintile, roughly the average hours of the median adult. We are limited to only five nations where we have annual hours of work in the LIS data at this time. Unfortunately, the United Kingdom and Sweden are not among the nations we examine. In both cases, other research shows that British single parents do not work very many hours, whereas Swedish women work a substantial number of hours (Smeeding 2002; McLanahan and Garfinkel 1994).

The patterns evident in the table, no surprise to international labor-market analysts, may surprise others: Americans of all stripes and situations work much longer hours than do any other nations'

Table 4.8 Mean Number of Annual Work Hours, by Quintile[a]

A. Actual Work Hours

1. All Non-Elderly Adults (Head and Spouse)

Nation (Year)	Lowest	Middle	Highest
United States (2000)	1,645	3,097	3,605
Netherlands (1999)	1,132	2,392	3,097
Germany (2000)	870	2,603	3,228
Canada (1997)	1,081	2,670	3,248
Belgium (1997)	1,114	2,531	3,064
Average	1,168	2,659	3,248

2. Single Parents (Head Only)[b]

Nation (Year)	Lowest	Middle	Highest
United States (2000)	1,104	1,938	2,115
Netherlands (1999)	585	1,158	1,340
Germany (2000)	659	1,859	1,456
Canada (1997)	440	1,648	1,799
Belgium (1997)	455	1,558	826
Average	649	1,632	1,507

B. Hours as Percentage of "Average Middle-Income Household"

1. All Non-Elderly Adults (Head and Spouse)

Nation (Year)	Lowest	Middle	Highest
United States (2000)	61.9	116.5	135.6
Netherlands (1999)	42.6	90.0	116.5
Germany (2000)	32.7	97.9	121.4
Canada (1997)	40.7	100.4	122.2
Belgium (1997)	41.9	95.2	115.2
Average	43.9	100.0	122.2

2. Single Parents (Head Only)[b]

Nation (Year)	Lowest	Middle	Highest
United States (2000)	67.6	118.7	129.6
Netherlands (1999)	35.8	70.9	82.1
Germany (2000)	40.4	113.9	89.2
Canada (1997)	27.0	101.0	110.2
Belgium (1997)	27.9	95.5	50.6
Average	39.7	100.0	92.3

(Table continues on p. 182.)

Table 4.8 Mean Number of Annual Work Hours, by Quintile[a] (*Continued*)

3. Two Parents (Head's Hours Only)[c]

Nation (Year)	Lowest	Middle	Highest
United States (2000)	1,708	2,218	2,426
Netherlands (1999)	1,164	2,024	2,311
Germany (2000)	1,267	2,133	2,211
Canada (1997)	1,258	1,952	2,138
Belgium (1997)	1,139	2,023	2,040
Average	1,307	2,070	2,225

3. Two Parents (Head's Hours Only)[c]

Nation (Year)	Lowest	Middle	Highest
United States (2000)	82.5	107.1	117.2
Netherlands (1999)	56.2	97.8	111.6
Germany (2000)	61.2	103.0	106.8
Canada (1997)	60.8	94.3	103.3
Belgium (1997)	55.0	97.7	98.6
Average	63.1	100.0	107.5

Source: Author's tabulations based on the Luxembourg Income Study.

[a]Mean annual hours of work per year in each nation for adults (18 to 64) classified by type of household.

[b]Single parents may have one adult who works and also perhaps an older child who works in some circumstances, but we only count hours of work for the single parent here.

[c]Two-parent households may have two adults and older children who work, but we only count the hours of the head here.

workers (Osberg 2002). The differences between American and other workers are least among the highest-quintile workers and are the largest among low-income parents, especially single parents. American single parents in the lowest-income quintile average over 1,000 hours per year—almost twice as many as those in the other four nations shown here. Lowest-quintile heads in two-parent units work almost full-time (over 1,700 hours per year). The next nearest nation is Germany, with 1,267 hours. Belgian parents work the least number of hours of any low-income parents. It seems that we have the hardest-working low-income parents extant, but that they are receiving the least assistance from the social safety net.

Table 4.9 confirms this fact by presenting data on children who are poor in terms of the hours worked by their parents and of their family situation. There are many numbers and many expected and unexpected patterns in this table. For instance—children of family heads who work less than 1,000 hours a year are very likely to be poor, regardless of the number of parents in the family unit, according to the data in panel B, center and right columns. Also, children in two-parent units where one parent works at least 1,000 hours are likely to have poverty rates that are below 10 percent except in the United States, where their poverty rate is 21.0 percent (panel C, right column)! But the key figure is in panel C in the middle column: almost a third of all United States children living with a single parent where the head works more than 1,000 hours are poor. The next nearest nation is the Netherlands, at 13.1 percent.

Summary of Results

Comparative cross-national poverty rankings suggest that United States poverty rates are at the top of the range when compared with those in other rich countries. The United States child and elderly poverty rates seem particularly troublesome. Poverty rates for U.S. elders are 28.4 percent, whereas all other nations' rates except those of the United Kingdom are less than half that. In most rich countries, the child poverty rate is 10 percent or less; in the United States, it is 21.9 percent. Part, though not all, of the explanation is that the United States devotes a relatively small share of its national income to social transfers for families with a non-aged head. Another part of the problem seems to be that even when parents, especially single mothers, work 1,000 hours a year or more, they still have

Table 4.9 Poverty Rate (Percentage Who Are Poor) by Number of Hours Worked and Income Source, for One-Parent Versus Two-Parent Families

A. All Hours Worked

Nation (Year)	All Children			Children in a One-Parent Family			Children in a Two-Parent Family		
	Market Income	Social Insurance	Social Assistance	Market Income	Social Insurance	Social Assistance	Market Income	Social Insurance	Social Assistance
United States (2000)	24.2	25.2	21.9	54.0	53.3	46.2	15.5	16.9	14.7
Netherlands (1999)	13.8	11.4	9.6	56.1	45.8	29.9	9.8	8.2	7.7
Germany (2000)	13.9	9.6	6.8	56.1	44.1	34.5	7.8	4.6	2.8
Canada (1997)	23.6	18.2	15.8	57.0	48.3	42.5	16.5	11.8	10.1
Belgium (1997)	17.3	8.6	7.6	46.3	17.3	11.3	13.8	7.5	7.2
Average	18.6	14.6	12.3	53.9	41.8	32.9	12.7	9.8	8.5

B. Less than 1,000 Hours Worked (Head)

Nation (Year)	All Children			Children in a One-Parent Family			Children in a Two-Parent Family		
	Market Income	Social Insurance	Social Assistance	Market Income	Social Insurance	Social Assistance	Market Income	Social Insurance	Social Assistance
United States (2000)	88.8	84.3	78.8	89.4	86.3	80.9	87.0	78.2	72.6
Netherlands (1999)	85.5	70.9	56.4	88.0	77.3	48.4	83.9	66.7	61.7
Germany (2000)	74.6	43.7	28.1	91.1	77.2	59.5	58.2	43.7	28.1
Canada (1997)	79.7	68.0	59.5	88.0	79.1	71.4	70.6	55.8	46.4
Belgium (1997)	72.1	35.5	30.5	89.3	35.0	22.0	65.4	35.7	33.5
Average	80.1	60.5	50.7	89.2	71.0	56.4	73.0	56.0	48.5

(Table continues on p. 186.)

Table 4.9 Poverty Rate (Percentage Who Are Poor) by Number of Hours Worked and Income Source, for One-Parent Versus Two-Parent Families

C. 1,000 Hours or More Worked (Head)

Nation (Year)	All Children			Children in a One-Parent Family			Children in a Two-Parent Family		
	Market Income	Social Insurance	Social Assistance	Market Income	Social Insurance	Social Assistance	Market Income	Social Insurance	Social Assistance
United States (2000)	27.9	29.8	25.1	40.3	40.6	32.9	21.5	24.2	21.0
Netherlands (1999)	5.7	4.2	3.6	26.9	17.0	13.1	3.9	3.2	2.8
Germany (2000)	6.0	2.9	1.9	20.7	10.6	9.2	4.2	2.0	1.0
Canada (1997)	17.9	11.7	9.9	22.4	13.9	10.2	16.7	11.1	9.8
Belgium (1997)	7.8	3.2	3.2	9.7	2.3	2.3	7.5	3.3	3.3
Average	13.1	10.4	8.7	24.0	16.9	13.5	10.8	8.8	7.6

Source: Author's calculations, based on the Luxembourg Income Study.

high poverty rates. Previous studies have shown that low wages and low spending (but not high unemployment) are highly correlated with high poverty rates (Burtless, Rainwater, and Smeeding 2002). The findings here suggest that we need to move beyond worrying about welfare and instead concentrate on a package of benefits for the working poor, especially for single parents and for the poorly educated.

Relative and Real Economic Well-Being

Although most would argue that economic well-being, at least in developed countries, is most crucially a function of the individual's relative position in the distribution of income, real levels of living standards are also important in comparing living standards and well-being across nations. Interest in real-income position is important for all persons, but especially for households with children. Interest in real economic position of children goes beyond the situation of poor children alone—in comparative studies one also wants to know about the real standard of living of average and well-off children when we assess equality of opportunity. These measures can also be understood as measures of the types of life chances that low-income parents can provide for their children.

Tables 4.10 through 4.13 compare the distribution of disposable income in eight countries at around the same time (1997 to 2000) by decile, for four populations of interest—all persons, elders, children and adults in two-parent units, and children and adults in single-parent units. Within each country, we focus on the relative differences between those at the bottom and those at the top of the income distribution. In the first panel (A), we calculate, in each country, for each population, the ratio of the income of a household at the 10th percentile (P10) to median income (P50), and the ratio of a household at the 90th percentile (P90) to median income. This tells us how far below or above the middle of the distribution the poor and the rich are located on the continuum of income within each country. We also calculate the decile ratio, that is, the ratio between the incomes of those at the 90th and 10th percentiles, or between the richest and the poorest, in each country. The bar graphs illustrate "economic distance," the gap between P10/P50 and

(*Text continues on p. 196.*)

Table 4.10   Relative and Real Economic Well-Being of All Persons in Eight Rich Countries[a]
(Numbers Given are Percentage of Median in Each Nation and Gini Coefficient)

A. Real Income Relative to Own Median Income

	P10/P50 (Low Income)	Economic Distance[e]	P90/P50 (High Income)	P90/P10 (Decile Ratio)	Gini Coefficient[b]
Sweden (2000)	57		168	2.95	.254
Finland (2000)	57		164	2.90	.247
Germany (2000)	55		173	3.17	.252
Belgium (1997)	53		170	3.19	.250
Netherlands (1999)	53		175	3.27	.253
United Kingdom (1999)	47		214	4.54	.345
Canada (1997)	47		186	3.99	.291
United States (2000)	39		210	5.43	.368
Average[c]	51		183	3.68	.283

B. Real Income as Percentage of Overall U.S. 2000 Median-Equivalent Income in PPP Terms[d]

	P10/P50 (Low Income)	Economic Distance[e]	P90/P50 (High Income)	P90/P10 (Decile Ratio)	Real-Income Gap Between Rich and Poor
Sweden (2000)	38		113	2.95	$18,263.17
Finland (2000)	38		111	2.90	$17,774.85
Germany (2000)	41		131	3.17	$21,827.90
Belgium (1997)	43		136	3.19	$22,755.71
Netherlands (1999)	41		133	3.27	$22,511.55
United Kingdom (1999)	35		157	4.54	$29,909.60
Canada (1997)	45		181	3.99	$33,083.68
United States (2000)	39		210	5.43	$41,897.86
Average[c]	40		146	3.68	$26,003.04

Source: Luxembourg Income Study and author's calculations.

[a]Figures given are adjusted dollars per equivalent person (child) in own currency as a percent of own overall national median income (P50), weighted for the number of persons in each unit. In panel A, the 10/50 and 90/50 columns are the country's 90th and 10th percentiles relative to the nation's median, and the 90/10 column is the country's 90th percentile relative to the country's 10th percentile. In panel B, the 10/50 and 90/50 columns are the country's 90th and 10th percentiles relative to the U.S. median.

[b]Gini coefficients are based on incomes that are bottom-coded at 1 percent of mean disposable income and top-coded at ten times the median disposable income.

[c]Simple average.

[d]Figures given are adjusted dollars per equivalent person 2000 U.S. dollars, weighted for the number of persons in each unit size, and relative to the overall U.S. median income of $24,416.

[e]Length of bar represents the gap between low- and high-income individuals.

Table 4.11 Relative and Real Economic Well-Being of Elderly Persons in Eight Countries,[a] as Percentage of Median Income in Each Country

A. Real Income Relative to Own Median Income

	P10/P50 (Low Income)	Economic Distance[d]	P90/P50 (High Income)	P90/P10 (Decile Ratio)
Sweden (2000)	52		123	2.39
Finland (2000)	50		120	2.40
Germany (2000)	48		145	3.01
Belgium (1997)	46		132	2.85
Netherlands (1999)	59		159	2.68
United Kingdom (1999)	38		125	3.30
Canada (1997)	54		146	2.71
United States (2000)	33		179	5.42
Average[b]	48		141	3.09

B. Real Income as Percentage of Overall U.S. 2000 Median-Equivalent Income in PPP Terms[c]

	P10/P50 (Low Income)	Economic Distance[d]	P90/P50 (High Income)	P90/P10 (Decile Ratio)	Real-Income Gap Between Rich and Poor
Sweden (2000)	35		83	2.39	$11,744.10
Finland (2000)	34		81	2.40	$11,573.18
Germany (2000)	36		110	3.01	$17,896.93
Belgium (1997)	37		105	2.84	$16,602.88
Netherlands (1999)	45		121	2.68	$18,482.91
United Kingdom (1999)	28		92	3.31	$15,650.66
Canada 1997	52		142	2.71	$21,827.90
United States (2000)	33		179	5.42	$35,696.19
Average[b]	38		114	3.09	$18,684.34

(Economic Distance axis: 0   50   100   150   200   250)

Source: Luxembourg Income Study and author's calculations.

[a] Figures given are adjusted dollars per equivalent person (child) in own currency as a percent of own overall national median income (P50), weighted for the number of elderly persons in each unit.

[b] Simple average.

[c] Figures given are adjusted dollars per equivalent person 2000 U.S. dollars, weighted for the number of persons in each unit size, and relative to the overall U.S. median income of $24,416.

[d] Length of bars represents the gap between low- and high-income individuals.

Table 4.12   Relative and Real Economic Well-Being of Two-Parent Families with Children in Eight Countries,[a] as Percentage of Median Income in Each Country

A. Relative to Own Median Income

	P10/P50 (Low Income)	Economic Distance[d]	P90/P50 (High Income)	P90/P10 (Decile Ratio)
Sweden (2000)	71		163	2.28
Finland (2000)	67		158	2.36
Germany (2000)	67		165	2.47
Belgium (1997)	58		163	2.80
Netherlands (1999)	57		154	2.72
United Kingdom (1999)	51		203	3.94
Canada (1997)	51		169	3.31
United States (2000)	45		197	4.41
Average[b]	58		171	3.04

Economic Distance[d]

0   50   100   150   200   250

B. Real Income as Percentage of Overall U.S. 2000 Median-Equivalent Income in PPP Terms[c]

	P10/P50 (Low Income)	Economic Distance[d]	P90/P50 (High Income)	P90/P10 (Decile Ratio)	Real-Income Gap Between Rich and Poor
Sweden (2000)	48		109	2.28	$26,686.69
Finland (2000)	45		107	2.36	$14,332.19
Germany (2000)	50		125	2.47	$19,386.30
Belgium (1997)	46		130	2.80	$19,386.30
Netherlands (1999)	43		117	2.72	$17,188.86
United Kingdom (1999)	38		148	3.94	$25,734.46
Canada (1997)	50		164	3.31	$30,788.58
United States (2000)	45		197	4.41	$35,891.52
Average[b]	46		137	3.03	$23,674.36

(Economic Distance bar chart, horizontal scale: 0, 50, 100, 150, 200, 250)

Source: Luxembourg Income Study and author's calculations.

[a]Figures given are adjusted dollars per equivalent person (child) in own currency as a percentage of own overall national median income (P50), weighted for the number of two parents with children in each unit.

[b]Simple average.

[c]Figures given are adjusted dollars per equivalent person 2000 U.S. dollars, weighted for the number of persons in each unit size, and relative to the overall U.S. median of $24,416.

[d]Length of bars represents the gap between high- and low-income individuals.

Table 4.13 Relative and Real Economic Well-Being of Single Parents with Children in Eight Countries,[a] as Percentage of Median Income in Each Country

A. Relative to Own Median Income

Economic Distance[d]

	P10/P50 (Low Income)	Economic Distance[d]	P90/P50 (High Income)	P90/P10 (Decile Ratio)
Sweden (2000)	49		100	2.06
Finland (2000)	52		114	2.22
Germany (2000)	26		103	3.97
Belgium (1997)	46		133	2.88
Netherlands (1999)	38		91	2.40
United Kingdom (1999)	42		112	2.70
Canada (1997)	30		118	4.00
United States (2000)	21		131	6.12
Average[b]	38		113	3.29

B. Real Income as Percentage of Overall U.S. 2000 Median-Equivalent Income in PPP Terms[c]

	P10/P50 (Low Income)	Economic Distance	P90/P50 (High Income)	P90/P10 (Decile Ratio)	Real-Income Gap Between Rich and Poor
Sweden (2000)	33		67	2.06	$8,472.35
Finland (2000)	35		77	2.22	$10,376.80
Germany (2000)	20		78	3.95	$14,210.11
Belgium (1997)	37		106	2.88	$16,895.87
Netherlands (1999)	29		69	2.40	$9,864.06
United Kingdom (1999)	31		82	2.69	$12,647.49
Canada (1997)	29		115	3.99	$21,046.59
United States (2000)	21		131	6.12	$26,759.94
Average[b]	29		91	3.29	$15,034.15

Economic Distance axis: 0   50   100   150   200   250

Source: Luxembourg Income Study and author's calculations.

[a]Figures given are adjusted dollars per equivalent person (child) in own currency as a percent of own overall national median income (P50), weighted for the number of single parents with children in each unit.

[b]Simple average.

[c]Figures given are adjusted dollars per equivalent person 2000 U.S. dollars, weighted for the number of persons in each unit size, and relative to the overall U.S. median of $24,416.

[d]Length of bars represents the gap between high- and low-income individuals.

P90/P50, or low income and high income, for each country. The countries in all eight panels are ranked by the P10/P50 ratio for all persons within each country (table 4.10, panel A). In panel B of each table, we convert the relative incomes of the seven other countries to 2000 U.S. dollars by purchasing power parities (PPPs). We then recalculate low, median, and high incomes in those countries as a fraction of the 2000 United States overall median adjusted disposable income per equivalent person ($24,416) to create "real income" figures to assess the relative richness of nations.

We use the OECD estimates of PPP exchange rates to convert household incomes in each country into U.S. dollars, but OECD's estimates of PPP are far from ideal for comparing the well-being of low-income households in different countries. In principle, the PPPs permit us to calculate the amount of money needed in country A to purchase the same bundle of consumption items in country B.[20] If relative prices on different consumption items differ widely between the two countries, however, the PPP exchange rate may only be correct for one particular collection of items. The exchange rates calculated by the OECD are accurate for overall national aggregate production and consumption (Castles 1996). Thus, the exchange rates are appropriate for comparing market baskets of all final consumption, including government-provided health care, education, and housing. These goods are paid for in different ways in different nations, however. In most countries, health care as well as some rental housing, child care, and education are subsidized more generously by the government than in the United States. Thus, disposable incomes in countries with publicly financed health and relatively generous education systems reflect the fact that health and education costs have already been subtracted from households' incomes in the form of tax payments. One implication is that in countries where in-kind benefits are larger than average, real incomes may be understated, and therefore, low incomes may be understated because citizens actually face a lower effective price level than is reflected by OECD estimates of the PPP exchange rate. The opposite is true for countries whose citizens must pay larger amounts for health care and education out of their disposable incomes. Since United States residents pay more out of pocket for these goods than residents of other nations, United States percentile points are likely overstated.[21] In contrast, Northern European countries provide high levels of tax-financed health care and education benefits; consequently their real-income positions are likely understated. However, the extent of these differences is unknown at this time.[22]

Another problem for comparing real incomes across countries arises because of differences in the quality of the household income survey data used to measure poverty. For example, the LIS survey for the United States is the Current Population Survey (CPS). The CPS captures about 86 percent of the total household incomes that are estimated from other sources, such as national income accounts data and agency administrative records. Most but not all of the other surveys used by LIS capture approximately the same percentage of total income (Atkinson, Rainwater, and Smeeding 1995). The household surveys of Finland and Sweden capture between 93 and 94 percent of the incomes reflected in the aggregate statistical sources. Unfortunately, not all of the countries shown here have performed the calculations that would allow us to determine the overall quality of their household survey data.[23] We used a rough methodology to compare the quality of survey data for the different LIS countries before our calculations were made.[24]

Assuming that the household surveys from different countries yield information about disposable incomes with comparable reliability, we should expect that once incomes are converted into a common currency unit, countries with higher average incomes will have higher real-income levels. This expectation is of course based on the assumption that income inequality is approximately the same across all countries. If income inequality differs significantly, countries with higher average incomes but greater income disparities may have "richer" high-income persons and "poorer" low-income persons than we find in lower-average-income countries with less income inequality. And indeed this is the case.

Table 4.10 provides the basic information for all persons in our eight nations. The United States has the highest level of disposable income inequality of all nations, with the United Kingdom second and Canada third. These patterns are reflected in both the Gini coefficients, taken from the LIS website, and in the decile ratios shown in table 4.10. Panel A shows that U.S. low-income persons are disadvantaged in relative terms, with incomes only 39 percent of the median compared to an average 51 percent. In other nations the next lowest "low-income" person is in either Canada or the United

Kingdom, where that person has 47 percent of the income of the average Briton or Canadian. At the top of the distribution, high-income Britons and Americans have more than twice the income of their average countryman, 214 percent and 210 percent, respectively. The combined effects of these are shown in the decile ratios, which show that rich Americans have 5.4 times as much as do poor Americans, rich Britons have 4.5 times as much, and the rich in all other nations have less than 4.0 times as much as the poor.

But these are relative amounts only. Britain is much poorer than America, with a GDP that is only about 70 percent of United States GDP. Therefore, the rich Briton whose income is 214 percent that of the average Briton has an income that is only 157 percent that of the average American, once PPPs have been applied to adjust for differences in living standards between the United States and the United Kingdom. This comparison validates the fact that rich Americans are really well-off compared to the "relative rich" in any other nation. The PPP adjustment also closes the gap between poor Americans and poor residents in other comparable nations so that the average poor American is roughly as well off as the average poor person in any other nation—having a living standard based on a real income that is about $9,770, or 40 percent of the average American median income of $24,416. Poor Americans are in general about as badly off as are the poor in any other nation—with Britons a bit worse off and Canadians a bit better off, but with no large differences across nations. This result is a modest improvement in American low-income living standards compared to the situation in the mid-1990s, when low-income Americans were about 5.0 percentage points lower (with a P10 of 35), below average (for example, see Blank and Schoeni 2003, on the growth of American children's real income in the second half of the 1990s). The overall gap between the rich and the poor in the United States is about $41,700 per equivalent person, and much larger than in any other nation.

Poor American elders' living standards are only about a third that of the average American (table 4.11) as measured by their disposable incomes; rich ones are considerably better off, and the gap between rich and poor, as measured by the differences in their real incomes, is larger than for the population as a whole. Among the elders, the gap between rich and poor is much greater than in any other nation by a wide amount (decile ratio of 5.4, compared to 3.3 in the United Kingdom, which is the next closest nation). Moving to real incomes in panel B, the gap between well-to-do elderly and their foreign counterparts widens even more. In fact, rich old Swedes, Finns, and Britons are not as well off as are average American elders. Poor American elders, however, are still poorer in real-income terms than those in other nations—only elder Britons living at the same standard are poorer—and low-income Swedes and Finns are at roughly the same living standard, not counting health-care costs or wealth levels, which pull these particular comparisons in different directions. Low-income Canadian elders have especially higher income compared to their American counterparts.

On average, children's real incomes if they live in a two-parent household are 45 percent of the median at the 10th percentile and are 197 percent of the median at the 90th percentile, producing a decile ratio of 4.41. The real income gap, or "economic distance," between low- and high-income children in these families averages almost $35,900 per child, as shown in panel B of table 4.12. This means that low-income families have resources of $10,987 per child, assuming all resources are evenly split among household members, compared to the $46,968 that high-income families have to spend on each child. The economic distance of $35,891 per child between rich and poor children in the United States is by far the largest, with Canada the only other one above the $30,000 level. It is hard to argue that all American children have an equal opportunity if one measures by their parents' incomes.

Looking at a measure of "fair chance," the nations with the highest low-income decile (P10) offer their children the best economic chance for future success. We agree with Susan E. Mayer (1997) and others that income alone is a poor proxy for measuring life chances for middle-class households with children. Another $500 or $1,000 per child for middle-income or well-to-do families makes little difference to their children's overall life chances compared to the difference made by other influences such as parents, schools, communities, and peers. But we also agree with Greg Duncan et al. (1998) that being born into a family with very low income (roughly 30 percent of the median) significantly decreases a child's overall life chances. Wendy Sigle-Rushton and McLanahan (2004) recently summarized the effects of parental absence on child development in rich nations. While they found that parental absence mattered, they also found that low incomes mattered to child development, even when parental structure is held constant. Thus, we believe that the relative level of a country's low-income decile (P10) for children is a meaningful and important indicator of a fair life chance.

On this basis, poor American children in two-parent units are no better or worse off than are poor children in other nations in the bottom panel of table 4.12, with the exception of British low-income children. American low-income children are at roughly the same level of living standard as average children, as long as they live with two parents. Of course on a relative basis, our poor children are still at a disadvantage: 45 percent of the median compared to a 51 percent average. At the other end of the scale, U.S. children in prosperous two-parent households have living standards 197 percent above the median U.S. person. In Sweden and Finland, the average high-income child in a two-parent family actually has a living standard just about 10 percent above that of the average United States person, measured by cash income. The gap between rich and poor children is lowest in Scandinavian nations.

Finally, we turn to low-income children in one-parent families. As expected, these children do less well than do children in two-parent units in every country and at any income level. In relative terms the income of the typical poor child in an American single-parent family is 21 percent that of the average American and less than 50 percent the typical income of a poor child from a two-parent family (in panel A of tables 4.12 and 4.13, compare the United States figure of 21 and 45). In table 4.13, panel B, this translates to a real-income level of $5,127 per child.[25] The situation delineated by these real-income comparisons is very damaging for our low-income children. The income differences across nations do not make up for how poorly we treat our low-income children in single-parent families. The average poor child in such a unit is not as well off as is his or her counterpart in any nation, who on average enjoys a living standard 29 percent of that of the average American. A low-income American child in a single-parent unit is better off only in comparison to the average German low-income child. In every other nation, a low-income child is better off than average and far better off than a low-income American child in a single-parent family.

Discussion

Many defenders of American economic and political institutions, while acknowledging that the United States has greater inequality than other industrialized nations, have argued that inequality plays a crucial role in creating incentives for people to improve their situations through saving, hard work, and investment in education and training. Without the powerful signals provided by big disparities in pay and incomes, the economy would operate less efficiently and average incomes would grow less rapidly. In the long run, goes this argument, poor people might enjoy higher absolute incomes in a society where wide income disparities are tolerated than in one where law and social convention keep income differentials small. According to this line of argument, wide income disparities may be in the best long-term interest of the poor themselves.[26] Of course, there is no evidence that this is true (Burtless and Jencks 2003).

In recent years, the United Kingdom and especially the United States economies have in fact performed better than other economies where income disparities are smaller. Employment growth has been faster, joblessness lower, and economic growth higher than in many other OECD countries where public policy and social convention have kept income disparities low. However, the evidence that lower social spending "caused" higher rates of growth is not found in the literature (for example, Arjona, Ladaique, and Pearson 2001). Our lower-income citizens' real incomes are at or below the incomes that poor people receive in other rich countries that have less inequality. The supposed efficiency advantages of high inequality have not accrued to low-income residents of the United States, at least so far. Although the real incomes of families with children did rise in the later 1990s (Blank and Schoeni 2003), most of the gains were captured by Americans much further up the income scale, producing a conspicuously wide gap between the incomes of the nation's rich and poor children, elders, and adults.

Low-income United Kingdom children in single-parent units experience real living standards that are above those found for United States children in similar units. Just four years before the U.K. data used in this study, in 1995, these low-income United Kingdom children were worse off than were United States children in real terms (Smeeding and Rainwater 2004). The reason for their improvement is that the United Kingdom's prime minister has set a national goal of improving living standards and eradicating child poverty in Britain over the next decade, and has matched his political rhetoric with some measure of real and continuing fiscal effort, which has already had an impact (Bradshaw 2003; Walker and Wiseman 2001; Micklewright 2001).

Policy and Research Implications

A substantial fraction of the variance in cross-national poverty rates appears to be accounted for by the cross-national variation in the incidence of low pay. Because the United States has the highest proportion of workers in relatively poorly paid jobs, it also has the highest poverty rate, even among parents who work half time or more (Burtless, Rainwater, and Smeeding 2002). Conversely, other countries have a significantly lower incidence of low-paid employment and also have significantly lower poverty rates than the United States. The prevalence of low-pay workers is, in fact, not the only reliable predictor of poverty rates. While low pay is a good predictor of United States poverty rates, and while poorly educated workers do not do well at keeping their families from poverty by means of earnings alone, other factors, such as the antipoverty efforts of the government, are also important predictors of the poverty rate. Social spending also reduces poverty, as we have seen. As a result of its low level of spending on social transfers to the non-aged, the United States has a very high poverty rate. All of the high-spending nations in Northern Europe and Scandinavia have child-poverty rates of 10 percent or less. And in Britain, Prime Minister Blair has spent an *extra* .9 percent of GDP for low-income families with children since 1999 (Hills 2003). Nine tenths of a percent of United States GDP is about $90 billion. This is more than we now spend on the EITC, the Food Stamp Program, and TANF combined. The result of this spending in Britain is that child poverty rates in 2001 were 23 percent below their 1996 level and, as is evident from the foregoing, real living standards for these children also rose (Bradshaw 2003).

Even though social spending in general has an inverse correlation with poverty rates, different patterns of social spending can produce different effects on national poverty rates. Antipoverty and social-insurance programs are in most respects unique to each country. There is no one kind of program or set of programs that is conspicuously successful in all countries that use them. Social-insurance, universal benefits (such as child allowances), and social-assistance transfer programs targeted on low-income populations are mixed in different ways in different countries. So, too, are minimum wages, worker preparation and training programs, work-related benefits (such as child care and family leave), and other social benefits. The United States differs from most nations that achieve lower poverty rates because of its emphasis on work and self-reliance for working-age adults, regardless of the wages workers must accept or the family situation of those workers. For over a decade, United States unemployment has been well below the OECD average, and until recently American job growth has been much faster than the OECD average. The strong economy coupled with a few specific antipoverty devices such as the expanded EITC has produced most of the United States' poverty reduction, such as it is, in recent years. But it has not produced much poverty reduction. And the longer-term effects of low income on poor American children are a topic which we are just beginning to grapple with.

As long as the United States relies almost exclusively on the job market to generate incomes for working-age families, changes in the wage distribution that affect the earnings of less-skilled workers will inevitably have a big effect on poverty among children and prime-age adults. Welfare reform has pushed many low-income women into the labor market and they have stayed there as TANF roles continue to fall. Even with the $25.4 billion spent on TANF today, only $11.2 billion is in the form of cash assistance; the rest is now in the form of child-care, transportation assistance, training, and other services (Pear 2003). While the switch from cash to services has undoubtedly helped account for higher earnings among low-income parents, it has not helped move many of them from poverty. In fact, serious gaps still exist, especially in the child-care arena (Smolensky and Gootman 2003) and in family leave policy (Gornick and Meyers 2003). Still, labor markets alone cannot reduce poverty because not all of the poor can be expected to "earn" their way out of poverty. Single parents with young children, disabled workers, and the unskilled will all face significant challenges earning an adequate income, no matter how much they work. The relationship between antipoverty spending and poverty rates is of course complicated, so the arguments discussed here are at best suggestive. United States poverty rates among children and the aged are high when compared with those in other industrialized countries. Yet United States economic performance has also been outstanding compared with that in other rich countries. Carefully crafted public policy can certainly reduce American poverty. Implementing the policies that would achieve lower poverty rates would also have budgetary costs and perhaps, some efficiency costs that are yet to be unearthed.

Of course, the direct and indirect costs of antipoverty programs are now widely recognized—and frequently overstated—in public debate.[27] The wisdom of expanding programs targeted at children and poor families and older women depends on one's values and subjective views about the economic, political, and moral trade-offs of poverty alleviation. For many critics of public spending on the poor, it also depends on a calculation of the potential economic efficiency losses associated with a larger government budget and targeted social programs. It is hard to argue that the United States cannot afford to do more to help the poor, particularly those who are working in the labor market.

Toward Solutions

A partial solution to the poverty problem that is consistent with American values lies in creating an income package that mixes work and benefits so that unskilled and semiskilled workers, including single parents, can support their families above the poverty level. Such a package could include more generous earnings supplements under the EITC, refundable child and daycare tax credits, and the public guarantee of assured child support for single parents with an absent partner who cannot or will not provide income to their children. A reasonable increase in the minimum wage over the next several years would also help low-skilled workers more than it would hurt them. Targeted programs to increase job access and skills for less-skilled workers could also help meet future growing labor demand in the United States economy. In the long run, a human-capital strategy that focuses on improving the education and marketable job skills of disadvantaged future workers, particularly younger ones, is the approach likely to have the biggest payoff. If the nation is to be successful in reducing poverty, it will need to do a better job of combining work and benefits targeted to low-wage workers in low-income families (see, for example, Ellwood 2000; Danziger, Heflin, and Corcoran 2000). There is already evidence that such programs improve outcomes for children (Clark-Kauffman, Duncan, and Morris 2003).

An expanded income-related program with a higher benefit guarantee for the aged and disabled who also receive Social Security could go a long way toward reducing poverty among these groups to levels that are common in Northern Europe. Canada achieved a major reduction in poverty when it implemented a targeted expansion of its social-assistance plan in the 1980s (Smeeding and Sullivan 1998; Osberg 2002), and we might do the same as part of a Social Security reform package.

Given the political disposition of the American public, a near-zero percent poverty rate is not a plausible goal, but a gradual reduction in the overall poverty rate to 10 percent using the 50 percent standard is certainly feasible. Although this rate would represent a considerable achievement by the standards of the United States, it is worth remembering that a 10 percent overall poverty rate is higher than the average poverty rate in the eight nations examined here, and would just put us on a par with our British and Canadian counterparts.

Appendix

Table 4A.1   Macro and Micro Comparisons

Nation (Year)	GDP per Capita (in 2000 US$)[a]	Index	LIS Median DPI (in 2000 US$)[a]	Index
United States (2000)	34,106	100	24,116	100
Netherlands (1999)	26,517	78	18,328	76
Sweden (2000)	25,363	74	16,206	67
Germany (2000)	25,329	74	18,208	76
Canada (1997)	25,044	73	21,005	87
Finland (2000)	24,530	72	16,327	68
United Kingdom (1999)	23,723	70	17,677	73
Belgium (1997)	23,541	69	19,245	80

Source: OECD and Luxembourg Income Study.
[a]Median DPI per equivalent adult in real 2000 PPP dollars, using OECD PPPs, price-adjusted in each nation to correct year.

Table 4A.2 Distribution of Household Types, as Percentage of All Persons

Nation (Year)	Mixed[a]	Elders	Non-Elderly Childless	Non-Elderly Single Parent	Two Parents with Children	Total
United States (2000)	8.4	8.7	29.8	10.6	42.5	100.0
Netherlands (1999)	3.7	10.8	36.0	3.5	45.9	100.0
Sweden (2000)	3.8	15.1	35.1	7.9	38.1	100.0
Germany (2000)	6.2	16.7	38.6	4.0	34.6	100.0
Canada (1997)	8.0	8.7	33.9	7.3	42.1	100.0
Finland (2000)	6.4	11.7	36.4	5.7	39.7	100.0
United Kingdom (1999)	7.0	12.0	34.4	9.0	37.5	100.0
Belgium (1997)	7.5	13.1	34.1	4.3	41.1	100.0
Average	6.4	12.1	34.8	6.5	40.2	100.0

Source: Author's calculations from Luxembourg Income Study.

[a]Mixed are likely to be elder and nonelderly families living together, and include very few elders with children.

The author would like to thank Lee Rainwater, Kim Desmond, Joseph Marchand, Mike Eriksen, Mary Santy, and especially Kati Foley for their help in preparing this manuscript. Also thanks go to John Quigley, Gary Burtless, and Lee Rainwater for many helpful conversations; to Joel Slemrod and David Wise for thoughtful comments; and finally to Gene Smolensky for long-term inspiration and guidance. The author thanks the Luxembourg Income Study sponsors for their support. The conclusions reached are those of the author alone.

Notes

1. Rich nations can have low relative (as well as low absolute) poverty as well as high incomes. For instance, Luxembourg's gross domestic product (GDP) is 50 percent larger than the United States', but its relative poverty rate is under 5 percent. While there is likely some tradeoff between one's overall standard of living and one's level of relative poverty, recent analysts have found no strong evidence of such tradeoffs in rich nations (see Osberg, Smeeding, and Schwabish 2004; Lindert 2004).

2. Poverty measurement began as an Anglo-American social indicator. In fact, "official" measures of poverty (or measures of "low income" status) exist in very few nations. Only the United States (U.S. Bureau of the Census 2003b) and the United Kingdom (U.K. Department of Social Security 1996) have regular "official" poverty series. Statistics Canada publishes the number of households with incomes below a "low income cutoff" on an irregular basis, as does Australia. In Northern Europe and Scandinavia the debate centers instead on the level of income at which minimum benefits for social programs should be set and on "social exclusion." In other words, their concept of insufficient "low income" directly leads to programmatic responses and they have moved on to other concerns.

3. See for UNICEF (2000), Bruce Bradbury and Markus Jäntti (1999); for the United Nations Development Programme (1998, 1999); for the OECD, see Michael Förster (1993, 2000); for the European Union, see Eurostat (1998) and Aldi Hagenaars, Klaas de Vos, and Asghar Zaidi (1994); and, for LIS, Jäntti and Sheldon Danziger (2000), Timothy Smeeding (1997), Hwanjoon Kim (2000), Lane Kenworthy (1998), Smeeding, Michael O'Higgins, and Lee Rainwater (1990), and Smeeding and Rainwater (2004).

4. In 1998 the ratio of the United States (four-person) poverty line to median family income was 35 percent while the ratio to median house-

hold income was 42 percent. Median household income ($38,855) is far below median family income ($47,469) because single persons living alone (or with others to whom they are not directly related) both are numerous and have lower incomes than do families. The ratio was unchanged in 2002, the most recent year for which we have data (U.S. Bureau of the Census 2003a, 2003b). Families include all units with two or more persons related by blood, marriage, or adoption; single persons (unrelated individuals) are excluded. In contrast, households include all persons sharing common living arrangements, whether related or not, including single persons living alone. Different adjustments for family or household size might also make a difference in making such comparisons.

5. The Penn World Tables Mark V purchasing power parities (PPPs) were judged to be accurate and consistent for the early 1990s for all nations except Italy (Summers and Heston 1991). However, they have not been updated, and now the OECD and World Bank have developed their own sets of PPPs, the latest benchmarked in 1999. We do not present comparisons of real poverty rates over time because of the intertemporal inconsistency of PPPs dating back to the mid-1980s and earlier. For additional comments on PPPs and microdata-based comparisons of well-being, see Peter Gottschalk and Smeeding (2000), Rainwater and Smeeding (1999), Smeeding and Rainwater (2004), Smeeding et al. (2000), Ian Castles (1996), and Bradbury and Jäntti (1999, appendix).

6. This income definition differs from the census income definition used in most poverty studies. Still, the internationally comparable measure of income does not subtract work-related expenses or medical-care spending. In particular, there is no account for provision of or costs of child care. The Earned Income Tax Credit and similar refundable tax credits and noncash benefits such as food stamps and cash housing allowances are included in this income measure, however, as are direct taxes paid.

7. Of course, our measures of the antipoverty effects of benefits are partial equilibrium in nature and assume no so-called "feedback" effects from transfers or taxes on economic activities such as work or earnings. That is, poverty measured *before* government benefits (using MI) is not the same as poverty in the *absence* of government benefits. If one's awareness of the impact of taxes and transfers on one's MI influences one's work behavior, there will be feedback effects. In the case of benefit programs for the elderly, we expect and find larger effects. The correlation between the size of benefits (percentage of GDP spending on cash benefits for the elderly) and MI poverty is .35, which means that different pension systems have a fairly large effect on MI poverty for the elderly. But in the case of the non-elderly, the correlation between social spending and MI-based poverty is only .14. Thus, we conclude that for the non-elderly, the feedback effects of the tax

benefit system on earnings are modest. For an excellent discussion of behavioral effects and benefit incidence, see Morgan Reynolds and Eugene Smolensky (1977).

8. Formally, adjusted disposable income (ADPI) is equal to *un*adjusted household income (DPI) divided by household size (S) raised to an exponential value (e), thus: ADPI = DPI/S^e. We assume the value of e to be .5. To determine whether a household is poor under the relative-poverty measure, we compare its ADPI to 50 percent of the national median ADPI. National median ADPI is calculated by converting all incomes into ADPI and then taking the median of this "adjusted" income distribution. The regime 2001 equivalence scale that we employ is robust, especially when used for comparing families of different size and structure (for example, elders and children). See Atkinson, Rainwater, and Smeeding (1995) for detailed and exhaustive documentation of these sensitivities.

9. Adding another Northern European or Scandinavian nation (Denmark or Norway) would mimic Sweden and Finland. LIS does not yet have year 2000 data from France or Australia. Southern European LIS data (Italy, Spain) are not well enough reported to include in measures of real well-being. The Central and Eastern European nations have much lower living standards than the others and are, therefore, excluded.

10. We present LIS data on unified Germany for 2000. However, trend data for Germany (table 4.3) are still restricted to the states of the former West Germany. The LIS West German poverty rates tend to be .9 to 1.2 percentage points below those for all of Germany.

11. Unemployment is, of course, cyclical and business cycles differ across nations. However, the period from 1997 to 2000 was one of strong economic performance in every nation studied here. In previous research on this topic, Atkinson, Rainwater, and Smeeding (1995) found no consistent effect of unemployment on overall inequality measured at a point in time. Rather, they concluded that institutional factors were more likely to explain the cross-sectional relationship between unemployment and inequality (or poverty) than were cyclical conditions. Smeeding (1997) found the same result. Still, we must conclude that economic cyclicity probably affects MI-based poverty via its effects on wages and employment. However, we do not know how much difference economic conditions make in a cross-national study such as this.

12. Children are all persons under age eighteen; elderly are all persons age sixty-five or over. We do not include racial or ethnic breakdown as only five to seven LIS nations have such variables. The poverty status of immigrants (foreign-born citizens) can be studied in only four or five LIS countries. These data show that about 15 percent of the poor in the United States (2000), Canada (1997), and the United Kingdom (1999), were foreign-born.

13. Given more time and space, it would be interesting to see how many single parents and elders live in such arrangements and whether they would be poor if they lived independently on their own income.

14. The reason why SSI and food stamps have no effect on elder poverty is because SSI benefits for the elderly max out at less than 90 percent of the official U.S. poverty line, and food stamp benefits max out at about 75 percent of the half-of-median DPI poverty line.

15. Robert L. Brown and Steven G. Prus (2003) show that nations with high levels of social retirement benefits have lower elderly poverty. When social retirement systems change from defined benefit to defined cost, less redistribution results. Both the generosity and nature (whether it is or is not a means-tested benefit) of the lowest tier in such systems are important determinants of elder poverty.

16. The careful reader will note that the poverty rates at the 50 percent standard in section B of table 4.5 are slightly or even substantially lower than in section A. The reason is that the rates in section B of the table are for all elders, including those living in mixed families. The rates in section A are for elders living only in units headed by persons sixty-five or older and not containing any non-elderly persons except spouses. The differences in poverty are mainly due to the economics of scale that are possible living with others.

17. In table 4.7 we see all children regardless of their family circumstances, a slightly different universe than is found in table 4.6, where poverty is selected by parent type.

18. Education is coded into low (less than high school), median (high school diploma), and high (some college or university) by LIS and OECD. The reader can find this code in LIS at http://www.lisproject.org/techdoc/variabdef.htm.

19. In fact, United States families whose MI is below the poverty level pay higher net taxes (even after the Earned Income Tax Credit) than do families in other nations. These taxes are mainly payroll taxes, which mean more poverty today but which may also contribute to reduced poverty in old age or in case of disability. This treatment of payroll taxes in current income, not as payments toward future benefits, should be noted by the reader.

20. In principle, we would like a common market basket of goods and services and the full prices (before and after subsidies) of each element of this market basket in each nation. Of course, different nations consume different baskets, and the differences between "full-priced" and "subsidized" goods for health care, education, housing, and transportation are large across nations. Still, the use of PPP is the preferred use of exchange rates, which vary as a result of a large number of causes, such as currency movements, that are largely unrelated to differences in living standards across nations. See Castles (1996) for more.

21. Smeeding et al. (1993) find that countries that spend more on cash social expenditures also spend more on noncash subsidies. The largest differences between the United States and other nations are in the realm of health-care costs. United States citizens spend roughly 15 percent of their disposable income on health care, as compared to 5 percent in France, 2 percent in Canada, and 1 percent in the United Kingdom (unpublished LIS results). See Irwin Garfinkel, Lee Rainwater, and Smeeding (2004) for more on noncash income and its effect on income distribution.

22. Although the arguments tend to suggest that United States real income levels may be overstated compared to those in other nations, some counterarguments can also be made. More than 85 percent of Americans are covered by health insurance. They do not pay for most of the health care they consume out of the disposable income measured on the CPS, though they do pay more out of pocket for health care on average (see note 14). In other words, the average insured American does not pay the full "price" of medical services reflected in the OECD's PPP estimates for the United States. For a large majority of low-income Americans, insurance is provided for free through the Medicaid program or at reduced cost under Medicare. For others, it is subsidized by an employer's contribution to a company-sponsored health plan. Low-income people in most, if not all, LIS nations pay lower net prices for medical care than do residents of the United States, and the United States probably has the highest final consumption prices for medical care of all OECD countries. The OECD's PPP estimates should therefore show that the United States has a high cost of living (at least for medical care). Second, Americans pay more for higher education (though not for K-through-twelve schooling) than citizens in other OECD countries. Many Americans pay for college out of their disposable incomes. But Americans with low income can obtain a decent college education about as cheaply as most Europeans, so the difference in higher-education costs may not be very relevant for comparing poverty market baskets across countries. Third, more than one-quarter of low-income Americans receive housing subsidies, either directly, through vouchers, or indirectly, through below-market rents on publicly subsidized apartments. European subsidies for housing vary by country, but are generally larger. Fourth, some consumption items that are more important to poor families than to the nonpoor are dramatically cheaper in the United States than they are in other OECD countries. Food is one such item. Because food consumption likely carries a greater weight in the consumption of the poor than it does in aggregate consumption, the OECD's PPP exchange rates are biased against the United States. In summary, although we could develop better PPP exchange rates for purposes of comparing low-income families across

OECD countries, it is not obvious that a superior set of PPPs would reveal systematically lower absolute earning standards in the United States than we see here. Hence, our comparisons in figures 4.3 to 4.6 are about as good as any that could be done at this time.

23. Underreporting of income has a large impact in comparing absolute levels of living standard across countries. The smaller the percentage of aggregate income that is reported in the household survey, the lower the measured level of well-being. Underreporting may also affect relative poverty comparisons or relative income rankings, if income at either the bottom or the top of the income distribution is differentially underreported. Unfortunately, we cannot currently assess the relative importance of income underreporting in different parts of the income distribution.

24. We compared aggregate LIS market incomes to OECD final domestic consumption aggregates. The ratio was 86 percent for the United States. Most of the other nations shown in figures 4.3 to 4.6 were close to the United States level; a few were above it.

25. Even "Murphy Brown"'s son lived at an income level only about 131 percent of that of the average American. *Murphy Brown* was a popular 1990s television show whose eponymous main character was a high-income woman who bore an out-of-wedlock child. Her character sparked a debate on the income of single parents and the public perception that many single mothers had relatively high incomes. Later research, for example, Sara S. McLanahan and Gary Sandefur (1994), has debunked this myth.

26. A lucid presentation and analysis of this viewpoint can be found in Arthur M. Okun (1975). See also Finis Welch (1999).

27. The efficiency costs of public programs are debatable. The recent increase in market work among single mothers who would otherwise be on public support after the 1996 welfare reform is taken by many to be strong evidence that labor supply responded in part to changes in this program. However, the literature debates the importance of TANF versus the EITC and the strong labor market of the late 1990s as primary causes of greater market work among low-income mothers. See Jeffrey Grogger (2003) and chapter 2 of this volume.

References

Arjona, Roman, Maxime Ladaique, and Mark Pearson. 2001. "Growth, Inequality, and Social Protection." Labour Market and Social Policy, occasional paper no. 51. Paris: Organization for Economic Cooperation and Development.

Atkinson, Anthony, Bea Cantillon, Eric Marlier, and Brian Nolan. 2002. *Social Indicators: The EU and Social Inclusion.* Oxford: Oxford University Press.

Atkinson, Anthony B., Lee Rainwater, and Timothy M. Smeeding. 1995. "Income Distribution in OECD Countries: Evidence from the Luxembourg Income Study (LIS)." Social Policy Studies 18. Paris: Organization for Economic Cooperation and Development.

Björklund, Anders, and Richard Freeman. 1997. "Generating Equality and Eliminating Poverty—the Swedish Way." In *The Welfare State in Transition: Reforming the Swedish Model,* edited by Richard B. Freeman, Robert Topel, and Birgitta Swedenborg. Chicago: University of Chicago Press.

Blank, Rebecca M., and Robert F. Schoeni. 2003. "Changes in the Distribution of Children's Family Income over the 1990s." *American Economic Review* 93(2): 304–8.

Bradbury, Bruce, and Markus Jäntti. 1999. "Child Poverty Across Industrialized Nations." Innocenti Occasional Papers, Economic and Social Policy Series, no. 71. Florence, Italy: UNICEF, Innocenti Research Centre.

Bradshaw, Jonathan. 2003. "Using Indicators at the National Level: Child Poverty in the United Kingdom." Unpublished manuscript. Heslington, York, U.K.: University of York, Social Policy Research Unit.

Brown, Robert L., and Steven G. Prus. 2003. "Social Transfers and Income Inequality in Old-Age: A Multi-National Perspective?" Luxembourg Income Study, working paper no. 355 (August). Luxembourg: LIS Center for Policy Research, The Maxwell School. Syracuse, N.Y.: Syracuse University.

Burtless, Gary, and Christopher Jencks. 2003. "American Inequality and Its Consequences." In *Agenda for the Nation,* edited by Henry J. Aaron, James M. Lindsay, and Pietro Nivola. Washington, D.C.: Brookings Institution.

Burtless, Gary, Lee Rainwater, and Timothy Smeeding. 2002. "United States Poverty in a Cross-National Context." In *Understanding Poverty,* edited by Sheldon H. Danziger and Robert H. Haveman. Cambridge, Mass.: Harvard University Press.

Castles, Ian. 1996. "Review of the OECD-Eurostat PPP Program." STD/PPP (97)5, Economic Studies Branch. Paris: Organization for Economic Cooperation and Development.

Citro, Constance F., and Robert T. Michael. 1995. *Measuring Poverty: A New Approach.* Washington, D.C.: National Academy Press.

Clark-Kaufman, Elizabeth, Greg Duncan, and Pamela Morris. 2003. "How Welfare Policies Affect Child and Adolescent Achievement." *American Economic Review* 93(2): 299–303.

Danziger, Sheldon, Colleen M. Heflin, and Mary E. Corcoran. 2000. "Does It Pay to Move from Welfare to Work?" Ann Arbor: University of Michigan, Poverty Research and Training Center.

Duncan, Greg, J., Wei-Jun J. Yeung, Jeanne Brooks-Gunn, and Judith Smith. 1998. "How Much Does Childhood Poverty Affect the Life Chances of Children." *American Sociological Review* 63(3): 406–23.

Ellwood, David T. 2000. "Anti-Poverty Policy for Families in the Next Century: From Welfare to Work—and Worries." *Journal of Economic Perspectives* 14(1): 187–98.

Erikson, Robert, and John H. Goldthorpe. 2002. "Intergenerational Inequality: A Sociological Perspective." *Journal of Economic Perspectives* 16(3): 31–44.

Eurostat. 1998. "Recommendations of the Task Force on Statistics on Social Exclusion and Poverty." Luxembourg: European Statistical Office.

———. 2000. *The Social Situation in the European Union, 2000.* Luxembourg: Statistical Office of the European Communities.

Förster, Michael. 1993. "Comparing Poverty in 13 OECD Countries: Traditional and Synthetic Approaches." Luxembourg Income Study, working paper no. 100. Syracuse, N.Y.: Center for Policy Research, Syracuse University.

———. 2000. "Trends and Driving Factors in Income Distribution and Poverty in the OECD Area." Social Policies Studies Division, paper no. 42. Paris: Organization for Economic Cooperation and Development.

Förster, Michael F., and Koen Vleminckx. 2004. "International Comparisons of Income Inequality and Poverty: Findings from the Luxembourg Income Study." *Socio-Economic Review* 2(2): 191–212.

Garfinkel, Irwin, Lee Rainwater, and Timothy M. Smeeding. 2004. "Welfare State Expenditures and the Redistribution of Well-Being: Children, Elders, and Others in Comparative Perspective." Unpublished manuscript. Available at: http://www-cpr.maxwell.syr.edu/faculty/smeeding/pdf/welfarestate_appam_10.20.04.pdf (accessed September 9, 2005).

Gornick, Janet C., and Marcia K. Meyers. 2003. *Families That Work: Policies for Reconciling Parenthood and Employment.* New York: Russell Sage Foundation.

Gottschalk, Peter, and Timothy M. Smeeding. 2000. "Empirical Evidence on Income Inequality in Industrialized Countries." In *Handbook of Income Distribution,* edited by Anthony B. Atkinson and François Bourguignon. New York: Elsevier–North Holland Publishers.

Grogger, Jeffrey. 2003. "Welfare Transitions in the 1990s: The Economy, Welfare Policy, and the EITC." NBER working paper no. 9472. Cambridge, Mass.: National Bureau of Economic Research.

Hagenaars, Aldi, Klaas de Vos, and Asghar Zaidi. 1994. "Patterns of Poverty in Europe." In *The Distribution of Welfare and Household Production: International Perspectives,* edited by Stephen P. Jenkins, Arie Kapteyn, and Bernard M. S. van Prag. Cambridge: Cambridge University Press.

Haskins, Ron, and Isabel V. Sawhill. 2003. "Work and Marriage: The Way to End Poverty and Welfare." Welfare Reform and Beyond Policy Brief No. 28, (September). Washington, D.C.: Brookings Institution. Available at: http://www.brookings.edu/es/research/projects/wrb/publications/pb/pb28.htm (accessed September 9, 2005).

Hertz, Thomas. 2004. "Rags, Riches, and Race: The Intergenerational Economic Mobility of Black and White Families in the United States." In *Unequal Chances: Family Background and Economic Success,* edited by Samuel Bowles, Herbert Gintis, and Melissa A. Osborne. New York: Russell Sage Foundation and Princeton University Press.

Hills, John. 2003. "The Blair Government and Child Poverty: An Extra One Percent for Children in the United Kingdom." In *One Percent for the Kids: New Policies, Brighter Futures for America's Children,* edited by Isabel V. Sawhill. Washington, D.C.: Brookings Institution.

Jäntti, Markus, and Sheldon Danziger. 2000. "Income Poverty in Advanced Countries." In *Handbook of Income Distribution,* edited by Anthony B. Atkinson and François Bourguignon. New York: Elsevier–North Holland Publishers.

Kenworthy, Lane. 1998. "Do Social-Welfare Policies Reduce Poverty? A Cross-National Assessment." Luxembourg Income Study, working paper no. 188. Syracuse, N.Y.: Syracuse University, Maxwell School, Center for Policy Research.

Kim, Hwanjoon. 2000. "Anti-Poverty Effectiveness of Taxes and Income Transfers in Welfare States." Luxembourg Income Study, working paper no. 228. Syracuse, N.Y.: Syracuse University, Maxwell School, Center for Policy Research.

Krueger, Alan B. 2002. "The Apple Falls Close to the Tree." *New York Times.* November 14.

Lindert, Peter H. 2004. *Growing Public.* Cambridge: Cambridge University Press.

Luxembourg Income Study. 2000. *LIS Quick Reference Guide.* Syracuse, N.Y.: Syracuse University, Maxwell School, Center for Policy Research.

Mayer, Susan E. 1997. *What Money Can't Buy: Family Income and Children's Life Chances.* Cambridge, Mass.: Harvard University Press.

McLanahan, Sara S., and Irwin Garfinkel. 1994. "Single Mother Families and Social Policy: Lessons for the United States from France, Canada, and Sweden." In *Poverty, Inequality, and the Future of Social Policy: Western States in the New World Order,* edited by Katherine McFate, Roger Lawson, and William J. Wilson. New York: Russell Sage Foundation.

McLanahan, Sara S., and Gary Sandefur. 1994. *Growing Up with a Single Parent: What Hurts, What Helps.* Cambridge, Mass.: Harvard University Press.

Micklewright, John. 2001. "Social Exclusion and Children: A European View for a U.S. Debate." Presented to the Conference on Social Exclusion and Children, Institute for Child and Family Policy. New York : Columbia University (May 3 to 4).

Okun, Arthur M. 1975. *Equality and Efficiency: The Big Tradeoff.* Washington, D.C.: Brookings Institution.

Organization for Economic Cooperation and Development. 2002. "1980–1998: 20 Years of Social Expenditures—The OECD Database." Paris:

Organization for Economic Cooperation and Development. Available at: http://www.oecd.org/dataoecd/3/63/2084281.pdf (accessed September 9, 2005).

———. 2003. "Annual National Accounts of OECD Countries: 1970–2003." Available at: http://cs4-hq.oecd.org/selected_view.asp?tableID=560& viewname=ANApart4.

Osberg, Lars. 2002. "Time, Money, and Inequality in the International Perspective." Luxembourg Income Study, working paper no. 334. Syracuse, N.Y.: Syracuse University, Center for Policy Research.

Osberg, Lars, Timothy M. Smeeding, and Jonathan Schwabish. 2004. "Income Distribution and Public Social Expenditure: Theories, Effects, and Evidence." In *Social Inequality,* edited by Kathryn Neckerman. New York: Russell Sage Foundation.

Pear, Robert. 2003. "Welfare Spending Shows Huge Shift from Checks to Service." New York Times, October 12, p. 1.

Rainwater, Lee, and Timothy M. Smeeding. 1999. "From 'Relative' to 'Real' Income: Purchase Power Parities and Household Microdata, Problems and Prospects." *Papers and Final Report of the Third Meeting on Household Income Statistics,* edited by Mike Sheridan, Louis Rouillard, and Anna Choquette. Ottawa, Canada: Statistics Canada.

Ravallion, Martin. 1994. *Poverty Comparisons. Fundamentals of Pure and Applied Economics* 56. Chur, Switzerland: Harwood Academic Press.

———. 1996. "Issues in Measuring and Modeling Poverty." *Economic Journal* 106(September): 1328–44.

Reynolds, Morgan, and Eugene Smolensky. 1977. *Public Expenditure, Taxes, and the Distribution of Income: The United States, 1950–1970.* New York: Academic Press.

Shapiro, Isaac, and Sharon Parrott. 2003. "Are Policies That Assist Low-Income Workers Receiving Appropriate Priority?" Washington, D.C.: Center on Budget and Policy Priorities.

Sigle-Rushton, Wendy, and Sara McLanahan. 2004. "Father Absences and Child Well-Being: A Critical Review." In *The Future of the Family,* edited by Daniel P. Moynihan, Lee Rainwater, and Timothy M. Smeeding. New York: Russell Sage Foundation.

Smeeding, Timothy M. 1997. "Poverty in Developed Countries: The Evidence from the Luxembourg Income Study." In *Poverty and Human Development,* editing, desktop composition, and production management by America Writing Division of Communications Development Incorporated. Washington, D.C., and New York: United Nations Development Programme. Available at: http://hdr.undp.org/reports/global/1997/en/ (accessed September 9, 2005).

———. 1999. "Social Security Reform: Improving Benefit Adequacy and Economic Security for Women." Policy Brief Series, no. 16. Syracuse, N.Y.: Syracuse University, Maxwell School, Center for Policy Research.

———. 2001. "SSI: Time for a Change?" Unpublished manuscript. Center for Policy Research. Syracuse, N.Y.: Syracuse University.

———. 2002. "No Child Left Behind?" *Indicators* 1(3): 6–30.

———. 2003. "Income Maintenance in Old Age: Current Status and Future Prospects for Rich Countries." *Genus* 59(1): 51–83.

Smeeding, Timothy M., and Andrej Grodner. 2000. "Changing Income Inequality in OECD Countries: Updated Results from the Luxembourg Income Study (LIS)." In *The Personal Distribution of Income in an International Perspective,* edited by Richard Hauser and Irene Becker. Berlin, Germany: Springer-Verlag.

Smeeding, Timothy M., Michael O'Higgins, and Lee Rainwater. 1990. *Poverty, Inequality and the Distribution of Income in a Comparative Context: The Luxembourg Income Study (LIS).* London and Washington, D.C.: Harvester Wheatsheaf and Urban Institute Press.

Smeeding, Timothy M., and Lee Rainwater. 2004. "Comparing Living Standards Across Nations: Real Incomes at the Top, the Bottom, and the Middle." In *What Has Happened to the Quality of Life in the Advanced Industrialized Nations?,* edited by Edward N. Wolff. Northampton, Mass.: Edward Elgar.

Smeeding, Timothy M., Lee Rainwater, and Gary Burtless. 2001. "United States Poverty in a Cross-National Context." In *Understanding Poverty,* edited by Sheldon H. Danziger, and Robert H. Haveman. New York and Cambridge, Mass.: Russell Sage Foundation and Harvard University Press.

Smeeding, Timothy M., Peter Saunders, John Coder, Stephen Jenkins, Johan Fritzell, Aldi Hagenaars, Richard Hauser, and Michael Wolfson. 1993. "Poverty, Inequality and Family Living Standards Impacts across Seven Nations: The Effect of Noncash Subsidies for Health, Education, and Housing." *Review of Income and Wealth* 39(3): 229–56.

Smeeding, Timothy M., and Dennis Sullivan. 1998. "Generations and the Distribution of Economic Well-Being: A Cross-National View." *American Economic Review, Papers and Proceedings* 88(2): 254–58.

Smeeding, Timothy M., Michael Ward, Ian Castles, and Haeduck Lee. 2000. "Making Cross-Country Comparisons of Income Distributions." Paper presented at Twenty-Sixth General Conference of the International Association for Research in Income and Wealth. Cracow, Poland (August 3).

Smeeding, Timothy M., and R. Kent Weaver. 2001. "The Senior Income Guarantee (SIG): A New Proposal to Reduce Poverty Among the Elderly." Unpublished manuscript. Syracuse, N.Y.: Syracuse University, Center for Policy Research.

Smolensky, Eugene, and Jennifer Appleton Gootman. 2003. *Working Families and Growing Children: Caring for Children and Adolescents.* Washington, D.C.: National Academy Press.

Social Security Administration. Office of Policy. 2003. "SSI Caseloads." Available at http://www.ssa.gov/policy/docs/statcomps/ssi_asr/2002/table03.html (accessed September 9, 2005).

Solon, Gary. 2002. "Cross-Country Differences in Intergenerational Earnings Mobility." *Journal of Economic Perspectives* 16(3): 59–66.

Summers, Robert, and Alan Heston. 1991. "The Penn World Table (Mark 5): An Expanded Set of International Comparisons, 1950–1988." *Quarterly Journal of Economics* 106(2): 327–68.

U.K. Department of Social Security. 1996. *Households Below Average Income.* London: Government Statistical Service.

UNICEF. Innocenti Research Centre. 2000. "A League Table of Child Poverty in Rich Nations." Innocenti Report Cards, no. 1. Florence: UNICEF.

United Nations Development Programme. 1998. *Human Development Report: Consumption for Human Development.* New York: United Nations.

———. 1999. *Human Development Report 1999: Globalization with a Human Face.* New York: United Nations.

U.S. Bureau of the Census. 2003a. "Income in the United States 2002: Current Population Reports." Washington: U.S. Department of Commerce, Economics and Statistics Administration.

———. 2003b. "Poverty in the United States 2002: Current Population Reports." Washington: U.S. Department of Commerce, Economics and Statistics Administration.

U.S. Department of Health and Human Services. 2003. "U.S. Welfare Caseloads Information, March-June 2003: Caseload Numbers, TANF Statistics." Washington, D.C.: Administration for Children and Families. Available at: http://www.acf.dhhs.gov/news/stats/newstat2.shtml (accessed September 9, 2005).

Walker, Robert, and Michael Wiseman. 2001. "The House That Jack Built." *Milken Institute Review,* Fourth Quarter, pp. 52–62.

Welch, Finis. 1999. "In Defense of Inequality." *American Economic Review, Papers and Proceedings* 89(2): 1–17.

Part II

Taxation and Social Insurance

Chapter 5

Income and Wealth Concentration in a Historical and International Perspective

Emmanuel Saez

Recent studies have used tax statistics to construct top-income and wealth-shares series over the twentieth century for the United States and Canada and for a number of European countries: the United Kingdom, France, the Netherlands, and Switzerland. In the first part of the century, all countries except Switzerland experienced a dramatic drop in top-income shares—the percentage of a country's wealth controlled by the wealthiest—owing to a precipitous drop in large-wealth holdings. A plausible explanation is that the development of very progressive tax systems prevented large fortunes from recovering from the shocks of the world wars and the Great Depression by reducing drastically the rate of wealth accumulation at the top of the wealth distribution.

Since 1980, however, top-income shares have increased substantially in English-speaking countries, but not at all in the countries of continental Europe. This increase is due to an unprecedented surge in top-wage incomes that started in the 1970s and accelerated in the 1990s. As a result, top wage earners have replaced capital income earners at the top of the income distribution in English-speaking countries. We discuss the proposed explanations and the main questions that remain open.

Introduction

The evolution of income and wealth inequality during the process of development of modern economies has attracted enormous attention in the economics literature. Liberals, concerned with issues of equity, have blamed income and wealth concentration for tilting the political process in favor of the wealthy. They have proposed progressive taxation as an appropriate counterforce against wealth concentration. Conservatives, on the other hand, consider concentration of income and wealth to be a natural and necessary outcome of an environment that provides incentives for work, entrepreneurship, and wealth accumulation, key markers of macroeconomic success. Progressive taxation may redistribute resources away from the rich and reduce wealth concentration, and in addition it might weaken those incentives and generate large efficiency costs. In order to cast light on this controversial political debate, it is of great importance to understand the forces driving income and wealth concentration over time and understand whether government interventions through taxation are effective or harmful to curbing wealth inequality. To make progress on those questions, the availability of long and homogeneous series of income or wealth concentration is clearly necessary.

Constructing such series, however, is a challenging task because of a lack of good data covering the top of the income and wealth distributions. Household surveys hardly existed before the 1960s and have become available in many countries only in recent decades. Moreover, household surveys such as the Current Population Survey in the United States cannot be used to analyze high incomes because of small samples and top coding issues. Therefore, to study the top of the income or wealth distributions, tax statistics remain the best data source. Those statistics have two important advantages relative to survey data. First, they often span very long time periods, for fiscal administrations in most countries have begun publishing such statistics since the creation of those taxes, in general in the early part of the twentieth century. Second, these statistics usually provide tabulations by brackets of income or wealth, and those brackets are generally are detailed enough to allow a precise analysis of very small groups at the top of the distribution, such as the top .1 percent, or even the top .01 percent.

Of course, such tax data have also important drawbacks. First and foremost, the data are based on income or wealth reported for tax purposes. As a result, the data might not reflect real income or wealth because of tax evasion (fraudulent underreporting or nonreporting) or tax avoidance (using legal means to repackage reported incomes in order to reduce tax liabilities). The extent of tax evasion or tax avoidance is related to the level of taxes, to the enforcement of the tax law, and to the more general legal tax environment, which might make it more or less difficult to avoid taxes. Therefore, when using tax data to study top incomes, it is necessary to analyze the tax structure at the same time in order to tell apart real changes in income or wealth concentration from changes in reported income or wealth due to changes in tax avoidance following a tax reform.[1]

Second, the tax statistics cover only the fraction of the population that files tax returns. In most countries, high exemption levels meant that in the first part of the century the fraction of filers was small (for example, less than 10 percent in the United States before World War II). As a result, tax data alone do not provide sufficient data to allow a comparison of the evolution of top incomes relative to average incomes. The key innovation of the famous 1953 study by Simon Kuznets of income concentration in the United States for the period 1913 to 1948 was to use National Accounts data in addition to income-tax statistics to compute total personal income and obtain shares of total personal income accruing to various upper-income groups.[2]

In the decades since Kuznets's study, the tax statistics have been used relatively rarely to study inequality, for two main reasons. First, in the 1960s microdata started becoming available, which made possible the analysis of not only the complete distribution but also of the relation between income and demographics such as age, gender, and education. Second, the decades following World War II were characterized by a relative stability of the upper ends of the income and wealth distributions in most countries. Following the example of Thomas Piketty (2001, 2003), who presented a comprehensive analysis of the income-tax statistics for France since the beginning of the twentieth century, the authors of a number of very recent studies have constructed series of shares of income or wealth accruing to upper groups of the income and wealth distribution for various countries. Top-income shares have been constructed by Anthony B.

Atkinson (2002) for the United Kingdom, by Piketty and Emmanuel Saez (2003) for the United States, by Saez and Michael R. Veall (2003) for Canada, by Atkinson and Wiemer Salverda (2003) for the Netherlands, and by Fabien Dell, Piketty, and Saez (2003) for Switzerland.[3] Shares of wealth accruing to top wealth groups have also been constructed for some countries as well using either estate or wealth individual tax data: Wojciech Kopczuk and Saez (2004) for the United States; Piketty, Postel-Vinay, and Rosenthal (2004) for France; and Dell, Piketty, and Saez (2003) for Switzerland.[4]

This paper summarizes the main empirical findings that have emerged out of this new top-incomes and top-wealth literature and the principal explanations that have been proposed to account for the facts; it also highlights issues that remain unresolved and discusses promising avenues of research.

Most of the series constructed share two important and striking characteristics. First, in all the countries except Switzerland, a dramatic reduction in top income and wealth shares is observed from the early part of the century until the decades following World War II. In virtually all cases, the share of income or wealth accruing to the top 1 percent has been divided by a factor of 2 and sometimes by a much greater factor. For example, in the United Kingdom, the top 1 percent income share falls from almost 20 percent in 1918 to around 6 percent in the 1970s (Atkinson and Salverda 2003, table 2). Second, in the same countries those dramatic decreases are concentrated in the very top groups of the income or wealth distribution. There are relatively minor secular changes for the bottom part of the top decile or even the bottom part of the top percentile—most of the decrease is actually concentrated in the top .1 percent. Those changes are the consequence of a drastic reduction in top-wealth holdings and the large capital income they generate.

In contrast to this earlier consistency, the evolution of top-income shares in the recent decades has been different across countries: the United States, Canada, and the United Kingdom have experienced a large increase in top-income shares, while France, the Netherlands, and Switzerland display hardly any change in top-income shares. For the Anglo-Saxon countries (the United States, the United Kingdom, and Canada), this dramatic increase has been due to a dramatic increase in top wages and salaries.[5] In both the United States and the United Kingdom, the increase in top-wealth shares has been small and almost negligible relative to the dramatic increase in top-income shares. This suggests that income concentration, which has increased sharply in the United States and the United Kingdom, has not yet translated into a significant increase in wealth concentration. As a result, in the English-speaking countries, the working rich, who receive very large salaries, have replaced at the top of the income distribution the rentiers, those deriving very large incomes from their capital.[6]

Following Piketty (2001, 2003), most authors have argued that the dramatic increase in tax progressivity that took place in the interwar period in all the countries studied and that remained in place at least until the recent decades has been the main factor preventing top income and wealth shares from coming back to the very high levels observed at the beginning of the century. Indeed, with marginal income-tax rates in excess of 60 percent and sometimes reaching even 90 percent for very high incomes, it is hypothesized that a wealthy individual has to pay in taxes a very large fraction of his returns on capital, and accumulating or sustaining a fortune requires much higher saving rates. However, because the effects of taxes on wealth concentration are a long-term process, it is nearly impossible to provide a rigorous, direct proof of this hypothesis.[7] The case of Switzerland, a country which did not experience the shocks of the two World Wars and never established a very progressive tax structure, offers an interesting test of the hypothesis. Dell, Piketty, and Saez (2003) analyze income and wealth concentration in Switzerland and their results support the tax explanation discussed above: Switzerland is the only country among those studies so far to display the same concentration of wealth and income in the early part of the century and in the decades following World War II.

Explaining the surge in top-wage incomes in the United States, Canada, and the United Kingdom over the last thirty years is more difficult, however, several points can be made. First, this change cannot be attributed solely to technological change, such as the computer revolution, because no such changes in top wages occurred in continental European countries (France, the Netherlands, or Switzerland), and they have experienced similar technological changes. Second, this surge in top-wage incomes cannot be entirely due to changes in tax avoidance, such as a shift from perquisites or deferred compensation to current cash compensation, following the large tax-rate cuts at the top in the United States and the United Kingdom, because Canada implemented much smaller tax changes and yet also experienced very large increases in top-wage incomes.

It is, however, plausible to think that such a surge in top-wage incomes might not have occurred if the United States and the United Kingdom had kept the extremely high marginal tax rates on very large incomes (in excess of 80 percent) that they implemented up to the 1960s or 1970s. The drastic change in the top of the earnings distribution in Anglo-Saxon countries was probably produced by a combination of technological changes, changes in the fiscal environment, and changes in corporate governance—although the relative contribution of each change is still open to debate as well as the causality relation between the various changes.

The next section describes briefly the general methodology and data sources that have been used to estimate top income and wealth shares, as well as the main potential sources of bias. The following section presents the central findings concerning the dramatic reduction in income and wealth concentration and discusses the tax-progressivity explanation. The final section focuses on the recent changes in income concentration that have taken place in English-speaking countries.

Data Sources, Methodology, and Potential Biases

Most top-income and top-wealth studies mentioned follow the same broad estimation methodology and use similar data sources. Atkinson (2003) describes in detail the methodological issues involved in those estimations, including the following.

Tax Units and Population Totals

Top-income or top-wealth groups are defined relative to the complete population, even if only a fraction of the population is required to file tax returns. The unit of analysis is defined as the tax-filing unit. The income-tax law can be family-based, as in the United States and France, or individually based, as in Canada and the United Kingdom since 1990.[8] In family-based systems, a tax-unit family is defined as a married couple with dependent children, or a single parent with dependent children, or a single adult. In individual-based systems each adult is taxed independently.[9] Thus, top groups such as the top decile or top percentile are defined relative to the total number of families (in the case of family-based systems) or the total number of adults (in the case of individual-based systems). Such totals for families or adults can be obtained from census or population survey data for most countries. It is important to note that individually and family-based top income-shares can differ both in levels and patterns, depending on the levels and patterns of correlation of incomes between spouses.[10] In the case of Canada, both family- and individual-based top-income shares can be constructed for the recent period using micro-data. Saez and Veall (2003) show that the level and the upward pattern of top-income shares is almost identical for individuals and families, suggesting that changes in the correlation of incomes between spouses do not explain any significant change in top-income shares, at least not in the case of Canada in recent decades.

Once the total tax-units series are obtained, all upper-income groups—the top 10 percent, the top 1 percent, and so on—are defined relative to that total, irrespective of the actual number of returns filed. When exemption levels are high, tax return data covers only the top of the distribution.

Interpolations from Tax Statistics

Tax statistics for individual incomes, wealth, or estates present in general the number of returns and amounts reported in terms of how many are in each income bracket. In all countries studied, the base for individual income taxes is comprehensive and includes both labor income (wages and salaries, pension income, self-employment income, and so forth) and capital income (profits from small businesses, dividends from stock, interest income, rents, and so forth). In most countries, capital gains and imputed rent of homeowners are not taxable and hence are excluded from the income definition. In certain countries—the United States is one—realized capital gains are in part taxable and can also be analyzed to check the sensitivity of results to the exclusion of capital gains (see later section). The definition of income that is used is income before personal and family exemptions and other deductions.[11] In all the series presented here, income is defined as total market income accruing to individuals (including labor, business, and capital income) but excluding realized capital gains and most transfers from the government such as welfare or unemployment benefits.

In most of the published tabulations, the top brackets contain few individuals and therefore allow for a very precise analysis of the groups at the very top, especially during the first part of the century.[12] In the United States today, the top bracket is for annual incomes above $10 million, and this group contains less than 20,000 taxpayers (see annual editions of the U.S. Treasury Department's *Statistics of Income: Individual Income Tax Returns*). In many cases, the amounts reported are further divided by source of income or wealth such as wages and salaries, business income, dividends, and interest income. Assuming that the income or wealth distribution is Pareto-distributed in each bracket, and using a simple interpolation technique, it is straightforward to obtain the thresholds corresponding to each percentile cutoff, such as the top 10 percent or the top 1 percent, and then compute the total amounts reported in each upper group. Linear interpolations can be used to compute the fractions of income from each source using the composition tables. In practice, the estimation is complicated by the fact that brackets are not always defined in terms of gross income but sometimes in terms of income after deductions. For a number of countries, micro-files of individual tax returns are also available and can be used to check the accuracy of the interpolations and other adjustments made when tabulated data are used.[13]

Income Denominators

Once the amounts of income in each upper group are obtained, a denominator representing total personal income is required to obtain shares of income accruing to upper groups. This denominator would be straightforward to obtain if everybody had been required to file a tax return, but when only a small fraction of individuals file tax returns, National Accounts must be used to estimate total personal income. Personal income estimated from National Accounts must be corrected to exclude items such as government transfers, imputed rent, imputed interest on bank accounts, and other forms of income that are not reported on tax returns. Government transfers are reported separately in National Accounts and are easy to correct, but other items must be estimated. In general, those correction coefficients are estimated using data for the recent period, in countries where almost all individuals with positive income file income-tax returns, and then extrapolated back to the earlier periods.

Figure 5.1 shows the average real income per family in France, the United Kingdom, the United States, and Switzerland, expressed in 2000 U.S. dollars. Incomes are first expressed in real value in each currency, using a price deflator based on year 2000, and then amounts are converted into dollars, using the exchange rate of February 20, 2004.

Although France, and to a lesser extent the United Kingdom, appear to have significantly lower average real income than the United States and especially Switzerland, one should be careful when comparing levels across countries because of large and fast exchange-rate fluctuations, as well as important differences in the level of payroll taxes.[14] Despite these issues, the four series display a strikingly similar pattern over time. In all countries, growth in real incomes is very small from 1913 to the beginning of World War II, with the

Figure 5.1 Average Real Incomes in the United States, the United Kingdom, France, and Switzerland, 1913 to 2000[a]

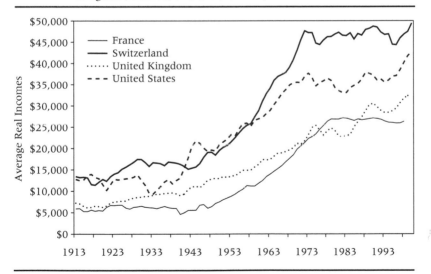

Sources: France: Piketty (2001, figure 1-6): United States: Piketty and Saez (2003, table 2); Switzerland: Dell, Piketty, and Saez (2003, table A); United Kingdom: Atkinson and Salverda (2003).
Note: All incomes figures are first expressed in real value in the domestic currency for year 2000 and then converted into dollars, using the exchange rate of February 20, 2004.
[a]Average real income per tax unit (defined at the family level as in the current U.S. tax code).

United States showing very large fluctuations owing to the extremely strong business cycle. Real-income growth is very fast in the decades following World War II and during World War II in the United States, but it has been much slower over the last thirty years. It is therefore important to keep in mind that the macroeconomic performance of these four countries has been quite similar over the twentieth century in spite of the quite different patterns of taxation and income and wealth concentration, which we describe later.

As we have noted, it is difficult to compare levels of income across countries because of movements in exchange rates. Similarly, even within countries, comparing real incomes over time is difficult because it requires the use of a price index and there is substantial controversy about how to construct such an index and account properly for the introduction of new goods.[15] As a result, it is important to measure inequality between and within countries in a way that is independent of exchange-rate fluctuations and price fluctuations. That is why top-income or top-wealth shares, which are by definition independent of price levels, are valuable measures to make over-time and cross-country comparisons.

Tax Evasion and Avoidance

As noted, top-income or top-wealth shares can be underestimated because of tax evasion or tax avoidance. Tax evasion is fraudulent nonreporting or underreporting of income for tax purposes. Fiscal administrations carry audits and impose penalties on tax evaders, and sometimes publish detailed reports on the extent of underreporting by income source.[16] The main lesson from those studies is that tax evasion is minimal for income sources such as wages and salaries, dividend, or interest income that are reported to the fiscal administration both by the payer and the payee, but tax evasion can be substantial for sources such as self-employment or informal small business income, where there is no such double reporting. Income from foreign accounts in tax havens is also likely to be underreported and might also escape audits. There are no good estimates of the amount of capital income earned by wealthy Northern Americans or Europeans residing in tax havens that escapes taxation, and it would be a very useful project to try systematically to collect information from tax havens.[17]

Most audit studies suggest that the extent of tax evasion has declined as the systems of reporting and especially double reporting have improved substantially. Today, virtually all wages and salaries at the high end of the distribution are accurately reported in all the countries studied as well as capital income in the form of dividends or interest income earned at home. Thus, if one could correct the series for tax evasion accurately, it is likely that the secular drop in top-income shares that has been documented in most countries would be even more dramatic.

Tax avoidance consists in using legal means to reduce tax liabilities. Tax avoidance is a concern when making top-income shares estimates because some forms of real economic income might fail to appear on individual tax returns. The extent of tax avoidance depends also to a large extent on the general fiscal environment: not only the level of taxes but also the interactions between various taxes and the laws regulating various forms of payments and legal structures. Tax avoidance can take three main forms.

First, individuals supplying labor might be paid with nontaxable perquisites such as better offices, health insurance, company cars or jets, conferences in attractive vacation locations, and so forth, instead of taxable salary compensation. All countries impose rules on perquisites in order to prevent excesses. As a result, perquisites are far from perfect substitutes to cash compensation, and thus should not be included in full in the definition of economic income. More important, the changes in top-wage incomes that have taken place in North America in the recent decades seem to be far too large to be explained by a shift away from perquisites toward cash compensation. Cash compensation can also be deferred through the use of pension plans (taxable in general when cashed out at retirement) or through stock-option plans (which are taxed only at the time they are exercised or when the shares are finally sold), creating a substantial delay between the compensation decision and the time the income is effectively realized.[18]

Second, individuals may rearrange the legal structures of their businesses in order to reduce their tax liability. The most important element is the interface between the corporate and the individual sectors. Businesses can be incorporated and taxed on their profits by the corporate income tax before those profits are distributed as dividends to shareholders. Also, under some important restrictions on the number of shareholders, businesses can also be unincorporated, in which case profits are reported and taxed uniquely at the individual level. Profits from incorporated businesses do not appear on individual returns until they are distributed as dividends or shares are sold and capital gains are realized (in those countries where capital gains are taxed). In principle, because capital gains are either not observed at all or are observed only at realization, one would like to impute profits instead of distributed dividends. Unfortunately, this is impossible owing to data limitations in general. That is why it is important, whenever possible, to supplement top-income shares series with information on the composition of those top incomes, pay-out ratios of corporations at the aggregate level, the importance of realized capital gains, and perhaps more important, with data on wealth distribution, either from wealth taxes or from estate taxes.

A change in the corporate status can dramatically change reported incomes on individual returns but have no real economic effect. The corporate status is sensitive to the relative levels of taxes on the corporate and the individual sector. In the United States, such shifts from the corporate to the individual sector have been documented in detail following the significant changes in the tax law that took place in the 1980s (see, for example, Roger Gordon and Jeffrey MacKie-Mason 1990, Joel Slemrod 1996, and Gordon and Slemrod 2000). The extent of those shifts also depends on whether the tax law imposes substantial restrictions on unincorporated businesses. Sole proprietorships and partnerships can always choose to be unincorporated, but in general, businesses with many shareholders have to be incorporated. In the United States, the so-called S-corporation entity, like unincorporated businesses, is taxed only at the individual level but can have up to sixty-five shareholders. As a result, for many closely held businesses there is little cost in switching from S-corporation status to the corporate sector; indeed, behavioral responses along that margin are large. In contrast, Canada only allows partnerships and sole proprietorships to be taxed at the individual level; hence, there is no evidence of behavioral responses at the individual-corporate interface in that country.

Finally, owners of closely held businesses, in addition to changing the legal status of their business, may also have substantial flexibility in the form of payment they choose: larger salaries for themselves versus accumulation of assets within the corporation; and paying dividends versus retaining earnings.[19] Those shifting strategies blur the distinction between labor and capital income for small business owners and make it important to supplement tax data on top-wage incomes with other data such as executive compensation data where management and ownership are separated.

The Pattern of Top-Income Shares

Figure 5.2, panel A, plots the top 1 percent income share in France and the United States since 1913.[20] The patterns are strikingly parallel from the beginning of the century up to the 1970s. In both countries the top 1 percent income shares were very high, around 18 to 20 percent, at the eve of the first World War.[21] The top 1 percent share is highest in the United States in 1929, at the onset of the Great Depression.

The top 1 percent income share falls in both countries during the Great Depression, and especially during World War II, and is more pronounced in France, which suffered much more directly from the shock of the war than the United States. By the end of World War II, top 1 percent income shares are around 11 percent in the United States and 9 percent in France, only about half of their pre–World War I level. It is striking that in the prosperous years and decades following World War II, top-income shares do not come back to their high levels of the prewar period but remain relatively stable in France or decrease further (and slowly) in the United States. In the 1970s, the top 1 percent income share is around 8 percent in both countries, but over the last thirty years the pattern of top-income shares in the two countries displays a striking contrast. While the top 1 percent income share in France remained stable at around 8 percent up to year 1998, the top 1 percent income share increased dramatically and was around 17 percent in 2000, almost as high as in 1913.

Figure 5.2, panel B, shows the top 10–1 percent income share (defined as the top decile excluding the top 1 percent) for France and the United States.[22] In sharp contrast to the top 1 percent, there are no secular changes for the upper-middle-income-class share. In both countries, the share of this group fluctuates around 25 percent, and the levels are almost identical at the beginning and at the end of the period. In both countries, the upper-middle class reaches a secular maximum of around 30 percent during the Great Depres-

Figure 5.2   Top 1 percent and Top 10–1 Percent Income Shares in the
United States and France, 1913 to 2000

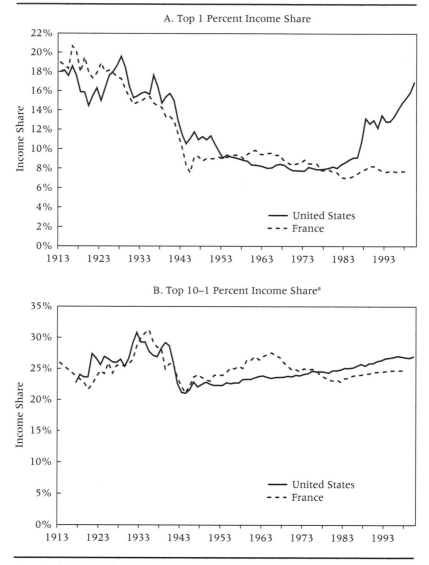

Sources: United States: Piketty and Saez (2003); France: Piketty (2001)
Note: The unit is the family.
[a]Top 10–1 percent is the top decile, excluding the top 1%.

sion and a secular minimum by the end of World War II of around 21 percent. Composition analyses in Piketty (2001) and Piketty and Saez (2003) show that incomes in this group are overwhelmingly composed of wages and salaries.[23] During the deflation of the Great Depression, because wages were nominally rigid downward, this upper-middle-class group did better than the top 1 percent incomes, composed primarily of capital and business income, and bottom or middle income earners, who suffered from unemployment.

This phenomenon can be observed more directly when one looks at wage series by occupation (wage earners are employees paid at an hourly or daily wage rate; salary earners are supervisory employees and officers paid at a monthly or annual salary rate). Saez and Veall (2003) use surveys of the manufacturing sector in Canada, which report the number and amounts paid to wage and salary earners. Those series show very clearly that during the downturns of the interwar period (1920 to 1921 and 1930 to 1932), both the number of salaried workers and the average salary rose substantially relative to the number of wage workers and the average wage. This is evidence that upper-income earners were gaining in the economy relative to the average worker during the depression episodes, which explains why the share of the top 10–1 percent increases during the downturns of the interwar period.

In contrast, World War II led to a significant wage compression, which reduced significantly the share of the upper-middle-income class. The wage compression during World War II for France and Canada is analyzed in detail by Piketty (2001) and Saez and Veall (2003). In the United States, a large literature has also documented the "Great Compression" of wages during World War II (see, for example, Goldin and Margo 1992; Piketty and Saez 2003). This explains why the share of the top 10–1 percent fell significantly during World War II.

Figure 5.2, panel B, shows that there is no secular trend in inequality, measured by the disparity between the upper-middle class and the average, which casts doubt on the traditional Kuznets (1955) theory of the inverted U-curve of inequality during the process of development.[24] It is striking to note the contrast between the flat pattern of the upper-middle-income class and the skyrocketing trajectory of the top 1 percent share over the last thirty years in the United States: while the top 1 percent share increased by nine percentage points, the upper-middle-income-class shares increased by only two percentage points.

Figure 5.3, panel A, shows the top .1 percent income share in three English-speaking countries: the United States, the United Kingdom, and Canada.[25] It shows that the pattern for this very-top-group income share has been quite similar across the three countries. A sharp drop in the first part of the century, especially in the United Kingdom and the United States, was followed by a slower decline during the post–World War II decades. Finally, all three countries display a substantial increase in the top .1 percent income share over the last thirty years. This increase is largest in the United States and lowest in the United Kingdom, but the timing is remarkably similar across the three Anglo-Saxon countries.

Figure 5.3, panel B, shows the same top .1 percent income share for two continental countries in Europe, France and the Netherlands. Those two series show a very similar pattern over the full century. As in the English-speaking countries, the top .1 percent income share experiences a dramatic drop in the first part of the century followed by a almost flat pattern afterward, and in contrast to English-speaking countries, those two countries did not experience any noticeable increase in the top .1 percent income share in recent decades. As a result, the secular decline in the share of income going to the top is dramatic. While the top .1 percent accounted for around 8 percent of total income in France and 10 percent in the Netherlands at the beginning of the twentieth century, by the late 1990s those shares were only 2 percent in France and around 1.2 percent in the Netherlands.

How can the two main empirical facts described here be explained: the dramatic decline in very top shares in the first part of the century and the recent and large increase in those top-income shares over the last thirty years in English-speaking countries?

The Secular Decline in Top Capital Incomes

The drop in top-income shares over the first part of the century is extremely concentrated. There is no similar decline below the top 1 percent, and even within the top 1 percent, most of decline is actually concentrated in the upper part of the top percentile—the top .1 percent. The fact that we expect very top incomes to be com-

Figure 5.3   Top .1 Percent Income Share in Anglo-Saxon Countries
Versus Continental Europe, 1913 to 2000

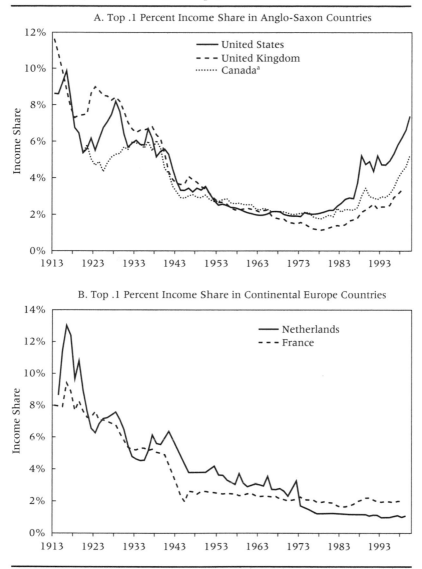

Sources: United States: Piketty and Saez (2003); United Kingdom: Atkinson (2002); Canada: Saez and Veall (2003); France: Piketty (2001); Netherlands: Atkinson and Salverda (2003).
[a]The unit for Canada is the individual adult.

posed primarily of capital income suggests that this decline in very top shares is primarily driven by a reduction in top capital incomes and hence by the top wealth holdings that generated such incomes.

Indeed, figure 5.4 displays the composition of the top .1 percent income share for France (panel A) and the United States (panel B). In both countries, in the first part of the century top .1 percent incomes are composed primarily of capital income and business income, while the fraction of wages and salaries is very small (around 15 percent). Capital income comprises dividends, which constitute by far the largest item in the category, and also interest income and rents but excludes capital gains. Business income is profits from non-incorporated businesses. At the beginning of the period, the relative fraction of business income is much larger in France than in the United States, probably because relatively fewer businesses were incorporated in France.

In both countries, the dramatic fall in the top .1 percent income share is thus due to a sharp decline in business income and capital income, which suggests that the reduction in income concentration was the consequence of a decline in large wealth holdings. If this is true, it might lead one to be tempted to interpret the significant upswing in top-income shares observed since the 1970s in English-speaking countries as a revival of very high-capital incomes, but this is not the case. Panel B shows that the main factor that has driven up the top .1 percent income share in the United States has been an unprecedented increase in the fraction of wages and salaries, which now represent about 60 percent of incomes in the top .1 percent group.[26] Therefore, the composition of high incomes at the end of the century in the United States (as well as in Canada and most likely in the United Kingdom as well) is very different from that earlier in the century: today, highly paid executives seem to have replaced the capitalists and rentiers of the early part of the century at the top of the income distribution.

It is important to note that the secular decline of top capital incomes is due to a decreased concentration of capital income rather than a decline in the share of capital income in the economy as a whole. First, National Accounts series from France and the United States show that the capital-income share of personal income has not declined over the century: it displays medium-term fluctuations but no secular trend down (see Piketty 2003; Piketty and Saez 2003).

Figure 5.4 Top .1 Percent Income Share and Composition in France and the United States, 1916 to 2000

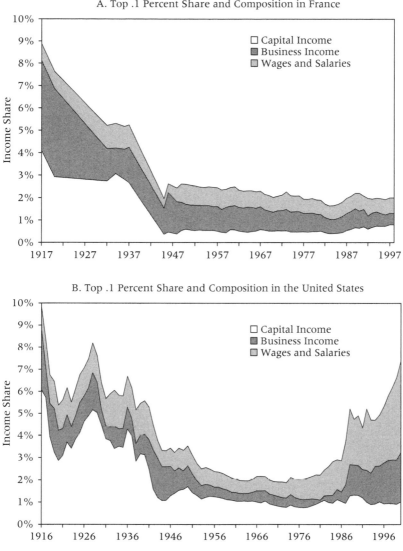

A. Top .1 Percent Share and Composition in France

B. Top .1 Percent Share and Composition in the United States

Sources: United States: Piketty and Saez (2003); France: Piketty (2001, table B-18).
Note: Capital income is dividends, interest income, rents, and so on, but excludes capital gains. Business income is self-employment income and profits from unincorporated businesses (and S-corporations in the U.S.). Wages and salaries include also pensions and exercises of stock options.

Second and more important, series on wealth concentration have been constructed for various countries from estate- or wealth-tax statistics. Although estimates from such tax statistics can also be biased,[27] they are a valuable alternative source to analyze and cast further light on the issue of wealth and capital-income concentration. Figure 5.5 shows the share of total personal wealth accruing to the wealthiest 1 percent of adults in the population for the United States, the United Kingdom, and France.[28] The figure shows that wealth concentration has indeed declined very significantly from the early part of the century to the decades following World War II. The top 1 percent share of wealth was around 60 percent in the United Kingdom and France, and around 40 percent in the United States in the early decades of the century. By the end of the century, those top 1 percent wealth shares have converged to around 22 percent in all three countries.

Figure 5.5   The Top 1 Percent Wealth Share in the United States, the United Kingdom, and France

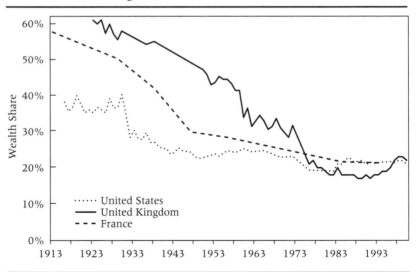

Sources: United States: Kopczuk and Saez (2003); United Kingdom: 1913–1972, Atkinson and Harrison (1978, 159); 1976 to 2000: Inland Revenue Personal Wealth ("Top 1% Marketable Net Worth Series for Adult Population," table 13.5) http://www.inlandrevenue.gov.uk/stats/personal_wealth/dopw_t05_1.htm; France: Piketty, Postel-Vinay, and Rosenthal (2004), table 4, "Top 1% Estate Share" (wealth shares not yet available).

Interestingly, in contrast to the surge in the top-income shares, there has been only a modest increase in the top-wealth shares in the United States and the United Kingdom over the last twenty-five years. This is consistent with the wage-income-surge explanation we described. The surge in top incomes seems to be due primarily to a dramatic increase in top-wage incomes and not to an increase in top-capital incomes. As a result, the increased income concentration has not yet translated into increased wealth concentration.

How can we explain the steep secular decline in capital-income concentration? The very large downturns of the interwar period and especially the Great Depression in the United States resulted in many business failures as well as a dramatic decline in corporate equity prices relative to other assets such as real estate or fixed-claims assets (such as bonds). As a result, top fortunes and top incomes composed primarily of corporate equities and dividends from those equities fell relative to the average.[29] At the eve of World War II, top fortunes and top incomes had clearly not yet recovered from the dramatic shock of the Great Depression.

The world wars and especially World War II produced additional shocks to top incomes and top fortunes. In countries such as France or the Netherlands (and to some extent the United Kingdom), the war directly destroyed a substantial fraction of the capital stock. The German occupation and the subsequent liberation of those countries also generated substantial confiscations and redistributions of businesses and assets. But figure 5.3 shows clearly that top-income shares also fell substantially in the United States and Canada, which did not experience war on their soil or direct destruction of property. As discussed in detail in Piketty and Saez (2003) and Saez and Veall (2003), these two countries substantially increased individual and especially corporate income taxes in order to finance the war effort. In spite of surging corporate profits during the war, profits after tax and especially dividends distributed to stockholders did not increase much during the war years. As a result, top incomes composed primarily of dividends declined relative to the increasing average income generated by the war economy, which explains the decline in the top .1 percent income share shown in figure 5.3.[30]

Financing World War I had also generated a fiscal shock, but one much less pronounced than that caused by World War II. During

World War I, top-income shares declined in the United States and the United Kingdom but remained stable in France and actually increased substantially in the Netherlands—showing that World War I benefited capitalists in some but not all countries.[31]

It is easy to understand how the macroeconomic shocks of the Great Depression and the world wars have had a negative impact on capital concentration; the question that is difficult to answer is why large fortunes did not recover from these shocks during the very prosperous decades following World War II. The most natural and realistic explanation seems to be the creation and the development of the progressive income tax, the progressive estate tax, and the corporate income tax. The very large fortunes that generated the top .1 percent incomes observed at the beginning of the century were accumulated during the nineteenth century, at a time when progressive taxes hardly existed and capitalists could use almost all their income to consume and to accumulate. The fiscal situation faced by capitalists as they attempted to recover from the shocks incurred during the 1914 to 1945 period was substantially different. All the countries for which we present top-income share results in figure 5.3 started to adopt very progressive income- and inheritance-tax structures during the interwar period, with top marginal tax rates often in excess of 75 percent, and those top rates remained extremely high after World War II. For example, the top marginal tax rate in the United States until 1963 was 91 percent. These very high marginal rates applied to only a very small fraction of taxpayers, but created a substantial burden on the very top income groups (such as the top .1 percent) whose income was primarily capital income.

It is difficult to prove in a rigorous way that the dynamic effects of progressive taxation on capital accumulation and pretax income inequality have the right quantitative magnitude and can account for the observed facts, because those dynamic effects are long-term and there is, unfortunately, no direct evidence on the savings rates and accumulation strategies of top wealth holders over time.

The case of Switzerland, which did not experience the shocks of the two world wars and never established a very progressive tax structure, offers an interesting test of the hypothesis. Dell, Piketty, and Saez (2003) analyze income and wealth concentration in Switzerland. For most of the century, and still true today, the majority of income taxes in Switzerland are levied at the local (county and municipal) level. Probably because of fiscal competition and mobility across counties, these local income and wealth taxes have a relatively flat rate structure with low marginal tax rates. The federal income- and wealth-tax rate has been only modestly progressive, with very low top rates for almost every year. Thus, over the twentieth century the average tax rate in Switzerland on capital income of the very wealthy, including federal and local income, wealth, and inheritance taxes, has been much lower than in the other countries that we have analyzed.

Figure 5.6, panel A, displays the top 1 percent wealth share for Switzerland (estimated using wealth-tax statistics) and the United States (as in figure 5.5) since 1915, and panel B displays the top 1 percent income share in Switzerland and the United States since 1933.

Top-wealth and top-income shares in Switzerland fell during the shocks of the world wars and the Great Depression, although less than in other countries, because Switzerland was noncombatant in both wars—although it did increase taxes substantially during each war in order to build up defense and discourage attacks. During World War II, the top 1 percent wealth share in Switzerland declined from almost 45 percent to about 37 percent and the top 1 percent income share declined from about 12 percent to 10 percent. Most important, though, is the fact that top-wealth and -income shares fully recovered from those shocks in the post–World War II period. As a result, Switzerland is the only country among those studied so far to display the same concentration of wealth or income in the early part of the century and in the decades following World War II. The results for Switzerland give some credence to the explanation that tax progressivity has been the main factor driving down top-income shares in the other countries. If the United States had not kept a very progressive tax system after World War II, it is conceivable that top-income shares would have rebounded during the 1950s and 1960s, as they did during the prosperous 1920s after the shocks of World War I and the downturn of 1920 to 1921.[32]

Finally, it is important to recall that the United States and Switzerland have had a remarkably similar pattern of real income growth per family, in spite of very different patterns of wealth and income concentration over time (see figure 5.1). This suggests that the dramatic reduction in top fortunes in the first part of the century in the United States did not impair its subsequent macroeconomic growth prospects.

Figure 5.6   Comparison of Switzerland and the United States

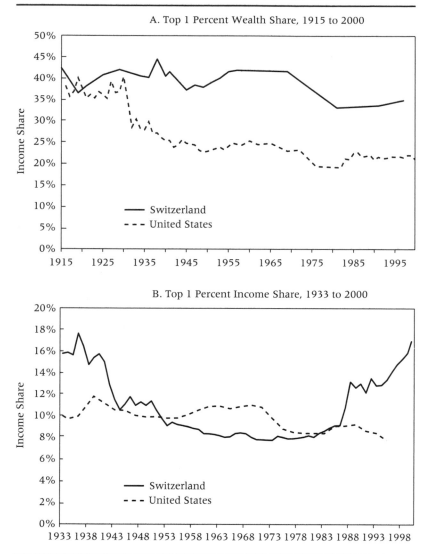

Sources: United States: Piketty and Saez (2003); Switzerland: Dell, Piketty, and Saez (2003).

The Recent Increase in Top-Income Concentration

We have documented a striking difference in the pattern of top-income share series over the last thirty years between the Anglo-Saxon countries and the countries of continental Europe. We have argued that the dramatic increase in top-income shares that has taken place in the United States, Canada, and the United Kingdom has been primarily driven by an unprecedented surge in top-wage incomes. A number of explanations for this state of affairs have been proposed.

For a few countries, such as the United States or France, which have published tax statistics on the distribution of wage income, it is possible to construct shares of total wages accruing to top-wage-income earners for most of the twentieth century.[33] Since the 1970s, for which micro-tax-return data are available for a number of countries, those series can be constructed for these countries as well.

Panel A in figure 5.7 shows the top 1 percent wage-income share in France and the United States since the 1920s. In France, there is no secular change in the top 1 percent wage-income share. The series displays moderate medium-run fluctuations, but nevertheless the levels are almost identical in the early 1920s and the late 1990s—around 6 percent. In contrast, the top 1 percent wage-income share in the United States displays striking fluctuations. Consistent with our previous discussion, figure 5.7 shows clearly that World War II generated a sharp wage-income compression in the United States. The top 1 percent wage-income share declines from more than 8 percent to less than 6 percent in just three years, from 1941 to 1944, and does not recover afterward.

The most impressive feature of the U.S. series, however, is the dramatic increase in the top wage-income share, which started in the early 1970s, accelerated in the 1980s, accelerated faster in the late 1990s, and has driven the top 1 percent share from about 5 percent in the 1960s to 12.5 percent in 2000, a level much higher than in the pre–World War II period. This feature confirms our previous explanation that the increase in top-income shares in the United States since the 1970s is a labor-income phenomenon driven by an unprecedented surge in top-wage incomes. Panel B in figure 5.7 displays the top .1 percent wage-income share in the United States and Canada. There is a striking parallelism between the two series. In

Figure 5.7 The Pattern of Top Wage-Income Shares

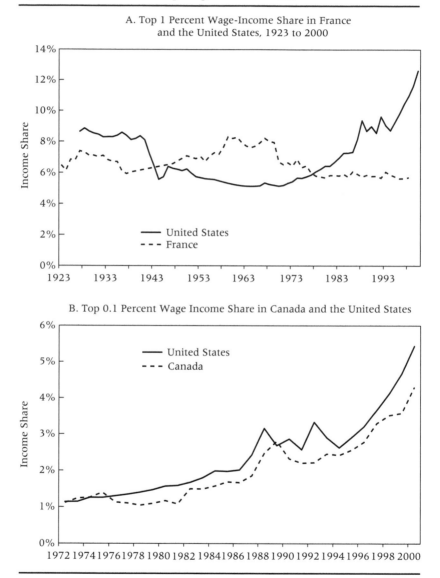

A. Top 1 Percent Wage-Income Share in France
and the United States, 1923 to 2000

B. Top 0.1 Percent Wage Income Share in Canada and the United States

Sources: United States: Piketty and Saez (2003); France: Piketty (2001).

both countries, the top .1 percent is around 1 percent in the early 1970s and grows to 5.4 percent in the United States and to 4.3 percent in Canada. Thus, the surge in top wages has been almost as large in Canada as in the United States.

All our evidence so far has been based on cross-sectional annual-income concentration. However, if the increased cross-sectional-income concentration that we documented in Anglo-Saxon countries has been associated with a substantial increase in income mobility, it might be the case that permanent income inequality has not changed much. For example, a substantial fraction of the increase in top-wage incomes in North America has been due to the explosion of stock-option compensation. Since stock options are reported as wage income on tax returns only when they are exercised, it is plausible to think that top-wage-income earners today experience much larger year-to-year fluctuations in earnings than thirty years ago. Permanent income inequality is a better measure of disparity in economic well-being, so it is very important to analyze how income mobility at the top has evolved in the recent decades.

In most countries, no longitudinal data on top-income earners exist for researchers to use to carry out such a study. Canada, however, has constructed a longitudinal administrative database (LAD) of individual tax returns since 1982, which is analyzed in Saez and Veall (2005). They explore income mobility at the top in two ways. First, they recompute top-income shares on the basis of average income over three or five years instead of a single year. If high incomes were relatively transitory, we would expect to see less concentration when incomes are measured over a longer time period. Figure 5.8, panel A, plots the top .1 percent income share using averages centered on one year, three years, and five years.

The three curves match almost perfectly, suggesting that income mobility has not increased significantly in recent years. Second, and more directly, panel B shows that the probability of remaining in the top .1 percent group is about 60 percent one year later, about 50 percent two years later, and between 40 percent and 50 percent three years later. This suggests that mobility at the top is quite modest. Consistent with the panel A results, there is no increase in mobility since 1982—perhaps there is even a slight decrease. These Canadian results suggest that the surge in annual-income concentration docu-

Figure 5.8   Mobility of High Incomes in Canada, 1982 to 2000

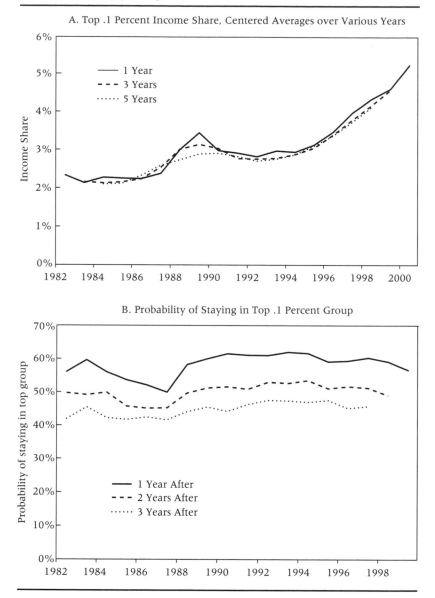

A. Top .1 Percent Income Share, Centered Averages over Various Years

B. Probability of Staying in Top .1 Percent Group

Source: Saez and Veall (2003). Computations based on the Longitudinal Administrative Database of individual Canadian tax returns.
Note: Panel A reports the top .1 percent income share for incomes averaged over one year, three years, and five years. Panel B reports the probability of staying in top .1 percent income group one year, two years, and three years

mented in Canada is associated with a similar increase in longer-term income concentration and welfare. From the Canadian findings it seems plausible to infer that the surge in top U.S. incomes is also not primarily due to increased mobility.

A number of studies (for example, Feldstein 1995; Feenberg and Poterba 1993, 2000) have argued that the dramatic increase in top incomes in the United States might have been the consequence of the very large marginal-tax-rate reductions that took place in the 1980s during the Reagan administration. Indeed, similar tax changes took place in the United Kingdom, a country that also experienced a rise in top-income shares; and no such reductions took place in France, which experienced no increase in top incomes.[34] Saez (2004) analyzes the link between top-income shares and marginal tax rates in the United States for the period from 1960 to 2000. Panel A of figure 5.9 displays the average (income-weighted) marginal income tax rate for the top .1 percent income group, along with the share of income accruing for this group in the United States from 1960 to 2000.

The figure clearly shows a jump in the top-income share from 1986 to 1988, exactly when the tax rates for high-income earners were reduced by the Tax Reform Act of 1986 from 50 percent to 28 percent (a point first noted by Feenberg and Poterba 1993).[35] However, although top tax rates decreased substantially in the early 1960s (from around 90 percent to 70 percent at the very top), the surge in top incomes did not start before the 1970s. Second, the surge in top incomes has been strongest in the late 1990s, when the top marginal tax rate increased significantly, from around 30 percent to around 40 percent.[36]

A more detailed analysis presented in Saez (2004) shows that there is clear evidence of income shifting from the corporate sector toward the individual sector, following the tax cuts of the 1980s and that there is evidence of short-term responses to top-wage income earners around the Tax Reform Act of 1986 and the tax increase of 1993.[37] However, the evidence suggests that the secular increase in top-wage incomes is not closely related to the timing of tax changes in the United States. If there is a substantial lag in the response of top-wage incomes to changes in tax rates, it becomes very difficult to distinguish the impact of tax effects from other effects on the top tail of the wage-income distribution.

Figure 5.9   Marginal Tax Rates and Income Share for the Top .1 Percent in
the United States and Canada, 1960 to 2000

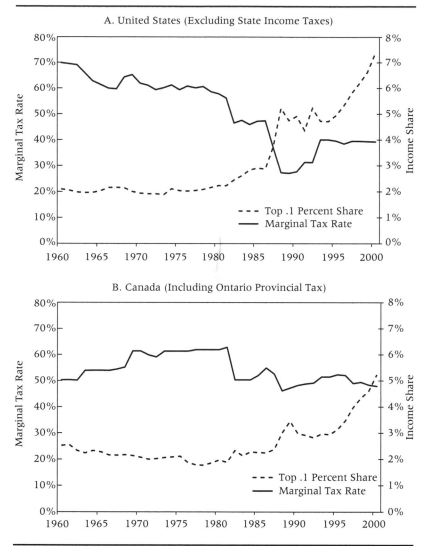

Source: Saez and Veall (2003) for Canada and Saez (2004) for the United States.
Note: Marginal income-tax rates are weighted by income. Marginal tax rates in Canada include
federal and Ontario provincial income taxes, as well as applicable surtaxes and credits. United
States marginal tax rates do not include state income taxes

The case of Canada, analyzed by Saez and Veall (2003), casts interesting light on this issue. As panel B of figure 5.7 shows, Canada experienced almost the same increase in top-wage incomes as the United States, but the fiscal developments in the two countries have been quite different. Panel B of Figure 5.9 displays the average marginal tax rate for the top .1 percent incomes in Canada, along with the top .1 percent income share. Whereas the top .1 percent income group in the United States experienced a reduction in marginal tax rates from 70 percent to less than 30 percent from the early 1960s to the late 1980s, marginal tax rates in Canada for the top .1 percent were about the same (around 50 percent) in the early 1960s and the 1990s. Therefore, it seems difficult to attribute the dramatic increase in top-wage income shares in Canada uniquely to the modest tax cuts that have been implemented there.

Saez and Veall (2003) show that Francophones in Quebec experienced a much smaller increase in top-wage income shares than Canadians in other provinces. This evidence, together with direct evidence on the migration of highly skilled and educated workers from Canada toward the United States, suggests that the surge in top wages in Canada might have been driven by brain-drain threats from the United States. As top wages in the United States increased, migrating to the United States became more attractive for highly skilled Canadians, and thus Canadian companies had to increase the salaries of their best-paid workers in order to retain them. If this explanation is true, it cannot be the case that the surge in top wages that has been observed in the United States can be entirely due to changes in tax avoidance such as shifts from the corporate to the individual sector or repackaging of income. If that were the case, the United States would not have become a significantly more attractive option for Canadians and wages would not have increased in Canada in response to this.

Thus, the extraordinary increase in top-wage incomes in Anglo-Saxon countries, a phenomenon certainly closely related to the explosion of the compensation of CEOs and other top executives and of sports, movies, and television stars, does not appear to be obviously and directly related to changes in tax codes. A more pertinent question to ask is perhaps whether this surge in top wages could have occurred in the United States if the tax structure had remained the same as it was in the early 1960s, and if the working rich had had to pay more than three quarters of their earnings in taxes. It is plausible to think that the drastic reduction in top marginal tax rates, which started in the 1960s, opened the possibility of the dramatic increase in top wages that started in the 1970s and accelerated in the 1980s and the 1990s. It is of course impossible to provide a convincing answer to that important question by looking only at individual income-tax statistics in the United States. A promising way to make progress would be to look more closely into the top-salaries-surge phenomenon by analyzing executive compensation data. There is a large literature on executive compensation (see Murphy 1999 for a survey). However, although there are many studies explaining disparity of CEO pay in cross-sectional data, no convincing explanation for the time-series evidence seems to have been provided.[38] There is strong evidence that pay might not reflect marginal productivity for top executives. For example, Marianne Bertrand and Sendhil Mullainathan (2001) have shown convincingly that CEOs' pay reacts to shocks outside of CEOs' control, such as oil-price shocks, which suggests that the standard model where compensation equals marginal productivity is excessively naïve. The question that arises is whether the recent surge in top-wage incomes has reduced or increased the gap between CEO pay and marginal productivity. If increased CEO pay represents increased skimming of corporations rather than increases in managerial productivity, it is important to understand whether tax policy (such as an increase in top income-tax rates) or regulatory policies (such as requiring the inclusion of stock-options grants as costs in corporations' public accounts) can be effective to curb this market failure.

This paper was prepared for the Berkeley Symposium "Poverty, the Distribution of Income, and Public Policy," a conference honoring Gene Smolensky. I thank Tony Atkinson and Thomas Piketty for very helpful discussions as well as for having provided the key impetus to the development of the new "high-incomes" studies, which this paper summarizes. I also benefited from comments and discussions with Alan Auerbach, David Card, Roger Gordon, John Quigley, and Karl Scholz, as well as with numerous other conference participants. Financial support from the Sloan Foundation and NSF Grant SES-0134946 is gratefully acknowledged.

Notes

1. The analysis of the behavioral responses to tax changes is of much interest in itself for tax policy analysis, and is quite developed in the case of the United States. See for example Saez (2004) for a recent survey.

2. Wealth or income tax statistics tabulated by brackets had been used, at least since Vilfredo Pareto (1897), to compute Pareto parameters of the top tails of the distributions, which amounts to computing income or wealth concentration *within* the upper end of the distribution, as opposed to relative to the average as in Kuznets (1953). See Atkinson (2003) for a more detailed presentation of that point.

3. Earlier historical studies on income concentration are summarized in Christian Morrison (2000) (for European countries) and Peter Lindert (2000) (for Britain and America). Series for Germany and for Australia and New Zealand are being constructed by Dell (2003) and Atkinson and Andrew Leigh (2003).

4. Such wealth-concentration series had also been constructed for the United Kingdom by Atkinson and A. J. Harrison (1978) and Atkinson, J. P. F. Gordon, and Harrison (1989), and for the United States by Robert J. Lampman (1962).

5. See Piketty and Saez (2003) for the United States, Saez and Veall (2003) for Canada and the recent study by Atkinson and Voitchovsky (2004) on top wage incomes in the United Kingdom.

6. In continental Europe, it is still the case that top incomes are composed primarily of capital income.

7. See, however, Atkinson and Leigh (2003) for an attempt at capturing this effect by regressing top-income shares on current and lagged tax rates.

8. Changes in the tax unit definition as happened in the United Kingdom in 1990 create an additional difficulty to construct homogeneous series.

9. In general, dependent minors are not taxed separately, their incomes are added to the incomes of the parents.

10. Atkinson (2003) discusses this point formally.

11. For example, in the United States, charitable contributions can be deducted from income for tax purposes.

12. In most cases, statistics reported for the top brackets are based on the universe of tax returns and not a sub-sample.

13. For example, for the United States, large micro datasets of individual tax returns with over-sampling of higher incomes are publicly available since 1960.

14. For example, the dollar depreciated by more than 30 percent relative to the Euro from the end of 2001 to the the beginning of 2004.

15. In the United States, for example, the methods for constructing the Consumer Price Index (CPI) have evolved over time. As a result, the

historical CPI series and the new series incorporating retrospectively the improvements in the methodology differ considerably with a cumulative gap of about 15 percent over the last 25 years. This gap implies that income series deflated using the official CPI underestimate real growth since 1978 by about 15 percent. See Kenneth J. Stewart and Stephen B. Reed (1999) for more details.

16. See, for example, U.S. Treasury Department (1996) for a recent U.S. analysis.

17. Evidence from Switzerland reported in Dell, Piketty, and Saez (2003) shows that the amounts earned in Switzerland from all non-residents and never reported by taxpayers in their own country of residence is very small relative to the amounts reported by high incomes in the United States (less than 10 percent than all incomes earned by the top .01 percent income earners in the United States).

18. This issue is especially important in the case of stock-options which are in general exercised in a lumpy way and are not an annual stream of income like salaries. In most countries, profits from exercised stock-options are reported as wages and salaries on income tax returns.

19. Gordon and Slemrod (2000) show evidence of tax minimization strategies along those lines for the United States.

20. In year 2000, in the United States, the top 1 percent is formed of tax units with annual incomes above $280,000, corresponding perhaps to the popular view of the affluent. In both countries, the series do not include realized capital gains.

21. This means that taxpayers in the top 1 percent earned 18 to 20 times the average income.

22. The average annual income of a tax unit in this group is $120,000 in the United States in year 2000 (and about $75,000 in France in 1998). This group corresponds perhaps to the popular view of the upper middle class.

23. At the end of the period, wages and salaries form about 85 percent of incomes in this group. The share of wage income for that group was around 60 percent at the beginning of the period.

24. The Kuznets theory is based on the comparison between wages in the old (agricultural) sector and the new (industrial) sector. Thus, one would expect the upper middle income class share, which amounts roughly to comparing skilled wage earners to unskilled wage earners, to capture well the Kuznets effect.

25. In the United States in 2000, the top .1 percent incomes represent the top 1.3 million tax units with annual incomes above around $1 million.

26. There is a discontinuous increase in the fraction of business income in the United States from 1986 to 1988. This was the consequence of shifting of income from the corporate sector toward the individual sector using the S-corporation status which had become fiscally more advan-

tageous than traditional corporations (C-status) following the Tax Reform Act of 1986. This shift has been documented in detail in Slemrod (1996) and Gordon and Slemrod (2000). Note however that this jump in business income remains small relative to the increase in wages and salaries over the last 25 years.

27. See Atkinson and Harrison (1978) for a detailed discussion on methodological issues.

28. In all three cases, the top wealth share is estimated from estate tax return data using the estate multiplier method which amounts to re-weight the sample of estates by the inverse of the probability of death in order to obtain the wealth distribution for the living.

29. Kopczuk and Saez (2004) who analyze the composition of top wealth holdings in the United States since 1916 discuss this point in detail.

30. It is interesting to note on figure 5.5. that wealth concentration did not decline as much as income concentration in the United States during World War II. This is consistent with a large temporary decline in dividend payments but a much smaller decrease in stock-prices during the war.

31. It would be interesting to analyze in detail the evolution of taxation during World War I in each of those countries to see whether the distribution of the fiscal burden to finance the war can explain the patterns of top-income shares that we observe across countries.

32. Of course, the shocks of the Great Depression and World War II were milder in Switzerland than in the United States. Therefore, we cannot be fully confident that top fortunes and top incomes in Switzerland would have fully recovered if Switzerland had experienced such large shocks as the United States.

33. Atkinson and Voitchovsky (2004) have constructed top earnings shares for the United Kingdom for the post–World War II period.

34. The Netherlands also experienced small top-tax-rate reductions and no increase in top incomes.

35. The top-income share also increased following the marginal tax cuts of the early 1980s (a point first noted by Lawrence Lindsey 1987), but much less than from 1986 to 1988.

36. Companies might, however, have started granting stock options more aggressively after the Tax Reform Act of 1986 because of the decrease in individual tax rates. Those options can be exercised (and thus appear on individual income-tax returns) only a number of years later. Brian Hall and Kevin Murphy (2003) show, however, that grants of new stock options, valued using the Black-Scholes formula, increased massively *after* the tax increase of 1993.

37. Austan Goolsbee (2000) showed convincingly, using executive compensation data, that most of the short-term response in wage income around the 1993 tax increase was due to a surge in stock-option exer-

cises in 1992 in order to take advantage of the last year with low tax rates. Goolsbee (2000) finds no evidence of a long-term response of executive compensation to changes in tax rates.

38. It is quite telling to read in the recent survey of Hall and Murphy (2003), two prominent and conservative researchers in this field, that their best explanation for the surge in stock-option compensation was that "boards and managers falsely perceive stock options to be inexpensive because of accounting and cash-flow considerations."

References

Atkinson, Anthony B. 2002. "Top Incomes in the United Kingdom over the Twentieth Century." Unpublished paper (mimeographed). Oxford: Oxford University, Nuffield College.

———. 2003. "Measuring Top Incomes: Methodological Issues." Unpublished paper (mimeographed). Oxford: Oxford University, Nuffield College.

Atkinson, Anthony B., James P. F. Gordon, and Alan J. Harrison. 1989. "Trends in the Shares of Top Wealth Holders in Britain, 1923–1981." *Oxford Bulletin of Economics and Statistics* 51(3): 315–32.

Atkinson, Anthony B., and Alan J. Harrison. 1978. *Distribution of Personal Wealth in Britain*. Cambridge: Cambridge University Press.

Atkinson, Anthony B., and Andrew Leigh. 2003. "The Distribution of Top Incomes in Anglo-Saxon Countries over the Twentieth Century." Unpublished paper (mimeographed). Oxford: Oxford University, Nuffield College.

Atkinson, Anthony B., and Wiemer Salverda. 2003. "Top Incomes in the Netherlands and the United Kingdom over the Twentieth Century." Unpublished paper (mimeographed). Oxford: Oxford University, Nuffield College.

Atkinson, Anthony B., and Sarah Voitchovsky. 2004. "The Distribution of Top Earnings in the United Kingdom since the Second World War." Unpublished paper (mimeographed). Oxford: Oxford University, Nuffield College.

Bertrand, Marianne, and Sendhil Mullainathan. 2001. "Are CEOs Rewarded for Luck? The Ones Without Principals Are." *Quarterly Journal of Economics* 116(3): 901–32

Dell, Fabien. 2003. "Top Incomes in Germany over the Twentieth Century: 1895–1995." Unpublished paper (mimeographed). Paris: INSEE.

Dell, Fabien, Thomas Piketty, and Emmanuel Saez. 2003. "The Evolution of Income and Wealth Concentration in Switzerland over the 20th Century." Unpublished paper (mimeographed). Berkeley: University of California, Berkeley.

Feenberg, Daniel, and James Poterba. 1993. "Income Inequality and the Incomes of Very High Income Taxpayers: Evidence from Tax Returns." In *Tax Policy and the Economy,* edited by James Poterba. Cambridge: MIT Press.

———. 2000. "The Income and Tax Share of Very High Income Households, 1960–1995." *American Economic Review* 90(2): 264–70.

Feldstein, Martin. 1995. "The Effect of Marginal Tax Rates on Taxable Income: A Panel Study of the 1986 Tax Reform Act." *Journal of Political Economy* 103(3): 551–72.

Goldin, Claudia, and Robert Margo. 1992. "The Great Compression: The Wage Structure in the United States at Mid-Century." *Quarterly Journal of Economics* 107(1): 1–34.

Goolsbee, Austan. 2000. "What Happens When You Tax the Rich? Evidence from Executive Compensation." *Journal of Political Economy* 108(2): 352–78.

Gordon, Roger, and Jeffrey MacKie-Mason. 1990. "Effects of the Tax Reform Act of 1986 on Corporate Financial Policy and Organizational Form." In *Do Taxes Matter? The Impact of the Tax Reform Act of 1986,* edited by Joel Slemrod. Cambridge: MIT Press.

Gordon, Roger, and Joel Slemrod. 2000. "Are 'Real' Responses to Taxes Simply Income Shifting Between Corporate and Personal Tax Bases?" In *Does Atlas Shrug? The Economic Consequences of Taxing the Rich,* edited by Joel Slemrod. New York: Russell Sage Foundation.

Hall, Brian, and Kevin Murphy. 2003. "The Trouble with Stock Options." NBER working paper no. 9784. Washington, D.C.: National Bureau of Economic Research.

Kopczuk, Wojciech, and Emmanuel Saez. 2004. "Top Wealth Shares in the United States, 1916–2000: Evidence from Estate Tax Returns." NBER working paper no. 10399. Washington, D.C.: National Bureau of Economic Research.

Kuznets, Simon. 1953. *Shares of Upper Income Groups in Income and Savings.* Washington, D.C.: National Bureau of Economic Research.

———. 1955. "Economic Growth and Economic Inequality." *American Economic Review* 45:1–28.

Lampman, Robert J. 1962. *The Share of Top Wealth-Holders in National Wealth, 1922–1956.* Washington, D.C., and Princeton: National Bureau of Economic Research and Princeton University Press.

Lindert, Peter 2000. "Three Centuries of Inequality in Britain and America." In *Handbook of Income Distribution,* edited by Anthony Atkinson and François Bourguignon. Amsterdam: North-Holland.

Lindsey, Lawrence. 1987. "Individual Taxpayer Response to Tax Cuts: 1982–1984, with Implications for the Revenue Maximizing Tax Rate." *Journal of Public Economics* 33: 173–206.

Morrison, Christian. 2000. "Historical Perspectives on Income Distribution: The Case of Europe." In *Handbook of Income Distribution,* edited by Anthony Atkinson and François Bourguignon. Amsterdam: North-Holland.

Murphy, Kevin J. 1999. "Executive Compensation." In *Handbook of Labor Economics,* edited by Orley Ashenfelter and David Card. Volume 3B. Amsterdam: North-Holland.

Pareto, Vilfredo. 1897. *Cours d'économie politique.* Volume 2. Paris: Pichon.

Piketty, Thomas. 2001. *Les Hauts Revenus en France au 20ème siècle—inégalités et redistributions, 1901–1998.* Paris: Editions Grasset.

———. 2003. "Income Inequality in France, 1901–1998." *Journal of Political Economy* 111(5): 1004–42.

Piketty, Thomas, Gilles Postel-Vinay, and Jean-Laurent Rosenthal. 2004. "Wealth Concentration in a Developing Economy: Paris and France, 1807–1994." CEPR Discussion Paper No. 4631.

Piketty, Thomas, and Emmanuel Saez. 2003. "Income Inequality in the United States, 1913–1998." *Quarterly Journal of Economics* 118(1): 1–39.

Saez, Emmanuel. 2004. "Reported Incomes and Marginal Tax Rates, 1960–2000: Evidence and Policy Implications." In *Tax Policy and the Economy,* edited by James Poterba. Cambridge: MIT Press.

Saez, Emmanuel, and Michael R. Veall 2003. "The Evolution of Top Incomes in Canada, 1920–2000." NBER working paper no. 9607. Washington, D.C.: National Bureau of Economic Research.

———. 2005. "The Evolution of High Incomes in Northern America: Lessons from Canadian Evidence." *American Economic Review* 95(3): 831–49.

Slemrod, Joel. 1996. "High Income Families and the Tax Changes of the 1980s: The Anatomy of Behavioral Response." In *Empirical Foundations of Household Taxation,* edited by M. Feldstein and James Poterba. Chicago: University of Chicago Press.

Stewart, Kenneth J., and Stephen B. Reed. 1999. "CPI Research Series Using Current Methods, 1978–98." *Monthly Labor Review* 122(6): 29–38.

U.S. Department of the Treasury. Internal Revenue Service. 1996. "Federal Tax Compliance Research: Individual Income Tax Gap Estimates for 1985, 1988, and 1992." Publication 1415. Washington: U.S. Government Printing Office.

U.S. Department of the Treasury. Internal Revenue Service. Various years. *Statistics of Income: Individual Income Tax Returns.* Published annually since 1916. Washington: U.S. Government Printing Office.

Chapter 6

Social Security and the Evolution of Elderly Poverty

Gary V. Engelhardt and Jonathan Gruber

One of the most striking trends in elderly well-being in the twentieth century was the dramatic decline in poverty among the elderly. The official poverty rate of those sixty-five years and older was 35 percent in 1960, more than twice that of the non-elderly (those aged eighteen to sixty-four), but by 1995 it had fallen to 10 percent, and to below that for the non-elderly. Eugene Smolensky, Sheldon Danziger, and Peter Gottschalk (1988) found similar steep declines in elderly poverty going back to 1939. This poverty reduction among the elderly exceeded that for any other group in society.

The rapid growth in Social Security benefits in the post–World War II period is often cited as a major factor in elderly poverty reduction. This conclusion is based on evidence such as that shown in figure 6.1, which plots both the elderly poverty rate and per-capita Social Security program expenditures over time (the figure is rescaled so that both series fit on the same graph). There is a striking negative association between these series: elderly poverty declined rapidly as the Social Security program grew quickly in the 1960s and 1970s, and then declined more slowly as program growth slowed in the 1980s and 1990s. One concern with potential reforms to the Social Security system is that the reduction of elderly poverty rates over the last forty years may be reversed to the extent such changes effectively involve benefit reduction.

Our goal in this chapter is to assess the role of Social Security in driving this reduction in elderly poverty.

Figure 6.1   Poverty Rate of Elderly Households and Social Security
Expenditures over Time

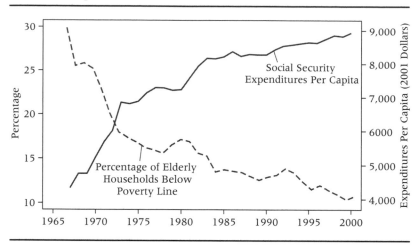

Source: Authors' compilation.

We begin with time-series evidence on the growth in Social
Security and the decline in elderly poverty. We consider both absolute
and relative measures of elderly poverty, as well as the heterogeneity in the evolution of elderly poverty. We consider two points
in particular: first, whether these changes in poverty were reflected
equally among the oldest old, who start with much higher poverty
rates, and the youngest old; and second, whether the trends were
comparable across marital-status groups: the married, divorced, widowed, and never-married.

We then assess the causal role of Social Security in explaining
these trends. We outline the econometric problems in the previous
literature on the impact of Social Security on elderly income poverty
and propose an instrumental-variable (IV) procedure to circumvent
these difficulties. We then examine the effect on poverty of the large
changes in Social Security benefits for cohorts born in the late nineteenth and early twentieth centuries. Of particular interest are the
sharp benefit changes for birth cohorts from 1906 through 1926. The
early cohorts in this range saw enormous exogenous increases in
Social Security benefits, partly because of the double indexing of
the system in the early 1970s. This double indexing was ended in
the 1977 Amendments to the Social Security Act, generating the so-

called "benefits notch." Because those born in 1916 would attain the early-retirement claiming age of sixty-two in 1978, when the 1977 law went into effect, the 1977 law grandfathered the old benefit rules for all individuals born before January 1, 1917; those born in 1917 to 1921 received benefit reductions that were as much as 20 percent lower than observationally equivalent individuals in the 1916 birth cohort. For those born after 1921, benefits were roughly constant in real terms. In particular, the "notch" birth cohorts (born in 1917 to 1921) received large, unanticipated, and permanent reductions in benefits very late in their working life, to which they had relatively less time to adjust than younger cohorts (Moffitt 1987). This variation was first identified by Alan Krueger and Jörn-Steffen Pischke (1992) as a fruitful means of identifying the behavioral effects of Social Security, in their case in the context of retirement decisions. We follow their methodology to define an instrumental variable for observed Social Security benefits that allows us to trace out the long-run impact of late-career changes in Social Security benefits on subsequent poverty in old age.[1]

Specifically, we carry out this analysis using data from 1967 through 2000 from the March Current Population Survey to study the elderly who were born in 1885 through 1930. We use these data to form income measures for elderly households and families. Elderly households are all living units in which an elderly person resides; elderly families consist of an elder and his or her spouse. So if an elderly couple co-resides with their children, they are in the same household, but different families.

We have several findings of interest. First, while there has been a major decline in absolute poverty among elderly households, that decline has been much smaller for relative poverty, which did not decrease in the 1980s and 1990s. This raises the important question of whether the elderly should or should not share in the increases in the standard of living realized by the non-elderly. Income inequality has also exploded among the elderly in the 1990s. Second, these changes in the income position of low-income elders are fairly similar across age groups, with all age groups following the same basic patterns outlined above. Third, there are important differences in these patterns by marital-status group. In particular, the declines in absolute poverty that we see in the data are much stronger for married than for unmarried elders. Fourth, we document a major causal role of Social Security in driving these time-series patterns. Increases in Social Security generosity over time are strongly negatively associated with changes in poverty. There is, however, a weak association with income inequality, suggesting that Social Security benefits higher-income elders at the same rate as or a higher rate than it benefits low-income elders over this period.

Finally, we illustrate the critical role of elderly persons' living arrangements in driving these conclusions. As we document, there were stark changes in the living arrangements of the elderly over the time period we study, with a large shift in living with others to living independently. Our regression results show that the effect of Social Security on poverty is much stronger for families than for households, in particular for widows and widowers and divorcées. This is consistent with the findings of Gary V. Engelhardt, Jonathan Gruber, and Cynthia D. Perry (2005), that higher Social Security benefits cause more independent living among widowed and divorced elders. When those elders move out on their own, they are in the same family, but they become relatively poor households, raising the poverty rate among households. This offsets to some extent the measured poverty reduction among the elderly from higher benefits.

After describing the Current Population Survey data, we chart the time-series evolution of elderly income and poverty from 1967 to 2000. Next we outline the principal method used to determine the impact of Social Security in the previous literature and describe the construction of the instrumental variable. We discuss the empirical results in the "Estimation Results" section. There is a brief conclusion.

Data Construction

This study uses data from the Current Population Surveys (CPS) of March 1968 through 2001. Each file is a cross-sectional, nationally representative sample of households. We restrict our analysis to cohorts born from 1880 to 1935. The year 1880 was chosen because our sample is very small before that cohort; the cohort born in 1935 is the youngest cohort that turns sixty-five in our data.

To construct our main sample, we first assign families within the CPS. For our purposes, a "family" is defined as the household head, his or her spouse, and any children of the household head that are living in the household and are under the age of eighteen. This differs from the CPS definition of a family in that we assume any other member of the household is a separate family, whereas all individuals related by birth, marriage, and adoption are considered members of the CPS family. Note that there may be more than one "family" in a given CPS "household" (if, say, multiple nonmarried elderly live together). Our family definition requires consistency in relational measures in the CPS household in the annual surveys. Because of changes in these measures, we were not able to construct our measure of the family prior to the March 1968 CPS. We use both families and households as our observational unit.

In order to measure outcomes for any age range for either households or families, we weight the full sample of households and families by the number of persons sharing that household or family in the relevant age range. That is, our estimated poverty rate for "households" aged sixty-five to sixty-nine is the poverty rate over all households containing a person aged sixty-five to sixty-nine, weighted by the number of persons in that age range in that household. So these are essentially person-weighted poverty rates.

The questions in the March CPS are about income earned in the previous calendar year, so that even though we use data from the 1968-to-2001 surveys, the income data refer to 1967 to 2000. Over time, the CPS has provided more disaggregated questions on income sources, and has changed the wording of questions for some types of income. For each year we used the most disaggregated income measures to make our poverty measures, which, following official poverty rates, are based on gross income.[2] All income measures were deflated into real 2001 dollars, using the all-items Consumer Price Index (CPI).

We begin our analysis with the classic absolute poverty measure: whether a family is below the federal poverty line. Specifically, for the household-level analysis we assigned to each household the poverty threshold for the appropriate household size. Similarly, for the family-level analysis we assigned to each family the threshold for the appropriate size, treating the family as the "household" in the federal threshold definition. So that we could compare elderly and non-elderly on an equal basis, we did not incorporate the adjustments for age sixty-five and older for one- and two-person households that are built into the federal thresholds. This absolute measure of poverty has a number of limitations, however. First, it holds standards of living constant and does not allow for productivity growth. Specifically, in a mechanical sense, if there is any real productivity growth over time, so that real wage growth is positive, then poverty based on the federal threshold likely will fall over time, because this measure only adjusts for inflation, not real-earnings growth. Second, it is a knife-edge measure that does not capture the depth of absolute deprivation.

As an alternative, we define a relative measure of the poverty line: 40 percent of the median income of the non-elderly in each calendar year per adult equivalent as defined by the Organization for Economic Development (OECD). Non-elderly are defined as individuals twenty-five to fifty-four years old. We adjust both elderly and non-elderly income by the OECD equivalence scale. An important feature of the relative measure is that it does not hold living standards constant. Holding real elderly income per equivalent constant, elderly poverty will rise as median non-elderly income rises. This relative measure will yield poverty rates that are more likely to be pro-cyclical, as median income rises and falls over the business cycle.

The potential importance of using this relative measure in addition to the absolute measure is shown in figure 6.2. This figure graphs real Social Security expenditures per capita as well as the ratio of Social Security expenditures per capita to mean non-elderly

Figure 6.2   Absolute and Relative Social Security Expenditures over Time as Percentage of Non-Elderly Income

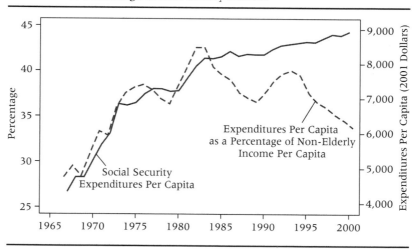

Source: Authors' compilation.

income per capita. The two series moved in tandem until the mid-1980s, at which point there was a decline in relative Social Security generosity, even as benefits continued to slowly rise in real terms.

In addition, we consider income inequality among the elderly, which we measure as the 90-10 coefficient of variation (that is, in each calendar year, the difference between the 90th and 10th elderly OECD-equivalent income percentiles normalized by mean elderly income). We also considered other variants of poverty measures. Specifically, we created three alternative measures of the absolute poverty line based on 133, 150, and 200 percent of the relative poverty line based on 25 and 50 percent of the non-elderly median income, respectively, and measures based on gross and net income. The results did not differ from those presented later. For the remainder of the analysis, all income measures were based on gross income to be comparable with the federal poverty thresholds.

Time-Series Evidence

We begin our time series analysis by considering trends for all elderly households, before turning to subsets of the elderly. Figure 6.3 shows the absolute poverty rate for elderly households; it replicates the

Figure 6.3   Absolute Poverty of Elderly and Non-Elderly Households over Time

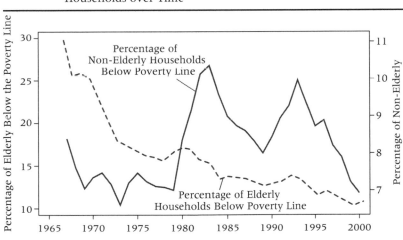

Source: Authors' compilation.

result from figure 6.1, but adds as well the trends in poverty for non-elderly households. This figure is rescaled so that elderly and non-elderly poverty can be shown in comparable terms. Recall that this graph includes only those born between 1885 and 1930, so it will not match published statistics for all elderly in each year; but the pattern is very similar to that shown in published statistics over this time period.

During the period of most rapid Social Security growth, during the late 1960s and early 1970s, both elderly and non-elderly poverty are declining. The difference between the elderly and non-elderly emerges in the recession of the elderly in the 1980s, when non-elderly poverty rose dramatically while elderly poverty rose only slightly, and the recession of the early 1990s, when elderly and non-elderly poverty followed a similar pattern. In the 1990s the decline in non-elderly poverty was much steeper than the decline in elderly poverty. These findings on the relative cyclicality of poverty highlight the protective role of Social Security for the elderly.

Figure 6.4 shows the relative poverty rate for the elderly and non-elderly. During the late 1960s and early 1970s, the relative poverty rate of the elderly was falling, as was the absolute poverty rate, although in this case the declines came against a backdrop of rising

Figure 6.4   Relative Poverty of Elderly and Non-Elderly
               Households over Time

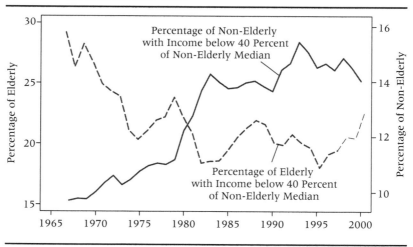

Source: Authors' compilation.

non-elderly relative poverty. During the 1980s and 1990s the decline stagnated, so that there was little net change in relative poverty from 1980 through 2000. The fact that relative poverty did not fall while absolute poverty did is consistent with the pattern of benefits during the 1980s and 1990s shown in Figure 6.2.

Figure 6.5 shows the evolution of inequality within the elderly over time. Relative to the non-elderly, inequality among the elderly declined significantly from the late 1960s through the early 1990s. But inequality exploded in the late 1990s among the elderly, rising at an even faster rate than inequality among the non-elderly.

Families Versus Households

The analysis thus far has focused on elderly households, a category that includes elders and others that share their residence. An alternative means of measuring poverty is just to focus on the elders themselves (and their own spouses and children under eighteen) in a family-level analysis. These analyses potentially can yield very different measures of poverty because changes in Social Security benefits can change the living arrangements of the elderly. A number of studies, most recently Engelhardt, Gruber, and Perry (2005), found that unmarried elders are more likely to live on their own as their

Figure 6.5   Income Inequality of Elderly and Non-Elderly Households over Time

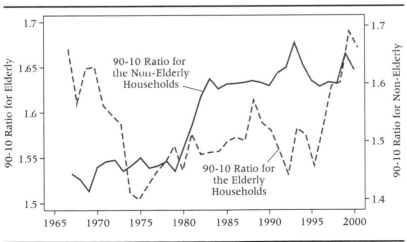

Source: Authors' compilation.

Social Security benefits rise. Specifically, they found that widows' living arrangements were quite sensitive to benefits: each 1 percent rise in benefits was found to lead to a 1.3 percent reduction in the share of widows living with others. Elderly divorcées were even more income elastic in their living arrangements. The never-married are less elastic, and the married are not at all elastic. Overall, averaging across all of these groups, there is a sizable elasticity of −0.4.

This time-series change in living arrangements is illustrated in figure 6.6, which shows the percent of elderly in shared living arrangements over time. This share dropped precipitously, from 34 percent in 1967 to 24 percent by 1982, and then was relatively constant thereafter. This is very consistent with the rapid run-up in benefits in the late 1960s and 1970s, and the flattening of benefits in the 1980s and 1990s, supporting the notion that Social Security benefits are a major determinant of living arrangements.

These findings can have important implications for the measurement of poverty. In particular, if higher Social Security benefits make the widowed and divorced more likely to live independently, then this will create more elderly households but keep the number of elderly families the same (because in our definition of family, elderly

Figure 6.6   Percentage of Elderly in Shared Living Arrangements over Time

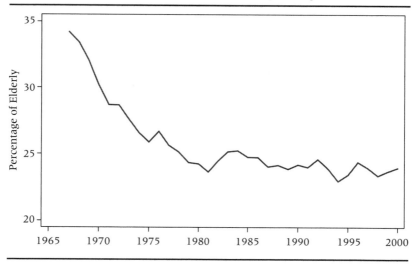

Source: Authors' compilation.

living alone or in shared arrangements are their own family). In addition, the "new" elderly households will be comparatively poor, because they only have elderly in them. Therefore, the endogenous response of living arrangements to benefits will bias downward any estimated poverty improvement among elderly households. This suggests that using a family-level analysis may be more appropriate for reflecting Social Security–induced poverty reductions.

Figure 6.7 shows the results for elderly families, rather than elderly households. Here, the pattern for absolute poverty for the elderly is similar, but in this case it is not mirrored by the non-elderly; the poverty rate of non-elderly families actually rises slightly. Poverty rates are much higher, consistent with the notion that there are economies of scale in shared living conditions. Nevertheless, in these time-series data, there is no evidence that using families rather than households for the analysis has any major effect.

Trends by Age Group

There are dramatic differences in the poverty rates of the "young" and "old" elderly. In 2000, households whose residents were aged sixty-five to sixty-nine had a poverty rate of 7.5 percent; households in which elders aged eighty and above resided had a poverty rate that

Figure 6.7   Absolute Poverty of Elderly and Non-Elderly Families over Time

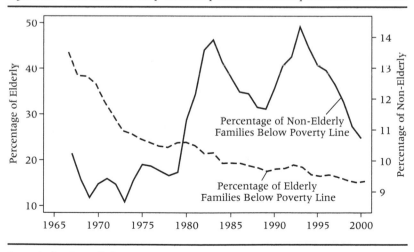

Source: Authors' compilation.

was almost twice as high, 13 percent. This raises the question of whether all age groups of elderly have shared equally in the dramatic changes in the income distribution.

Figure 6.8 shows the poverty rates by age group, at the household level (compare figures 6.3 and 6.4). In fact, the patterns are remarkably similar across these age groups. In every case we see the steep decline in poverty in the late 1960s and early 1970s, and the much slower decline in the 1980s and 1990s. Thus, there is no evidence here of a relatively large effect on one particular age group.

Trends by Marital Status

Another important source of dispersion in poverty rates among the elderly is marital status. At the household level, the poverty rate of married elders in 2000 was only 5 percent; for never-married elders, it was almost 22 percent. For divorced and widowed elders, it was about 16 percent.

Figure 6.9 illustrates differences in the evolution of income for elderly households by marital status. When we interpret these figures it is important to recognize that the composition of each group is

Figure 6.8   Elderly Absolute Poverty by Age Group over Time

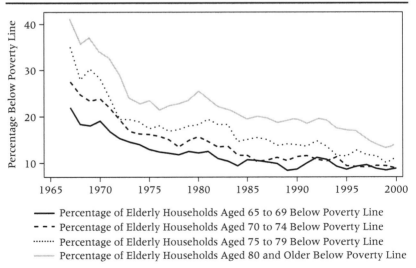

Source: Authors' compilation.

Figure 6.9 Elderly Absolute Poverty by Marital Status over Time

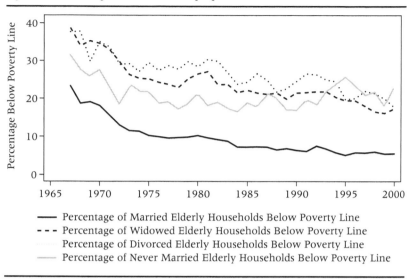

- Percentage of Married Elderly Households Below Poverty Line
- - - Percentage of Widowed Elderly Households Below Poverty Line
Percentage of Divorced Elderly Households Below Poverty Line
Percentage of Never Married Elderly Households Below Poverty Line

Source: Authors' compilation.

changing over time. Where the number of married or widowed elders rose by 50 percent from 1967 to 2000, the number of divorced elders rose by almost 500 percent, and the number of never-married elders rose by over 300 percent. Thus, patterns in poverty over time could reflect changes in group composition.

Given this caveat, the results for changes in poverty by marital status are quite interesting. It appears that the changes over time for all elderly are driven by the married elderly. The patterns are much stronger for married elderly than for other groups. Particularly striking is the lack of poverty decline for never-married elderly, who start out with the second highest poverty rate in 1967 and have the highest rate of these groups by 2000.

Identifying the Impact of Social Security

The existing literature on poverty is voluminous, and we do not attempt to review it here.[3] Instead, we focus on the primary method used to measure the impact of public policies on poverty and how that relates to our instrumental-variable identification strategy. Following Markus Jäntti and Danziger (2000), let i and t index the elderly subgroup and the calendar year, respectively, and let F be a function of resources, then $P_{it}[F(y);z]$ is a poverty measure for some income y and poverty line z. In addition, let b denote Social Security income, so that:

(6.1) $$y = y' + b$$

where y′ is market capital and labor income. In principle, the impact of Social Security on poverty is:

(6.2) $$\tilde{\Delta} = P_{it}\left[\tilde{F}(y');z\right] - P_{it}\left[F(y);z\right]$$

where $\tilde{F}$ is the counterfactual distribution of market labor and capital income in the absence of Social Security. In practice, the primary method for analyzing the impact of Social Security on poverty has been to calculate the *actual* difference in poverty using market income and income net of taxes and transfers,

(6.3) $$\Delta = P_{it}\left[F(y');z\right] - P_{it}\left[F(y);z\right]$$

There are three problems with Δ as a measure of the impact of Social Security on poverty. First, it misses any "crowd-out" of real behavior. In particular, observed capital and labor income, y′, itself may be a function of benefits, b, if, for example, when faced with an unanticipated and permanent increase in benefits, the elderly leave the labor force earlier, reduce postretirement hours of labor supplied, increase consumption and reduce saving, or substitute independent for shared living arrangements.[4] Second, survey-based measures of income might be subject to reporting error. Third, to the extent that most of the variation in Social Security benefits that identifies Δ is time-series in nature, there may be omitted variables that are correlated with changes in poverty rates and Social Security. For example, lifetime earnings, which enter into Social Security benefit calculations, are affected by aggregate productivity and human-capital accumulation that have been changing across time. However, because the federal poverty thresholds are inflation-adjusted but not average earnings–adjusted, in a mechanical sense poverty rates for successive birth cohorts should be predicted to fall as productivity, human-capital accumulation, and real lifetime earnings have risen. Thus, what might appear as an inverse correlation between elderly poverty based on absolute measures and Social Security, as in our figures, may simply be due to rising aggregate productivity. That is, even given that Social Security has no causal impact, elderly poverty would appear to have fallen as benefits rose. This would bias estimates toward finding that Social Security lowered elderly poverty.

Construction of the Instrument

To circumvent these problems we place equation (6.3) in a regression framework and construct an instrumental variable for Social Security benefits independent of omitted time-varying factors and based on an exogenous measure of lifetime labor income. The variation in this instrument derives solely from legislative changes in benefits.

To construct our instrument, we note that all of the identifying variation from the Social Security "notch" is based on year of birth, and divide the underlying CPS microdata into age-by-calendar-year cells, which of course are also year-of-birth cells. The year of birth refers to the "Social Security beneficiary," defined as the male person in the family sixty-five and older. If there is no male sixty-five and older, the beneficiary is the oldest never-married female in the family. These two groups consist of people most likely to have had Social Security benefits based on their own earnings history, rather than that of their spouse. If there is neither a male nor a never-married female sixty-five and older, we assign the Social Security beneficiary to be the divorced or widowed female that is sixty-five and older. We assume that her Social Security benefits are based on the earnings of her former or deceased spouse, assumed to be three years older than her, so that the "age" of beneficiary is the woman's age plus three for the purposes of calculating our instrument.[5]

The instrument is based on the notion that Social Security benefits should be constructed to be identical for each year of birth *except for changes in the benefits law*. We first assign an earnings history to the 1916 birth cohort. The *Annual Statistical Supplement* produced by the Social Security Administration each year contains the median Social Security earnings by gender for five-year age groups on a yearly basis for the current year as well as years past. We use median male earnings from these tables. We assign median earnings at age twenty-two (from the median earnings for ages twenty to twenty-four in

1938), age twenty-seven (from median earnings for ages twenty-five to twenty-nine in 1943), and so on, in five-year intervals. We then assume a linear trend in earnings in between these five-year intervals. This method is used through age sixty, and earnings are assumed to grow with inflation for ages beyond sixty. We do not use median earnings for workers over sixty because many of these workers have entered "bridge" jobs, so that the median worker's earnings at these ages may not be representative of workers who remain in their lifetime jobs through age sixty-five. This generates an earnings history for a median male earner in the cohort born in 1916. We use the *same* earnings profile even when assigning benefits to never-married females, because we assume that their earnings profile would more closely resemble that of a male worker than that of the median female worker.[6]

It is important to note that we want our instrument to vary only with changes in Social Security benefit rules and do not want to capture changes in earnings profiles that are due to human-capital and productivity changes in cohorts over time. Therefore, we use the earnings history that we constructed for the 1916 cohort for *all* birth cohorts, and simply use the Consumer Price Index to adjust this earnings profile for inflation for earlier and later cohorts. Thus, all birth cohorts have the same real-earnings trajectory over time. Holding lifetime earnings constant when we construct the instrument ensures that all of the variation in the instrument comes from variation in the benefit formula resulting from the change in the law. We also assume that this prototypical earnings history ends at age sixty-five, to avoid incorporating any variation across cohorts in average retirement ages. So we assume all workers retire at age sixty-five; our results are very similar when we use an instrument that employs a fixed distribution of retirement ages from the 1916 cohort.

Our next step is to input the constructed earnings histories into the Social Security Administration's ANYPIA program, which, given a date of birth, date of retirement, and earnings history, calculates the monthly benefit at the date of retirement (the "primary insurance amount"). To yield a PIA, we assign birthdays of June 2 in the year of birth and assume that people retire and claim benefits in June of their retirement year.[7] Married couples are assigned 150 percent of this PIA.

The Social Security Administration periodically increases nominal benefits to adjust for inflation. To obtain a value for the predicted benefit for a given age and year-of-birth cohort, we need to account for all "cost-of-living adjustments" (COLA) until the date of the CPS interview. We calculate the median month in which a given age and year-of-birth cell was interviewed, and administer all COLA adjustments from the time that the person would have retired through this date. For each age and year-of-birth cell, this produces a predicted (COLA-adjusted) Social Security monthly benefit. We then multiply by 12 to get the predicted annual benefit, which we refer to as the "simulated benefit."

Figure 6.10 shows the plot of cell mean annual household Social Security income versus the instrument by year of birth. The variation in simulated benefits, even conditional on constant earnings histories, is readily apparent in the figure. Benefits rose steadily until 1910, and then ramped up quickly from 1910 through 1916, before falling precipitously in the 1917-to-1921 period and then rising more slowly thereafter. Actual Social Security income tracks this pattern well, with the benefits "notch" apparent in the data. So there is a

Figure 6.10   Real Actual and Simulated Annual Social Security Benefits, by Year of Birth

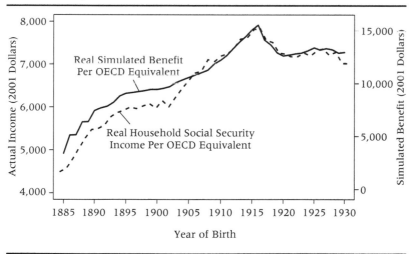

good first-stage relationship here: our legislative-variation instrument clearly predicts actual Social Security incomes.

Regression Specification

To examine the effect of Social Security on elderly poverty, we estimate the following basic specification,

$$(6.4) \qquad P_{it} = \delta' \mathbf{X}_{it} + \theta SSIncome_{it} + u_{it}$$

where i and t index single year of age and calendar year, respectively. P is poverty (or one of the other outcome measures used here), SSIncome is the cell mean reported annual Social Security income, and u is a disturbance term. The parameter θ indicates the change in the proportion of elderly in poverty for a change in Social Security income. $\mathbf{X}$ is a vector of all other explanatory variables. We specify $\delta' X$ as:

$$(6.5) \qquad \delta' \mathbf{X}_{it} = \beta' x_{it} + \sum_{i=65}^{90} \gamma_i D_{it}^{Age\,i} + \sum_{t=1967}^{1999} \alpha_t D_{it}^{Year\,t}$$

where X is a vector of demographic variables that includes controls for cell means of educational attainment of the head (high school diploma, some college, and college or advanced degree), marital status (married, widowed, and divorced in the pooled sample), white, and female. By controlling for these cell characteristics, we control for any other trends in cohort characteristics that might be correlated with both the legislative changes in benefits determination and with poverty. Following Krueger and Pischke (1992), we also include in equation 6.5 a full set of dummies for the age of the head, $D^{Age\,i}$, and calendar-year dummies, $D^{Year\,t}$.[8] The age dummies control for differences across age groups in the outcome measure; the year dummies control for any general time trends in the outcome measure.

Thus, after controlling for age and calendar year, the variation in SSIncome is based only upon year of birth. When we then instrument with the variable described above, which we denote as Z, our model is identified solely by legislative variation in benefits generosity across birth cohorts, and not by any differences in cohort members' earnings history. The regression analysis is based on 950 elderly age-by-year cells. The means of the dependent variable and primary explanatory variable are shown in table 6.1.

Visual Inspection

To illustrate the nature of the regression results that follow, we begin with a visual inspection of the data. Figure 6.11 shows the average poverty rate at ages sixty-five and older for each birth cohort, graphed against our instrument for that birth cohort. There is a rapid decline in poverty for early cohorts, where benefits are rising, and this rate of decline slows substantially after the 1916 cohort, although the decline does continue. This is suggestive of a role for benefits, but the correspondence is not particularly striking.

Figure 6.12 shows a parallel graph for shared living arrangements. Once again, there is a steep decline in the early years of the sample, when benefits are rising most rapidly, then a turnaround and rise in shared living arrangements when Social Security benefits fall and flatten. This evidence is very consistent with a benefits effect on shared living arrangements.

Estimation Results

Table 6.2 shows the grouped ordinary least squares (OLS) and instrumental-variable (IV) estimation results for the full sample that

Table 6.1 Sample Means

Variable	(1) Mean	(2) Standard Deviation
Simulated benefit	$10,507	$2,761
Household SS income per equivalent	$6,896	$1,396
Household absolute poverty rate	18.5%	6.9%
Household relative poverty rate	23.7%	6.3%
Household 90-10 ratio	1.56	0.14
Family SS income per equivalent	$7,288	$1,441
Family absolute poverty rate	27.9%	12.7%
Family relative poverty rate	31.4%	10.9%
Family 90-10 ratio	1.54	0.19
Percentage in shared living arrangements	0.28	0.09

Source: Authors' compilation.
Note: Table shows means and standard deviations for selected variables from the CPS data set described in text.

Figure 6.11   Absolute Poverty of Elderly Households Versus Benefits, by
Year of Birth

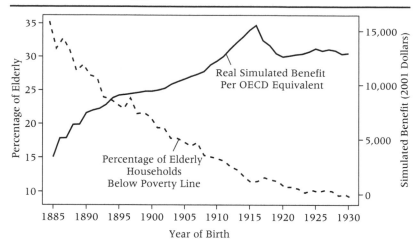

Source: Authors' compilation.

Figure 6.12   Elderly Shared Living Arrangements Versus Benefits, by Year
of Birth

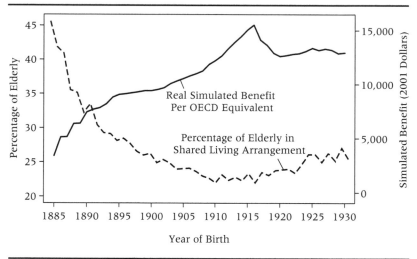

Source: Authors' compilation.

Table 6.2 Estimation Results for Full Sample

Dependent Variable	(1) OLS	(2) IV, Without Controls	(3) IV, with Controls	(4) Log IV	(5) Log IV, with Controls
A. Household level					
Absolute poverty	−.028	−.035	−.031	−.752	−.722
	(.002)	(.003)	(.003)	(.146)	(0.165)
Relative poverty	−.028	−.034	−.035	−1.025	−1.155
	(.002)	(.003)	(.004)	(.127)	(.151)
90-10 ratio	−.055	−.083	−.035	−.478	−.221
	(.009)	(.013)	(.016)	(.072)	(.085)
B. Family level					
Absolute poverty	−.055	−.068	−.057	−1.721	−1.383
	(.003)	(.004)	(.004)	(.174)	(.176)
Relative poverty	−.049	−.057	−.052	−1.693	−1.575
	(.003)	(.004)	(.004)	(.163)	(.178)
90-10 ratio	−.049	−.065	−.018	−.286	−.017
	(.011)	(.015)	(.019)	(.104)	(.118)
Shared living	−.036	−.047	−.038	−2.382	−1.787
	(.003)	(.004)	(.004)	(.221)	(0.211)

Source: Authors' compilation.
Notes: N = 950 for all regressions. Table shows coefficients of interest from regressions that also include the full set of age and year dummies. Standard errors are in parentheses. Regressions "with controls" also include controls for the percentage in age or year cell that are female, white, high school graduate, some college, college graduate, advanced degree, married, divorced or separated, widowed. The IV regressions instrument with the simulated Social Security benefit described in the text. First three columns are estimated in levels; remaining columns, in logs.

includes all elderly, where the weights were based on the cell sizes. Standard errors are shown in parentheses. Each row shows the estimate of θ for the associated outcome measure. Columns 1 and 2 give the grouped OLS and IV estimates of θ with no other controls, respectively. Column 3 gives the IV estimates with other controls.

In columns 1 to 3, in which the outcome and Social Security measures are in levels, all coefficients are multiplied by 1,000 for ease of interpretation, so the coefficient shows the impact of a real $1,000 rise in annual Social Security benefits on the outcome. In column 4, the outcome and the Social Security measures are in logs, so that the coefficients are interpreted as elasticities, and column 5 shows the results in logs with the X controls. Panel A gives estimates for elderly households and panel B, for families.

Using the fraction of elderly households below the federal poverty threshold (the head-count ratio) as the dependent variable (panel A, row 1), a $1,000 increase in annual benefits reduces the poverty rate by 2.8 percentage points (column 1). The IV estimates in columns 2 and 3 imply decreases in the poverty rate of 3.5 and 3.1 percentage points without and with controls, respectively. The IV estimates from the log specification with controls in column 5 imply an elasticity of the poverty rate to Social Security benefits of –0.72, so that if benefits were cut by 10 percent, the poverty rate would be expected to rise by 7.2 *percent* (not percentage points).

Over the 1967-to-2000 period, the poverty rate for this sample fell from 28.3 percent to 11.6 percent, or by 16.7 percentage points, while the simulated Social Security benefit Z rose by $5,760, or 91 percent. Hence, the IV linear estimate in column 3 implies that the increase in Social Security benefits of $5,760 would lead to a 17.8 percent decline in poverty rates. The IV log estimate in column 5 implies that the 91 percent rise in benefits should have led to a 66 percent decline in poverty rates. Both of these estimates are almost exactly the same as the poverty decline experienced by these elderly, suggesting that Social Security can explain all of the decline.

The first row of panel B shows the estimates of θ for the family-level data set. The results for elderly families are much stronger. In column 5, the estimated elasticity of the poverty rate to Social Security benefits is –1.38, which suggests that a cut in benefits of 10 percent would increase the proportion of elderly families in poverty by 13.8 percent. The IV linear estimate in column 3 implies that each $1,000 increase in Social Security benefits would cause a 5.7 percent decline in elderly poverty.

At the family level, the poverty rate fell from 39.4 to 16.9 percent, a decline of 22.5 percentage points (57 percent of base value). Applied to the $5,760 (91 percent) rise in benefits over this period, both of these estimates suggest that, at the family level, poverty actually fell less than it should have, given the rise in benefits. The log estimate suggests that family-level poverty should have fallen by 126 percent (twice the actual fall), and the level estimate suggests that family-level poverty should have fallen by 33 percent (50 percent larger than the actual fall).

The second row of table 6.2 gives the estimates of θ for the relative poverty rate. Increases in Social Security benefits appear to play a strong causal role in reducing poverty for both the levels and log specifications. Once again, there is a much stronger effect for elderly families than for households, a consistent finding throughout the empirical analysis, and one to which we return.

The third row of each panel shows the estimated impact of Social Security on our measure of inequality (the 90-10 difference divided by mean income). For elderly households, there is a significant reduction in inequality, but for elderly families, this finding is very sensitive to the inclusion of controls in the model. Overall, the results in table 6.2 indicate that Social Security has played a very significant role in reducing elderly poverty, measured as (absolute and relative) rates and gaps. However, it may be a fairly blunt instrument at the family level, where there are only insignificant declines in inequality.

The final row of the table shows the impact of Social Security benefits on shared living arrangements. There is a sizable negative effect, with the log estimate suggesting an elasticity of shared living arrangements of 1.8 with respect to the benefit level. This is an enormous effect, much larger than is found in Engelhardt, Gruber, and Perry (2005) for their full sample.

Restricting the Time Period

One disadvantage of the estimation strategy thus far is that it does not focus explicitly on the "notch" variation in benefits. Much of the identification of the results in table 6.2 comes from the run-up in benefits from 1885 onward. If there is a simple birth-cohort trend in poverty, this could be driving a significant portion of the results.

To address this issue, in table 6.3 we reduce the sample of years of birth used to the ten years before and after the benefits peak in 1916. We show the results only for the two IV specifications, with controls, in levels and in logs.

Overall, using these "notch" years for identification confirms our main finding from table 6.2: there is a sizable and significant effect of Social Security benefits in reducing elderly poverty. The log results are very similar to those of table 6.2. The effect on poverty for households rises and for families falls, with both converging in an elasticity of −0.8 to −1, which is still large enough to more than

Table 6.3 Estimation Results When Time Period Restricted to
1906 to 1926

Dependent Variable	(1) IV, with Controls	(2) Log IV, with Controls
A. Household level		
Absolute poverty	−.022	−1.062
	(.004)	(.243)
Relative poverty	−.032	−1.372
	(.005)	(.246)
90-10 ratio	−.016	−.097
	(.022)	(.118)
B. Family level		
Absolute poverty	−.025	−.989
	(.004)	(.206)
Relative poverty	−.030	−1.117
	(.005)	(.189)
90-10 ratio	−.027	−.158
	(.024)	(.137)
Shared living	−.009	−.341
	(.004)	(.174)

Source: Authors' compilation.
Notes: N = 419 for all regressions. Table shows coefficients of interest from regressions that also include the full set of age and year dummies and controls for the percentage in age or year cell that are female, white, high school graduate, some college, college graduate, advanced degree, married, divorced or separated, widowed. Standard errors are in parentheses. The regressions instrument with the simulated Social Security benefit described in the text. First column estimated in levels; the second, in logs.

explain the time-series trends in poverty rates. For the level specification, the convergence between household and family results also occurs, but to a much lower level.

The inequality results also weaken when the sample is restricted, confirming the insignificant effect on inequality of these policy changes. There is also a dramatic reduction in the elasticity of shared living arrangements, which falls to −0.34 and is marginally significant. This is much closer to the full-sample estimate of −0.4 in Engelhardt, Gruber, and Perry (2005), which was estimated on a more restricted set of birth cohorts.

Results by Marital Status

The pooled sample used in table 6.2 combines households of different marital types, some of which might be expected to display quite different responsiveness of Social Security to poverty. For example, because most married couples live independently (of other adults) and have many potential sources of income with which to support themselves, they may be expected to have relatively low sensitivity of poverty to Social Security a priori. Married couples have a much lower baseline rate of poverty than the other groups in our sample: over our sample period, the rate of absolute poverty for married couples is 9.5 percent, whereas it is 26.5 percent for divorcées, 24.2 percent for widows, and 21.3 percent for those never married.

Table 6.4 shows estimation results for four different subsamples, split out by marital status. Once again we show only the level and log IV specifications, including control variables. Surprisingly, married couples appear to have the most elastic poverty response to Social Security, with very large estimated elasticities in table 6.4 across the various outcome measures. The responses for other groups are much smaller, and are only significant at the household level for widows. At the family level, the effects are much larger for widows, although they remain smaller in elasticity form than for married households. The results are also significant in levels, although much smaller, for widows and the never-married at the family level.

One finding that is consistent across all specifications in our analysis is that the impact of Social Security on poverty is stronger for elderly families than for households. Indeed, the final row of the table shows that for all marital status groups, there is a strong effect of Social Security benefits on living in shared arrangements. The findings here are different than those of Engelhardt, Gruber, and Perry (2005), who found a strong effect on living arrangements for widows and divorcées, but not for married couples. These differences are due to differences in birth cohorts used; when the sample is restricted to the narrower set of birth cohorts from 1900 to 1930, the effects on shared living arrangements are much stronger for the widows and divorcées relative to married couples.

As noted earlier, the fact that Social Security impacts living arrangements can explain the much stronger response of family-level poverty measures. If higher Social Security benefits make the

Table 6.4 Results by Marital Status

Dependent Variable	Married		Widowed		Divorced		Never Married	
	(1) IV, with Controls	(2) Log IV, with Controls	(3) IV, with Controls	(4) Log IV, with Controls	(5) IV, with Controls	(6) Log IV, with Controls	(7) IV, with Controls	(8) Log IV, with Controls
A. Household level								
Absolute poverty	-.033	-2.810	-.032	-.574	-.020	-.183	-.012	-.598
	(.004)	(.518)	(.006)	(.168)	(.014)	(.446)	(.016)	(.496)
Relative poverty	-.044	-2.620	-.039	-1.012	-.023	-.427	-.029	-1.122
	(.004)	(.385)	(.006)	(.156)	(.015)	(.430)	(.016)	(.431)
90-10 ratio	-.038	-.240	-.075	-.370	-.024	.090	.060	.117
	(.021)	(.173)	(.023)	(.096)	(.065)	(.307)	(.078)	(.277)
B. Family level								
Absolute poverty	-.040	-3.506	-.093	-1.644	-.041	-.545	-.034	-.731
	(.004)	(.599)	(.007)	(.163)	(.014)	(.405)	(.015)	(.264)
Relative poverty	-.049	-2.827	-.085	-1.803	-.036	-.557	-.032	-.785
	(.005)	(.451)	(.007)	(.170)	(.014)	(.362)	(.015)	(.273)
90-10 ratio	-.026	-.055	-.008	.220	-.001	.252	.014	.170
	(.023)	(.209)	(.031)	(.160)	(.074)	(.439)	(.075)	(.250)
Shared living	-.017	-2.131	-.093	-2.509	-.050	-1.692	-.061	-1.036
	(.004)	(.496)	(.009)	(.229)	(.016)	(.655)	(.019)	(-.305)

Source: Authors' compilation.

Notes: N = cells for married regressions (first set of two columns), 950 for widowed regressions (second set of two columns), 815 cells for widowed regressions (third set of two columns), and 808 for never married regressions (last set of two columns). Table shows coefficients of interest from regressions that also include the full set of age and year dummies and controls for the percentage in age and year cell that are female, white, high school graduate, some college, college graduate, advanced degree. Standard errors are in parentheses. The regressions instrument with the simulated Social Security benefit described in text. First column in each panel estimated in levels; second, in logs.

widowed and divorced more likely to live independently, they will cause the creation of many elderly households that are comparatively poor because they only have elderly in them. Therefore, the endogenous response of living arrangements to benefits will bias downward any estimated poverty improvement among elderly households.

Conclusion

The most frequently cited "victory" in the war on poverty of the 1960s is the dramatic decline in elderly poverty. This poverty decline typically is attributed to the growth in Social Security over this period, but to date there has been little direct assessment of the causal role of the Social Security program in determining elderly poverty. We provide such a direct assessment by using the variation in the generosity of the Social Security program across the 1885-to-1930 birth cohorts. Our analysis suggests that the growth in Social Security indeed can explain the entire decline in poverty among the elderly over this period.

We also highlight the important sensitivity of poverty measurement to living arrangements. Poverty measured at the family level is much more sensitive to increases in program generosity than is poverty measured at the household level. This is consistent with the notion that part of the response to rising Social Security benefits is to encourage increased independent living among lower-income elders.

Although our results are striking, they are not the final word on this important topic. A particularly important question remains: What are the implications of this increase in elderly income for broader measures of well-being, such as consumption? For example, was this rise in income associated one for one with increased consumption, or did it serve to crowd out other sources of consumption smoothing, such as transfers from family members? Analysis of these types of questions is important for a richer understanding of the welfare implications of changes in the Social Security program.

We are very grateful to David Card, Ronald Lee, John Quigley, Timothy Smeeding, symposium participants, and two anonymous referees for comments and to Cindy Perry for excellent research assistance. The views presented in this paper are those of the authors and do not reflect the views of the National Bureau of Economic Research, MIT, or Syracuse University.

Notes

1. In related papers, Stephen E. Snyder and William N. Evans (2002) and Engelhardt, Gruber, and Perry (2005) used the "notch" to examine the effect of income on mortality and living arrangements, respectively.

2. In addition, we constructed poverty measures using a set of more aggregated income measures consistently measured across surveys, and the results of our statistical analysis below did not change. We made no attempt to quantify in-kind transfers (Smeeding 1986) into our gross-income measures.

3. See Jäntti and Sheldon Danziger (2001), Frank A. Cowell (2001), and Gottschalk and Smeeding (2002) for comprehensive recent reviews of various aspects of this literature.

4. See Martin Feldstein and Jeffrey B. Liebman (2001) for a comprehensive recent review of studies on labor supply and saving behavior, and Isabel V. Sawhill (1988), Michael D. Hurd (1990), and Danziger, Haveman, and Plotnick (1981) for earlier reviews. Engelhardt, Gruber, and Perry (2005) review the literature on elderly living arrangements.

5. Three years was the median difference in age between male and female spouses in the 1981 New Beneficiary Survey. An additional factor that influences actual Social Security benefit levels for widows is the age at which the spouse dies (for widows). A widow whose husband dies at a relatively young age will receive less than a widow whose spouse dies at an older age, due to a longer earnings history for the deceased spouse. For a divorcée, the age at which the marriage ends and the duration of the marriage (for divorcées) are also important factors, as divorcées may only make a claim on their former spouses' earnings histories if the marriage lasted at least ten years. Because the March survey did not ask the duration of previous marriages for divorcées or the age at death of the spouse for widows, we could not incorporate these factors into the construction of our instrument.

6. In separate tabulations in the CPS, the median earnings of never-married females are significantly more highly correlated with male earnings than with the earnings of all females.

7. We assume that they claim in June because some cost-of-living (COLA) adjustments were administered in June of a given year, rather than December of a given year. We assume that the beneficiary claims in June so that he or she will receive any COLA in that year. This prevents variation across years of birth resulting simply from the timing of the COLA.

8. The excluded group consists of families with heads' age over ninety, observed in calendar year 2000.

References

Cowell, Frank A. 2001. "Measurement of Inequality." In *Handbook of Income Distribution*, edited by Anthony B. Atkinson and François Bourguignon. Volume 1. Amsterdam: Elsevier.

Danziger, Sheldon, Robert Haveman, and Robert Plotnick. 1981. "How Income Transfers Affect Work, Savings, and the Income Distribution." *Journal of Economic Literature* 19(3): 975–1028.

Engelhardt, Gary V., Jonathan Gruber, and Cynthia D. Perry. 2005. "Social Security and Elderly Living Arrangements." *Journal of Human Resources* 40(2): 354–72.

Feldstein, Martin, and Jeffrey B. Liebman. 2001. "Social Security." In *Handbook of Public Economics*, edited by Alan J. Auerbach and Martin Feldstein. Volume 4. Amsterdam: Elsevier.

Gottschalk, Peter, and Timothy Smeeding. 2002. "Empirical Evidence on Income Inequality in Industrialized Countries." In *Handbook of Income Distribution*, edited by Anthony B. Atkinson and François Bourguignon. Volume 1. Amsterdam: Elsevier.

Hurd, Michael D. 1990. "Research on the Elderly: Economic Status, Retirement, and Consumption." *Journal of Economic Perspectives* 28(2): 565–637.

Jäntti, Markus, and Sheldon Danziger. 2001. "Income Poverty in Advanced Countries." In *Handbook of Income Distribution*, edited by Anthony B. Atkinson and François Bourguignon. Volume 1. Amsterdam: Elsevier.

Krueger, Alan, and Jörn-Steffen Pischke. 1992. "The Effect of Social Security on Labor Supply: A Cohort Analysis of the Notch Generation." *Journal of Labor Economics* 10(4): 412–37.

Moffitt, Robert A. 1987. "Life-Cycle Labor Supply and Social Security: A Time-Series Analysis." In *Work, Health, and Income Among the Elderly*, edited by Gary Burtless. Washington, D.C.: Brookings Institution.

Sawhill, Isabel V. 1988. "Poverty in the U.S.: Why Is It So Persistent?" *Journal of Economic Literature* 26:3.

Smeeding, Timothy. 1986. "Nonmoney Income and the Elderly: The Case of the 'Tweeners.' " *Journal of Policy Analysis and Management* 5(4): 707–24.

Smolensky, Eugene, Sheldon Danziger, and Peter Gottschalk. 1988. "The Declining Significance of Age in the United States: Trends in the Well-Being of Children and the Elderly Since 1939." In *The Vulnerable*, edited by John L. Palmer, Timothy Smeeding, and Barbara Boyle Torrey. Washington, D.C.: Urban Institute.

Snyder, Stephen E., and William N. Evans. 2002. "The Impact of Income on Mortality: Evidence from the Social Security Notch." NBER working paper no. 9197. Cambridge, Mass.: National Bureau of Economic Research.

U.S. Social Security Administration. Various years. *Annual Statistical Supplement.* Washington: U.S. Social Security Administration.

Chapter 7

The Measurement and Evolution of Health Inequality: Evidence from the U.S. Medicare Population

JONATHAN SKINNER AND WEIPING ZHOU

The technological revolution in health care has brought both great benefits with respect to survival and general well-being, and substantial increases in costs.[1] Whether these changes have reduced inequality in health care or in health outcomes is not well understood. Earlier research suggested that medical-care innovations, such as the use of antibiotics in the treatment of tuberculosis, reduced health-care disparities by race (McDermott 1978). On the other hand, studies of health-care expenditures by income group found higher income groups accounting for a larger fraction of spending, particularly after accounting for health status.[2] Recent studies also suggest that better-educated patients get access to newer drugs (Lleras-Muney and Lichtenberg 2002), survive longer following the diagnosis of cancer (Glied and Lleras-Muney 2003), and comply better with regimens for the treatment of AIDS (Goldman and Smith 2002).

This chapter returns to the question of whether technological advances and increases in health-care expenditures have been associated with an increase or a decrease of inequality in health or in health care. The group studied is the over-sixty-five population in the United States during the 1990s, which is of interest given their high rates of utilization and very high rates of insurance coverage under the Medicare program. Initially, two conventional measures of inequality are considered: health-care expenditures and health-care outcomes as measured by ten-year survival rates. Using detailed Medicare claims data on a panel of several million people in the over-sixty-five population in the United States back to 1987, we matched individuals to income deciles on the basis of median income in their zip code of residence. Between 1987 and 2001, we found a dramatic increase in health-care expenditures among the lowest-income groups, accounting for a 78 percent increase ($2,624) in real terms, compared to a 34 percent increase ($1,214) for those in the top-income decile. Using expenditures as a marker for health inequality, one would conclude that inequality has lessened, and if anything the higher (annual) expenditures for lower-income households would help to compensate for earlier years during which insurance coverage and preventive care were minimal.[3]

There are, however, a variety of disadvantages to using expenditures for health care as a measure of access. Expenditures may reflect patient preferences, health status, and access to care, nor is it clear how expenditures on health care translate into health outcomes (for example, Fisher et al. 2003). For example, much of the differential increase in expenditures by income group during this period was accounted for by home health care. One government investigation found that 40 percent of Medicare home health care spending was deemed "inappropriate" (Havemann 1997), suggesting that the actual benefits accruing to patients fell short of the money spent on them.

A different picture emerges in the evolution of outcomes as measured by ten-year survival rates. All income groups experienced a survival gain during the 1990s, but those in higher-income groups did better: life expectancy rose by .2 years in the bottom income decile, compared to .8 years in the top-income decile. But this measure is not immune from criticism either. Individual decisions regarding healthy behavior exert an important influence on health outcomes over the life course, and it is rarely clear whether these choices should be attributed to "preferences," education, or economic status per se (Graham 2002; Contoyannis and Jones 2004; Smith 2003). As well, long and variable lags in outcomes make it difficult to evaluate the impact of current health-care expenditures on changes in current health outcomes, particularly when income itself is endogenous to health status (Case and Deaton 2003).

That the two measures of health inequality are contradictory suggests the need for a different approach. We propose focusing on a more limited set of effective (or high-quality) utilization measures with well-established benefits.[4] These measures include mammography screening among women aged sixty-five to sixty-nine, eye examinations for diabetics, smoking-cessation advice, aspirin, beta-blockers, and reperfusion in the first twelve hours following a heart attack. The latter three treatments accounted for the vast majority of improvement in thirty-day survival following heart attacks (Heidenreich and McClellan 2001). The advantage of these measures over expenditures is that one need not control for health status; nearly everyone in the appropriate universe should be receiving these treatments. Nor does one need to control for preferences toward health care or for lifestyle differences; every appropriate heart attack patient should be receiving beta-blockers upon admission, regardless of whether they are marathon runners or couch potatoes.[5] The use of these measures is not dependent on genetic or environmental factors that might further confound differences in survival rates across income groups. As well, there is increasing effort to use these measures as components of health-care quality indices, for example, by the National Committee for Quality Assurance (NCQA) at the hospital level or at the state level (for example, Stephen F. Jencks, Edwin D. Huff, and Timothy Cuerdon 2003).

Using the Medicare claims data augmented with the Cooperative Cardiovascular Project (CCP) data for heart-attack patients from 1994 to 1995, we find distinct income gradients with regard to the use of effective care. For mammography, in 1993 examination rates for the top-income decile were 16 percentage points higher than that for the lowest decile, and by 2001 the gap had shrunk only slightly, to 15 percentage points. For the inpatient treatment of heart attacks in 1994/95, where the use of effective care is unlikely to have any incremental impact on patient costs and where noncompliance is minimal, the income gradients are smaller; seven percentage points for beta-blockers and five percentage points for reperfusion therapy within twelve hours, with no significant differences in aspirin or ACE-inhibitor use.[6]

In sum, the dramatic increases in relative Medicare expenditures for low-income neighborhoods during the past several decades have not translated into similar improvements in health outcomes. The apparent lack of relative improvement in effective care among the lowest-income groups makes this puzzle less surprising, but by itself cannot explain the *widening* of survival trends by income group.[7] Still, the use of effective care measures can allow the government to work toward actually doing something about inequality in health care. Monitoring and rewarding providers and patients to raise rates of effective care close to the 100 percent ideal for all Medicare enrollees would have the additional salutary effect of erasing inequality in the dimension of effective care.

The Measurement of Health and Health-Care Inequality

It is important to distinguish between inequality in health care and inequality in health. There is a long history of measuring inequality in health care by the use of utilization or expenditures measures. Julian LeGrand (1978, 1982) and others found a positive gradient between expenditures and income after controlling for measures of health status in the United Kingdom, even several decades after the establishment of the National Health Insurance. Although there was a lively debate about how best to measure income-based gradients in health care (Wagstaff, van Doorslaer, and Paci 1991; LeGrand 1991), the positive association between expenditures and income has been found in many countries, with just a few exceptions (Wagstaff, van Doorslaer, and Paci 1991). The earlier evidence from the United States pointed toward the same positive association between expenditures and income (Davis and Reynolds 1975; Link, Long, and Settle 1982), although more recent data on Medicare expenditures in the 1990s suggests that lower-income households have begun to account for higher levels of spending (Lee, McClellan, and Skinner 1999; McClellan and Skinner, forthcoming).

Health-care expenditures have been used to construct measures of "full income" that include both money income and government-financed health-care expenditures. This approach was pioneered by Eugene Smolensky and his colleagues at the University of Wisconsin during the 1970s in the study of income distribution (Reynolds and Smolensky 1977; Moon 1977), and was extended to valuing health-care benefits in a money-metric context (Smolensky et al. 1977). More recently, Victor Fuchs (1998a, 2001) has used this approach to document the very large fraction of full income among the elderly in the United States made up of health-care expenditures, most of which is paid for by younger generations. The implicit message in creating full-income measures is the opportunity cost of health-care spending, that a reduction in health-care spending could have a large impact on money income, particularly among low-income groups.

The interest in illness-adjusted expenditures or utilization can be motivated by a concern about access to care, where the null hypothesis of perfect equality is presumably one where high-income and low-income individuals with similar medical ailments would be treated with the same procedures and with the same degree of intensity. But some have questioned whether equal rates of utilization are really the same as equal access, for example if people with high incomes experienced different preferences for care (Mooney et al. 1991; Culyer, van Doorslaer, and Wagstaff 1992). While economists are generally comfortable taking preferences as given, the issue is less clear in the health-care literature. For example, Said A. Ibrahim (2001, 2002) documented more distrust of surgery among black candidates for hip or knee replacement than among whites; they placed greater reliance on alternative (nonsurgical) approaches such as copper bracelets or prayer. Jeffrey N. Katz (2001) has distinguished between preferences "guided by informed decisions" and those "limited by truncated opportunities or historical circumstances." Thus, if low-income households are less likely to seek care because of past adverse encounters with the health-care system, their choices today may be related less to immutable preferences and more to past financial or cultural barriers in access to care.

Another shortcoming of using health expenditures is that higher levels of expenditures may not translate into better health outcomes. James A. Glover (1938) counseled against the overuse of tonsillectomies at a time when the risk of surgical complications was high. He and his colleagues noted that children of anxious high-income parents were more likely to receive the procedure and hence were more likely to be exposed to the risk of operative mortality. More generally, Elliott S. Fisher et al. (2003) have suggested that regions with greater use of health care were no more likely to experience better outcomes or even improved satisfaction of patients and improved access to care. In other words, higher expenditures do not always translate into better health.

In the past decade, there has been an increasing interest in the inequality of health, whether measured as life span, quality-adjusted life years, healthy life years, or self-reported health.[8] Measuring health outcomes avoids the problem of inferring the effectiveness of health-care expenditures on outcomes. It also has the advantage of capturing income-based differences in a variety of factors such as health behavior, diet, and life-course events that have a larger impact on health outcomes than does the health-care system alone. In sum, the estimated gradient between income and health outcomes tends to be considerably stronger than the estimated gradient between income and health-care utilization.

Inequality in health outcomes can be present even in the absence of inequality in health care. Suppose that the health-care system were perfectly equal and provided instant access to all people in society. Inequality in outcomes could still occur, for a variety of reasons. The first is simply luck, or genetic differences across the population (Gakidou, Murray, and Frenk 2000). However, most summary measures of income-based health inequality remove this source of inequality by averaging over large numbers of individuals. For example, the "concentration index" compares the cumulative distribution of income on the horizontal axis and the cumulative distribution of healthy life years (however measured) on the vertical axis, thereby averaging out variation occurring within income categories.[9]

The second source of life-span inequality arises from potential differences in health behavior such as diet, smoking, exercise, drinking, and other factors associated with income and socioeconomic status. In effect, "Inequalities in health reflect the wider inequalities in society" (LeGrand 1982, 45). For example, Paul Contoyannis and Andrew M. Jones (2004) report that these measures of "healthy living" in 1984 were strong predictors of positive good health in 1991. Of course, this raises the very difficult question again of how one can separate "preferences" for health-related behavior from income per se. Exogenous health-care shocks can also have long-lasting effects on health, for example, as in Douglas Almond's (2003) study of the long-term negative repercussions of being in utero during the 1918 influenza epidemic. Long-term health shocks can also affect both earnings capacity and health, muddying the causal link between income and health outcomes even further (Case and Deaton 2003; Elstad and Krokstad 2003; Graham 2002).

We suggest a more restrictive but theoretically cleaner measure of health-care inequality: the utilization rates of effective care, where effective care is defined as procedures that are efficacious for every appropriate patient. Examples include mammography screening for women aged sixty-five to sixty-nine, and the use of beta-blockers, aspirin, reperfusion therapies, and ACE inhibitors for heart-attack patients. (ACE inhibitors are angiotensin-converting enzyme-inhibiting vasodilator drugs that were introduced in 1981.) Mammography has been adopted as a measure of preventive care in other studies as well (for example, see Decker, forthcoming); Card, Dobkin, and Maestas 2004).

There are several advantages in using such measures. The first is the existence of a reliable link between utilization and health outcomes. Second, there is no need to control (however imperfectly) for health status, since among appropriate or ideal patients, nearly everyone should receive the treatment. Finally, preferences should generally not play a strong role in the use of such interventions, given that the objective benefits are so much larger than the costs.[10] Trends or levels in several of these effective-care measures will be considered further, but first we will examine the empirical record on the evolution of health-care expenditures and survival by income group.

The Distribution of Medicare Expenditures by Zip Code Income

The Continuous Medicare History Survey (CMHS), a 5 percent sample of Medicare enrollees, is used to consider the secular trends of overall Medicare expenditures by income decile. Because individual income is not available in the Medicare claims data, we instead use median zip code income from the 1990 U.S. Census, which is assigned to each individual in the Medicare denominator file on the basis of their mailing-address zip code. (The results are not sensitive to the use of the 2000 census income data.) There are advantages and disadvantages of using zip code income from the census instead of individual income data from surveys. On the one hand, the neighborhood that a person lives in may better reflect permanent income than self-reported income, which may be infested with measurement error and transitory income and, particularly for the elderly population, may not reflect important components of household wealth. On the other hand, zip code income is subject to "ecological bias," such that poor Medicare enrollees in rich neighborhoods could be treated differently from rich enrollees in poor neighborhoods. One previous study, however, has suggested that zip code income provides a reasonably good characterization of income in health-related research (Geronimus, Bound, and Neidert 1996).

In quantifying health-care expenditures for the population over sixty-five, we express all expenditures in 2001 dollars and estimate age- and sex-specific expenditures in five-year age increments (plus those over eighty-five) for each of ten income deciles. In aggregated data, we use direct adjustment to normalize the per-capita Medicare expenditures to a constant age and sex composition over time by use of the sample frequencies of the ten age and sex categories.[11] Only fee-for-service Medicare enrollees are included in the sample, which means that expenditures made on behalf of enrollees in Medicare managed care plans will not be included.[12] The sample size is sufficiently large (30.8 million person-years) that standard errors are small, and so are not reported.

Table 7.1 and figure 7.1 present expenditures for selected income deciles, 1987 to 2001. Not surprisingly, real Medicare expenditures

Table 7.1 Medicare Expenditures by Year and Zip-Code-Income Decile, in 2001 Dollars

	Decile 1	Decile 3	Decile 5	Decile 8	Decile 10
1987	3,346	3,159	3,228	3,478	3,588
1988	3,548	3,309	3,343	3,556	3,656
1989	3,926	3,619	3,590	3,817	3,980
1990	4,068	3,637	3,698	3,904	3,970
1991	4,265	3,852	3,811	4,050	4,022
1992	4,457	4,039	3,914	4,119	4,123
1993	4,740	4,140	4,102	4,199	4,219
1994	5,365	4,553	4,465	4,432	4,464
1995	5,743	4,736	4,702	4,605	4,611
1996	5,998	4,931	4,804	4,596	4,675
1997	6,120	5,073	4,778	4,651	4,666
1998	6,337	5,311	5,031	4,804	4,908
1999	6,153	5,299	5,002	4,719	4,946
2000	5,895	5,068	4,885	4,614	4,725
2001	5,970	5,080	4,873	4,574	4,802
Dollar change, 1987 to 2001	2,624	1,921	1,645	1,096	1,214
Percentage change, 1987 to 2001	78.4	60.8	51.0	31.5	33.8

Source: Authors' calculations using the Continuous Medicare History Survey.
Notes: These estimates of expenditures adjust for age and sex. All expenditures are in real 2001 dollars, adjusted using the GDP deflator.

Figure 7.1   Medicare Annual Expenditures 1987 to 2001, by Income Decile

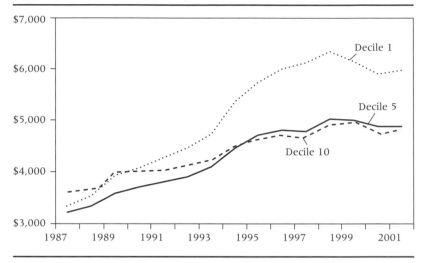

Source: Authors' calculations using the Continuous Medicare History Survey.
Note: These estimates of expenditures adjust for age and sex.

have increased during this period. However, the rates of growth by income group are quite different; the bottom decile experienced a 78 percent increase in real expenditures, in contrast to the top decile, which had just a 34 percent increase.

The advantage of health-care dollar expenditures is that these changes in spending can be compared to changes over the same period of time in median money income, as measured in the Current Population Survey. The real median increase in family income during the period 1987 to 2001 was $2,551.[13] In 1993, the average household size of elderly people living either alone or with a spouse was 1.47,[14] so the per-capita increase in income per elderly person was $1,735 ($2,551 divided by 1.47). Note that the dollar increase in expenditures for the lowest-income decile was $2,624, compared to $1,214 for the highest-income group. Thus, the size of the differential increase (or "twist") in Medicare expenditures was $1,410 ($2,624 minus $1,214), or the amount of money that would have been left "on the table" had Medicare costs for the lowest-income group grown at the same rate as the highest-income group. This differential increase is therefore 81 percent of the total increase in money income for the elderly population during the period 1987 to 2001. It is also larger than the average *level* of per-capita benefits from the Earned Income Tax Credit (EITC) program, estimated to be $1,287 (in 2001 dollars) among the near-poor (Short and Garner 2002). Unlike the EITC, the redistribution occurring in the Medicare program was largely unintended, and the differential benefits to the lowest-income group are still not well understood.[15]

Why the differential growth in expenditures? One reason was the growth in the Disproportionate Share Hospitals (DSH) program, which provided higher reimbursements for hospitals in low-income neighborhoods (see Baicker and Staiger 2004). Another factor was the rapid expansion of home health care during the 1990s. Beginning in the late 1980s, when restrictions on the use of home health care were eased, there were dramatic increases in the use of home health care, particularly in certain regions of the country such as Texas, Florida, and Tennessee (Wennberg and Cooper 1999). Because of the rapid growth in expenditures, and an accompanying increase in scandals, Congress restricted its use sharply in 1997. These expenditures for home health care were concentrated to a large extent in the poorest zip codes of the United States.[16] Figure 7.2 shows average home-health-care spending for the eighty-plus population (the most common users of home health care) by year for deciles 1 (the lowest-income decile), 5, and 10 (the highest-income decile). These are measures of spending per Medicare enrollee age eighty and older, and are not restricted just to users of home health care. There was rapid growth in home-health-care expenditures for all income groups, but the growth for decile 1 was particularly notable, rising to $1,635 per elderly enrollee before dropping after 1997, when the Balanced Budget Act clamped down on unrestricted use.

How much of this spending benefited low-income patients, either through improved survival or improved quality of life? In 1997, a report by the General Accounting Office suggested that 40 percent of all home-health-care costs were "inappropriate" (Havemann 1997). In this case, "inappropriate" meant care resulting from fraud (for example, a physician prescribing tests for sexually transmitted diseases to all of his home-health-care patients in order to get the payments) or care that the patient simply was not eligible to receive. A recent paper by Robin McKnight (2004) did not find adverse health consequences caused by the sharp decline in home-health-care

Figure 7.2 Home Health Care Expenditures for Medicare Enrollees Aged 80 and Over, 1987 to 2001

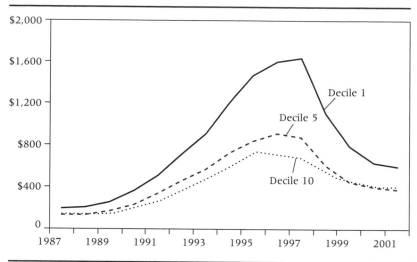

Source: Authors' calculations using the Continuous Medicare History Survey.
Note: These estimates of expenditures adjust for age (two categories: eighty to eighty-four and eighty-five and older) and sex.

benefits in 1997, although there was a modest consequent increase in out-of-pocket medical expenses. In short, one should be cautious about attributing all dollar increases in Medicare expenditures to the people who nominally "receive" the benefit.[17] Home health care is not the only service provided during the 1990s that may have fraudulently inflated providers' bank accounts, but it was certainly the most visible.[18]

The Distribution of Survival Gains by Income

We next consider overall survival gains in the Medicare population. Here the sample includes not just the fee-for-service population but also the HMO enrollees; this is to avoid potential selection bias caused by healthier individuals' joining managed-care organizations. We consider two different cohorts from the Continuous Medicare History Survey. The first cohort consists of people in 1982 who were either aged sixty-five to sixty-nine or aged seventy-five to seventy-nine. The second cohort consists of people in 1992 who were in the same age groups, sixty-five to sixty-nine and seventy-five to seventy-nine. For both the 1982 and 1992 cohorts, figure 7.3 shows the ten-year survival rate, in percentage terms, for the younger age groups (aged sixty-five to sixty-nine). There is a clear income gradient for both cohorts; people living in higher-income zip codes were more likely to survive whether in the 1980s or 1990s. In table 7.2 a similar pattern is shown for those aged seventy-five to seventy-nine.

Comparing the 1982 and 1992 cohorts, it is important to note all income groups benefited in the sense of experiencing a higher ten-year survival probability. However, the highest-income groups

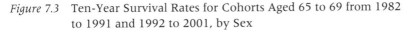

Figure 7.3   Ten-Year Survival Rates for Cohorts Aged 65 to 69 from 1982 to 1991 and 1992 to 2001, by Sex

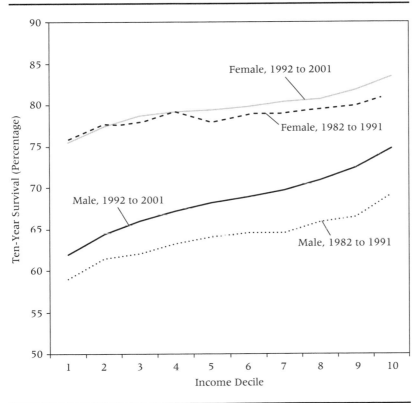

Source: Authors' compilation.

Table 7.2 Ten-Year Survival Probabilities 1982 to 1991 and 1992 to 2001, by Age and Sex

| | Aged 65 to 69 | | | | Aged 75 to 79 | | | |
| | Male | | Female | | Male | | Female | |
Income Decile	82 to 91	92 to 01	82 to 91	92 to 01	82 to 91	92 to 01	82 to 91	92 to 01
1	59.0	61.9	75.8	75.4	34.6	35.1	51.2	51.8
2	61.5	64.3	77.5	77.4	35.3	36.5	53.3	53.1
3	62.0	66.0	77.8	78.7	35.0	37.6	53.6	54.1
4	63.2	67.2	79.2	79.2	34.8	37.6	53.8	55.0
5	64.1	68.2	77.9	79.4	36.0	39.7	53.9	55.1
6	64.5	68.9	78.8	79.8	36.1	39.8	53.9	54.8
7	64.6	69.7	79.0	80.4	35.4	39.9	53.8	55.7
8	65.8	70.9	79.4	80.7	37.3	41.0	54.1	56.2
9	66.5	72.5	79.8	81.8	38.2	42.9	54.1	56.3
10	69.2	74.8	81.1	83.4	38.7	44.8	54.7	57.1
Sample	188,177	217,272	229,308	263,093	98,053	126,011	152,606	187,554

Source: Authors' calculations using the Continuous Medicare History Survey.

gained the most, both in terms of relative odds ratios, or in terms of absolute gains in expected lifespan.

To quantify these changes in terms of the change in expected survival years, we chain together the two panels of ten-year survival curves for the younger and older cohorts, and estimate the change in expected survival years for a synthetic cohort over a twenty-year period (from sixty-five to sixty-nine to eighty-five to eighty-nine) with fixed weights for men and women based on the fraction of women in the cohort aged sixty-five to sixty-nine (54.8 percent). There was a .2 increase in expected life years in the bottom income decile, a .5 increase in the fifth decile, and a .8 increase in the top-income decile.[19]

Inequality in the Provision of Effective Care

Here we focus on specific measures of effective care, considering first mammography rates (percentage of women who receive mammographies) among women aged sixty-five to sixty-nine in the Medicare population.[20] The advantage of using mammography rates is that we have a time series on rates of screening from 1993 to 2001 and so can measure changes over time in screening rates. A 5 percent sample of part B physician-claims data is used from 1993 to 1997, and a 20 percent sample is used from 1998 to 2001. The later 20 percent sample also includes hospital outpatient data as separate from physician-based claims; these would include women who were screened, for example, in a hospital-based clinic. In theory, excluding such outpatient records for all years could bias our results if low-income women were more likely to receive care in an outpatient setting. In practice, as we show using data from 1998 to 2001, the bias is small or nonexistent.

Table 7.3 reports these mammography screening rates by selected income deciles, but also include (in brackets) the 1998 to 2001 rates that include the outpatient screening data. Although all the rates rose, the relative magnitudes by income group remained largely unchanged (see figure 7.4).

A pronounced income gradient in mammography rates persists throughout the period of analysis. In 1993, the range in screening rates between decile 1 and decile 10 was sixteen percentage points, whereas in 2001 the range had shrunk slightly, to fifteen percentage

Table 7.3   Mammography Rates of Women Aged 65 to 69, by Year and Zip-Code-Income Decile

	Decile 1	Decile 3	Decile 5	Decile 8	Decile 10
1993	20.7	25.9	28.2	30.6	34.6
1994	22.8	28.3	30.1	32.2	35.7
1995	24.0	30.1	31.7	33.0	36.8
1996	23.8	29.0	30.0	32.4	36.1
1997	24.7	29.3	31.6	33.3	37.1
1998	32.0	39.5	41.0	43.5	46.7
	[34.8]	[42.0]	[43.9]	[45.7]	[48.5]
1999	34.3	41.9	43.6	45.4	48.1
	[36.8]	[44.2]	[45.8]	[47.5]	[49.8]
2000	34.6	42.6	44.7	45.9	48.3
	[36.9]	[44.8]	[46.6]	[47.8]	[49.9]
2001	36.5	44.0	45.3	47.0	49.4
	[38.5]	[45.9]	[47.0]	[48.5]	[50.7]
Change from 1993 to 2001	15.8	18.1	17.0	16.4	14.8
Change from 1997 to 2001	11.7	14.7	13.7	13.7	12.3

Source: Authors' calculations using the Medicare Part B data.
Note: Numbers in brackets use both the Medicare Part B data and the Medicare outpatient data to estimate the frequency of mammograms.

points. A notable feature of the data is the sharp jump in rates between 1997 and 1998—the consequence of removing the $100 co-insurance payment on January 1, 1998, and allowing reimbursement for annual rather than biannual screening. It is surprising that rates for all income groups appear to have risen by about the same amount, given that low-income households should have been most sensitive to the relaxation of the $100 co-payment.

Similar results for 1998 to 2001 were also found when rates of screening for eye examinations among patients with diabetics were compared (available upon request from the authors). These examinations check for damage to the vascular system caused by high uncontrolled blood-glucose levels. Despite the shorter time period covered, it was possible to establish that there was, again, no evidence of trends in the income-based gradient of diabetes-related eye examinations.

Figure 7.4 Change in Mammography Rates for Females Aged 65 to 69 During 1993 to 2001, by Income Decile

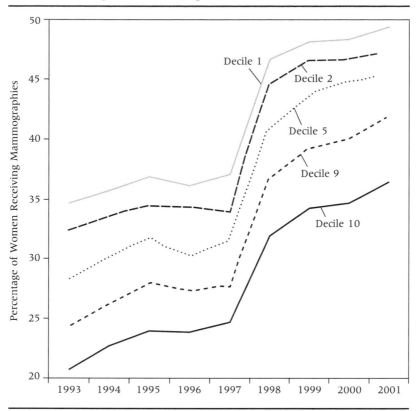

Source: Authors' calculations using the Medicare Part B data.
Note: The 100-dollar co-insurance fee was removed on January 1, 1998.

Of course, some part of the income-based differential could be the consequence of noncompliance—that is, that lower-income patients don't sign up or show up for their screening appointments. We therefore considered physician directives or procedures performed in the first few days following acute myocardial infarction, where the primary goal of the physician is to keep the patient alive, and patient preferences and noncompliance issues should play a small role. The measures of effective care for heart-attack patients are derived from the Cooperative Cardiovascular Project (CCP) survey of more than 160,000 AMI (acute myocardial infarction) patients over the age of sixty-five in 1994 to 1995. The survey information included detailed clinical data from chart reviews along with information on the patient's treatment. This allowed clinical researchers to determine from the chart data patients who were "ideal" or appropriate for the use of the specific treatment; thus the right rate should be a number near 100 percent, regardless of health status, income, age, or any other characteristic.[21] For this reason, we do not control for covariates or health indices, but consider simple averages by income decile. Table 7.4 presents income-based differences in utilization of effective care and, in the bottom row, the total sample size. Approximate 95 percent confidence intervals are presented at the bottom of the table; these apply to each of the means in the column because the deciles ensure equal sample sizes and the exact binomial confidence intervals are based on the average ratio.

Table 7.4 suggests that in 1994 to 1995, utilization of these measures was remarkably low. For example, the beta-blockers were used

Table 7.4   Rates of Effective Care for Acute Myocardial Infarction in 1994 to 1995, by Income Decile

Zip-Code-Income Decile	Beta-Blocker Use at Discharge[a]	Ace Inhibitor at Discharge[b]	Reperfusion Within 12 Hours	Smoking Advice Given[c]
1	40	57	32	33
2	39	57	32	35
3	43	60	33	34
4	45	59	33	35
5	45	59	34	37
6	44	57	35	34
7	45	59	37	34
8	47	59	37	37
9	45	59	36	35
10	47	59	37	35
Approximate 95 percent confidence interval	±1.4	±2.2	±1.7	±2.3
Sample size	50,156	19,286	32,097	17,151

Source: Authors' calculations using the Cooperative Cardiovascular Project (CCP) dataset.
[a]Universe: appropriate (beta-blocker) or eligible (for reperfusion).
[b]Universe: ideal patients.
[c]Universe: smokers.

for less than half of appropriate patients when the target rates should have been closer to 100 percent. Second, rates of use for effective care were modestly elevated among higher-income groups; for example, rates of beta-blockers ranged from 40 percent among the lowest-income decile to 47 percent in the top-income decile. Indeed, for some treatments, such as the use of ACE inhibitors to control hypertension, there were no income-based difference in utilization.

One additional question is whether high-income individuals are more likely to receive higher-quality care because of treatment differences within regions, or because they are more likely to live in regions where overall effective-care rates are higher (Chandra and Skinner 2003). Figure 7.5 shows utilization rates for beta-blockers estimated with and without categorical regional variables. First the previous results were replicated in a logistic-regression with coefficients converted to percentage screening rates. Second, state

Figure 7.5   Income Gradient for the Use of Beta-Blockers Among Ideal Patients, 1994 and 1995

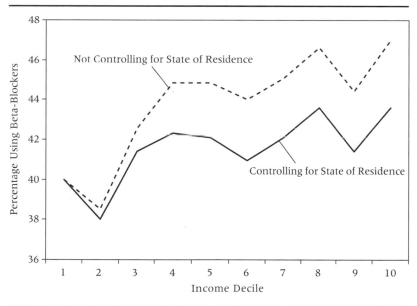

Source: Authors' calculations using the Cooperative Cardiovascular Project data.

dummy variables were then added to the regression, and it was re-estimated, again with odds ratios converted to probabilities, as shown in figure 7.5.

The adjusted probability of beta-blocker use, holding constant the state of residence, shows just a 3.6-percentage-point difference by income group rather than a 7-percentage-point difference. (In this latter regression, only the eighth- and tenth-decile coefficients were significantly different from zero.) That is, half of the income gradient here is the consequence of where patients live and not how patients are treated within regions. The result does not generalize, however. A similar analysis for mammography and diabetes-related eye exams in 1998 to 2001 did not suggest any diminution in the effects of income on utilization rates after controlling for region of residence.[22]

In theory, we would like to know how the income gradient in beta-blocker use evolved over time, but we have just one observation from the survey, in 1994 to 1995. Since the use of beta-blockers for heart-attack patients was rare before the early 1980s, we may safely infer that the observed difference in 1994 to 1995 reflects a somewhat higher growth rate in the use of beta-blockers among the top-income deciles, at least through 1994 to 1995. Since then compliance has improved, but in 2001, median compliance was still less than 70 percent (Jencks, Huff, and Cuerdon 2003). It is possible that rates of compliance have risen more rapidly in low-income regions, but Alabama was low in the use of beta-blockers in 1994 to 1995 and it remained relatively low in 2001.

Conclusions and Discussion

How should one judge whether inequality of health care and of health has improved or worsened during the past several decades? This paper has considered several alternative approaches to measuring inequality using U.S. data from the elderly Medicare population over the age of sixty-five. Medicare expenditures grew much more rapidly among the lowest-income deciles than among higher deciles, but health outcomes improved much less rapidly for this group than for other groups. Beginning at least with Victor Fuchs's comparison of Nevada and Utah, two states with similar health-care expenditures but very different mortality rates (Fuchs 1998b), economists and health-services researchers have long recognized the distinction between inequality in health care as measured by expenditures and inequality in health as measured by survival.

We suggest a different approach to measuring inequality, one that relies on effective care, or measures of health-care quality. The efficacy of these treatments is well proven and benefits most patients (aside from those with contraindications for the treatment), regardless of health status or preferences. An examination of the past decade suggests that there has been little or no relative improvement in the utilization of effective-care measures among lower-income deciles. Thus the discordance between rapidly rising health expenditures of low-income households and rapidly rising longevity of high-income households is not quite so puzzling. Overall expenditures may have risen disproportionately among low-income Medicare recipients, but the use of effective care with a proven impact on health outcomes has not.

It should be cautioned that the magnitudes of the differences in effective care observed in the data would not be expected to have a large impact on overall mortality rates. The predicted impact on heart-attack patients of an increase of seven percentage points in the range of use of beta-blockers (the difference between the rates of use in the highest- and lowest-income deciles) is a decline in mortality of .21 percentage point, or an overall impact on the general population of about .01 percent, since just 5 percent of the Medicare population experience a heart attack in any year.[23] The fact that these measures of effective care account for a small fraction of overall expenditures and a small fraction of the overall variation in health outcomes motivates interest in other measures of quality, for example, the overuse of marginally effective procedures (Fisher et al. 2003).

There are three important limitations of this study. The first is that in using outcome data, we have focused only on survival and not on quality-adjusted or "healthy life years." To capture a fuller measure of health, it would be necessary to include income-based differentials in treatments with proven effectiveness for improving functioning, not just survival per se. Examples include hip or knee replacements for the treatment of osteoarthritis or the use of angioplasty for patients with ischemic heart disease. However, measuring true income-based differences in health status is more difficult, since it would be necessary to adjust for differential health needs such as rates of osteoarthritis of the hip by income group and for preferences—however defined—regarding surgical intervention.[24]

Second, the study is limited to the population over sixty-five. Focusing just on income-based differences in mammography rates within the Medicare program ignores the fact that Medicare itself contributes to a substantial increase in mammography rates at age sixty-five among those who were previously uncovered by insurance or are in lower educational groups (Decker, forthcoming; Card, Dobkin, and Maestas 2004). Focusing just on inequality within a specific age group ignores changes in inequality across age groups, for example differences between those under age sixty-five, who increasingly lack health insurance, and those over age sixty-five, who are generally covered (Danziger, Haveman, and Smolensky 1977).

Finally, we have not considered the financing side of the Medicare program. During the 1990s payments rose and also became more progressive as general income taxes became a larger source of revenue (McClellan and Skinner, forthcoming). The new prescription drug benefits passed into law in 2003 should also contribute to an increasing degree of redistribution to the extent that future growth in benefits is financed out of general tax revenue. It seems unlikely that this increased future progressivity in the Medicare program should justify the more rapid increases in the longevity of higher-income households, however.

A singular advantage of focusing on equality in effective care (or quality of care) is that there are reasonable approaches to fixing the problem of inequality in health outcomes. Monitoring claims data in real time with the objective of raising rates to ideal levels of near 100 percent among appropriate candidates is one sure way to at least reduce income-based inequality. Of course, inequality in outcomes due to other factors would continue to persist for many years, but at least such differences would not be exacerbated by inequality in health care. Indeed, one could imagine "nondiscrimination" rules like those developed for 401(k) pension plans, whereby hospitals or health-care systems would experience a partial loss in Medicare funding if effective-care measures for their low-income patients fell too far below those for their high-income patients.

This chapter was prepared for the symposium in honor of Eugene Smolensky, Berkeley, California, December 12 to 13, 2003. We are grateful to Alan Auerbach, Katherine Baicker, David Card, Victor Fuchs, Julian LeGrand, John Quigley, and seminar participants for helpful comments. Tom Bubolz generously shared his Continuous Medicare History Survey data files, and Dan Gottlieb provided invaluable data assistance. Financial support was provided by the National Institute on Aging grant no. PO1-AG19783.

Notes

1. See David Cutler et al. (1998); Cutler and Mark McClellan (2001); Cutler (2004); Jonathan Skinner, Douglas Staiger, and Elliott Fisher (2005).
2. For the older literature, see LeGrand (1978, 1982); LeGrand (1991); Wagstaff, van Doorslaer, and Paci (1991); Karen Davis and Roger Reynolds (1975); Link, Long, and Settle (1982). More recently, see McClellan and Skinner (forthcoming), although see Kanika Kapur et al. (2004); and Jay Battacharya and Darius Lakdawalla (2004). Alex Y. Chen and José Escarce (2004) find a pronounced negative association between income and expenditures, but reverse the association after controlling for a host of covariates measuring well-being and disease burden. Other studies find quite nuanced patterns, for example, Alan M. Gittelsohn, Jane Halpern, and Ricardo L. Sanchez (1991) and Stephen Morris, Matthew Sutton, and Hugh Gravelle (2003).
3. See Decker (forthcoming); J. Michael McWilliams et al. (2003); Card, Dobkin, and Maestas (2004).
4. This terminology follows that in Wennberg, Skinner, and Fisher (2002).
5. In some cases, preferences can still play a role in screening programs, see Walter et al. (2004). The question is then raised as to whether those preferences against effective care reflect past adverse encounters with the health care system.
6. Reperfusion therapy (twelve-hour surgical angioplasty, or "clot busting" thrombolytics) is effective at removing the blockage or clots restricting blood flow to the heart. Aspirin is effective at breaking down platelets that interfere with blood flow, while ACE-inhibitors (angiotensin-converting enzyme-inhibiting drugs) attenuate the body's natural tendency to constrict vascular walls. Finally, beta-blockers reduce the demands of the body on the heart.
7. See also Katherine Baicker and Amitabh Chandra (2004), who have shown this lack of association between Medicare expenditures and effective care measures at the regional level.
8. See Gabriella Berloffa, Agar Brugiavini, and Dino Rizzi (2003); Anne Case and Angus Deaton (2003); Contoyannis and Jones (2004); Jon Ivar Elstad and Steiner Krokstad (2003); E. E. Gakidou, C. J. L. Murray, and J. Frenk (2000); Sherry Glied and Adriana Lleras-Muney (2003); D. P. Goldman and J. P. Smith (2002); Marian E. Gornick et al. (1996); Samuel Preston and Paul Taubman (1994); Eddy van Doorslaer et al. (1997); Wagstaff and van Doorslaer (2004).

9. The measure of inequality is then calculated much like the Gini coefficient; for a general discussion of health inequality decompositions, see Contoyannis and Martin Forster (1999).

10. In practice, Louise C. Walter et al. (2004) have pointed out that preferences could play a legitimate role for some patients who may not want to be screened. These arguments are harder to make in the case of heart attack treatments; it seems unlikely that anyone should prefer not to take aspirin following a heart attack. Alternatively, one may view the benefits as being sufficiently high to justify paternalistic efforts on the part of the government to encourage such practices.

11. Thus the age-sex frequencies are averages from 1987 to 2001. Just the eighty-plus population is considered in quantifying home health care, and for this group there are four age-sex categories: males eighty to eighty-four, males eighty-five or older, females eighty to eighty-four, and females eighty-five or older.

12. Until 1997, managed-care organizations were reimbursed for their Medicare enrollees by a capitated fee based on 95 percent of the lagged value of regional fee-for-service expenditures, so that fee-for-service expenditures within a region would have been a reasonable measure of the managed-care capitation fee. Although the Balanced Budget Act of 1997 severed that close link, it is not expected that the relatively small fraction of Medicare managed-care enrollees would bias these results.

13. See http://www.census.gov/hhes/income/histinc/f11.html.

14. See Frank Hobbs and Bonnie Damon (1996, 6.6). To estimate the average household size, we excluded people sixty-five and older living with other relatives or with unrelated people, and assumed the spouse was also age sixty-five or older.

15. One shortcoming with these changes in Medicare expenditures is that we do not have similar data on Medicaid expenditures. In theory, a decline in Medicaid expenditures among the low-income groups could have been offset by this sharp increase in Medicare expenditures with no net impact on transfers to lower-income neighborhoods. However, Medicaid expenditure data by state and by year for home-health-care expenditures provides little support for this explanation. In 1991, Medicaid programs in New York were spending more on recipients than in Texas ($623 versus $74); by 1997 the spending levels had not changed appreciably ($647 in New York, $146 in Texas). See http://www.cms.hhs.gov/statistics/nhe/state-estimates-resident/medicaid-per-capita50.asp.

16. See Julie Lee, McClellan, and Skinner (1999).

17. This is the basic insight of tax incidence studies: the tax burden does not necessarily fall on the people who pay the tax. Similarly, government benefits do not necessarily flow to the people whose names are on the checks.

18. Another cause for the rapid increase in health-care expenditures during the 1990s was upcoding whereby hospitals switched patients from low-reimbursement to high-reimbursement diagnostic related groups, or DRGs (Silverman and Skinner 2004) and effectively increased the price charged per DRG. Upcoding, which is distinguishable from "bracket creep" by the absence of supporting evidence for the more expensive coding, was curtailed sharply also around 1997 following well-publicized investigations of a large for-profit hospital chain.

19. Recent work has focused on placing a dollar value to increased survival; see Gary S. Becker, Thomas J. Philipson, and Rodrigo R. Soares (2003) or Gabriella Berloffa, Agar Brugiavini, and Dino Rizzi (2003). A different approach to quantifying the changes over time in survival is the concentration index, a variant of a Gini coefficient (Contoyannis and Forster 1999). However, changes in the index were very small, since we were just considering inequality in the over-sixty-five population and not over the entire life-course.

20. The CPT codes are 76090 (unilateral mammography), 76091 (bilateral mammography) and 76092 (screening mammography).

21. See David E. Wennberg and John D. Birkmeyer (1999, chapter 3) for a discussion of this measure.

22. In this case, because the sample sizes were so much larger, we were able to use the 306 hospital referral regions (Wennberg and Cooper 1999) as regional controls instead of states as in the analysis of beta blockers.

23. According to Heidenreich and McClellan (2001), the (thirty-day) marginal impact of beta-blockers on mortality is estimated to be .88 in terms of odds-ratios. Converting this to one-year probabilities suggests that the use of beta-blockers is associated with a reduction in mortality of three percentage points. Between the lowest and highest income group, there is a seven-percentage-point difference in the use of beta-blockers. The implied impact is therefore seven times three, or .21 percent.

24. Chen and Escarce (2004), for example, attempt to control for income-based differences in health status along a wide variety of dimensions.

References

Almond, Douglas. 2003. "Is the 1918 Influenza Pandemic Over? Long-term Effects of *In Utero* Influenza Exposure in the Post-1940 U.S. Population." Unpublished paper. Department of Economics, Columbia University.

Baicker, Katherine, and Amitabh Chandra. 2004. "Medicare Spending, the Physician Workforce, and Beneficiaries' Quality of Care." *Health Affairs* (web exclusive), April 7.

Baicker, Katherine, and Douglas Staiger. 2004. "Fiscal Shenanigans, Targeted Federal Health Care Funds, and Patient Mortality." *Quarterly Journal of Economics* 120(1): 345–86.

Battacharya, Jay, and Darius Lakdawalla. 2004. "Does Medicare Benefit the Poor? New Answers to an Old Question." NBER working paper no. 9215. Cambridge, Mass.: National Bureau of Economic Research.

Becker, Gary S., Thomas J. Philipson, and Rodrigo R. Soares. 2003. "The Quantity and Quality of Life and the Evolution of World Inequality." NBER working paper no. 97645. Cambridge, Mass.: National Bureau of Economic Research.

Berloffa, Gabriella, Agar Brugiavini, and Dino Rizzi. 2003. "Health, Income and Inequality: Evidence from a Survey of Older Italians." Working paper. Venice: University of Venice.

Card, David, Carlos Dobkin, and Nicole Maestas. 2004. "The Impact of Nearly Universal Insurance Coverage on Health Care Utilization and Health: Evidence from Medicare." NBER working paper no. 10365. Cambridge, Mass.: National Bureau of Economic Research.

Case, Anne, and Angus Deaton. 2003. "Broken Down by Work and Sex: How Our Health Declines." NBER working paper no. 9821. Cambridge, Mass.: National Bureau of Economic Research.

Chandra, Amitabh, and Jonathan Skinner. 2003. "Geography and Racial Disparities in Health," NBER Working Paper. Cambridge, Mass.: National Bureau of Economic Research.

Chen, Alex Y., and José Escarce. 2004. "Quantifying Income-Related Inequality in Healthcare Delivery in the United States." *Medical Care* 42(1): 38–47.

Contoyannis, Paul, and Martin Forster. 1999. "The Distribution of Health and Income: A Theoretical Framework." *Journal of Health Economics* 18(5): 605–22.

Contoyannis, Paul, and Andrew M. Jones. 2004. "Socio-Economic Status, Health, and Lifestyle." *Journal of Health Economics* 23(5): 965–95.

Culyer, A. J., Eddy van Doorslaer, and Adam Wagstaff. 1992. "Comment: Utilisation as a Measure of Equity by Mooney, Hall, Donaldson, and Gerard." *Journal of Health Economics* 11(1): 93–98.

Cutler, David M. 2004. *Your Money or Your Life: Strong Medicine for America's Health Care System.* New York: Oxford University Press.

Cutler, David M., and Mark McClellan. 2001. "Is Technological Change in Medicine Worth It?" *Health Affairs,* September–October, pp. 11–29.

Cutler, David, Mark McClellan, Joseph Newhouse, and Dahlia Remler. 1998. "Pricing Heart Attack Treatments." *Quarterly Journal of Economics* 113(4): 991–1024.

Danziger, Sheldon, Robert Haveman, and Eugene Smolensky. 1977. "The Measurement and Trend of Inequality: Comment." *American Economic Review* 67(3): 505–12.

Davis, Karen, and Roger Reynolds. 1975. "Medicare and the Utilization of Health Care Services by the Elderly." *Journal of Human Resources* 10(3): 361–77.

Decker, Sandra. Forthcoming. "Medicare and the Health of Women with Breast Cancer." *Journal of Human Resources.*

Elstad, Jon Ivar, and Steinar Krokstad. 2003. "Social Causation, Health-Selective Mobility, and the Reproduction of Socioeconomic Health Inequalities over Time: Panel Study of Adult Men." *Social Science and Medicine* 57(8): 1475–89.

Fisher, Elliott S., David Wennberg, Therese Stukel, Daniel Gottlieb, F. L. Lucas, and Etoile L. Pinder. 2003. "The Implications of Regional Variations in Medicare Spending." Parts 1 and 2. *Annals of Internal Medicine* 138(4): 283–99.

Fuchs, Victor. 1998a. "Provide, Provide: The Economics of Aging." NBER working paper no. 6642. Cambridge, Mass.: National Bureau of Economic Research.

———. 1998b. *Who Shall Live? Health, Economics, and Social Choice.* Hackensack, N.J.: World Scientific Publishing.

———. 2001. "The Financial Problems of the Elderly: A Holistic Approach." NBER working paper no. 8236. Cambridge, Mass.: National Bureau of Economic Research.

Gakidou, E. E., C. J. L. Murray, and J. Frenk. 2000. "Defining and Measuring Health Inequality: An Approach Based on the Distribution of Health Expectancy." *Bulletin of the World Health Organization* 78(1): 42–54.

Geronimus, Arline, John Bound, and Lisa Neidert. 1996. "On the Validity of Using Census Geocode Characteristics to Proxy Individual Socio-economic Characteristics." *Journal of the American Statistical Association* 91(434): 529–37.

Gittelsohn, Alan M., Jane Halpern, and Ricardo L. Sanchez. 1991. "Income, Race, and Surgery in Maryland." *American Journal of Public Health* 81(11): 1435–41.

Glied, Sherry, and Adriana Lleras-Muney. 2003. "Health Inequality, Education, and Medical Innovation." NBER working paper no. 9738. Cambridge, Mass.: National Bureau of Economic Research.

Glover, James A. 1938. "The Incidence of Tonsillectomy in School Children." *Proceedings of the Royal Society of Medicine* 31: 1219–36.

Goldman, Dana P., and James P. Smith. 2002. "Can Patient Self-Management Help Explain the SES Health Gradient?" *Proceedings of the National Academy of Sciences of the United States of America* 99(16): 10929–934.

Gornick, Marian E., Paul Eggers, Thomas Reilly, Renee Mentnech, Leslye Fitterman, Lawrence Kucken, and Bruce Vladeck. 1996. "Effects of Race and Income on Mortality and Use of Services Among Medicare Beneficiaries." *New England Journal of Medicine* 335(11): 791–99.

Graham, Heather. 2002. "Building an Inter-Disciplinary Science of Health Inequalities: The Example of Lifecourse Research." *Social Science and Medicine* 55(11): 205–16.

Havemann, Judith. 1997. "Fraud Is Rife in Home Care for the Elderly; Medicare Investigators Find 40 percent of Services Unjustified." *Washington Post,* July 29, p. A01.

Heidenreich, Paul A., and Mark McClellan. 2001. "Trends in Treatment and Outcome for Acute Myocardial Infarction: 1975–1995." *American Journal of Medicine* 110: 165–74.

Hobbs, Frank, and Bonnie Damon. 1996. "65-Plus in the United States." *Current Population Reports: Special Studies,* series P23, no. 190. Washington: U.S. Government Printing Office for U.S. Bureau of the Census.

Ibrahim, Said A., Laura A. Siminoff, Christopher J. Burant, and C. Kent Kwoh. 2001. "Variations in Perceptions of Treatment and Self-Care Practices in the Elderly with Osteoarthritis: A Comparison Between African American and White Patients." *Arthritis and Rheumatism* 45: 340–45.

———. 2002. "Understanding Ethnic Differences in the Utilization of Joint Replacement for Osteoarthritis." 2002. *Medical Care* 40(supplement 1): 144–55.

Jencks, Stephen F., Edwin D. Huff, and Timothy Cuerdon. 2003. "Change in the Quality of Care Delivered to Medicare Beneficiaries." *Journal of the American Medical Association* 289(3): 305–12.

Kapur, Kanika, Jeanette A. Rogowski, Vicki A. Freedman, Steven L. Wickstrom, John L. Adams, and José J. Escarce. 2004. "Socioeconomic Status and Managed Care Expenditures in Medicare Managed Care." NBER working paper no. 10757. Cambridge, Mass.: National Bureau of Economic Research.

Katz, Jeffrey N. 2001. "Patient Preferences and Health Disparities." *Journal of the American Medical Association* 286: 1506–9.

Lee, Julie, Mark McClellan, and Jonathan Skinner. 1999. "The Distributional Effects of Medicare Expenditures." in J. Poterba (ed.) *Tax Policy and the Economy,* edited by James Poterba. Volume 13. Cambridge, Mass.: MIT Press.

LeGrand, Julian. 1978. "The Distribution of Public Expenditure: The Case of Health Care." *Economica* 45(178): 125–42.

———. 1982. *The Strategy of Equality.* London: George Allen & Unwin.

———. 1991. "The Distribution of Health Care Revisited: A Commentary on Wagstaff, van Doorslaer and Paci, and O'Donnell and Propper." *Journal of Health Economics* 10: 239–45.

Link, Charles R., Stephen H. Long, and Russell F. Settle. 1982. "Equity and the Utilization of Health Care Services by the Medicare Elderly." *Journal of Human Resources* 17(2): 195–212.

Lleras-Muney, Adriana, and Frank R. Lichtenberg. 2002. "The Effect of Education on Medical Technology Adoption: Are the More Educated

More Likely to Use New Drugs?" NBER working paper no. 9185. Cambridge, Mass.: National Bureau of Economic Research.

McClellan, Mark, and Jonathan Skinner. Forthcoming. "The Incidence of Medicare." *Journal of Public Economics.*

McDermott, Walsh. 1978. "The Public Good and One's Own." *Perspectives in Biology and Medicine* 21(1978): 167–88.

McKnight, Robin. 2004. "Home Health Care Reimbursement, Long-Term Care Utilization, and Health Outcomes." NBER working paper no. 10414. Cambridge, Mass.: National Bureau of Economic Research.

McWilliams, J. Michael, Alan M. Zaslavsky, Ellen Meara, and John Z. Ayanian. 2003. "Impact of Medicare Coverage on Basic Clinical Services for Previously Uninsured Adults." *JAMA* 290: 757–64.

Moon, Marilyn. 1977. "The Economic Welfare of the Aged and Income Security Programs." In *Improving Measures of Economic Well-Being,* edited by Marilyn Moon and Eugene Smolensky. New York: Academic Press.

Mooney, Gavin, Jane Hall, Cam Donaldson, and Karen Gerard. 1991. "Utilisation as a Measure of Equity: Weighing Heat?" *Journal of Health Economics* 10: 475–80.

Morris, Stephen, Matthew Sutton, and Hugh Gravelle. 2003. "Inequity and Inequality in the Use of Health Care in England: An Empirical Investigation." Center for Health Economics, technical paper no. 27. York, England: University of York.

Preston, Samuel, and Paul Taubman. 1994. "Socioeconomic Differences in Adult Mortality and Health Status." In *Demography of Aging,* edited by Linda G. Martin and Samuel Preston. Washington, D.C.: National Research Council and the National Academy Press.

Reynolds, M., and Eugene Smolensky. 1977. *Public Expenditures, Taxes, and the Distribution of Income: The U.S., 1950, 1961, 1970.* New York: Academic Press.

Short, Kathleen, and Thesia I. Garner. 2002. "Experimental Poverty Measures Under Alternative Treatments of Medical Out-of-Pocket Expenditures: An Application of the Consumer Expenditures Survey." Bureau of Labor Statistics Working Paper No. 358 (March). Washington: U.S. Department of Labor. Available at: http://www.bls.gov/ore/pdf/ec020070.pdf (accessed September 8, 2005).

Silverman, Elaine, and Jonathan Skinner. 2004. "Hospital Ownership and Medicare Upcoding." *Journal of Health Economics* 23(2): 369–89.

Skinner, Jonathan, and Douglas Staiger. 2004. "The Diffusion of Technology: From Hybrid Corn to Beta Blockers." Unpublished paper (mimeographed). Hanover, N.H.: Dartmouth College.

Skinner, Jonathan, Douglas Staiger, and Elliott Fisher. 2005. "Is Technological Change in Health Care Always Worth It? The Case of Acute

Myocardial Infarction." Unpublished paper (mimeographed). Hanover, N.H.: Dartmouth Medical School.

Smith, James. 2003. "Unraveling the SES-Health Connection." Unpublished paper (mimeographed). Santa Monica, Calif.: RAND Corporation.

Smolensky, Eugene, Leanna Stiefel, Maria Schmundt, and Robert Plotnick. 1977. "In-Kind Transfers and the Size Distribution of Income." In *Improving Measures of Economic Well-Being*, edited by Marilyn Moon and Eugene Smolensky. New York: Academic Press.

van Doorslaer, Eddy, Adam Wagstaff, Han Bleichrodt, Samuel Calonge, Ulf-G. Gerdtham, Michael Gerfin, José Geurts, Loma Gross, Unto Häkkinen, Robert E. Leu, Owen O'Donnell, Carol Propper, Frank Puffer, Marisol Rodriguez, Gun Sundberg, Olaf Winkelhake. 1997. "Income–Related Inequalities in Health: Some International Comparisons." *Journal of Health Economics* 16: 92–112.

Wagstaff, Adam, and Eddy van Doorslaer. 2004. "Overall Versus Socioeconomic Health Inequality: A Measurement Framework and Two Empirical Examples." *Health Economics* 13: 297–301.

Wagstaff, Adam, Eddy van Doorslaer, and Pierella Paci. 1991. "On the Measurement of Horizontal Inequity in the Delivery of Health Care." *Journal of Health Economics* 10: 169–205.

Walter, Louise C., Natalie P. Davidowitz, Paul A. Heineken, and Kenneth E. Covinsky. 2004. "Pitfalls of Converting Practice Guidelines into Quality Measures: Lessons Learned from a VA Performance Measure." *Journal of the American Medical Association* 291(20): 2466–70.

Wennberg, David E., and John D. Birkmeyer, eds. 1999. *The Dartmouth Atlas of Cardiovascular Health Care*. Hanover, N.H.: Dartmouth Medical School, Center for Evaluative Clinical Sciences.

Wennberg, John E., and Megan M. Cooper. 1999. *The Dartmouth Atlas of Health Care*. Chicago: American Hospital Association.

Wennberg, John E., Jonathan Skinner, and Elliott Fisher. 2002. "Geography and the Debate over Medicare Reform." *Health Affairs* (web exclusive), February 13, pp. W96–W114.

Part III

Government Policies and Outcomes

The Socioeconomic Status of Black Males: The Increasing Importance of Incarceration

Steven Raphael

Over the past three decades, the average socioeconomic status of African American males has deteriorated, absolutely and relative to men from other racial and ethnic groups. Despite gains in relative earnings immediately following passage of the Civil Rights Act, the relative earnings of black men have stagnated since the mid-1970s (Bound and Freeman 1992). In addition, employment rates among noninstitutionalized black men have declined markedly, with pronounced declines for the relatively less-educated (Holzer and Offner 2002).

Concurrent with these adverse labor-market trends is a phenomenal increase in the proportion of black men involved in one form or another with the criminal justice system. Between 1970 and 2000, the proportion of working-age black males who are institutionalized increased from 3 to 8 percent. Over the same time period, the proportion of black males who have ever served a prison sentence increased from approximately 7 to 17 percent (Bonczar 2003). For both measures, these increases were considerably larger for certain subgroups of the black male population, such as the relatively less-educated and the young.[1]

For the increasing proportion of black men who are either currently incarcerated or have been incarcerated in the past, this fact is likely to worsen their relative socioeconomic status. Having served a prison sentence worsens one's labor-market prospects for a variety of reasons, and thus aggravates stubborn racial differences in employment and pay. In addition, the interruption of life represented by a prison sentence and the consequent lengthy absence of African American males from their spouses, partners, and children is likely to hamper family formation and hasten the dissolution of existing family units. Given the high fraction of black men with felonious criminal history records, these collateral consequences of incarceration are quickly becoming an increasingly important source of racial inequality in the United States. In fact, one might argue that in light of the potentially permanent consequences of a spell of incarceration, the high incarceration rate among black males is perhaps one of the chief barriers to their socioeconomic progress.

How important is the increasing incarceration of black males in determining their average socioeconomic status in the United States? This chapter attempts to answer that question: by documenting national trends in the proportion of black males who are institutionalized and the way this proportion varies by age and level of educational attainment; by analyzing data concerning employer demand for ex-inmates; and by using U.S. census data to assess whether increasing incarceration rates provide a possible explanation for the drastic declines in employment rates observed among noninstitutionalized black males.

Changes in Incarceration Rates, 1970 to 2000

This section documents incarceration trends over the past three decades. I focus on two principal measures of incarceration: the proportion of men institutionalized at a given point in time and the proportion of men who are either currently incarcerated or have served time at some point in the past. The large fraction of currently incarcerated black men suggests that a much larger fraction of this population is in a nonproductive status than the traditional focus on the employment rates of the noninstitutionalized would suggest. In addition, the increasing proportion of black men with previous prison experience indicates that many noninstitutionalized blacks face the same employment barriers as ex-offenders.

Documenting Trends in Institutionalization from the U.S. Census

The decennial Census of Population and Housing enumerates both the institutionalized as well as the noninstitutionalized population. The Public Use Microdata Samples (PUMS) for each census includes a flag for the institutionalized as well as micro-level information on age, education, race, and all other items that noninstitutionalized long-form respondents supply. Within the institutionalized population one can separately identify individuals residing in nonmilitary institutions. This category includes inmates of federal and state prisons, local jail inmates, residents of in-patient mental hospitals, and residents of other non-aged institutions. I use residence in a nonmilitary institution as the principal indicator of incarceration.[2]

To gauge the validity of using the census data in this manner, I compared estimates of the institutionalized population from the census to estimates of the incarcerated populations from other sources, shown in figure 8.1. The figure presents a comparison of the number of institutionalized adult black, white, and Hispanic males from the 2000 census to counts of the number of prison and jail inmates at midyear 2001, as calculated by the U.S. Bureau of Justice Statistics (BJS) (Beck, Karberg, and Harrison 2002).[3] The census definition of institutionalization is more inclusive than that of the BJS, so the census estimates are slightly larger than the BJS numbers

Figure 8.1   Comparison of BJS Estimates of the Number of Men in Federal Prison, State Prison, and Local Jails (2001) to Estimates from the 2000 1 Percent Census Public Use Microdata Sample of the Number of Men Institutionalized, by Race and Ethnicity

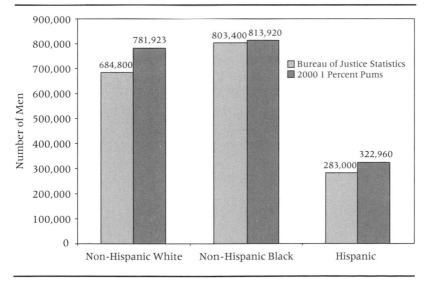

Source: One percent PUMS files, 2000; Beck, Karberg, and Harrison (2002).

for all groups. Nonetheless, the two sets of estimates correspond quite closely and the differences are small.

Table 8.1 documents employment and incarceration trends by race and educational attainment using data from the 1970, 1980, 1990, and 2000 1 percent PUMS. The table presents the proportion of non-Hispanic black and white males eighteen to sixty-five years of age who are employed, who are not working but are not institutionalized, who are in the armed forces, and who are institutionalized.

For all black men, the proportion employed declines markedly over this thirty-year period, from .73 in 1970 to .57 in 2000. This decline occurs within all education groups, although the drop is largest for black high school dropouts (from .71 to .34). Employment rates decline slightly for white males overall, and decline substantially for white high school dropouts, but these changes are small in comparison to those observed for blacks.

Over the thirty-year period, the proportion of black men who were institutionalized, especially less-educated black men, increased considerably. For all black males, the proportion institutionalized increased nearly threefold, from .03 in 1970 to .08 in 2000. For black high school dropouts, the institutionalization rate increased nearly fivefold. At the end of the century, roughly one-fifth of black men with less than a high school diploma were institutionalized. There was no increase in institutionalization among black males with at least a college degree. Among whites, changes in institutionalization rates, overall and within educational groups, are small by comparison.

Table 8.2 presents similar tabulations by age. For black men, the proportion institutionalized increases within every age group, with the most pronounced increases for the young. In 2000, roughly 11 percent of black men between 18 and 40 are institutionalized. Again, slight increases in the proportion institutionalized among young white men notwithstanding, the changes are small in comparison to what we observe among African Americans.

Tables 8.1 and 8.2 indicate that both age and educational attainment are strong predictors of current incarceration. Table 8.3 explores the interaction between these two dimensions for black men only. The table presents comparable tabulations for the subset of black men who are relatively young (under forty) and relatively less educated (dropouts and high school graduates). For young high school dropouts, the declines in the proportion employed are considerably

Table 8.1 Employment and Institutionalization Status for Non-Hispanic Black and Non-Hispanic White Males 1970 to 2000, by Educational Attainment

Age	Black Males				White Males			
	1970	1980	1990	2000	1970	1980	1990	2000
All								
Employed	.73	.64	.63	.57	.82	.80	.80	.79
NILF	.20	.29	.30	.33	.13	.17	.17	.18
Armed forces	.04	.04	.03	.02	.04	.02	.02	.01
Institutionalized	.03	.03	.04	.08	.01	.01	.01	.01
Less than high school								
Employed	.71	.57	.46	.34	.80	.69	.63	.59
NILF	.23	.38	.44	.47	.17	.28	.34	.37
Armed forces	.01	.01	.00	.00	.01	.01	.00	.00
Institutionalized	.04	.05	.10	.19	.02	.02	.03	.04
High school graduate								
Employed	.75	.66	.63	.56	.85	.81	.80	.77
NILF	.15	.25	.28	.35	.10	.15	.17	.20
Armed forces	.08	.06	.04	.02	.05	.03	.02	.01
Institutionalized	.02	.03	.05	.08	.01	.01	.01	.02
Some college								
Employed	.71	.69	.68	.66	.77	.81	.81	.80
NILF	.22	.25	.23	.26	.18	.17	.16	.17
Armed forces	.06	.04	.05	.03	.04	.02	.02	.02
Institutionalized	.01	.02	.05	.05	.00	.00	.01	.01
College plus								
Employed	.87	.84	.85	.81	.89	.91	.90	.89
NILF	.09	.13	.11	.16	.07	.07	.08	.10
Armed forces	.04	.02	.03	.01	.04	.02	.02	.01
Institutionalized	.01	.01	.01	.01	.00	.00	.00	.00

Source: PUMS from the U.S. Census of Population and Housing, 1970, 1980, 1990, and 2000.

Table 8.2 Employment and Institutionalization Status for Non-Hispanic Black and Non-Hispanic White Males 1970 to 2000, by Age

Age	Black Males				White Males			
	1970	1980	1990	2000	1970	1980	1990	2000
18 to 25 years								
Employed	.55	.48	.46	.43	.63	.69	.68	.68
NILF	.32	.40	.41	.43	.26	.26	.25	.27
Armed forces	.08	.08	.06	.03	.10	.04	.05	.03
Institutionalized	.05	.04	.07	.11	.01	.01	.01	.02
26 to 30 years								
Employed	.80	.69	.64	.61	.89	.86	.86	.85
NILF	.13	.22	.23	.25	.07	.10	.10	.11
Armed forces	.04	.04	.04	.02	.04	.02	.03	.02
Institutionalized	.04	.05	.09	.12	.01	.01	.01	.02
31 to 40								
Employed	.82	.76	.70	.64	.91	.90	.89	.87
NILF	.11	.18	.21	.23	.05	.07	.08	.10
Armed forces	.04	.03	.03	.02	.03	.02	.02	.01
Institutionalized	.03	.03	.06	.11	.01	.01	.01	.02
41 to 50								
Employed	.83	.77	.74	.65	.92	.90	.90	.86
NILF	.14	.21	.21	.28	.06	.09	.10	.12
Armed forces	.01	.01	.01	.01	.01	.01	.01	.00
Institutionalized	.02	.02	.04	.06	.01	.01	.01	.01
51 to 65								
Employed	.72	.61	.58	.53	.81	.72	.69	.70
NILF	.26	.37	.40	.44	.18	.27	.31	.29
Armed forces	.00	.00	.00	.00	.00	.01	.00	.00
Institutionalized	.02	.01	.02	.03	.01	.01	.01	.01

Source: PUMS from the U.S. Census of Population and Housing, 1970, 1980, 1990, and 2000.

more drastic than the declines in employment for black male high school dropouts overall (presented in table 8.1). For dropouts between eighteen and twenty-five, the employment rate declines from .50 to .27. For those 26 to 30, the proportion employed declines from .76 to .30, whereas for 31 to 40 year olds, employment rates decline from .81 to .35.

Similarly, increases in the proportions institutionalized are much larger than those observed for dropouts overall. For dropouts between eighteen and twenty-five, the institutionalization increases from .08 to .23. For those between twenty-six and forty, the institutionalization rates increase from approximately .05 to .30. For all dropouts less than forty years of age, the institutionalized population is only slightly smaller than the population of employed men from this demographic group. For black dropouts between twenty-six and thirty, there are actually more institutionalized than employed. Comparable, although somewhat muted, patterns are observed for black high school graduates.

One factor that qualifies the figures presented in tables 8.1 through 8.3 concerns the fact that African American men have historically been undercounted in the census. Although the 2000 enumeration made a concerted effort to improve coverage—and in fact undercounting was considerably less than that observed in the 1990 census—disparities remain, with black men again the most likely to be missed. According to the Accuracy and Coverage Evaluation (A.C.E.) results released by the Census Bureau (U.S. Census Bureau 2003), roughly 7 percent of noninstitutionalized black men were missed in the 2000 census. The net undercount of noninstitutionalized black men is 6 percent for those eighteen to twenty-nine, 10 percent for those thirty to forty-nine, and 4 percent for those fifty or over.

To assess the effect of this undercount on my estimates of black male incarceration rates, I calculated the following adjustment for the 2000 figures. Let "Institution" be the unadjusted estimates of the proportion institutionalized, "Noninstitution" be the comparable unadjusted estimate for the household population, and "Coverage" be the proportion of the household population measured in the census (1 minus the net undercount rate). An adjusted institutionalization rate can be calculated by the equation:

$$\text{Institution}^* = \frac{\text{Institution}}{\text{Institution} + \text{Non-Institution}/\text{Coverage}}.$$

For all black men, this adjustment decreases the estimate of the proportion institutionalized from .08 to .075. The undercount adjustment reduced the proportion institutionalized from .11 to .105 for those eighteen to twenty-five, from .12 to .114 for those twenty-six to thirty, from .11 to .10 for those thirty-one to forty, from .06 to .054 for those forty-one to fifty, and from .03 to .029 for those fifty-one and over. Thus, accounting for the undercount in the noninstitutional population does not appreciably affect the reported patterns.

The A.C.E. does not disaggregate net undercount estimates to produce values by race, age, and level of educational attainment. Thus it is difficult to present adjusted estimates for the results in table 8.3, where we observe the starkest patterns. However, we can assume an arbitrarily high undercount rate for this population and provide some lower-bound results. For example, if we assume that one-fifth of black male high school dropouts are missed by the census (assuming an undercount rate that is twice the highest of the age-specific rates for black males), the estimate of the proportion incarcerated among black high school dropouts declines from .23 to .19 for those eighteen to twenty-five, from .34 to .29 for those twenty-six to thirty, and from .28 to .24 for those thirty-one to forty. Although these are notable declines, these lower-bound estimates of the proportion incarcerated are still quite high.

Thus, institutionalization rates for black men have increased considerably since 1970. These increases have been largest for the young and the relatively less-educated. Interacting these two dimensions reveals that the most dramatic increases in incarceration occurred among black males with less than a high school education who were between the ages of twenty-five and forty.

Estimating the Proportion with Prior Prison Experience

The fraction of black men who have served time in state or federal prison at some point in their lives is certainly larger than the sizable minority that is currently incarcerated. Turnover rates in state and federal prisons are high, and the median sentences are fairly short. For example, the median sentence for new prison admissions in the United States in 1999 was roughly three years for the maximum sentences and thirteen months for the minimum sentences. Moreover, many inmates will serve considerably less time than their maximum sentences.

Table 8.3 Employment and Institutionalization Status for Non-Hispanic Black Males 40 and Under with a High School Education or Less, 1970 to 2000

	High School Dropouts				High School Graduates			
Age	1970	1980	1990	2000	1970	1980	1990	2000
18 to 25 years								
Employed	.50	.38	.30	.27	.62	.52	.49	.44
NILF	.38	.51	.55	.50	.23	.32	.36	.44
Armed Forces	.04	.04	.00	.00	.13	.13	.10	.04
Institutionalized	.08	.08	.15	.23	.02	.03	.06	.09
26 to 30 years								
Employed	.76	.58	.40	.30	.83	.70	.64	.58
NILF	.16	.32	.38	.36	.09	.21	.24	.29
Armed Forces	.01	.01	.00	.00	.06	.05	.04	.02
Institutionalized	.06	.10	.22	.34	.02	.04	.08	.12
31 to 40								
Employed	.81	.70	.52	.35	.82	.76	.69	.62
NILF	.13	.25	.34	.37	.08	.17	.24	.27
Armed Forces	.01	.00	.00	.00	.08	.04	.02	.01
Institutionalized	.05	.05	.13	.28	.02	.03	.06	.11

Source: PUMS from the U.S. Census of Population and Housing, 1970, 1980, 1990, and 2000.

Consistent with the high degree of turnover among prisoners, the majority of inmates will eventually be released. In 1997, 65 percent of surveyed inmates in state and federal prison indicated that they had a definite release date. An additional 32 percent indicated that they anticipated eventually leaving prison. Of the 97 percent of inmates who anticipated eventually leaving, nearly 60 percent reported that they would be released within the next three calendar years (Raphael and Stoll 2004). Taken together, these figures suggest that the large increases in the prison populations occurring over the last few decades have certainly left in their wake a much larger population of former inmates.

Gauging the population of former prison inmates is difficult because none of the major household surveys in the United States ask respondents whether they have served time. Consequently, estimating the size of this population requires indirect methods. The BJS estimates the number of former inmates by combining population data, birth cohort estimates of the likelihood of entering prison for the first time at each age (often separately by race and gender), and cohort- and age-specific mortality rates (Bonczar 2003).[4] Using this methodology, the BJS estimates that in addition to the 1.3 million current inmates in 2001, an additional 4.3 million noninstitutionalized persons had served a prison term in the past. In 2001, the current and former prison inmates accounted for 4.9 percent of the adult male population in 2001.

Of course, the percentages of current or ever-incarcerated males vary significantly by race and ethnicity. The BJS estimates indicate that 2.6 percent of non-Hispanic white males, 16.6 percent of non-Hispanic black males, and 7.7 percent of Hispanic males have served prison time (figures that are roughly double the institutionalization rates listed in table 8.1). The comparable figures for whites, blacks, and Hispanics for 1974 were 1.4, 8.7, and 2.3 percent, respectively.

The BJS uses the same methodology to calculate lifetime probabilities of entering either the state or federal prison system. Given that the risk of incarceration has increased over the past three decades, lifetime probabilities should exceed the current proportion of a specific population that is either currently incarcerated or formerly incarcerated.[5] Figure 8.2 presents these estimates for 1974 and 2001. For whites, the lifetime likelihood of men born in 1974 of going to prison is estimated to be 2.2 percent. For those born in

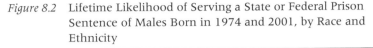

Figure 8.2   Lifetime Likelihood of Serving a State or Federal Prison
Sentence of Males Born in 1974 and 2001, by Race and
Ethnicity

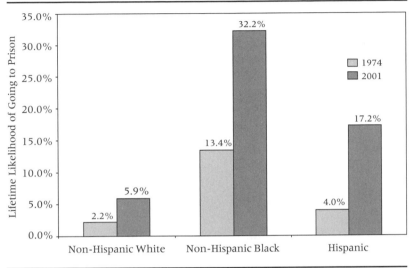

Source: Beck, Karberg, and Harrison (2002).

2001, the risk increases to 5.9 percent; for black males, from 13.2 to
32.2 percent; and for Hispanics, from 4 to 17.2 percent.

The analysis of institutionalization rates revealed large differences
within racial groups between less-educated and more-educated men
and between groups of men stratified by age. The BJS provides
race-specific estimates of the proportion that has ever served time
by age, but there are no estimates of how this proportion varies by
level of educational attainment. The results presented above indicate that education is a stronger predictor of current incarceration
than is age; thus, education is also likely to be more strongly associated than age with ever having served time.

I am able to fill this data gap somewhat with administrative
prison data from California. Using administrative records on all
prison terms served during the 1990s in a California state prison, I
first calculated an unduplicated count of prisoners entering the system during the 1990s, by race and by how old each prisoner would
be in the year 2000.[6] I then use the 1997 Survey of Inmates in
State and Federal Correction Facilities to estimate the distribution

of inmates across age-education cells within racial and ethnic groups. These distribution estimates are then used to allocate the number of unduplicated prisoners within each age-race cell across educational attainment groups.[7] Dividing these counts by the estimated 2000 California population (institutional plus noninstitutional) within each age-race-educational attainment cell yields estimates of the proportion of males in each cell serving a prison term during the 1990s.

Table 8.4 presents these results. The first column presents national estimates from the BJS of the proportion ever serving time by race-ethnicity and age. The second column presents comparable estimates of the proportion serving time in California. The final four columns present estimates by level of educational attainment that allot prisoners within race-age cells across education groups according to the estimated educational distributions of inmates during the late 1990s.

The tabulations by age indicate that the California estimates and the BJS estimates are fairly similar for males between the ages of eighteen and fifty-four. For older males, the California estimates indicate a smaller proportion ever having served time. This is sensible considering that the California administrative records only cover the 1990s, and that former prisoners over fifty-four in the year 2000 are likely to have served time prior to the 1990s. Both sets of estimates indicate that the proportion ever having served time increases with age through the late thirties and early forties and then declines. Black men between twenty-five and forty-four have the highest rates of current or previous incarceration (roughly one fifth of this group, using both the California and BJS estimates).

The estimates by race, age, and education reveal dramatic differences. For black high school dropouts between the ages of twenty-five and forty-four, the number of unduplicated prisoners serving time during the previous decade exceeds census population counts (the ratio is greater than 1).[8] Ninety percent of black high school dropouts between forty-five and fifty-four are estimated to have served a prison term during the past decade. These figures suggest that for black high school dropouts, serving time in prison is practically a certainty. The proportion of blacks with prison time in the past decade is considerably lower for those with higher levels of educational attainment, although the figures for black high school graduates are still quite high (between .12 and .16). By contrast, the

Table 8.4 BJS Estimates of the Proportion of the Male Population Ever Having Served Time in a State or Federal Prison by Race-Ethnicity and Age and Estimates of the Proportion Serving Time in a California State Prison During the 1990s, by Race, Age and Educational Attainment

	BJS Estimates for the Nation[a]	Estimates for California from CDC Administrative Records				
		All[b]	High School Dropouts[c]	High School Graduates[c]	Some College[c]	College Plus[c]
Non-Hispanic white males						
18 to 24	0.01	0.01	0.03	0.00	0.00	0.00
25 to 34	0.03	0.03	0.31	0.03	0.01	0.00
35 to 44	0.04	0.03	0.30	0.04	0.02	0.01
45 to 54	0.03	0.02	0.17	0.02	0.01	0.01
55 to 65	0.03	0.01	0.04	0.01	0.00	0.00
Non-Hispanic black males						
18 to 24	0.09	0.04	0.19	0.02	0.01	0.00
25 to 34	0.20	0.19	1.14	0.15	0.05	0.03
35 to 44	0.22	0.19	1.23	0.16	0.07	0.04
45 to 54	0.18	0.15	0.90	0.12	0.06	0.05
55 to 65	0.13	0.05	0.18	0.04	0.01	0.02
Hispanic males						
18 to 24	0.04	0.01	0.02	0.00	0.00	0.00
25 to 34	0.09	0.05	0.08	0.03	0.02	0.02
35 to 44	0.10	0.05	0.07	0.04	0.02	0.03
45 to 54	0.10	0.03	0.04	0.03	0.02	0.03
55 to 65	0.07	0.01	0.02	0.02	0.01	0.01

Sources:
[a]Estimates drawn from Bonczar (2003, table 7).
[b]Estimates in this column are calculated as follows: The administrative term records for all terms served in California were sorted by a CDC internal ID number. The first term for each unique ID was selected out to construct a sample of unduplicated prisoners. For each prisoner, we calculated how old the prisoner would be in the year 2000. We then calculated counts of prisoners by age and race for 2000. Using the 2000 1 percent PUMS, we then estimated the California population size for each age-race cell listed in the table. The figures in the table are the ratio of the prisoner counts to the 2000 census population estimate for each cell.
[c]Estimates in this column are calculated as follows: We first calculated the counts of unduplicated prisoners by age and race following the procedures in note b. We then used data from the 1997 Survey of Inmates in State and Federal Corrections Facilities to estimate the educational attainment of prison inmates in the United States by race-ethnicity and age. We used these estimates to allocate the number of unduplicated prisoners within each age-race cell across the four educational groups (the CDC administrative data do not contain information on educational attainment). We then used the 2000 1 percent PUMS to estimate the California population size of each age-race-education cell in the table. The figures in the table are the ratio of the prisoner counts hypothetically allocated across education groups to the 2000 census population estimate for each cell.

comparable proportions of whites as well as Latinos with prison time in the previous ten years are smaller for all comparisons.

The Effect of Changing Incarceration Rates on Estimates of Black-White Employment and Earnings Trends

To summarize the patterns documented thus far, the current incarceration rates of black men as well as the proportion of black men with prior prison experience have increased considerably over the past three decades. These increases have been most pronounced for black men who have not graduated from high school and who are between the ages of twenty-five and forty. For white men, the increase is minuscule by comparison.

One interesting implication of these trends concerns the fact that traditional gauges of black-white inequality, such as relative wages, unemployment rates, or employment-to-population ratios, are likely to suffer increasingly from selection bias. For example, the monthly unemployment rate estimated by race and ethnicity by the Bureau of Labor Statistics and reported widely in the press is calculated using data from the monthly Current Population Survey (CPS). The sampling frame of the CPS is based on housing units, and thus pertains to the noninstitutionalized population. To the extent that incarcerated felons are highly likely to be unemployed when not institutionalized, the increasing incarceration rate of blacks suggests that monthly black unemployment rates are being calculated with an increasingly select sample. Moreover, given the generally higher unemployment rate for blacks relative to other racial and ethnic groups, estimates of the overall unemployment rate may be similarly biased downward relative to the counterfactual with lower incarceration rates.[9] In general, use of noninstitutionalized samples to estimate labor-market aggregates is likely to bias research findings toward a greater degree of racial convergence.

Perhaps the most glaring example of selection bias is observed when the relative employment-to-population ratios of blacks and whites are compared. Bruce Western and Becky Petit (2000) demonstrate that by adding the incarcerated to the denominator of the employment-to-population ratio, white-black employment rate differentials increase considerably, especially for the relatively young and the relatively less-educated. To illustrate this point, figure 8.3 presents estimates of the difference in employment-to-population ratios between white and black men using two alternative base pop-

Figure 8.3 White-Black Employment-Rate Differentials for the
Noninstitutionalized, and for the Noninstitutionalized and
Institutionalized Combined

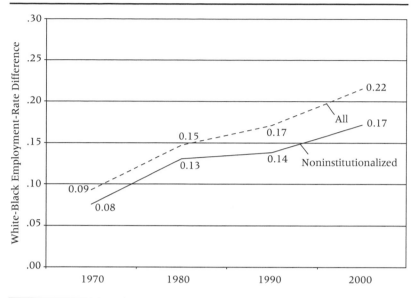

Source: One percent IPUMS files, 1970, 1980, 1990, and 2000.

ulations: the noninstitutionalized and the noninstitutionalized plus the institutionalized (labeled "All" on the graphs).[10]

The difference between the two sets of estimates increases in each decade: in 1970, including the institutionalized increases the white-black difference in employment rates by one percentage point, in 1980 by two, in 1990 by three, and in 2000 by five percentage points. In 2000, the white-black employment rate differential is 30 percent larger when the institutionalized are accounted for.

Table 8.5 presents comparable estimates by level of educational attainment. As would be expected, the differences between the estimates based on the noninstitutionalized and estimates based on the entire population are largest for the least-educated and smallest for the most-educated. In 2000, including the institutionalized increases the white-black employment rate differential by six percentage points for high school dropouts, four points for high school graduates, three points for those with some college education, and one point for those with at least a college degree.

Table 8.5   Comparisons of the White-Black Employment Rate
            Differentials, by Year and Level of Education Attainment, Using
            Alternative Base Populations to Calculate Employment Rates

	1970	1980	1990	2000
High school dropouts				
Noninstitutionalized	.07	.11	.13	.19
Total population	.09	.12	.17	.25
Difference	.02	.01	.04	.06
High school				
Noninstitutionalized	.05	.10	.13	.17
Total population	.06	.11	.16	.21
Difference	.01	.01	.03	.04
Some college				
Noninstitutionalized	.04	.08	.08	.10
Total population	.04	.10	.10	.13
Difference	.00	.02	.02	.03
College graduates				
Noninstitutionalized	.02	.05	.03	.06
Total population	.02	.06	.04	.07
Difference	.02	.01	.01	.01

Source: One percent PUMS files, 1970, 1980, 1990, and 2000.
Note: The figures in the table are the differences between the employment-to-population ratios for white males and black males by education group. In the rows labeled "Noninstitutionalized," the noninstitutionalized population is used as the base for calculating the underlying employment rates. In the rows labeled "Total population," the noninstitutionalized plus the institutionalized are used as the base for calculating the underlying employment rates.

The effect of increased incarceration on estimates of black-white wage convergence is likely to impart less of a selection bias than that created by the more general decline in black employment rates. That is to say, such a large fraction of noninstitutionalized black men are non-employed in any given week that incarceration is unlikely to select out a substantial fraction of wage earners. Thus, researchers interested in black-white wage trends have focused more generally on estimating the selection effect of declining relative employment rates on aggregate black-white wage ratios (accounting for both the incarcerated and the nonincarcerated unemployed).

To the extent that black labor-market dropouts are disproportionately concentrated in the lower tail of the wage-offer distribution, the declining relative employment rate of black men will bias aggregate wage trends toward convergence. Assessing this selection bias requires recovering the wage-offer distribution for labor-market dropouts and recalculating measures of the central tendency of wage offers taking into account the entire distribution—both observed offers for the employed and the unobserved offer distribution for the non-employed (Chandra 2003). Several authors have attempted to tackle this problem. Charles Brown (1984) provides one of the earliest examples. Brown assumes that the noninstitutionalized non-employed of each racial group would earn wages below their group-specific median, and calculates hypothetical trends in black-white median-wage ratios based on this assumption.[11] The author argues that the majority of observed wage convergence during the 1970s is directly attributable to the declines in black labor-force participation rates.

More recent efforts to account for both the noninstitutionalized jobless as well as the incarcerated are offered by Chinhui Juhn (2003) and Amitabh Chandra (2003). Juhn assigns the average wage of similarly situated employed workers (of similar race, age, and education) to the non-employed and recalculates relative black-white wage trends with and without this adjustment. Juhn finds that whereas wage ratio estimates that are not adjusted for selection bias find convergence during the 1960s and 1970s, and stagnation thereafter, adjusting for selection bias reveals a widening of racial wage differentials during recent decades.

The most thorough research on this question is provided by Chandra (2003). Chandra presents a series of alternative adjustments for selection bias, including the following:

- A matching estimator that assigns the mean earning for comparable workers to the non-employed (a la Juhn 2003)

- A matching estimator that assigns the median earnings for comparable workers to the non-employed

- Calculating race-age-education cell-specific median earnings based on the assumption that nonparticipants are negatively selected from the offer distribution within cells and then calculating overall medians based on these tabulations

- Modifying the selection specification in the previous calculation so that only the long-term non-employed are negatively selected within the group

All four selection corrections find that black-white wages diverged during the 1980s, with the methods based on the assumptions that labor-market dropouts are negatively selected within the group yielding the largest increases in racial wage differentials. Moreover, Chandra shows that incarceration contributed significantly to the divergence during the 1980s.[12]

The Effect of Incarceration on Future Labor-Market Prospects

Serving prison time is likely to adversely affect one's labor-market prospects for a number of reasons. First, a prison term interrupts one's work career. Incarcerated felons cannot accumulate employment experience while serving time.

Second, the quality of one's noninstitutionalized social network, a main source of employment information, is likely to erode with time incarcerated.

Third, serving time in prison is stigmatizing. Employers consistently express reservations about applicants with prior criminal records. Many employers who offer low-skilled jobs either ask about criminal records or perform formal reviews of applicant criminal records. In some instances, employers are prohibited from hiring convicted felons.

These adverse effects of incarceration are sure to be an increasingly important determinant of black employment outcomes. This section explores these factors in detail.

To What Extent Does Prison Interrupt One's Potential Work Career?
The extent to which being sentenced to prison interrupts a felon's potential work career depends on both the expected amount of time served on a typical term as well as the likelihood of serving subsequent terms. Newly admitted prisoners during the late 1990s were generally serving time for a maximum sentence of three years and a minimum sentence of one year—many served time closer to the minimum (Raphael and Stoll 2004). If this were the only time served, the interruption would not be that substantial.[13]

In fact, however, many felons serve multiple terms in prison, because they have either committed new felonies or violated their parole conditions after being released from the initial spell. A large body of criminological research consistently finds that nearly two-thirds of ex-inmates are rearrested within a few years of release from prison (Petersilia 2003), and a sizable majority of these will serve subsequent prison terms. Thus, for many offenders, the period of time between the ages of eighteen and thirty is characterized by multiple short prison spells, with intermittent, and relatively short, spells outside of prison.

Data from the California state prison system makes it possible to chart the prison histories of young offenders entering the California state prison system. Although there are several reasons to suspect that California may not be representative of the nation, there are also several reasons why such an exercise is instructive.[14] First, the state incarceration rate in California (453 per 100,000) is near the national average (422 per 100,000); thus the state is comparable to the nation along this dimension. Second, the California state prison system is the largest in the nation (accounting for 13 percent of the nation's state prison population), so the experience of California inmates is an important contributor to the weighted-average experience. Finally, these detailed administrative records permit linking subsequent spells and characterization of personal prison histories, something that can't be done with publicly available inmate surveys.

The focus is on offenders between eighteen and twenty-five who enter one of the state's prisons on a new court commitment (not for a parole violation) during the year 1990, and on several aspects of their prison experiences over the subsequent decade. The analysis is based on administrative records obtained from the California Department of Corrections for all prison terms served in the state with a start date during the 1990s. Figures 8.4 and 8.5 present the relative frequency distributions for the number of separate prison terms served by our cohort, inclusive of the initial term caused by the 1990s court commitment and any subsequent terms due to either additional court commitments or parole revocations. Figure 8.4 presents the distribution for all inmates and figure 8.5 shows separate distributions by race and ethnicity.[15]

The majority of inmates serve more than one prison term. Only 32 percent of inmates entering prison during the year 1990 serve just one term during the decade. The median inmate serves two terms over the decade, while a substantial fraction (approximately 48 percent) serve three or more terms.

Figure 8.4   The Distribution of Prisoners Eighteen-to-Twenty-Five Years Old Entering the California State Prison System in 1990, by the Number of Terms Served over the Subsequent Decade

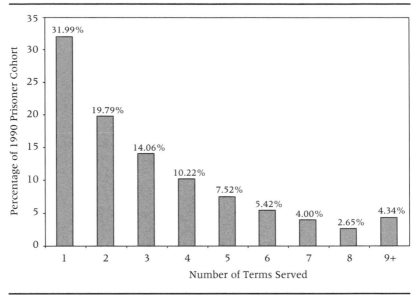

Source: California Department of Corrections Administrative Records, 1990 to 2000.

There are notable differences by race and ethnicity. Only 28 percent of white inmates and 23 percent of black inmates serve one term during the decade, whereas the comparable figure for Hispanic inmates is nearly 40 percent. The median white and black inmates serve three terms while the median Hispanic inmate serves two terms. Again, substantial fractions of this 1990 cohort serve three or more terms, with 54 percent of white inmates, 58 percent of black inmates, and 39 percent of Hispanic inmates entering prison at least three times.

In California, the time served on each term tends to be relatively short. Although there are many California inmates serving long sentences and several thousand who are serving twenty-five years to life under the state's "three strikes" sentencing provision, the majority of inmates are sentenced to relatively short terms of less than a year or two. Table 8.6 shows the median time served for inmates in our 1990 cohort. The table provides figures for all inmates, by race-ethnicity,

Figure 8.5   The Distribution of Prisoners Eighteen-to-Twenty-Five Years
Old Entering the California State Prison System in 1990 by the
Number of Terms Served over the Subsequent Decade, by Race
and Ethnicity

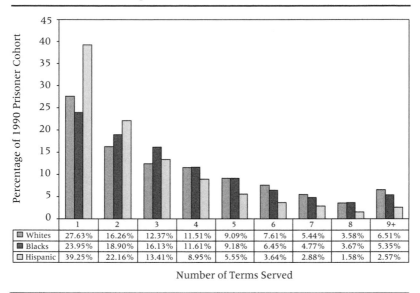

	1	2	3	4	5	6	7	8	9+
☐ Whites	27.63%	16.26%	12.37%	11.51%	9.09%	7.61%	5.44%	3.58%	6.51%
■ Blacks	23.95%	18.90%	16.13%	11.61%	9.18%	6.45%	4.77%	3.67%	5.35%
☐ Hispanic	39.25%	22.16%	13.41%	8.95%	5.55%	3.64%	2.88%	1.58%	2.57%

Number of Terms Served

Source: California Department of Corrections Administrative Records, 1990 to 2000.

and by whether the term is the first, second, third, fourth, or fifth or
higher term. For the first term served (which, for our sample, also corresponds to the first term served on a specific court commitment), the
median time served for all inmates is approximately one year. The
median time for white inmates is somewhat lower (.94 years),
the median for black inmates is somewhat higher (1.17 years),
and the median for Hispanics is equal to the overall median.

Median time served declines uniformly with subsequent terms
served, declining to .68 years for the second term, .62 years for third,
and so one. This decline reflects the fact that many of these subsequent prison terms are served for parole violations rather than new
felony court commitments, and thus represent time served on the
remaining sentence from the initial court commitment that sent the
offender to prison in the first place.

The figures in table 8.6 suggest that for most felons committed
to prison the actual amount of time behind bars is fairly short, even

Table 8.6   Median Time Served (Years) in the California State Prison
System by Term and by Race-Ethnicity for the 1990 Prisoner
Cohort, Eighteen-to-Twenty-Five Years of Age

	Terms Served				
	First	Second	Third	Fourth	Fifth or Higher
All Inmates	1.02	0.68	0.62	0.53	0.49
White	0.94	0.62	0.58	0.53	0.48
Black	1.17	0.71	0.65	0.53	0.50
Hispanic	1.01	0.72	0.63	0.55	0.47

Source: California Department of Corrections Administrative Records, 1990 to 2000.
Note: Tabulations are based on all individuals between the ages of eighteen and
twenty-five who entered the California state prison system during 1990 to serve the
first term of a commitment. The "Terms Served" column refers to the first and subsequent terms served by the 1990 cohort of inmates over the subsequent ten years.

accounting for the likelihood of serving multiple spells. Panel A of
table 8.7 presents estimates of the total amount of time served
accounting for multiple terms (summing time served across all
terms for each inmate) for the inmate at the 25th, 50th and 75th
percentiles of this distribution. During the 1990s, the median inmate
spent 2.8 years in one of California's state prisons, with the median
white inmate (3.09 years) and median black inmate (3.53 years)
serving more time and the median Hispanic inmate (2.23 years)
serving less time. Roughly 25 percent of inmates served at least
5 years during the 1990s while another 25 percent served less than
1.5 years.

These figures show cumulative time spent behind bars, but they
are misleading as a gauge of the extent to which incarceration potentially interrupts the accumulation of legitimate labor market experience. Cumulative time served does not account for the short periods
of time between prison spells where inmates may find employment,
yet are not able to solidify the employment match with any measurable amount of job tenure. A more appropriate measure of the
degree to which incarceration impedes experience accumulation
would be the time between the date of admission to prison for the
first term served and the date of release from the last term.

Panel B of table 8.7 presents the quartile values from the distribution of this variable. For the median inmate, 5 years elapsed
between the first date of admission and the last date of release. For

Table 8.7 Quartile Values of the Total Time Served During the 1990s and the Time Between the Date of First Admission and Date of Last Release for the 1990 Prison Cohort Eighteen-to-Twenty-Five Years of Age

	25th Percentile	50th Percentile	75th Percentile
Panel A: Distribution of total time served			
All inmates	1.44	2.79	4.81
White	1.43	3.09	5.12
Black	1.93	3.53	5.45
Hispanic	1.29	2.23	3.97
Panel B: Distribution of time between the date of first admission and the date of last release			
All inmates	1.86	4.99	8.71
White	2.01	6.17	9.11
Black	2.88	6.42	9.16
Hispanic	1.44	3.65	7.62

Source: California Department of Corrections Administrative Records, 1990 to 2000.
Note: Tabulations are based on all individuals between the ages of eighteen and twenty-five who entered the California state prison system during 1990 to serve the first term of a commitment. Tabulation of the percentiles of the two time distributions are based on all terms served over the subsequent ten years.

median white, black, and Hispanic inmates, the comparable figures were 6.2, 6.5, and 3.2 years, respectively. For approximately one quarter of inmates (and more than one quarter of white and black inmates), 9 years passed between their initial commitment to prison and their last release. In other words, one quarter of these inmates spent almost the entire decade cycling in and out of prison.

Moreover, the estimates of the work-life interruption in panel B of table 8.7 are likely to be lower-bound estimates.

Our cohort comprises inmates eighteen to twenty-five years old who entered the state prison system on a new court commitment in 1990. Surely many of the older offenders in this group have served prison time on previous commitments, a factor that would add to our estimates of both cumulative time served and entrance and exit from the prison system if we had information on earlier time served. Not only that, but many of the younger offenders are likely to have had juvenile records and may have been previously incarcerated in the California Youth Authority system. In addition, we do not have data on time served for commitments with start dates occurring after 1999—our study arbitrarily places a cap on the amount of time one can be involved with the prison system. Finally, time served in jail while an inmate is awaiting trial or a parole revocation hearing is not recorded in the available data and thus cannot be tabulated. Accounting for the jail time that usually accompanies the transition between being noninstitutionalized and imprisonment would surely increase these estimates.

Regardless, spending five years of one's early life (6.5 years for the median black offender) cycling in and out of prison must impact one's earnings prospects. Clearly, being behind bars and having just short spans of time outside of prison prohibit the accumulation of job experiences during a period of one's life when the returns to the accumulation of experience are the greatest.

Does Having Been in Prison Stigmatize Ex-Offenders?

The potential impact of serving time on future labor-market prospects extends beyond the failure to accumulate work experience. There is considerable evidence that employers are averse to hiring former prison inmates and often use formal and informal screening tools to weed ex-offenders out of the applicant pool. Given the high proportion of low-skilled black men with prison time on their criminal records, such employer sentiments and screening practices represent an increasingly important employment barrier for African American males. Moreover, this stigmatization of prisoners, coupled with the informal screening methods used by employers, may also be adversely impacting the employment prospects of young black men without criminal history records.

Employers consider criminal records when screening job applicants for a number of reasons. For starters, certain occupations are closed to felons under state and in some instances federal law (Hahn 1991). Examples include jobs requiring contact with children, certain health-services occupations, public employment in some states and localities, and employment in firms providing security services. In addition, in many states employers can be held liable for the criminal actions of their employees. Under the theory of negligent hiring, employers can be required to pay punitive damages as well as damages for loss, pain, and suffering for acts committed by an employee on the job (Craig 1987). Finally, employers looking to fill jobs where employee monitoring is imperfect may place a premium on trustworthiness. To the extent that past criminal activity signals a lack of trustworthiness, employers may take such information into account when screening applicants.

In all known employer surveys where employers are asked about their willingness to hire ex-offenders, employer responses reveal employers' strong aversion to hiring applicants with criminal records (Holzer, Raphael, and Stoll 2003, 2005; Pager 2003). Figure 8.6 presents tabulations from the employer survey of the Multi-City Study of Urban Inequality (MCSUI).[16] The figure presents employer responses to questions as to the likelihood that the employer would hire various types of job applicants, including applicants with a criminal record. Over 60 percent indicated that they would "probably not" or "definitely not" hire applicants with criminal records, with "probably not" being the modal response.

Since these data pertain to employers who have recently hired low-skilled workers (employers who are perhaps the most likely

Figure 8.6 Self-Reported Employer Willingness to Hire Applicants from Various Groups from the Establishment Survey of the Multi-City Study of Urban Inequality

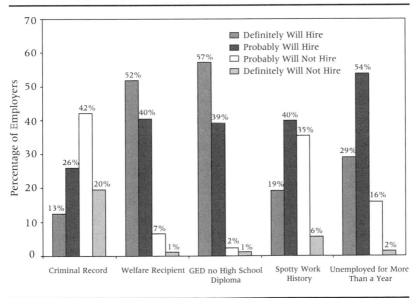

Source: Holzer, Raphael, and Stoll (2005).

to employ an ex-offender), these results imply that a large majority of employers are unwilling to hire former prison inmates.

Employer aversion to applicants with criminal records is stronger than employer aversion to hiring other types of applicants displayed in figure 8.6. For example, 60 percent of employers indicate that they are unlikely to hire ex-offenders,[17] but only 8 percent say this in regard to welfare recipients, 3 percent for applicants with a GED, 41 percent for applicants with spotty work histories, and 18 percent for applicants unemployed for over a year. It is interesting that employers exhibit a reluctance to hiring applicants with spotty work histories, a characteristic that one might interpret as signaling past incarceration. But the proportion of employers unwilling to hire such workers was just 75 percent of the proportion unwilling to hire ex-offenders.[18]

The ability of employers to act on an aversion to ex-offenders and the nature of the action in terms of hiring and screening behavior will depend on employers' access to criminal record information. To the extent that employers can and do access criminal records, they may simply screen out applicants on the basis of their actual arrest and conviction records. Among the employers interviewed in the MCSUI sample, 32 percent indicated that they always check the criminal records of applicants, 17 percent indicated that they check sometimes, while 51 percent indicated that they never check. More recent employer surveys (the MCSUI data are from the early 1990s) indicate that the use of formal background checks has increased. For example, a 2001 survey of employers in Los Angeles with questions similar to those in the earlier MCSUI survey found that 46 percent of employers indicated that they always performed criminal background checks, 18 percent indicated that they sometimes checked, and 37 percent indicated that they never checked.[19] The comparable tabulations for Los Angeles from the earlier MCSUI data indicated that 32 percent always check, 16 percent sometimes check, and 52 percent never check.

In the absence of a formal background check, employers may act on their aversion to hiring ex-offenders using perceived correlates of previous incarceration, such as age, race, or level of educational attainment to screen out those who they think may have criminal histories. In other words, employers may engage in statistical discrimination against applicants who are thought to come from demographic groups with high rates of involvement in the criminal justice system. Harry J. Holzer, Steven Raphael, and Michael A. Stoll (2005) find employer-hiring patterns consistent with such statistical discrimination against black men. Specifically, the authors find that employers who check criminal history records are more likely to hire blacks than employers who do not, and that this positive effect of criminal background checks is strongest among those employers with the strongest stated aversion to hiring ex-offenders.[20] Via such statistical discrimination, even young black men who have never been incarcerated or involved with the criminal justice system are harmed by the rise in incarceration among young black men overall.

A study by Devah Pager (2003) offers perhaps the clearest evidence of employer aversion to ex-offenders and the stigma associated with having served time in prison. Pager conducted an audit study of employer hiring activity in the year 2001 for employers located in the Milwaukee metropolitan area. Using male job applicants matched on observable characteristics including age, education, general appearance, demeanor, and race, Pager assessed the effect of prior prison experience on the likelihood that each applicant would be called back for an interview. The applicant assigned the criminal record signaled having served time by indicating six months of prison-work experience on his resume.

Figure 8.7 presents the main results from this study. For both black and white applicants, the call-back rate for the applicant with a criminal record is less than half the rate for auditors with no criminal record. Interestingly, the call-back rate for blacks who do not signal prior prison time is less than the call-back rate for whites with a prior prison term.

Such a pattern is consistent with either taste-based discrimination or employers statistically discriminating against black applicants without a signaled record in an attempt to avoid ex-offenders. Regardless, the results presented by Pager are stark and indicative of the employment barriers faced by ex-offenders.

Increasing Incarceration Rates and the Decline in Black Employment Rates

So far we have documented several facts. First, the rate of current incarceration among black men has increased considerably over the past three decades, with particularly pronounced increases among

Figure 8.7   Percentage of Applicants Called Back for an Interview by Race and Likelihood the Applicant Was Assigned a Criminal Record

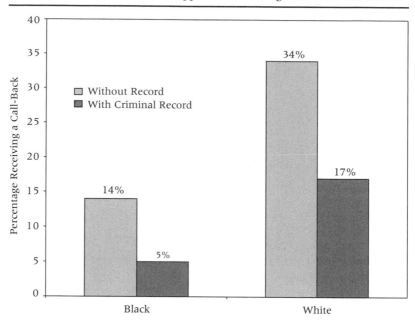

Source: Pager (2003).

prime-working-age, less-educated black men. Second, the proportion of black men with prison time on their criminal records has increased by even greater amounts. Third, serving time in prison substantially interrupts the potential work lives of young offenders, leading to at least six years of lost labor market experience for the median black offender in California, and more time for a sizable minority of offenders. Fourth, employers are averse to hiring ex-inmates, and use formal and informal screening methods to weed such individuals out of the applicant pool.

In addition to these criminal justice trends, we have also demonstrated that the employment rate of noninstitutionalized black men has declined over the same period. Between 1970 and 2000 the white-black employment-rate differential widened from eight percentage points to seventeen percentage points among noninstitutionalized men. For high school dropouts, this differential increased from seven to nineteen percentage points.

The preceding discussion suggests at least two avenues by which the increase in black incarceration rates may be related to the relative decline in black employment rates. First, with an increasing incarceration rate, the proportion of noninstitutionalized black men with prior prison time has increased. These men have less legitimate labor-market experience than otherwise similar men who have not been to prison and must contend with strong employer reluctance to hire ex-offenders. Second, men without criminal histories who are members of demographic groups where a large proportion has a criminal record may face statistical discrimination in the labor market and difficulty finding employment.

In this section, I test for a partial correlation between the proportion of a given subgroup of men who are institutionalized and the proportion of comparable noninstitutionalized men who are employed. These estimates are then used to provide an estimate of the proportion of the black-white employment rate differential among the noninstitutionalized that may be attributable to incarceration trends.

Using data from the 1970, 1980, 1990, and 2000 PUMS, I first estimate the proportion of noninstitutionalized men who are employed and the proportion of all men who are institutionalized for 320 demographic subgroups. The subgroups are defined by the interaction of four mutually exclusive race-ethnic groups, five age groups, four education groups, and four years. I use the five age groups and four education groups listed in tables 8.1 and 8.2, and compute separate figures for non-Hispanic whites, non-Hispanic blacks, non-Hispanic Asians, and Hispanics. I then estimate a series of regression models where the key dependent variable is the proportion of noninstitutionalized men who are employed and the key explanatory variable is the proportion of all men from the given demographic group who are institutionalized.

Table 8.8 presents these estimation results. Each model regresses the noninstitutionalized employment rate on dummy variables indicating the race-ethnicity of the group and interaction terms between these dummies and a set of year dummies.

The coefficients on these dummies provide estimates of the employment-rate differentials relative to whites in 1970 and changes in these differentials across decades. The first three regression models include a complete set of dummy variables indicating the age-education cell. The last three regressions include a complete set of

Table 8.8 Regressions of the Proportion Employed Among the Noninstitutionalized on the Proportion Institutionalized

	(1)	(2)	(3)	(4)	(5)	(6)
Black	-.045	-0.029	-0.073	-.058	-0.038	-0.045
	(.022)	(0.021)	(0.025)	(.013)	(0.010)	(0.015)
Black × 1980	-.073	-0.070	-0.010	-.060	-0.057	-0.019
	(.027)	(0.027)	(0.031)	(.016)	(0.013)	(0.019)
Black × 1990	-.085	-0.056	0.002	-.069	-0.041	-0.008
	(.028)	(0.027)	(0.032)	(.016)	(0.013)	(0.019)
Black × 2000	-.116	-0.064	-0.026	-.097	-0.049	-0.056
	(.027)	(0.027)	(0.030)	(.015)	(0.013)	(0.017)
Asian	-.104	-0.099	-0.109	-.096	-0.090	-0.092
	(.054)	(0.052)	(0.051)	(.031)	(0.025)	(0.025)
Asian × 1980	.027	0.024	0.035	.021	0.017	0.022
	(.064)	(0.061)	(0.060)	(.036)	(0.029)	(0.029)
Asian × 1990	.038	0.035	0.045	.027	0.023	0.025
	(.060)	(0.057)	(0.056)	(.035)	(0.028)	(0.027)
Asian × 2000	.024	0.019	0.029	.010	0.005	0.007
	(.057)	(0.055)	(0.054)	(.033)	(0.027)	(0.025)
Hispanic	-.025	-0.010	-0.048	-.035	-0.017	-0.024
	(.016)	(0.016)	(0.019)	(.009)	(0.008)	(0.012)
Hispanic × 1980	.027	0.008	0.051	.037	0.018	0.023
	(.027)	(0.026)	(0.028)	(.016)	(0.013)	(0.015)

	(1)	(2)	(3)	(4)	(5)	(6)
Hispanic × 1990	.037	0.028	0.072	.051	0.039	0.049
	(.024)	(0.023)	(0.026)	(.014)	(0.011)	(0.015)
Hispanic × 2000	−.035	−0.046	−0.007	−.014	−0.035	−0.028
	(.022)	(0.020)	(0.025)	(.013)	(0.014)	(0.014)
Institutionalized	—	−1.007	0.938	—	−1.076	−0.687
		(0.183)	(0.659)		(0.098)	(0.602)
Institutionalized × 1980	—	—	−2.518	—	—	−1.851
			(0.710)			(0.759)
Institutionalized × 1990	—	—	−2.220	—	—	−0.968
			(0.065)			(0.639)
Institutionalized × 2000	—	—	−1.861	—	—	−0.167
			(0.637)			(0.612)
Age-education dummies	Yes	Yes	Yes	Yes	Yes	Yes
Age-education dummies × year	No	No	No	Yes	Yes	Yes
R²	.837	.898	.903	.971	.981	.983
N	320	320	320	320	320	320

Source: One percent PUMS files, 1970, 1980, 1990, and 2000.

Note: All models include a constant term and year dummy variables. The dependent variable is the proportion of the noninstitutionalized age-race-education-year cell that is employed. The key explanatory variable is the proportion of each cell (including the institutionalized) that is institutionalized.

dummies indicating the age-education-year cells (thus allowing the effect on employment of being in a specific age-education group to change over time). Within these two groups of regressions, the first specification omits the variable measuring the proportion institutionalized, the second specification adds the institutionalization variables, and the final specification adds the institutionalization variable with a full set of interactions with the year dummies.[21]

Within both sets of regressions (those including and those omitting the age-education-year interaction terms), adding the proportion of institutionalized men reduces the coefficients on the interaction terms between the black and the year dummies. In other words, the proportion of institutionalized men explains part of the widening of the black-white employment rate differential in all decades between 1970 and 2000. For example, the results in regression model (1) indicate that after adjusting for age and education effects and year effects, the black-white employment-rate differential widened by twelve percentage points between 1970 and 2000. In contrast, the comparable estimate from regression (2) indicates a widening of 6.4 percentage points. The findings are similar in the models where the age-education dummies are interacted with year.

The proportion institutionalized has a strong negative effect on the proportion of noninstitutionalized men who are employed. In the models where the institutionalization variable is interacted with year, the proportion institutionalized has the largest effect on employment rates in 1980, followed by 1990, and 2000. Again, the regression results are comparable when the age-education-year interaction terms are included.

Figure 8.8 summarizes the effect of controlling for the proportion institutionalized on the white-black difference in employment rates among noninstitutionalized men. The employment rate differentials omitting controls for institutionalization come from the model (4) regression results, whereas the differentials adjusting for institutionalization come from the model (6) regression results. Adjusting for institutionalization reduces the residual employment-rate differential in all years, although the largest reductions occur in 1990 and 2000. In 1990, adjusting for institutionalization reduces the residual difference from 12.7 percentage points to 5.3 percentage points. In 2000, adjusting for institutionalization reduces this differential from 15.5 percentage points to 10.1 percentage points.

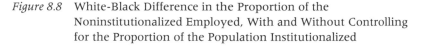

Figure 8.8 White-Black Difference in the Proportion of the Noninstitutionalized Employed, With and Without Controlling for the Proportion of the Population Institutionalized

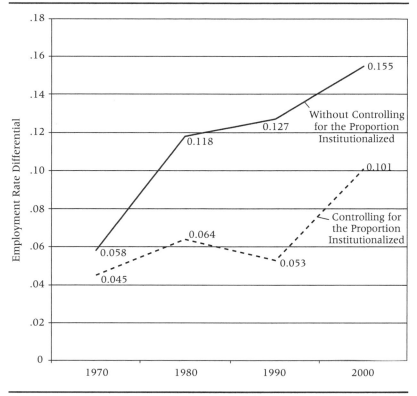

Source: One percent PUMS files, 1970, 1980, 1990, and 2000.

Thus, this very simple exercise yields a quite high upper-bound contribution of changes in incarceration rates to recent employment trends. To be sure, there are problems with this approach to the question. In particular, the proportion institutionalized within a given group is likely to be correlated with unobservable characteristics of men that vary within age-education cells and that determine their employability. Moreover, while the variation used to identify the effect of the institutionalization variable accounts for cross-year changes in the employment rates of the age-education subgroups, these employment-rate differentials may have changed within racial and ethnic groups, and in a manner correlated with changes in incarceration rates.[22] Nonetheless, the results suggest that incarceration trends may explain a large portion of currently observed racial employment-rate differentials.

Conclusion

This chapter documents several trends in the incarceration of black men and highlights the potential lasting effects of high incarceration rates on their future employment prospects and on their relative socioeconomic status. To summarize:

- The current incarceration rates of black men are extraordinarily high by historical comparison, especially for less-educated and relatively young black men.

- The proportion of black men ever having served time is even higher.

- Prison time substantially interrupts the potential work careers in the legitimate labor market of imprisoned young men.

- Employers are extremely reluctant to hire applicants who have served time in state or federal prison.

In addition, simple estimates presented suggest that a sizable portion of the black-white employment rate differentials may be attributable to the high rate of involvement of blacks with the criminal justice system. Across demographic groups defined by education, age, and race there is a strong inverse correlation between the proportion of the group currently institutionalized and the employment rate of the noninstitutionalized. Moreover, this partial correlation is strong enough to explain roughly one-third of the black-white employment-rate differential in 2000.

The continual increase in the lifetime likelihood of blacks going to prison between 1970 and 2000 suggests that the proportion of blacks with prior prison time is likely to increase in the coming years, even if current incarceration rates remain unchanged. This follows from the fact that the risk of incarceration is highest early in one's adult life, and that young men coming of age today face higher incarceration rates than those faced by comparable young men during the 1980s and 1990s. Thus, the barriers faced by ex-offenders are likely to hamper the socioeconomic progress of many black men for the foreseeable future.

Clearly, this is a topic that deserves future attention from both researchers and policymakers. There are several potentially fruitful directions that researchers can pursue. While the incarceration trends documented here are often attributable to changes in sentencing policy and potential changes in offending among young men, there are few systematic evaluations of the relative impact of behavioral trends and key policy choices as causal agents. For example, little work has been done on the relative impact of state versus federal sentencing reforms on black incarceration rates. At the state level, likely contributors to the trends in the incarceration of blacks are the shift from indeterminate to determinate sentencing, sentence enhancements for drug-related crime, such as those enacted under Governor Nelson Rockefeller in New York, three-strikes laws, and state-level sentence enhancement for violent crimes and crimes committed with a firearm. Additional potential contributors at the federal level are differential sentences for crimes involving crack versus powder cocaine, systematic efforts to try felons in possession of firearms in federal courts, and the federal sentencing reforms that limited judicial discretion. It would be most useful to assess the extent of these state and federal sentencing changes' disparate impact on blacks. Such research may be of help in deciding how to deploy criminal justice resources more efficiently and in assessing whether current sentencing policy is unnecessarily impacting the long-term employment prospects of an already disadvantaged group.

Despite the many qualitative evaluations of the effects of prisoner education and in-prison treatment programs, careful empirical studies employing rigorous experimental or quasi-experimental research designs are few and far between. Early nonexperimental evaluations of state employment programs tailored to paroled ex offenders (reviewed in Bushway and Reuter 2002) arrived at quite pessimistic conclusions regarding the ability of training and job-search assistance to lower the recidivism of parolees. Evaluations of more recent state programs, however, are uniformly more positive. In a review of recent research, Joan Petersilia (2002) cites several program evaluations that found program effects on the increased likelihood that parolees would find employment on the order of 20 percentage points, and effects on the reduced likelihood of rearrest and being returned to prison custody on the order of 10 percentage points. A review of nineteen studies by David B. Wilson et al. (2000) finds similar program effects.[23]

Careful reviews of the more recent evaluations tend to attribute the high estimates from the latter research to flaws in methodological design. Shawn Bushway and Peter Reuter (2002) as well as Wilson et al. (2000) note that few of the program evaluations are based on randomized designs where program participation is determined by random assignment rather than self-selection. Moreover, many of the evaluations do not control for differences in offender characteristics that may simultaneously explain program participation and recidivism or parole violation rates. Thus, there is much room for additional work.

In general, prisoner reentry policy is and will be an important determinant of the relative socioeconomic status of low-skilled black men. There is a great need for creative thinking on how to combine existing services for the economically disadvantaged (such as workforce development programs) with services targeting ex-offenders in a manner that will meet their needs and minimize the negative collateral consequences of prior prison time.

Notes

1. In addition to these race-specific trends, the overall U.S. incarceration is particularly high relative to those of other industrialized nations. Marc Mauer's (2003) international comparison of incarceration rates finds that the U.S. incarceration rate is roughly five times that of England, six times that of Canada, and over seven times that of Germany and France.
2. See Kristin Butcher and Anne Morrison Piehl (1998) for an analysis of incarceration among immigrant men that also uses the group-quarter variable to identify the incarcerated.
3. The BJS population estimates come from custody counts from the National Prisoner Statistics database and the 2001 Annual Survey of Jails. Thus, the census data and the BJS data come from entirely different sources.
4. The likelihood of entering prison is estimated from annual surveys of recent prison admissions, and mortality rates are based on mortality rates for the entire population adjusted upward by a fixed factor to account for observed average differences in mortality rates between ex-offenders and the general population.

5. This is due to the fact that earlier cohorts faced lower risks of incarceration during the high-criminal-activity portion of their life cycle.

6. Each record contains information on an internal California Department of Corrections (CDC) identity number that can be used to identify each inmate. Thus, the administrative records can be purged of inmates who serve multiple prison spells. See Raphael and David Weiman (2003) for a complete description of this administrative data set.

7. The prisoner survey estimates of the joint age-education-race density are needed because the California administrative records do not contain information on educational attainment.

8. To be sure, this does not mean that more than 100 percent of black men in this cell have served time in the past ten years. There are a number of factors that are likely to bias upward the count of unduplicated prisoners relative to the 2000 population. First, I calculated prisoner counts by age in 2000 without taking into account either the likely mortality of many of the inmates serving time during the 1990s or the likelihood that many of these inmates may have moved to another state after being released. In addition, a prisoner may be assigned additional internal CDC prisoner identification numbers for subsequent prison terms, which artificially inflates the number of unduplicated spells. This is unlikely to be a substantial source of bias, however, since tabulation based on prisoner Social Security numbers yields quite similar counts as the tabulations based on CDC identification codes. Finally, an undercount of black males in the census will suppress the denominator of this ratio below its actual level and inflate the rates reported earlier.

9. Lawrence F. Katz and Alan B. Krueger (1999) estimate that the decline in the national unemployment rate of 2.6 percentage points between 1985 and 1998 would have been .1 to .5 points lower if incarceration rates had not increased over this time period.

10. The "employed" classification comprises those who have a job and those who are in the armed forces. Excluding the armed forces from these calculations has little impact on the estimates in figures 8.3 through 8.7. These calculations make use of the 1970, 1980, 1990, and 2000 1 percent PUMS data.

11. This strategy is also employed by Derek Neal and William Johnson (1996) in their analysis of the effect of adjusting for scores on the Armed Forced Qualifying Test (AFQT) on estimates of residual racial wage differentials. Ignoring labor-market dropouts, Neal and Johnson find that accounting for AFQT scores explains nearly all of the residual wage differential between black and white workers observed in the National Longitudinal Survey of Youth. However, in least-absolute-deviation regressions that assign wage values of zero to all nonparticipants, a substantial AFQT-adjusted racial wage differential reappears.

12. The study does not provide an analysis of wage trends during the 1990s. Additional attempts to assess the importance of selection bias to estimates of trends in black-white wage ratios is provided by James J. Heckman, Rom Lyons, and Petra Todd (2000) and James P. Smith and Finis Welch (1986).

13. Of course, we are not saying that a year in prison is not costly. However, a year's absence from the labor market during the beginning of one's career would have only a small effect on accumulated experience.

14. In particular, California's high rate of parole violation and the fact that nearly all released inmates are released to parole status is unique among the fifty states.

15. White, Hispanic, and black inmates each account for approximately one third of the California state prison population. Asians and members of other racial groups account for a small proportion of inmates.

16. These data where collected in 1993 and 1994 from establishments in the Atlanta, Boston, Detroit, and Los Angeles metropolitan statistics areas. See Holzer, Raphael, and Stoll (2005) for a complete description of this survey.

17. We define "unlikely to hire" as responding that one would "probably not" or "definitely not" be willing to hire an applicant with the given characteristic.

18. Using a more detailed survey of employer preferences, Holzer, Raphael, and Stoll (2003) uncover a fair degree of nuance in employer sentiments with regard to ex-offenders. For example, employers are willing to consider such factors as specific offense and the amount of time lapsed since the offense was committed in evaluating applicants with criminal records.

19. See Holzer, Raphael, and Stoll (2003) for a description of this latter survey and the results.

20. In addition, the authors find this relative effect for the hiring of black men (but not black women) and for employer willingness to hire applicants from other stigmatized groups, especially workers with gaps in their employment histories.

21. Each regression is weighted by cell frequency. In addition, each regression includes a constant term and a set of base-year effects.

22. An alternative estimation strategy that may be used to address this issue would be to calculate the 320 sets of means for each state, and then include a full set of race-age-education-year fixed effects in the final specification. I experimented with this approach and found that the sample sizes using the 1 percent PUMS yielded extremely small cells for many states and thus quite imprecise estimates. Revisiting this exercise with the 5 percent samples, however, may solve this problem.

23. For detailed descriptions of three state-level job-training and placement programs, see Peter Finn (1998a, 1998b, 1998c).

References

Beck, Allen J., Jennifer C. Karberg, and Paige M. Harrison. 2002. *Prison and Jail Inmates at Midyear 2001.* Bureau of Justice Statistics report, NCJ 191702. Washington: U.S. Department of Justice, Bureau of Justice Statistics.

Bonczar, Thomas P. 2003. *Prevalence of Imprisonment in the U.S. Population, 1974–2001.* Bureau of Justice Statistics special report, NCJ 197976. Washington: U.S. Department of Justice, Bureau of Justice Statistics.

Bound, John, and Richard B. Freeman. 1992. "What Went Wrong? The Erosion of the Relative Earnings and Employment of Young Black Men in the 1980s." *Quarterly Journal of Economics* 107(1): 201–32.

Brown, Charles C. 1984. "Black-White Earnings Ratios Since the Civil Rights Act of 1964: The Importance of Labor Market Dropouts." *Quarterly Journal of Economics* 95(1): 31–44.

Bushway, Shawn, and Peter Reuter. 2002. "Labor Markets and Crime." In *Crime: Public Policies for Crime Control,* edited by James Q. Wilson and Joan Petersilia. Oakland, Calif.: Institute for Contemporary Studies Press.

Butcher, Kristin F., and Anne Morrison Piehl. 1998. "Recent Immigrants: Unexpected Implications for Crime and Incarceration." *Industrial & Labor Relations Review* 51(4): 654–79.

Chandra, Amitabh. 2003. "Is the Convergence in the Racial Wage Gap Illusory?" NBER working paper no. 9476. Cambridge, Mass.: National Bureau of Economic Research.

Craig, Scott R. 1987. "Negligent Hiring: Guilt By Association." *Personnel Administrator,* October, pp. 32–34.

Finn, Peter. 1998a. *Chicago's Safer Foundation: A Road Back for Ex-Offenders,* Washington, D.C., National Institute of Justice.

———. 1998b. *Successful Job Placement for Ex-Offenders: The Center for Employment Opportunities,* Washington, D.C.: National Institute of Justice.

———. 1998c. *Texas' Project RIO (Re-integrating of Offenders),* Washington, D.C., National Institute of Justice.

Hahn, J. M. 1991. "Pre-Employment Information Services: Employers Beware," *Employee Relations Law Journal,* 17(1): 45–69.

Heckman, James J., Rom Lyons, and Petra Todd. 2000. "Understanding Black-White Wage Differentials." *American Economic Review* 90(2): 344–49.

Holzer, Harry J., and Paul Offner. 2002. "Trends in the Employment Outcomes of Young Black Men, 1979–2000." Discussion paper no. 1247-02. Institute for Research on Poverty, University of Wisconsin-Madison.

Holzer, Harry J., Steven Raphael, and Michael A. Stoll. 2003. "Employer Demand for Ex-Offenders: Recent Evidence from Los Angeles." Working paper. Los Angeles: Center for the Study of Urban Poverty.

————. 2005. "Perceived Criminality, Racial Background Checks, and the Racial Hiring Practices of Employers." *Journal of Law and Economics.*

Juhn, Chinhui. 2003. "Labor Market Dropouts and Trends in the Wages of Black and White Men." *Industrial and Labor Relations* 56(4): 643–62.

Katz, Lawrence F., and Alan B. Krueger. 1999. "The High-Pressure U.S. Labor Market of the 1990s." *Brookings Papers on Economic Activity,* edited by William C. Brainard and George C. Perry. Volume 1. Washington, D.C.: Brookings Institution.

Mauer, Marc. 2003. "Comparative International Rates of Incarceration: An Examination of Causes and Trends." Report. Washington, D.C.: The Sentencing Project.

Neal, Derek, and William Johnson. 1996. "The Role of Pre-Market Factors in Black-White Wage Differences." *Journal of Political Economy* 104(5): 869–95.

Pager, Devah. 2003. "The Mark of a Criminal Record." *American Journal of Sociology* 108(5): 937–75.

Petersilia, Joan. 2002. "Community Corrections." In *Crime: Public Policies for Crime Control,* edited by James Q. Wilson and Joan Petersilia. Oakland, Calif.: Institute for Contemporary Studies Press.

————. 2003. *When Prisoners Come Home: Parole and Prisoner Reentry.* Oxford: Oxford University Press.

Raphael, Steven, and Michael Stoll. 2004. "The Effect of Prison Releases on Regional Crime Rates." In *Brookings-Wharton Papers on Urban Affairs,* edited by William G. Gale and Janet Rothenberg Pack. Washington, D.C.: Brookings Institution.

Raphael, Steven, and David Weiman. 2003. "The Impact of Local Labor Market Conditions on the Likelihood That Parolees Are Returned to Custody." Unpublished manuscript.

Smith, James P., and Finis Welch. 1986. *Closing the Gap: Forty Years of Economic Progress for Blacks.* Santa Monica: Rand Corporation.

U.S. Census Bureau. 2003. "Technical Assessment of A.C.E. Revision II." Accessed on March 17, 2004, at http://www.census.gov.dmd/www/ace2.html.

Western, Bruce, and Becky Petit. 2000. "Incarceration and Racial Inequality in Men's Employment," *Industrial and Labor Relations Review* 54(1): 3–16.

Wilson, David B., Catherine A. Gallagher, and Doris L. MacKenzie. 2000. "A Meta-Analysis of Corrections-Based Education, Vocation, and Work Programs for Adult Offenders." *Journal on Research in Crime and Delinquency* 37(4): 347–68.

Chapter 9

Public Health and Mortality:
What Can We Learn from the Past?

Dora L. Costa and Matthew E. Kahn

City life in the nineteenth and early twentieth century was dirty and dangerous (Melosi 2000). The water and milk supply of cities was contaminated with bacteria that caused typhoid fever, dysentery, and diarrhea. Cities did not remove sewage and their streets were filled with garbage and carrion. The influx of migrants from abroad and from rural areas who crowded into dank and dark urban tenements provided new foci of infection and new victims, and the rapid transmission of disease from host to host increased the diseases' virulence. An infant in a large city in 1890 was 88 percent more likely to die than an infant in a rural area and 48 percent more likely to die in the 1900s (Haines 2001), and nowhere was the urban mortality penalty as large as in the poor areas of cities, where crowding was greatest and parents could not afford to buy clean water and milk (Rochester 1923). City life left those who survived to age sixty permanently scarred, their lives shortened even when later residential moves are controlled for (Costa 2003; Costa and Lahey 2005). By 1940, however, the urban mortality penalty had disappeared and life in a city was in many ways healthier than life in the countryside (Haines 2001). Between 1902 and 1929, the urban death rate from waterborne causes had fallen by 88 percent (Cain and Rotella 2001).

This chapter focuses on the mortality transition in American city life between 1910 and 1930, a change that was only possible because of very expensive investments in city infrastructure. These investments dwarfed all other forms of public assistance. In 1913, the United States was spending twice as much on hospitals and health as it was on public poor relief and welfare (Lindert 2004). In contrast, in 1980 the United States was spending three times as much on public poor relief and welfare as on hospitals and health for the poor. Although later public policies, such as those of the New Deal, were also effective in reducing mortality (Fishback, Haines, and Kantor 2002), the reduction in mortality prior to 1930 was perhaps the foremost public policy success of the twentieth century.

When one investigates the determinants of state and local generosity in this time period (the federal government played only a minor role), an intriguing puzzle emerges. In the present day, several empirical studies of the determinants of local generosity (see Orr 1976; Luttmer 2001; Bahl, Martinez-Vazquez and Wallace 2002; Alesina and Glaeser 2004) have documented that support for redistribution (typically, welfare payments) is lower in areas where more minorities live and higher in areas with greater ethnic and racial homogeneity (see, for example Luttmer 2001; Poterba 1997). Unlike in the present day, we find that in the early twentieth century United States, support for redistribution was higher in areas with more blacks and immigrants. Our argument is not that the middle class has become less altruistic over time. Instead, we focus on the self-interest of the middle class as a motivating factor in catalyzing support for large public health investments.

Increased government expenditure for the poor is intended to increase their quality of life, but such expenditures can have unintended consequences. Today, some look at San Francisco's large homeless population and wonder whether this tolerant city's generosity has acted as a magnet attracting more homeless to move there. Public-finance economists have conducted analyses of "crowd-out"—the notion that increased government expenditure "crowds out" private donations to charity—to test the concept's validity. Where the vast majority of tests related to the unintended consequences of government redistribution have focused on modern data, we use our historical data to test for whether generous cities are immigrant magnets and for whether there is a negative correlation between city charity expenditure and private charity.

What is the effectiveness of government expenditure in improving the health of the population? In short, did public health investments save lives? And if so, whose? Urban blacks faced much higher death rates than urban whites. Did public health investments help close this racial mortality gap? Our findings contribute to a growing urban economic-history literature that measures the health benefits from increased public expenditure (Cain and Rotella 2001; Haines 2003; Troesken 2004).

We estimate individual-level and city-level health-production functions to test whether, holding other factors constant, cities that spend more on public health have lower death rates from diseases with a public health component. Complicating the process of resolving this important public policy issue is the potential endogeneity of public health spending. Louis B. Cain and Elyce J. Rotella (2001) argue that city public health investment is likely to be high in cities that had a public health epidemic in previous years. In this case, ordinary least squares regression estimates of the city-level health-production function could yield the surprising finding that increased government expenditure *raises* a city's death rate! We present instrumental-variable strategies for examining this issue.

This section's contribution to the urban historical public health literature is to examine the effectiveness of public spending using a larger sample, using individual-level data to control for individual covariates, and extending our analysis to 1940, when the urban mortality penalty had disappeared. By examining individual-level data we can determine whether the poor benefited more than the middle class from increased public spending.

By estimating individual-level infant mortality regressions, we provide new evidence on whether blacks benefited more from public health expenditures, as argued by Werner Troesken (2004), or whether they benefited less, as argued by Robert Higgs (1980). In addition to examining microdata, we also use a large city panel data set covering the years 1912 to 1925 and a state-year panel data set with death rates by race from 1910 to 1940 to provide a more comprehensive analysis of the effectiveness and incidence of public spending.

Of life-long interest to Eugene Smolensky was the ongoing challenge of designing programs that improve the quality of life of the poor by providing resources for this group without creating perverse incentives that discourage work or human-capital accumulation. Today's welfare-reform debate wrestles with this issue (Smolensky,

Evenhouse, and Reilly 1997). As compared to public assistance, public health investment is a likely example of a program that benefits the poor without distorting incentives.

First the determinants of city and state public health expenditures in the past are examined, using cross-city-level data to determine what the correlates of urban redistribution were in the past. We present two tests of the unintended consequences of these expenditures. We then investigate the public health gains achieved through public health investments, utilizing a combination of individual-, city-, and state-level data to estimate health-production functions and to test whether death rates decline when local governments spend more on public health.

Finally, "value of life" estimates and new compensating differential estimates are used to value the benefits of public spending. We find that the average city was underinvesting in public health. We conclude with some conjectures explaining why under-investments could occur.

Early-Twentieth-Century Local Redistributionary Expenditure

The United States has traditionally spent little on social transfers. In 1910 the United States was below the median of what are now the OECD countries for social transfers as a percentage of gross domestic product (Lindert 2004). The United States redistributed .56 percent of its GDP while Denmark's social transfers equaled 1.75 percent of GDP. In 1995, even though the share of its GDP that the United States spent on social transfers ballooned to 14 percent, it was still below the median. Examining redistribution within the United States can help us understand why the United States has always been a low spender.

We first study the determinants of redistribution differentials, using three measures of government redistribution in the past:

1. Total per-capita expenditures in 1913 by state and local (county and incorporated places) government on the two categories of charities, hospitals, and corrections, and recreation, health, and sanitation.

2. Per-capita expenditures in 1907 by cities on three subcategories: health, sanitation, and charities.

3. Per-capita expenditures in 1930 by cities on boards of health.

Although these three measures are not strictly comparable, they all work as indicators of government generosity. The 1907 data, which can be broken down into its subcomponents, show that the largest component of health expenditures was expenditures on sanitation. In 159 cities, median per-capita expenditure in 1907 dollars on health, sanitation, and charities combined was $1.59 (the maximum was $6.47). Median per-capita expenditures on the individual categories of health, sanitation, and charities were 17 cents, 40 cents, and 82 cents, respectively. The greater the expenditure on a single category, the greater the expenditure on all categories. The correlations between per-capita spending on health and sanitation, sanitation and charities, and health and charities were .42, .39, and .20, respectively.

In order to examine what local attributes are correlated with relative state and city generosity and whether the political variables that we hope to use later as instrumental variables have any explanatory power, ordinary least squares (OLS) regressions were run, of the form:

$$(9.1) \qquad \log(E_{lt}) = \beta_0 + \beta_1 X_{lt} + \beta_2 P_{lt} + u_{lt}$$

where E is expenditures per capita in city l at time t, X is a vector of demographic and socioeconomic characteristics, and P is a vector of political variables. Three OLS regressions were run: one for combined state and local expenditures on charities and health in 1913; a second for 1907 city expenditures on health, charities, and sanitation; and a third for city expenditure on boards of health in 1930.

Table 9.1 shows that both demographic characteristics and city heterogeneity matter when it comes to these expenditures. Larger cities are more generous. In 1907 the population elasticity is .22; in 1930 it is .19. Locations with older residents spend more on redistribution, but this coefficient is only statistically significant in the state-level regression.

Table 9.1   Determinants of Per-Capita State and City Expenditure
Generosity

City and State Characteristics	Log(1913 Combined State and City Expenditures)	Log(1907 City Health, Charities, and Sanitation Expenditures)	Log(1930 City Health Board Expenditures)
Log(population)	0.056	0.223***	0.185*
	(0.035)	(0.047)	(0.094)
Mean age	0.086***	0.047	0.027
	(0.016)	(0.033)	(0.038)
Duncan index	0.029	0.053***	0.002
	(0.020)	(0.020)	(0.025)
Standard deviation	0.070*	−0.087**	−0.042
of Duncan index	(0.041)	(0.036)	(0.046)
Fraction black	1.081*	1.675***	3.849***
	(0.614)	(0.621)	(1.484)
Fraction foreign-	5.980***	3.838**	2.500***
born	(0.701)	(1.666)	(1.098)
State share of	0.047***	1.138***	−0.270
Democrats, U.S.	(0.013)	(0.339)	(0.373)
House of			
Representatives			
State share of	−0.009	−0.747***	0.312
Democrats, U.S.	(0.008)	(0.226)	(0.239)
Senate			
Average years of			
service of state			
representatives:			
House	0.047***	0.149**	0.011
	(0.013)	(0.060)	(0.019)
Senate	−0.009	−0.008	0.031*
	(0.008)	(0.144)	(0.015)
R^2	0.895	0.587	0.300
Observations	48	132	116

Source: Authors' compilation; see Data Appendix.
Note: Ordinary least squares regressions are of state and city health-care and sanitation spending on state and city characteristics, including region fixed effects (four regions) and a constant. See equation 9.1 in the text. Robust standard errors (clustered on state in the city regressions) are in parentheses. The symbols *, **, and *** indicate that the coefficient is statistically different from 0 at the 10, 5, and 1 percent level respectively.

Richer locations (as proxied by the Duncan Index), an indicator of occupational status based upon average occupational earnings in 1959, spend more (Orr 1976; Lindert 1994).[1] Cities where income fragmentation (as proxied by the standard deviation of the Duncan Index) was high, distributed less, consistent with Dora L. Costa and Matthew E. Kahn's (2003) results of the importance of income fragmentation to such social-capital proxies as volunteering. Surprisingly, at the state level greater income fragmentation predicted greater spending.[2] It was also surprising, given that the literature on modern spending finds less spending when ethnic and racial fragmentation is high, that expenditures were greater in cities and states with a higher fraction of blacks and the foreign-born. A ten-percentage-point increase in the foreign-born increased 1907 city expenditures by 38 percent. A ten-percentage-point increase in the city's black population increased spending by 16 percent. Breaking out total spending into each of the three subcategories—charities, health, and sanitation—yields the same finding. Per-capita redistributionary spending is higher in cities where a larger share of the population is black.

To be sure, a benevolent planner might allocate greater spending per capita to areas where there are greater numbers of needy poor people, but why would self-interested middle-class taxpayers be so generous?[3] Relatively recent studies of the determinants of cross-state differences in AFDC (Aid to Families with Dependent Children) generosity such as Larry Orr's (1976) have reported that a state's generosity was negatively correlated with its minority population share. Were cities more generous toward minorities in the past than in the present? One plausible explanation is the ongoing decline in transportation costs over the last hundred years. When the vast majority of a city's employment was located in its downtown and the suburbs were not developed, the rich and poor lived in much closer physical proximity. Although these groups lived in separate communities, there was a greater potential that a public health shock such as infectious disease in the poor community could have a contagion effect on the richer community. Middle-class and rich taxpayers might view public health investments as a type of insurance policy. Today, as employment has been suburbanized and transportation costs between home and office have fallen, the middle-class and the rich are separated by "a moat" from the day-to-day life of the poor and have less of an incentive to vote for redistribution that benefits the poor. "In a world, where blacks and whites lived in close proximity 'sewers for everyone' was an aesthetically sound strategy. Failing to install water and sewer mains in black neighborhoods increased the risk of diseases spreading from black neighborhoods to white ones," writes Troesken (2004, 10).

Chinatown in San Francisco offers an interesting case study (Craddock 2000). Within the city, typhoid rates were highest in the immigrant Chinatown area. To reduce the chances of a public health crisis emerging from Chinatown, steps were taken proactively to invest in public health. Civic leaders recognized that this poor, densely populated community interacted with the native middle-class community and hence there existed the possibility of disease contagion. A rather large percentage of Chinese immigrants who lived in Chinatown worked outside of Chinatown in laundries and as cooks and domestic workers. Many also traveled to outlying farm areas and transported produce and other commodities from truck farms to the city of San Francisco (personal communication with Susan Craddock). "The Chinese were in the very center of the city, strategically located to infect the rest of San Francisco with their diseases" (Craddock 2000, 135). Table 9.1 shows a fairly large positive population elasticity in raising per-capita redistribution rates. This positive population coefficient may partially reflect an urban density effect.

Political variables also predict state and city spending. We hypothesize that states and cities whose congressmen and senators are Democrats and who have greater seniority spend more on redistribution. With the exception of those from the South, Democrats (controlling for regional fixed effects) have traditionally had an ideology that emphasized more redistribution, and seniority positively correlates with more money for the home state. We find that both 1913 state and 1907 city generosity is positively correlated with the share of Democrats in the House of Representatives and with average years of service. The same was not true of the Senate, and in 1930 our political variables were poor predictors.

Unintended Consequences of Public Expenditure for the Poor

Local public redistribution can affect the decisions of poor households as to where to live and the charity decisions of well-off households. An ongoing public policy debate focuses on whether state and local generosity triggers "welfare magnet" effects and a "race to the bottom" whereby more and more poor people move to the location where they can get charity, with the result that their circumstances actually worsen. The literature on welfare magnets has examined whether in the present day the poor migrate and seek out more generous places (Borjas 1999; Blank 1988). George Borjas (1999) has argued that international migrants have the largest "welfare arbitrage" responses, disproportionately moving to high-welfare-benefit states such as California relative to native poor people, because they have already made the decision to move. This hypothesis was tested in the past. Using microdata from the 1900 and 1920 micro census data, for each city the total number of immigrants over the age of eighteen who moved to the United States in the preceding ten years was counted. A cross-city regression was estimated where the dependent variable was the log of the count of immigrants in the city in 1920. This was regressed on the log of the count of immigrants in that city in 1900, the log of city population in 1907, and the log of that city's per-capita redistribution in 1907, controlling for nine region-fixed effects.

$$\text{Immigrants in 1920} = .229 \times (\text{city population}) + .706$$
$$(.118) \qquad\qquad (.095)$$
$$\times (\text{Immigrants in 1990}) + .078 \times \text{Redistribute}$$
$$(.135)$$

$$N = 132$$
$$R^2 = .77$$

The conclusion was that there is no statistically significant evidence that in the past, immigrants migrated to cities that redistributed more generously.

The second hypothesis tested was whether public generosity crowds out private generosity or whether the two complement each other. To study whether people living in generous cities contributed less to private charity we used microdata from the 1917-to-1919 Consumer Expenditure Survey, which provides detailed information on expenditures, including charitable expenditures (which were less than 1 percent of total expenditures for the mean household), and also includes geographical identifiers for cities. We first regressed the share of total expenditures spent on charity, called "Charity," for family i in city j on the logarithm of total expenditures and on demographic characteristics, X, and on city fixed effects, called "City,"

$$(9.2) \qquad \text{Charity}_{it} = \beta_0 + \beta_1 X_{il} + \beta_2 \left(\text{City}_1 \right) + u_{il}$$

where u is an error term. We recovered the city fixed effects from our estimated regression and merged these city fixed effects to our data on city expenditures. Finally, we graphed the relationship between private generosity within cities and per-capita public expenditures (see figure 9.1). The negative and statistically significant relationship between the private-charity city fixed effects and public city generosity suggests that private charity and city expenditures were substitutes for each other.[4]

Did Money Matter in Improving Public Health?

Death rates offer us an important, measurable outcome indicator for determining whether public expenditure improved the poor's qual-

Figure 9.1   Cross-City Variation in Charity Versus Public-Goods Expenditure

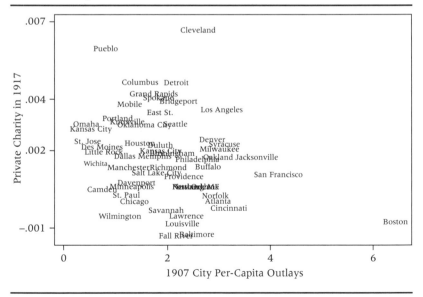

ity of life. There are two different empirical strategies for measuring the benefits of greater public health expenditure. One approach looks within specific cities on a community-by-community basis to establish whether investments in sewage and water supplies reduced mortality from typhoid fever, dysentery, and diarrhea (Condran and Cheney 1982). A second type of evidence focuses on cross-city analysis. In this section, we will estimate health-production regressions at the individual, city, and state level, using new data sets, each with its own strengths and weaknesses. All else being equal, does greater expenditure on public health reduce the urban death rate? Details of the data construction are provided in the appendix.

Individual-Level Data

We used the 1910 and 1940 microdata from the Census of Population and Housing to study the probability that a mother experienced an infant death as a function of her household's characteristics, the city size, and either the city's expenditures on health and sanitation or such health characteristics of the city as water filtration. Following Samuel H. Preston and Michael R. Haines (1991), we calculated a mortality index for each married woman equal to the number of child deaths experienced divided by the expected number of deaths for her marital duration. We calculated number of deaths in 1910 as the difference between the number of children ever born and the number of children surviving. In 1940 we calculate the number of deaths as the difference between the number of children ever born and the number of own children in the household. We limit the sample to women whose marital duration was less than fifteen years.

Our health-production functions, estimated separately for whites and for blacks, allow us to determine whether, all else being equal, death rates are lower in cities that spend more on health and sanitation. The functions we estimate are of the form:

$$(9.3) \qquad m_{ilt} = \beta_0 + \beta_1 \log(E_{lt}) + \beta_2 C_{lt} + \beta_3 X_{ilt} + u_{ilt}$$

where m is the mortality index for each individual i in city j at time t, E is per-capita city-level health expenditures, C is a vector of dummies indicating city size (greater than 1,500,000, between 300,000 and 1,500,000, between 100,000 and 300,000, and less than 100,000), X is a vector of socioeconomic and demographic characteristics, and u is an error term. We report estimates of equation 9.3 using OLS and instrumental variables.

Our OLS estimates for whites indicate that controlling for a range of household attributes, white child death rates declined as the city spent more on redistribution (see table 9.2). The mean mortality index in the white sample is .88, which implies an infant mortality rate of roughly .11 in a Model West life table.

Increasing expenditures by one standard deviation therefore would decrease the mortality index by .08 and the infant mortality rate by roughly .01. In contrast, black children did not benefit from increased city expenditure. Consistent with Preston and Haines's (1991) results, we find that a large city population raised death risk for both white and black children but disproportionately raised it for blacks. Note that for black children the effect of being in one of the largest cities was five times worse than for white children (a coefficient of 1.053 versus .242).

We recognize that city-level health expenditure is unlikely to be randomly assigned. Cities are likely to spend more if in the past they have had a health crisis (Cain and Rotella 2001). If the error term is serially correlated, this means that OLS estimates of β_1 are biased toward zero. We therefore instrument for city expenditures using the city-level variables in table 9.1, that is, a city's demographic and socioeconomic characteristics and the political characteristics of the state. In the white sample, our estimated coefficient on city spending increases (in absolute value) from −.127 to −.172 and is still statistically significant. In the black sample the coefficient on city spending increases and becomes statistically significant, but its positive sign implies that higher spending increases black child mortality. We suspect that because large cities spent more, our estimated coefficients on spending in part reflect city size. Our suspicion is reinforced by the much smaller coefficient on city size in the IV (instrumental-variable) regression.

The results in table 9.2 raise a puzzle. As shown in table 9.1, per-capita redistribution is higher in cities with a larger black population. Table 9.2 shows that in 1910, black mortality was not declining in response to this expenditure. Troesken (2004) argues that black health gains occurred more slowly in more segregated cities. Using the dissimilarity measure of racial residential segregation of David M. Cutler, Edward L. Glaeser, and Jacob L. Vigdor (1999) for sixty-four

Table 9.2 Effect of City Population and City Expenditures on Child Mortality, 1910 Census Microdata

	OLS		IV	
	White	Black	White	Black
Dummy = 1 if city population is				
More than 1,500,000	0.242***	1.053*	0.286***	0.726
	(0.068)	(0.562)	(0.101)	(0.594)
300,000 to 1,500,000	0.264***	0.617*	0.316***	0.526
	(0.089)	(0.327)	(0.118)	(0.455)
100,000 to 300,000	0.091	−0.176	0.107	−0.287
	(0.075)	(0.375)	(0.079)	(0.416)
Less than 100,000				
Log(per-capita expenditures on health, sanitation, and charities in city) in 1907	−0.127**	0.351	−0.172*	0.878*
	(0.059)	(0.269)	(0.104)	(0.512)
R^2	0.027	0.144	0.026	0.512
Observations	7,061	372	6,693	352
Number of cities	143	67	142	66

Source: Authors' compilation.

Notes: Estimated from the 1910 census integrated public use microdata sets for all married women whose husbands were present in the household, who had ever had children, whose marital duration was less than fifteen years, and for whom the number of children ever born was no greater than marital duration. Health expenditures are from the 1907 *Statistics of Cities,* U.S. Census Bureau (1910). Mean per-capita health expenditures in 1907 dollars in cities were $2.69 in the white sample and $2.50 in the black sample. Ordinary least squares regressions are of the mortality index on city health expenditures controlling for the logarithm of city population. Additional control variables include the woman's age, a dummy variable equal to 1 if the household owned its own home, dummies for the husband's occupational class (professional, managerial, clerical and sales, crafts, service, operative, laborer, and no occupation), a dummy equal to 1 if the mother worked, dummies for the mother's place of birth if white (United States, Canada, Scandinavia, Britain, Ireland, Germany, Poland or Russia, Italy, other southern Europe, other Eastern Europe, and other), average July temperature in the state, and nine region dummies. See equation 9.3 in the text. Instruments in the IV regressions are the fraction of the city population that is black and the fraction that is foreign-born, the city's average Duncan socioeconomic index, the city's standard deviation in the Duncan socioeconomic index, the state's share of Democrats in the U.S. Senate, the state's share of Democrats in the U.S. House, the average number of years of service of the state's representatives in the U.S. Senate, and the average number of years of service of the state's representatives in the U.S. House. Washington, D.C., is excluded from the IV regression. Robust standard errors clustered on city in parentheses. The symbols *, **, and *** indicate that the coefficient is significantly different from 0 at the 10, 5, and 1 percent level.

cities, we find that controlling for a city's population and the percentage of its population that is black, more segregated cities spend more on redistribution. This finding is borderline statistically significant.

City expenditures measured in dollars may represent different "treatments" in different cities. Large expenditures may translate into little tangible improvements in the health of the poor if expenditures are high because of urban patronage. Cities obtaining their water from wells or mountain springs instead of lakes or rivers would need to make fewer health investments. Still other cities may have invested before the year 1907 in fixed cost infrastructure with little variable cost. Based on our "flow" data from 1907, we would classify them as low-expenditure cities when in fact they had made their health investments in the past.

We therefore turn to "stock" indicators of city public health infrastructure investment. Our two stock indicators are the fraction of the city population whose dwelling had a sewer connection and a dummy variable indicating whether the city filtered its water by 1905. We estimate equation 9.2 substituting these "real" investments for the expenditure variable results reported in table 9.2.

Table 9.3 shows that child mortality among whites was lower in cities where a high proportion of the population had a sewer connection and in cities that filtered their water by 1905. The effects of water filtration were particularly strong, probably because there was much more variation among cities.

When we interact whether or not a city filtered its water by 1905 with a dummy variable indicating home ownership, we find that the poor whites (the non-owners) were the primary beneficiaries of water filtration, perhaps because in the absence of water filtration they could take fewer steps to protect themselves. Blacks benefited very little from city health investments. Our coefficients in table 9.3 are almost all positive (but insignificant). The interaction of water filtration with home ownership suggests that black home owners were the primary beneficiaries of water filtration, perhaps because water service and water filtration had not yet come to the poorer black neighborhoods. As in our previous regressions, it may not be possible to disentangle the effects of city health investments from those of city size. When we exclude city-size indicators from our regressions, we find that in the black sample the coefficient on the fraction of the city population with a sewer connection becomes −.115 ($\hat{\sigma} = .093$). Although the coefficient is still statistically insignificant, the point

Table 9.3 Effect of City Health Characteristics on Child Mortality, 1910 Census Microdata

	Number of Regional Dummies	White		Black	
		Coefficient	R^2	Coefficient	R^2
Independent variable is sewer connection					
1. Log(fraction of city with sewer connection)	4	−0.058** (0.029)	0.025	0.048 (0.122)	0.116
2. Log(fraction of city with sewer connection)	9	−0.036 (0.031)	0.026	0.021 (0.107)	0.148
Observations		7,226		372	
Number of cities		157		69	
Independent variable is water filtration					
1. Dummy = 1 if city filtered water by 1905	4	−0.202*** (0.070)	0.028	0.115 (0.402)	0.113
2. Dummy = 1 if city filtered water by 1905	9	−0.196*** (0.079)	0.030	0.234 (0.393)	0.135

(Table continues on p. 374.)

Table 9.3 Effect of City Health Characteristics on Child Mortality, 1910 Census Microdata (*Continued*)

	Number of Regional Dummies	White		Black	
		Coefficient	R^2	Coefficient	R^2
Independent variables are water filtration and interaction					
1. Dummy = 1 if city filtered water by 1905	9	−0.247*** (0.089)	0.030	0.294 (0.409)	0.137
2. City filtered water by 1905 × (dummy = 1 if owned home)		0.154 (0.088)		−0.988 (0.806)	
Observations		6,562		351	
Number of cities		147		59	

Source: Authors' compilation.

Notes: Estimated from the 1910 census integrated public use microdata sets for all married women whose husbands were present in the household, who had ever had children, whose marital duration was less than fifteen years, and for whom the number of children ever born was no greater than marital duration. Information on sewer connections and on water filtration comes from the 1909 and 1916 *Social Statistics of Cities*, respectively, U.S. Census Bureau (various years). The mean percentage of the population with a sewer connection in the city was 81 percent in the white sample and 70 percent in the black sample. The mean percentage of the population in a city that filtered water by 1905 was 33 percent in the white sample and 32 percent in the black sample. Regressions are ordinary least squares regressions of the mortality index on city health characteristics controlling for city size. (Regressions are similar except city health characteristics are substituted for city expenditures.) In examining water filtration the sample is restricted to cities with information on their water supply system. Additional control variables include the woman's age, a dummy variable equal to 1 if the household owned its own home, dummies for the husband's occupational class (professional, managerial, clerical and sales, crafts, service, operative, laborer, and no occupation), a dummy equal to 1 if the mother worked, dummies for the mother's place of birth if white (United States, Canada, Scandinavia, Britain, Ireland, Germany, Poland or Russia, Italy, other southern Europe, other Eastern Europe, and other), and average July temperature in the state. Robust standard errors clustered on city in parentheses. The symbols *, **, and *** indicate that the coefficient is significantly different from 0 at the 10, 5, and 1 percent level.

estimate implies that blacks benefited more than whites from city investments in sewage connections.

Table 9.4 presents our results for 1940. Note that neither city health board expenditures in 1930 nor city size was a significant predictor of child mortality for either whites or blacks.

Our findings on city size are consistent with Haines's (2003) account of the disappearance of the urban mortality penalty. By 1930 most cities had solved most of their sanitation problems, though health problems did remain. A survey conducted by the White House Conference on Child Health revealed that only 51 percent of the preschool children surveyed in cities and 37 percent of the preschool children surveyed in rural areas had ever had a health checkup and that only 13 percent of children in both urban and rural areas had ever had a dental exam. Among children in this age group only 21 percent of those in cities were vaccinated against smallpox and diphtheria (Palmer et al. 1931).

Table 9.5 shows that child mortality among whites was lower in cities where a higher percentage of children had had a health exam. Generally this health examination was given prior to age one (and none were given after age one) and roughly 10 percent of all children who had an exam got it from a public dispensary (Palmer et al. 1931).

However, health examinations may still have been valuable in lowering child mortality because most child mortality was below age one and because information about child health may have been transmitted to mothers. In addition, however, a high percentage of health examinations could reflect the availability of children's health services in dispensaries. We do not believe that it reflects general health consciousness, because vaccination and dental examinations should also be indicators of health consciousness and these are not statistically significant predictors of child mortality. Cities with a greater percentage of children who had had health exams also spent more; although aggregate health board expenditures may not have been beneficial, at least spending on public dispensaries was effective.

Table 9.5 shows that only whites benefited from health examinations; in fact, the greater the number of health examinations in the city per unit of population, the higher the black child mortality rate. We also found that among whites, non-owners benefited more than owners. When we interacted our home-ownership dummy variable with the logarithm of the percentage of children having health exam-

Table 9.4　　Effect of City Population and City Expenditures on Child Mortality, 1940 Census Microdata

	OLS		IV	
	White	Black	White	Black
Dummy = 1 if city population is				
More than 1,500,000	0.010	−0.113	0.013	−0.187
	(0.071)	(0.339)	(0.071)	(0.339)
300,000 to 1,500,000	−0.000	−0.412	0.008	−0.475
	(0.072)	(0.291)	(0.075)	(0.285)
100,000 to 300,000	0.022	−0.086	0.024	−0.133
	(0.080)	(0.334)	(0.080)	(0.319)
Less than 100,000				
Log(per-capita health	0.032	0.085	0.016	0.061
expenditures) in 1930	(0.020)	(0.082)	(0.036)	(0.064)
R^2	0.021	0.138	0.029	0.150
Observations	4,364	289	4,318	281
Number of cities	64	39	63	38

Source: Authors' compilation.
Notes: Estimated from the 1940 census integrated public use microdata sets for all married women whose husbands were present in the household, who had ever had children, whose marital duration was less than 15 years, and for whom the number of children ever born was no greater than marital duration. Health-expenditure information is from *the White House Conference on Child Health and Protection.* Mean per-capita health expenditures (including those on hospitals, medical poor relief, and plumbing) were $1.17 in 1930 dollars in the white sample and $1.13 in 1930 dollars in the black sample. Regressions are ordinary least squares regressions of the mortality index on city health expenditures controlling for the logarithm of city population. Additional control variables include the woman's age, a dummy variable equal to 1 if the household owned its own home, dummies for the husband's occupational class (professional, managerial, clerical and sales, crafts, service, operative, laborer, and no occupation), a dummy equal to 1 if the mother worked, dummies for the mother's place of birth if white (United States, Canada, Scandinavia, Britain, Ireland, Germany, Poland or Russia, Italy, other southern Europe, other eastern Europe, and other), average July temperature in the state, and nine region dummies. See equation 9.3 in the text. Instruments in the IV regressions are the fraction of the city population that is black and the fraction that is foreign-born, the city's average Duncan socioeconomic index, the city's standard deviation in the Duncan socioeconomic index, the state's share of Democrats in the U.S. Senate, the state's share of Democrats in the U.S. House, the average number of years of service of the state's representatives in the U.S. Senate, and the average number of years of service of the state's representatives in the U.S. House. Washington, D.C., is excluded from the IV regression. Robust standard errors clustered on city in parentheses. The symbols *, **, and *** indicate that the coefficient is significantly different from 0 at the 10, 5, and 1 percent level. Population weights are used in all regressions.

Table 9.5   Effect of City Health Characteristics on Child Mortality, 1940
Census Microdata

	White	R^2	Black	R^2
Log(percentage of children in city who had had health exam by 1930)	−0.169** (0.063)	0.022	0.594** (0.260)	0.136
Log(percentage of children in city who had had diphtheria immunization by 1930)	−0.027 (0.028)	0.021	0.028 (0.116)	0.127
Log(percentage of children in city who had had smallpox vaccination by 1930)	−0.019 (0.031)	0.021	0.151 (0.208)	0.128
Log(percentage of children in city who had had dental exam by 1930)	−0.022 (0.040)	0.021	0.097 (0.157)	0.127
Observations	4,427		307	
Number of cities	67		41	

Source: Authors' compilation.

Notes: Estimated from the 1940 census integrated public use microdata sets for all married women whose husbands were present in the household, who had ever had children, whose marital duration was less than fifteen years, and for whom the number of children ever born was no greater than marital duration. Health information is from the *White House Conference on Child Health and Protection* and is based upon city surveys. The mean percentage of children in the city who had had a health examination by 1930 was 53 percent in the white sample and 50 percent in the black sample. The mean percentage of children who had had a diphtheria immunization by 1930 was 24 percent in the white sample and 21 percent in the black sample. The mean percentage of children who had been vaccinated for smallpox by 1930 was 25 percent in the white sample and 21 percent in the black sample. The mean percentage of children who had had a dental examination by 1930 was 12 percent in both the white and black samples. Ordinary least squares regressions are of the mortality index on city health characteristics. (The regression is a variant of equation 9.3 in the text in which city health characteristics are substituted for city expenditures.) Additional control variables include dummies for city population, the woman's age, a dummy variable equal to 1 if the household owned its own home, dummies for the husband's occupational class (professional, managerial, clerical and sales, crafts, service, operative, laborer, and no occupation), a dummy equal to 1 if the mother worked, dummies for the mother's place of birth if white (United States, Canada, Scandinavia, Britain, Ireland, Germany, Poland or Russia, Italy, other southern Europe, other Eastern Europe, and other), average July temperature in the state, and nine region dummies. Robust standard errors clustered on city in parentheses. The symbols *, **, and *** indicate that the coefficient is significantly different from 0 at the 10, 5, and 1 percent level. Population weights used in all regressions.

inations, we found that in the white sample the coefficient on health examinations was −.200 ($\hat{\sigma}$ = .078) and the coefficient on the inter-action between home ownership and health examinations was .121 ($\hat{\sigma}$ = .113). In contrast, when we used the same specification in the black sample, the coefficient on health examinations was .635 ($\hat{\sigma}$ = .281) and the coefficient on the interaction between health and home ownership was −.383 ($\hat{\sigma}$ = .434), providing some suggestive evidence that if there were any benefits to blacks, the benefits accrued to the better-off in the black population.

City-Level Data

We recognize that there is a thirty-year gap between our two micro data sets. Detailed city-level death-rate data are available between the years 1912 and 1925, which allow us to "fill in the blanks." For each city and year between 1912 and 1925 except for 1918 we observe the case and death rate for diphtheria, measles, polio, smallpox, tuberculosis, and typhoid and link these cities to our 1907 redistribution data for 130 major cities.[5] (The case rate is the number of diagnosed cases per 100 people and the death rate is the number of deaths per 100 people.)

We study whether cities with greater health expenditures in 1907 have a steeper negative time trend in mortality and case rates for our six major diseases, controlling for a city-specific intercept. That is, we estimate OLS regressions for each of the six diseases,

$$(9.4) \quad \log(m_{lt} + 0.01) = \beta_0 + \beta_1 T_{lt} + \beta_2 T_{jt} \log(E_j) + \beta_3 City + u_{lt}$$

$$(9.5) \quad \log(c_{lt} + 0.01) = \beta_0 + \beta_1 T_{lt} + \beta_2 T_{jt} \log(E_j) + \beta_3 City + u_{lt}$$

where m is the mortality rate and c is the case rate, T is a time trend, "City" is a vector of city-fixed effects, u is an error term, and the subscript l indexes the city and the subscript t indexes time t. Note that case and death rates may be higher in cities with better public health offices because the better offices may have been able to enforce more precise diagnoses on the part of physicians. We are therefore likely to underestimate the effect of city expenditures on case and death rates.

Table 9.6 shows the predicted time trend for each disease for a city that spends the sample mean on redistribution and the predicted time

Table 9.6   Time Trends in City Case and Death Rates for Reportable
Diseases 1912 to 1925, by City Expenditure Class

City Illness Indicator	Time Trend for City Spending, Mean Amount	Time Trend for City Spending, 1 Standard Deviation Above Mean Amount
Diphtheria case rate	−.028	−.030
Diphtheria death rate	−.043	−.044
Measles case rate	−.031	−.044 (10% level)
Measles death rate	−.042	−.053 (10% level)
Polio case rate	−.021	−.014
Polio death rate	−.018	−.014
Smallpox case rate	.010	.011
Smallpox death rate	.020	.016
TB case rate	−.038	−.044 (10% level)
TB death rate	−.052	−.056
Typhoid case rate	−.125	−.119
Typhoid death rate	−.103	−.099
Typhoid case rate (unweighted regression)	−.119	−.126 (5% level)
Typhoid death rate (unweighted regression)	−.102	−.106

Source: Authors' compilation.
Note: The unit of analysis is a city-year. The dependent variable differs by row and is the logarithm of the case or death rate plus 0.01. See equations 9.4 and 9.5 in the text. The control variables are a city fixed effect, time trend, and time trend interacted with city per-capita redistribution expenditure in 1907. All regressions, except where indicated, are weighted by population. The table gives time trends predicted for mean city spending and one standard above mean city spending. One hundred thirty observations from 1912 to 1925, excluding 1918. Statistical significance levels are for the interaction of the logarithm of per-capita health expenditures times the time trend.

trend for each disease for a city that spends one standard deviation above the mean on redistribution. For measles, we find statistically significant evidence that the case-rate and the death-rate time trend are steeper for cities that spend more on redistribution.

The average city during this time period had a 4.2 percent annual decline in its measles death rate while a city whose redistributionary spending was a standard deviation above the mean had time trend of 5.3 percent annual decline in its measles death rate. One surprise that emerges is for typhoid. When we weight the regressions for population, we find that cities that spent more on redistribution had a less steep reduction in their death rates from typhoid than cities that spent the average. This result is driven by New York City. When we do not weight the regression, this "wrong sign" vanishes.

We also examined the effect of city expenditures in 1907 on infant mortality in 1910 for 120 cities, for all races combined, for whites, and for blacks. That is, we run OLS regressions of the form,

$$(9.6) \qquad \log(m_1) = \beta_0 + \beta_1 \log(E_1) + \beta_2 X_1 \neq u_1$$

where m is the mortality rate (deaths per 100 children under age one), E is per-capita health expenditures, X is a vector of city demographic characteristics, u is an error term, and l indexes the city. We also ran IV regressions in which we instrumented for per-capita health expenditures using our state political variables. Since reverse causality will bias OLS estimates toward zero, we expected that IV estimates of equation 9.6 would yield a larger negative coefficient estimate of β_1 than OLS estimates.

Table 9.7 shows that when we instrumented for city expenditures, the coefficient on the logarithm of city expenditures was both strongly negative and was statistically significant for all races combined and for whites. An increase of a standard deviation in city expenditures lowered total infant mortality rates from a mean of 14.9 per 100 to 11.5 per 100.

Although city expenditures did not have a statistically significant effect on black mortality rates, the magnitude of the coefficient on expenditures implied that blacks benefited as much as whites from city spending. The contrast with our microdata results suggested that perhaps the sample of blacks in the microdata was too small to draw reliable conclusions. As in our regressions using the census microdata, the urban penalty for blacks is much higher than the urban penalty for whites. In larger cities in 1910, blacks were living in more segregated areas.[6]

State-Level Data

State-level data allow us to further investigate the effect of expenditures on mortality rates by race and by cause. We linked total 1913 expenditures on the broad categories of charities, hospitals, and corrections, and recreation, health, and sanitation by state and local governments to an unbalanced panel on death rates for all ages at every

Table 9.7 Effect of City Population and City Expenditures on City Infant Mortality, 1910 City-Level Data

	Total		White		Black	
	OLS	IV	OLS	IV	OLS	IV
City size						
Within top 10 percent	.162***	.462***	2.720***	2.954***	4.210***	4.346***
	(.047)	(.156)	(0.422)	(0.494)	(0.693)	(0.868)
Within next 50 to 90 percent	.084*	.162***	1.005***	.989***	1.683***	1.669***
	(.044)	(.062)	(0.349)	(0.376)	(0.547)	(0.598)
Log(city expenditures)	−.014	−.351**	−0.194	−0.606*	−0.367	−0.621
	(.039)	(.167)	(0.212)	(0.307)	(0.392)	(0.694)
R²	0.531	0.162	0.898	0.890	0.709	0.702
Observations	120	119	62	61	60	59

Source: Authors' compilation.

Note: The infant mortality rate is calculated as the total number of deaths divided by the total population below age one. City expenditures include expenditures on health, sanitation, and charities. City size percentiles are calculated within the sample of 120 cities. Additional control variables include mean age, the fraction black, the fraction foreign-born, the fraction illiterate, the Duncan socioeconomic index, and eight regional dummies. See equation 9.6. Instrumental variables are the state's share of Democrats in the U.S. Senate, the state's share of Democrats in the U.S. House, the average number of years of service of the state's representatives in the U.S. Senate, and the average number of years of service of the state's representatives in the U.S. House. Washington, D.C., is excluded from the IV regression. Robust standard errors clustered on the state are in parentheses. The symbols *, **, and *** indicate that the coefficient is significantly different from 0 at the 10, 5, and 1 percent level, respectively.

five-year interval from 1910 to 1940 for ten different conditions.[7] The conditions that we examined are all causes—typhoid fever, scarlet fever, whooping cough, diphtheria, dysentery, tuberculosis, bronchitis, measles, pneumonia, influenza, diarrhea, and hernia. We used hernia as a placebo because although expenditures on hospitals toward the end of the time period may well have reduced deaths from hernias, most public health expenditures would have only a very small causal impact. We examined the effect on death rates of only 1913 state expenditures because the expenditure data are not comparable over time. Expenditures should therefore be interpreted as more of a rank ordering.

The regressions that we estimated are of the form:

$$(9.7) \qquad \log(m_{st}) = \beta_0 + \beta_1 T_{st} + \beta_2 \log(E_s) + \beta_3 X_{st} + u_{st}$$

where m is the mortality rate for each state s at time t, T is a time trend, E is per-capita state and local government expenditures in 1913, X is a vector of demographic characteristics, and u is an error term. We estimate separate regressions by disease and by race. In addition to OLS regressions, we also estimate IV regressions in which we instrument for expenditures using our political variables. Because states with health problems in the past were likely to be spending more, our OLS coefficients are lower-bound estimates of the effectiveness of state expenditures in reducing death rates.

Tables 9.8 and 9.9 show that state expenditures were mainly effective in reducing death rates from typhoid fever, diphtheria, and dysentery. Expenditures had a statistically significant effect in reducing deaths among whites from typhoid and diphtheria and a statistically significant effect in reducing deaths among blacks from diphtheria and dysentery.

However, the magnitude of the coefficient on expenditures suggests that expenditures also played a role in reducing deaths among whites from dysentery and in reducing deaths among blacks from typhoid. In addition, the coefficients on expenditures are quite large for both white and black deaths from pneumonia. Expenditures have no effect on death rates from hernias, our placebo, for whites but raise deaths from hernias for blacks, perhaps because states that spent more were more likely to attribute cause of death accurately to hernias. State expenditures appear to have played a slightly larger role

Table 9.8   Effect of State Expenditures on State Mortality 1910 to 1940, by Cause, by Race, Ordinary Least Squares Regressions

	White, Coefficient on			Black, Coefficient on		
Log(Mortality Rate)	Log (Expenditures)	Time Trend	R^2	Log (Expenditures)	Time Trend	R^2
All causes	0.023	−0.014***	0.490	0.130**	−0.017***	0.326
	(0.045)	(0.001)		(0.060)	(0.002)	
Typhoid fever	−0.396*	−0.088***	0.864	−0.416*	−0.097***	0.757
	(0.212)	(0.006)		(0.212)	(0.007)	
Scarlet fever	0.220**	−0.038***	0.692	0.047	−0.023***	0.479
	(0.101)	(0.005)		(0.098)	(0.004)	
Whooping cough	−0.172	−0.056	0.739	−0.097	−0.054***	0.487
	(0.115)	(0.004)		(0.180)	(0.006)	
Diphtheria	−0.462***	−0.092***	0.851	−0.293**	−0.062***	0.598
	(0.169)	(0.007)		(0.115)	(0.005)	
Dysentery	−0.191	−0.044***	0.753	−0.263*	−0.042***	0.780
	(0.174)	(0.006)		(0.134)	(0.005)	
Tuberculosis	0.256	−0.052***	0.805	0.144	−0.032***	0.491
	(0.169)	(0.005)		(0.189)	(0.010)	

(Table continues on p. 384.)

Table 9.8   Effect of State Expenditures on State Mortality 1910 to 1940, by Cause, by Race, Ordinary Least Squares Regressions *(Continued)*

	White, Coefficient on			Black, Coefficient on		
Log(Mortality Rate)	Log (Expenditures)	Time Trend	R²	Log (Expenditures)	Time Trend	R²
Bronchitis	-0.045	-0.064***	0.816	0.389	-0.081***	0.703
	(0.116)	(0.004)		(0.180)	(0.007)	
Measles	0.065	-0.054***	0.541	0.169	-0.039***	0.255
	(0.152)	(0.007)		(0.169)	(0.006)	
Pneumonia	-0.855	-0.058***	0.340	-0.571	-0.049***	0.421
	(0.640)	(0.017)		(0.368)	(0.007)	
Diarrhea	-0.286	-0.086***	0.861	-0.086	-0.070***	0.736
	(0.188)	(0.006)		(0.110)	(0.005)	
Hernia	-0.015	-0.011***	0.610	0.371***	-0.008***	0.378
	(0.056)	(0.001)		(0.056)	(0.002)	

Source: Authors' compilation.

Note: Ordinary least squares regressions are of state mortality rates by cause and by race on a time trend and on the logarithm of per-capita expenditures on charities, hospitals, and corrections and recreation, health, and sanitation by state and local governments within a state. Each row reports two regressions, one in which the dependent variable is the logarithm of the mortality rate for whites and one in which the dependent variable is the logarithm of the mortality rate for blacks. These state mortality rates are for the years 1910, 1915, 1920, 1925, 1930, 1935, and 1940 for the death registration states. Per-capita expenditures are for the year 1913. Additional control variables include the age distribution of the population, the Duncan socioeconomic index, and four regional dummies. See equation 9.7. Robust standard errors, clustered on the state, in parentheses. The symbols *, **, and *** indicate significance at the 10, 5, and 1 percent level, respectively. All regressions are weighted by state population.

Table 9.9 Effect of State Expenditures on State Mortality 1910 to 1940, by Cause, by Race, Instrumental-Variables Regressions

Log(Mortality Rate)	White, Coefficient on			Black, Coefficient on		
	Log (Expenditures)	Time Trend	R²	Log (Expenditures)	Time Trend	R²
All causes	-0.049	-0.015***	0.483	0.207*	-0.016***	0.138
	(0.104)	(0.002)		(0.108)	(0.002)	
Typhoid fever	-0.941**	-0.098***	0.850	-0.424	-0.097***	0.757
	(0.009)	(0.009)		(0.351)	(0.008)	
Scarlet fever	0.095	-0.040***	0.692	0.070	-0.022***	0.478
	(0.226)	(0.005)		(0.118)	(0.004)	
Whooping cough	-0.154	-0.056***	0.739	-0.087	-0.054***	0.487
	(0.195)	(0.005)		(0.262)	(0.006)	
Diphtheria	-0.613**	-0.095***	0.850	-0.459***	-0.063***	0.591
	(0.252)	(0.006)		(0.177)	(0.005)	
Dysentery	-0.530	-0.051***	0.743	-0.596**	-0.044***	0.761
	(0.341)	(0.009)		(0.290)	(0.006)	
Tuberculosis	-0.114	-0.059***	0.786	0.053	-0.033***	0.488
	(0.292)	(0.007)		(0.263)	(0.010)	
Bronchitis	0.262	-0.059***	0.808	0.106	-0.083	0.431
	(0.241)	(0.005)		(0.326)	(0.006)	

(Table continues on p. 386.)

Table 9.9   Effect of State Expenditures on State Mortality 1910 to 1940, by Cause, by Race, Instrumental-Variables Regressions (Continued)

	White, Coefficient on			Black, Coefficient on		
Log(Mortality Rate)	Log (Expenditures)	Time Trend	R^2	Log (Expenditures)	Time Trend	R^2
Measles	0.039	-0.054***	0.541	0.197	-0.039***	0.593
	(0.172)	(0.007)		(0.302)	(0.007)	
Pneumonia	-1.316	-0.067***	0.588	-0.455	-0.048***	0.493
	(1.057)	(0.023)		(0.350)	(0.008)	
Diarrhea	-0.276	-0.086***	0.861	-0.289	-0.071***	0.727
	(0.352)	(0.009)		(0.201)	(0.005)	
Hernia	-0.024	-0.011***	0.610	0.381***	-0.008***	0.377
	(0.099)	(0.002)		(0.115)	(0.002)	

Source: Authors' compilation.

Note: Instrumental-variables regressions are of state mortality rates by cause and by race on year and on the logarithm of per-capita expenditures on charities, hospitals, and corrections and recreation, health, and sanitation by state and local governments within a state. Each row reports two regressions, one in which the dependent variable is the logarithm of the mortality rate for whites and one in which the dependent variable is the logarithm of the mortality rate for blacks. These state mortality rates are for the years 1910, 1915, 1920, 1925, 1930, 1935, and 1940 for the death registration states. Per-capita expenditures are for 1913. Additional control variables include the age distribution of the population, the Duncan socioeconomic index, and four regional dummies. See equation 9.7 in the text. Instrumental variables are the share of the state's Democrats in the U.S. House, the share of the state's Democrats in the U.S. Senate, the average number of years of seniority of the state's representatives in the House, and the average number of years of seniority of the state's representatives in the Senate. Robust standard errors, clustered on the state, in parentheses. The symbols *, **, and *** indicate significance at the 10, 5, and 1 percent level, respectively. All regressions are weighted by state population.

in lowering white deaths from typhoid fever, diphtheria, and pneumonia than in lowering black deaths. In addition, the time trend in deaths from diphtheria and pneumonia is bigger for whites than for blacks.

Valuing Public Health Investments in the Early Twentieth Century

We have shown that on the whole government expenditures played an important role in lowering mortality rates, particularly in the first few decades of the twentieth century. But is it possible to place a dollar value on the benefits of these expenditures? To answer this, we must combine our estimates of how much extra health was produced through greater public health expenditure with estimates of how much the population valued improvements in health. We answer this question in two ways. We first estimate a rental hedonic using the 1917-to-1919 Consumer Expenditure Survey and city-level infant mortality rates in 1920. We then use estimates of the value of life calculated from wage hedonics and industry risk to value the statistical lives saved.

The rental regression that we estimate is:

$$(9.8) \qquad \log(r_{il}) = \beta_0 + \beta_1 \log(m_1) + \beta_2 X_{il} + u_{il}$$

where r is the yearly rent (imputed for home owners) for dwelling i in city l, m is the infant mortality rate in city l, X is a vector of housing characteristics, and u is an error term. Assuming that migration costs are low and that people not living in a city are aware of the attributes of the city, the coefficient estimate on the infant mortality rate represents the "compensating differential" to living in a high-mortality city (Williamson 1981). If preferences over risk exposure and consumption are homogenous, then this hedonic sketches out the representative agent's indifference curve. It is important to note that in estimating equation 9.8, we are assuming that the disease environment proxied for by m_l varies across cities but not within cities. Table 9.10 shows that apartment dwellers paid higher rents for a lower city-level infant mortality rate, controlling for city population and dwelling characteristics.

Table 9.10   Compensating Differential for Infant Mortality Risk

	Apartments		Nonapartments	
Log(city population	0.048***	0.051***	0.015	0.017
in thousands)	(0.018)	(0.016)	(0.020)	(0.021)
Log(city infant	−0.198	−0.227**	0.086	0.073
mortality)	(0.170)	(0.107)	(0.119)	(0.105)
With four region	Yes	No	Yes	No
dummies				
Probability dummies	0.860		0.456	
are jointly significant,				
from F-test				
R²	0.519	0.518	0.476	0.472
Observations	3,128	3,128	6,437	6,437
Number of cities	94	94	112	112

Source: Authors' compilation.
Note: Estimated from the 1917 to 1919 Consumer Expenditure Survey. Regressions are of the logarithm of rental value (imputed by homeowners for owned properties) on the logarithm of city infant mortality controlling for city population. Infant mortality is 1919 mortality for the registration cities. Average yearly rent in July 1918 dollars was $190 in the apartment sample and $198 in the nonapartment sample. The mean city infant mortality rate was .123 in both samples. Additional control variables include the number of rooms, the number of windows, the number of windows squared, whether the dwelling had a bathroom, whether the dwelling had a WC inside, whether the dwelling had a sewer connection, whether the dwelling had a pantry, whether the dwelling had an attic, whether the dwelling had a cellar, and whether the dwelling contained stationary laundry tubs. See equation 9.8 in the text. Robust standard errors in parentheses. The symbols *, **, and *** indicate significance at the 10, 5, and 1 percent level, respectively.

We seek to measure how much a city's residents would value the health benefits of increased public health expenditure. Recall that in table 9.7, a standard-deviation increase in per-capita city expenditures (roughly $19.66 in 2002 dollars), decreased total infant mortality from 14.9 per 100 to 11.5 per 100. This decrease of 3.4 deaths per 100 would have raised yearly rents by approximately $127.36 in 2002 dollars at a time when average rents in the sample were $2,264 in 2002 dollars. The implied value of a statistical infant's life was only $51,585 in 2002 dollars, a very small number. We believe that this very small estimate is due to intracity variation in community disease exposure. Within a city, there are safer low-density communities and riskier, high-density communities. This introduces measurement error in the explanatory variable, which in turn biases toward zero the estimate of the value of a statistical life. Susan Craddock's (2000) map of San Francisco's typhoid rates across communities supports this "hot spots" hypothesis. Two additional negative results further support the intracity-variation hypothesis. We find no evidence that city-level infant mortality rates were capitalized into the rents of non-apartment dwellers. We also find no evidence that city-level infant mortality rates were capitalized into wages. We expected that cities with high mortality rates would pay higher wages as a compensating differential.

Given that we do not fully trust the estimates in table 9.10 for recovering the historical value of a statistical life, we pursue an alternative strategy of valuing the benefits of health investments. We use estimates of the value of life derived from hedonic wage regressions on industry fatality risk. Costa and Kahn (2003, 2004) used microcensus data from 1940 to 1980 to estimate changes in the value of life over this period and concluded that the income elasticity of the value of life ranged between 1.5 and 1.7. Using an elasticity of 1.7 and interpolating back to 1920 yields an estimated value of life of $895,000 in 2002 dollars (Costa and Kahn 2003). Thus the decrease of 3.4 deaths per hundred infants gained from an increase in per-capita expenditures of $19.66 in 2002 dollars would yield benefits of at least $30,430 in 2002 dollars. Using our 1980 estimate of the value of a statistical life of $7,393,000 yields a benefit of $251,362 in 2002 dollars. Both of these estimates underestimate the benefits of city expenditures because they only account for changes in infant mortality, not for changes in child and adult mortality.

Were expenditures in reducing mortality worth it to cities? Because average population size in the cities for which we estimated a health-production function was 181,778, total city expenditures would have had to rise by $3,573,765 in 2002 dollars to save 3.4 infant lives per 100 and some unknown number of child and adult lives. Since the average number of infants in our cities was 4,265, the rate of lives saved implies that 145 infants would have been saved. Using the value of life of $895,000 interpolated from Costa and Kahn's (2003, 2004) wage regressions implies that the total benefit was $3,817,175,000 in 2002 dollars for city expenditures of $3.5 million. Using the value of an infant life of $51,585 derived from our rental hedonic yields total benefits of $7,479,825 in 2002 dollars, suggesting that under a broad range of value-of-life estimates cities were underinvesting in health.

Conclusion

How effective were public health expenditures in lowering mortality rates at the beginning of the twentieth century? Early work (summarized in United Nations 1953, 1973) emphasized the importance of public health reforms together with advances in medical technology and improved living standards in lowering infectious-disease rates. Thomas McKeown (1976), arguing by a process of elimination, upset this consensus view and claimed that because mortality declines began prior to any changes in medical technology or in public health reforms, the primary explanation had to be improved nutrition. But, as Robert W. Fogel (1997) pointed out, what matters is net nutrition, that is the difference between food intake and the demand made on that intake by disease, climate, and work. Those with parasitic diseases suffer depletion of iron supplies despite their consumption of an otherwise healthy diet. Recurrent sufferers from gastrointestinal diseases cannot digest all of the ingested nutrients.

This paper has emphasized the efficacy of public health reforms. We have shown that state expenditures on public health lowered mortality rates from typhoid, dysentery, and diphtheria between 1910 and 1940 and that city public health expenditures circa 1910, particularly those on sewage and water filtration, were very effective in reducing childhood and infant mortality. By 1940, however, cities had solved their sanitation problems and the biggest gains in mortality begin to come from spending on preventive medical care. We find some evidence that the poor benefited disproportionately from early public health spending. Renters, who lived in higher-density areas with a more severe disease environment and whose income afforded them fewer self-protection options, benefited from water filtration in the early 1900s, whereas home owners did not. Renters also disproportionately benefited from city expenditures on child health exams in the early 1930s. Such improvements in health capital could help to reduce poverty by increasing economic opportunities for this group (Wolfe 1994).

Our evidence on the relative importance of city spending to blacks and whites is mixed. Our microdata suggest that blacks did not benefit whereas our state- and city-level data suggest that they benefited as much as whites. Furthermore, the disappearance of the very large urban penalty for blacks in both the micro- and city-level data suggests that changes within cities benefited blacks more than whites. We may not find very large effects for blacks because the extension of water filtration and sewage connections to black neighborhoods generally lagged behind service provision to white neighborhoods by about five to seven years (Troesken 2004). It is possible that blacks did eventually benefit from the extension of services into their communities but that our 1910 data samples were generated "too soon," before the benefits of these infrastructure expansions were realized.

The public health expenditures undertaken by cities circa 1910 were very low relative to the value of the lives saved, under a wide range of plausible value-of-life estimates. Why didn't cities increase their public expenditures? Perhaps it was because the poor were getting the greater benefits from such investments as water filtration and publicly financed child health exams. Alternatively, it may have taken time for cities to learn how to reduce mortality. Cleaning sewage, water, and the milk supply, establishing disease reporting and quarantining systems, disseminating health information to citizens, and ensuring that all babies and children have medical exams and vaccinations required setting up new organizations and cooperation between citizens, doctors, private philanthropists, and city public health departments.

Our results speak to trends in inequality in overall well-being in the early twentieth century. More comprehensive measures of economic inequality should incorporate the value of government services, unpaid services in the home, leisure, natural environment, and work satisfaction (Reynolds and Smolensky 1978). Our estimates of the health gains from public expenditure provide a guide to the value of government services.

Data Appendix

City-Level Data We use city-level data on spending, sewer connections, and water filtration from U.S. Bureau of the Census's *Statistics of Cities Having a Population of Over 30,000: 1907* (1910), and *General Statistics of Cities* (1909 and 1916), respectively. We used reported infant deaths for the death registration cities in 1919 as published by the Census Bureau and calculated mortality rates using 1920 population.

We used disease cases and deaths as compiled by the Center for Population Economics at the University of Chicago from annual notifiable disease tables published by the Public Health Service between 1912 and 1925 and calculated mortality rates and case rates using estimated populations. Reportable disease cases and deaths for 1918 were not available at the time of writing. We used spending on boards of health and the percentage of children under age six who had ever had a health examination, a dental examination, diphtheria immunization, or a smallpox immunization from the 1931 White House Conference on Child Health and Protection (see Palmer et al. 1931). The 1909 and 1916 *Social Statistics of Cities* and reportable disease cases and deaths for 1912 to 1925 are available from http://www.cpe.uchicago.edu. The data we use from the 1907 *Social Statistics of Cities* (U.S. Census Bureau, various years) and from Palmer et al. (1931) are available at http://web.mit.edu/costa/www/data.html. We thank Michael Haines for his files on city deaths and populations for 1909 to 1911 and 1919 to 1920. We obtained demographic and socioeconomic characteristics of cities from the integrated public use census samples, at http://www.ipums.umn.edu.

State-Level Data Information on state and local (county and incorporated place) expenditures on charities, hospitals, and corrections and recreation, health, and sanitation was obtained from Richard E. Sylla, John B. Legler, and John Wallis's Interuniversity Consortium for Political and Social Research dataset, *State and Local Government: Sources and Uses of Funds* (study no. 6304; various years). We aggregate all of these expenditures into total state expenditures per capita. We obtained state mortality rates by cause for five-year intervals from 1910 to 1940 from Forrest Edward Linder's *Vital Statistics of the United States, 1900–1940* (1947). We obtain demographic and socioeconomic characteristics of cities from the integrated public use census samples. The source for the politics data used in table 9.1 as a set of explanatory variables and used throughout the other tables as instrumental variables is available at the Vote View website, http://voteview.com.

Micro-Level Data We used the 1910 and 1940 integrated public use microdata census samples (http://www.ipums.umn.edu) to estimate the effect of city spending and city health infrastructure on child mortality. We restricted both samples to currently married women whose husbands are in the household and who have had children. We restricted the sample to women who were married for fifteen years (using the variable on marriage duration in 1910 and the variable on age at first marriage in 1940). We excluded from the analysis observations where the number of children ever born was greater than the duration of the marriage. The 1910 census had questions on both the number of children ever born and the number of children surviving. The 1940 census only had a question on the number of children ever born. We therefore imputed the number of children surviving from the number of own children present in the household. We further restricted the 1940 census to women who had not moved across counties within the last five years and excluded eleven observations where the number of children ever born was greater than eight and there were no children in the household. Our dependent variable is a mortality index calculated as the total number of deaths for every woman divided by the expected number of deaths for women within that marital-duration category, where the marital duration categories are zero to four years, five to nine years, and ten to fourteen years. The expected number of deaths is simply the mean number of deaths per woman within each census, calculated over all races and over all urban and rural areas.

We use the 1917-to-1919 Consumer Expenditure Survey (available from the Interuniversity Consortium for Political and Social Research as *Cost of Living in the United States, 1917–1919,* study no. 8299 [U.S. Department of Labor 1986]) to estimate the effect of city-level infant mortality rates on yearly rental prices. Families were selected from employer records and were restricted to families in which both spouses were present and where there was at least one child in the household, where salaried workers did not earn more than $2,000 a year ($13,245 in 1982-to-1984 dollars), families had resided for a year in the same community prior to the survey, families did not take in more than three boarders, families were not classified as either slum or charity, and non-English families had been in the United States five or more years. We restrict the sample to whites.

This paper was written for the December 2003 Berkeley Symposium on Poverty, the Distribution of Income and Public Policy. We thank Peter Lindert, Barbara Wolfe, John Quigley, and the conference participants for extensive comments. We thank Jacqueline del Castillo for research assistance. This paper was written while both authors were visiting Stanford University. We both gratefully acknowledge the support of NIH Grant R01 AG19637, and Dora Costa also gratefully acknowledges the support of the Robert Wood Johnson Foundation, NIH Grant P01 AG10120, and the Center for Advanced Study in the Behavioral Sciences.

Notes

1. Our results are not driven by outlier cities. When we re-estimated these regressions using quintile regressions we made similar findings.
2. State spending on redistribution is surprisingly persistent over time. The correlation between a state's 1990 average monthly AFDC payment to a recipient and its 1913 per-capita redistribution is .65.
3. In 1907 the correlation between the proportion of a city's population that was black and the proportion that was illiterate was .82. When we included the proportion of the city that was illiterate in our 1907 regression, the coefficient on the proportion that was black became small and insignificant, whereas the coefficient on the proportion illiterate was 3.844, statistically significant at the 5 percent level.
4. We recognize that our finding is simply based on cross-sectional data. Peter Lindert (2004, chapter 3, 61) argues that history rejects the notion that government aid to the poor crowds out private aid. "Back in the late 1920s, when government aid to the poor was only 1/6 of one percent of national product, private charity to the poor was the same. The subsequent rise of government 'welfare' aid to around four percent of GNP by 1995 could not just crowd out private charity because there was only 1/6 of one percent of GNP in private philanthropy that could have been crowded out in the first place."
5. The data for 1918 were unavailable at the time of writing, but because of the influenza pandemic, 1918 may be an unusual year.
6. Using Cutler, Glaeser, and Vigdor's (1999) 1910 measure of residential racial segregation (the dissimilarity index), for sixty-four cities the correlation of the log of city population and this dissimilarity index is .42.
7. This measure of total 1913 local government per-capita expenditure is highly positively correlated with Charles V. Chapin's (1915) ranking of the quality of state public health departments.

References

Alesina, Alberto, and Edward L. Glaeser. 2004. *Fighting Poverty in the U.S. and Europe: A World of Difference*. Oxford: Oxford University Press.

Bahl, Roy, Jorge Martinez-Vazquez, and Sally Wallace. 2002. "State and Local Government Choices in Fiscal Redistribution." *National Tax Journal* 60(4): 723–42.

Blank, Rebecca. 1988. "The Effect of Welfare and Wage Levels on the Location Decisions of Female Households." *Journal of Urban Economics* 24(2): 186–211.

Borjas, George. 1999. "Immigration and Welfare Magnets." *Journal of Labor Economics* 17(4): 607–37.

Cain, Louis P., and Elyce J. Rotella. 2001. "Death and Spending: Urban Mortality and Municipal Expenditure on Sanitation." *Annales de Démographie Historique* 1: 139–54.

Chapin, Charles V. 1915. "A Report on State Public Health Work Based on a Survey of State Boards of Health." Chicago: American Medical Association.

Condran, Gretchen A., and Rose A. Cheney. 1982. "Mortality Trends in Philadelphia: Age- and Cause-Specific Death Rates, 1870–1930." *Demography* 19(1): 97–123.

Costa, Dora L. 2003. "Understanding Mid-Life and Older Age Mortality Declines: Evidence from Union Army Veterans." *Journal of Econometrics* 112(1): 175–92.

Costa, Dora L., and Matthew E. Kahn. 2003. "Civic Engagement in Heterogeneous Communities." *Perspectives on Politics* 1(1): 103–12.

———. 2004. "Changes in the Value of Life 1940–1980." *Journal of Risk and Uncertainty* 29(2): 159–80.

Costa, Dora L., and Joanna Lahey. 2005. "Becoming Oldest-Old: Evidence from Historical US Data." *Genus* 51(1): 125–61.

Craddock, Susan. 2000. *San Francisco: City of Plagues, Disease, Poverty and Deviance*. Minneapolis: University of Minnesota Press.

Cutler, David M., Edward L. Glaeser, and Jacob L. Vigdor. 1999. "The Rise and Decline of the American Ghetto." *Journal of Political Economy* 107(3): 455–506.

Fishback, Price V., Michael R. Haines, and Shawn Kantor. 2002. "The Welfare of Children During the Great Depression." NBER working paper no. 8902. Cambridge, Mass.: National Bureau of Economic Research.

Fogel, Robert W. 1997. "Secular Trends in Nutrition and Mortality." In *Handbook of Population and Family Economics*, edited by Mark R. Rosenzweig and Oded Stark. Volume 1A. Amsterdam: Elsevier.

Haines, Michael R. 2001. "The Urban Mortality Transition in the United States, 1800 to 1940." *Annales de Démographie Historique* 1: 33–64.

———. 2003. "Ethnic Differences in Demographic Behavior in the United States: Has There Been Convergence?" *Historical Methods* 36(4): 157–95.

Higgs, Robert. 1980. *Competition and Coercion: Blacks in the American Economy, 1865–1914*. Chicago: University of Chicago Press.

Linder, Forrest Edward. 1947. *Vital Statistics of the United States, 1900–1940.* Washington: Federal Security Agency. Available at: http://purl.access. gpo.gov/GPO/LPS50817 (accessed September 12, 2005).

Lindert, Peter H. 1994. "The Rise of Social Spending, 1880–1930." *Explorations in Economic History* 31(1): 1–37.

———. 2004. *Growing Public: Social Spending and Economic Growth Since the Eighteenth Century.* Cambridge: Cambridge University Press.

Luttmer, Erzo F. P. 2001. "Group Loyalty and the Taste for Redistribution." *Journal of Political Economy* 109(3): 500–28.

McKeown, Thomas. 1976. *The Modern Rise of Population.* London: Edward Arnold.

Melosi, Martin V. 2000. *The Sanitary City: Urban Infrastructure in America from Colonial Times to the Present.* Baltimore: Johns Hopkins University Press.

Orr, Larry. 1976. "Income Transfers as a Public Good: An Application to AFDC." *American Economic Review* 66(3): 359–71.

Palmer, George, Mayhew Derryberry, Philip Van Ingen, and Samuel McClintock Hamill. 1931. *Health Protection for the Preschool Child: A National Survey of the Use of Preventive Medical and Dental Service for Children Under Six.* Report prepared for the White House Conference on Child Health and Protection. New York, London: Century Co.

Poterba, James. 1997. "Demographic Structure and the Political Economy of Public Education." *Journal of Policy Analysis and Management* 16(1): 48–66.

Preston, Samuel H., and Michael R. Haines. 1991. *Fatal Years: Child Mortality in Late 19th Century America.* Princeton: Princeton University Press.

Reynolds, Morgan, and Eugene Smolensky. 1978. "The Fading Effect of Government on Inequality." *Challenge,* July–August, pp. 32–37.

Rochester, Anna. 1923. "Infant Mortality: Results of a Field Study in Baltimore, Maryland, Based on Births in One Year." U.S Department of Labor, Children's Bureau, publication 119. Washington: U.S. Government Printing Office.

Smolensky, Eugene, Eirik Evenhouse, and Siobhan Reilly. 1997. "Welfare Reform: A Primer in 12 Questions." Background Papers Series. San Francisco: Public Policy Institute of California (May).

Sylla, Richard E., John B. Legler, and John Wallis. Various years. *State and Local Government (United States): Sources and Uses of Funds, City and County Data [computer file].* Ann Arbor, Mich.: Interuniversity for Political and Social Research.

Troesken, Werner. 2004. *Water, Race and Disease.* Cambridge: MIT Press.

United Nations. 1953. *The Determinants and Consequences of Population Trends.* Population Studies, no. 17. New York: United Nations.

———. 1973. *The Determinants and Consequences of Population Trends.* Population Studies, no. 50. New York: United Nations.

U.S. Census Bureau. 1910. *Statistics of Cities Having a Population of over 30,000: 1907.* Washington: U.S. Government Printing Office.

————. Various years. *Statistics of Cities.* 1909 and 1916 Volumes. Washington: U.S. Government Printing Office.

U.S. Department of Labor. Bureau of Labor Statistics. 1986. *Cost of Living in the United States, 1917–1919* [Computer file]. 5th ICPSR ed. Ann Arbor, Mich.: Interuniversity Consortium for Political and Social Research.

Williamson, Jeffrey G. 1981. "Urban Disamenities, Dark Satanic Mills, and the British Standard of Living Debate." *Journal of Economic History* 41(1): 75–83.

Wolfe, Barbara L. 1994. "Reform of Health Care for the Nonelderly Poor." In *Confronting Poverty: Prescriptions for Change,* edited by Sheldon H. Danziger, Gary D. Sandefur, and Daniel H. Weinberg. New York and Cambridge, Mass.: Russell Sage Foundation and Harvard University Press.

Index

Boldface numbers refer to figures and tables.